America's Wars in Asia

A Study of the Maureen and Mike Mansfield Foundation

America's Wars in Asia

A Cultural Approach to History and Memory

Edited by

Philip West

Steven I. Levine

Jackie Hiltz

An East Gate Book

M.E. Sharpe
Armonk, New York
London, England

An East Gate Book

Copyright © 1998 by The Maureen and Mike Mansfield Center

Library of Congress Cataloging-in-Publication Data

America's wars in Asia : a cultural approach to history and memory /
edited by Philip West, Steven I. Levine, and Jackie Hiltz.
p. cm.
"An East gate book"
Includes bibliographical references and index.
ISBN 0-7656-0236-9 (hardcover : alk. paper). —
ISBN 0-7656-0237-7 (paperback : alk. paper)
1. Asia—History—20th century.   2. United States—History, Military—
20th century.   3. Asia—Military relations—United States.
4. United States—Military relations—Asia.   5. War and society—
United States—History—20th century.   6. War and society—Asia—
History—20th century.   7. Memory—Social aspects—United States.
8. Memory—Social aspects—Asia.   I. West, Philip, 1938–
II. Levine, Steven I.   III. Hiltz, Jackie.
DS35.A55   1997
950.4–dc21   97-27652
CIP
Printed in the United States of America

The paper used in this publication meets the minimum requirements of
American National Standard for Information Sciences—
Permanence of Paper for Printed Library Materials,
ANSI Z 39.48-1984.

EB (c)   10   9   8   7   6   5   4   3   2   1
EB (p)   10   9   8   7   6   5   4   3   2   1

Contents

Preface

This is a book about war. More precisely, it is about three wars the United States fought in Asia between 1941 and 1975: the Pacific War, the Korean War, and the Vietnam War. It is not a book about military strategy and tactics or campaigns and battles, nor does it focus on the politics and diplomacy of war. In the broadest sense its subject matter is the human dimensions of war as experienced by those who fought in, lived through, and later remembered these wars. It is an exercise in history and memory.

The book is one of the fruits of a 1995 Summer Institute held at The University of Montana's Maureen and Mike Mansfield Center.* Since 1984 the work of the Center has been supported primarily by the Maureen and Mike Mansfield Foundation. The Institute itself was funded by the National Endowment for the Humanities. It brought together twenty-two American and three Chinese college professors from around the country for an intensive study of the United States and Asia at war. We employed a *cultural approach* that is explained in the Introduction. Over a six-week period, we studied these wars with the help of presentations by historians, authors, filmmakers, film critics, and literary specialists from East Asia and the United States as well as war veterans and others. We read many American and Asian novels, short stories, and poems, and viewed dozens of American and Asian feature films, documentaries, and television series that dealt with the wars. In animated discussions that sometimes turned rancorous and even confrontational, we grappled with one another, deepening our appreciation of the multiple meanings of these wars. As we deployed our varying disciplinary approaches, our positions were constantly under fire from colleagues who sharply, and sometimes painfully, challenged our assumptions, preconceptions, and accustomed modes of understanding. Our understanding of the United States and Asia at war was both complicated and clarified by this

*We would especially like to acknowledge the cheerful and able assistance of Cathy Brown and Susan Gibb in the planning and administration of the National Endowment for the Humanities Summer Institute. Because of their hard work, the Institute proceeded smoothly and pleasantly.

process. Now, through this book, we would like to share our experience.

The purpose of this multiauthored volume is to encourage others, particularly teachers and students, to develop an understanding of the experience of war in Asia that is variegated, fragmented, and often contradictory. For us the image of a tangled web best conveys the multiple meanings of the wartime experiences. Like all good teaching, ours is an open-ended, ongoing project. We hope that readers will respond in the same spirit, using this volume not as a terminus but as a point of departure for their own explorations of the subject of the United States and Asia at war.

* * *

Note: John Dower has placed the surname first while the other authors place the surname last.

Philip West
Steven I. Levine
Jackie Hiltz
Missoula, Montana, March 1997

America's Wars in Asia

Introduction

Sounding the Human Dimensions of War

Philip West, Steven I. Levine, and Jackie Hiltz

> Up behind the front lines a bird used to chirp
> its mating call at sundown for several days.
> And his call was answered from amidst the
> desolation. It was beautiful, a sign maybe
> that there still remained a God somewhere.
> Only one evening there was no answering chirp.

> —Merrel Clubb
> Iwo Jima, March 1945

Relations between the United States and Asia are increasingly economic in nature, but it was not always so. As veteran Asia hand Frank Gibney writes, "For many of us it began in war."[1] Less than five years after the end of the Pacific War in August 1945, the United States intervened in a new war that erupted in Korea in June 1950. By the time that war sputtered out in July 1953, Washington had already embarked upon its fateful involvement in Vietnam that would drag on until April 1975. For three generations of American men and women who served in the armed forces, and for everyone on the home front who listened to the radio, watched newsreels and television, and anxiously scanned newspaper headlines, Asia was a battlefield long before it became a marketplace. For hundreds of millions of Japanese, Koreans, Chinese, and Vietnamese, the United States was either an enemy or an ally. The American soldier, dispenser of bullets and Hershey bars, napalm and chewing gum, was the ambiguous symbol of American culture and civilization.

During and after these wars, the U.S. military presence in Asia had a significant impact upon the culture, politics, and economies of the countries concerned.

The impact of these wars upon the United States was scarcely less profound. More than any other single factor, the experiences and the memories of war defined the relationship between the United States and Japan, Korea, China, and Vietnam from the 1940s through the 1970s. Even now, when economic interaction has replaced military confrontation, the experiences of war refracted through the prisms of memory influence how Americans and Asians perceive and deal with each other.

Memories, Voices, and History

Memory and history are not the same, and as many of the chapters in this volume suggest, the relationship between them is extremely complex. That relationship is further complicated by the phenomenon of war, which plays a central role in the self-definition of many countries, including the United States and its wartime allies and enemies in Asia. In his panoramic study of American history, Michael Kammen observes that wars have played a "fundamental role in stimulating, defining, justifying, periodizing, and eventually filtering American memories and traditions." Such memory, however, as critics point out, is necessarily selective as societies "reconstruct their pasts rather than faithfully record them" in order to serve the "needs of contemporary culture . . . manipulating the past in order to mold the present."[2] Other scholars amplify these points. Charles Hill posits a "political culture of memory" that creates "fighting stories" which help to integrate political communities, shape national and cultural narratives, and contribute to how peoples view each other.[3] Memories of war, Lucian Pye argues, are particularly important in reinforcing "myths of legitimacy" since they possess "an emotional substance and a higher level of truth than just the objective accounts of historians."[4]

It would be naïve, however, to suppose that the "objective accounts of historians" are simply what they purport to be. Reflecting upon the "tragic element in modern international conflict," Herbert Butterfield suggested that interpretations of war offered by contemporary historians are often tendentious accounts emphasizing the virtues of their own country and the failings of their enemies. It can take years, decades, or even longer for the study of international conflict to move into what he called an "academic" phase or mode. In this phase, the simplistic national moralism of earlier interpretations yields to examinations of the "structural features of the conflict which was inherent in the dialectic of events." Such historiographical progress, according to Butterfield, reveals "situations hardening, events tying themselves into knots, human beings faced by terrible dilemmas," and "it uncovers at the basis of the story a fundamental human predicament—one which we can see would have led to a serious conflict of wills even if all men had been fairly intelligent and reasonably well-intentioned."[5]

Kammen is doubtless correct in saying that societies reconstruct their pasts rather than faithfully record them. So is Pye when he adds that memories are significant even when they "may not accurately report actual historical events." The memories of different observers vary widely on something as seemingly simple as a traffic accident or a stickup. How much more so when the phenomenon is as confused and complicated as war. Moreover, as the chapters by John Dower and Edward Linenthal in particular emphasize, historical memory is almost always contested, often as hotly as the blood-soaked ground of a major battle.

Acknowledging these truths, we nonetheless reject the notion that the reconstruction that is history can be carried out arbitrarily. History is not a free-for-all or even a buffet. One need not choose between one extreme that sees history as the fossilized and unalterable past and another that would accept all reconstructions of the past, however arbitrary or fantastical some may be, as equally valid. It goes without saying not only that our historical understanding is constantly changing but also that the contestation between competing truths is integral to the profession of history. But this does not free historians from the obligation to root their new interpretations in documentary and other forms of evidence. We agree with Michael Schudson that "the past imposes itself upon us," which we take to mean that as historians we have an obligation to preceding and succeeding generations as well as our own. We also agree with his view that there is much work to be done "along the borders between conventional and post-conventional ways of understanding the world."[6] The present volume contains examples of such work along with conventional and postconventional approaches.

Precisely because of our openness to a variety of different perspectives, we can speak only for ourselves rather than all our contributors. It would be folly, of course, to deny the challenge of complexity that the proliferation of historical memories from many Asian and American sources presents. Yet we refuse to surrender to either a utopian or a cynical relativism that abandons the quest to create even-handed history, however quaint or quixotic such a quest may strike some readers. Good history must be sensitive to authentic memories on all sides of the wars we study, but memories are not a substitute for other kinds of historical evidence.

Some reflections upon the Vietnam Veterans Memorial in Washington, DC, may serve as a useful point of departure for our views about memory and help introduce our cultural approach to the study of America's wars in Asia. This memorial is unlike any of the other numerous war memorials that dot the American landscape. Absent from Maya Lin's original design were any of the familiar symbols of battle and heroic sacrifice or even the American flag, though these were added later at the insistence of veterans' groups. Instead, in the black marble wall of the memorial are etched the names of the 58,022 American men and women who died in the war or are missing and unaccounted for. (Imagine, incidentally, how long a wall would be needed to memorialize in like fashion the millions of Vietnamese who died in the war.) The absence of an explicit patriotic message in the design of the memorial served to highlight the complex human dimensions of the experience of war and honor those whose lives were sacrificed for their country. The emotional power of this roll call of the dead invites the visitor to meditate upon the connection between the abstraction that is war and the individuals who fought and died in war. Depending upon one's perspective, their sacrifice may be seen as either heroic tragedy or tragic waste. But the memorial mutely implores the visitor to rise above, if not set aside, the familiar conflicts of ideology and politics that lead to such judgments and that structured the American discussion of the war along a divide between pro-war and anti-war voices, hawks and doves. Its very silence inspires us to meditate upon the complexity and variegatedness of war, and to listen in the silence for the voices we ignore or shut our ears to. The Vietnam Veterans Memorial, then, may be read as a kind of "text" subject to as many variant readings as the war itself.

One of the extraordinary things about this memorial is that its designer, Maya Lin, was still in grade school during the Tet offensive of 1968 and claims never to have read a book about Vietnam or thought about the war before the design competition. Her "memory" of the war is derivative or secondary, but no less powerful or authentic for being so. It is this secondary voice that alike inspires soldiers and civilians, prowar and antiwar activists, officials and ordinary people. It is one of the paradoxes of historical memory that secondary voices like Maya Lin's, and others of her generation from Japan, Korea, China, and Vietnam, contribute to our understanding of the United States and Asia at war through their artistic, literary, and cinematographic creativity. Authenticity is not simply a function of having "been there and done that."

In mapping the complex and elusive territory of memory as part of our examination of the human dimensions of war, we recognize the oft-used divide between official and unofficial memory. Official memory expresses the powerful role of the state both during and after conflicts. The state controls access to its archives and releases documents pertaining to the origins and management of wars. These official documents are the primary archive for scholarly research about wars. National governments typically commission the design and construction of war memorials that express official policy and channel memory. Local war memorials usually follow. Unofficial memory created by writers, artists, filmmakers, and ordinary persons may overlap with and reinforce official memory. But unofficial memory inevitably speaks with a plurality of voices offering contrasting and contradictory views.

This dichotomy, like others in the discussion of memory, fails to capture the complexity of reality. For one thing, as Edward Linenthal's chapter demonstrates, official memory itself is both openly constructed and openly contested, particularly in pluralist societies where competing groups and interests struggle to exert control over it. The artifacts of official memory, even when carved in stone, acquire meaning only as the sites of human interaction—commemorative services, individual and group visits, and so forth. Moreover, as noted, the Vietnam Veterans Memorial itself transcends the dichotomy between official and unofficial memory as well as reminding us, too, that memory is constantly evolving.

That is no less true in Asia than in the United States as aspects of the past are emphasized, de-emphasized, and re-emphasized, recalled, suppressed, or forgotten for a variety of contemporary reasons connected to a multiplicity of contending forces. This is another reason why it is so difficult at any given moment to create an even-handed history that draws upon both official and unofficial memories on all sides of a conflict and is sensitive to the changing contexts in which wars are remembered.

Although monuments endure until they crumble or rust, are dismantled or forgotten, official and unofficial views of a war can change even while the war is still being waged, as the Vietnam War demonstrates. Such changes in perception influence what might be called the short-term memory of the origins and early stages of a protracted war. In the case of Vietnam, a decade after a nearly unanimous Senate supported the Tonkin Gulf Resolution of 1964, Washington and the American people had lost their taste for the Vietnam War. Defeat was seen as preferable to its further prolongation. Just five years after the fall of Saigon, the Senate voted unanimously to approve a war memorial in the central space of Constitution Mall next to the Lincoln Memorial. Republican Senators Charles McC. Mathias, John Warner, and Barry Goldwater were instrumental in generating official support for this project.

The polyphonic silences of the Vietnam Veterans Memorial also caution the historian not to rely exclusively on the powerful unofficial memories of the antiwar movement. For those of us who were part of that movement in the 1960s and 1970s, the memorial implores us to recognize that our passions, too, were more polarizing and less healing than we liked to think at the time. The polished black marble of the Vietnam Veterans Memorial reflects a tragic vision of the war that over time can transcend the division between the proponents and opponents of the conflict.

Additional ways of structuring the discussion of memory point to the differences between primary and secondary and firsthand and secondhand memories of war. For all three wars, oral histories are now available in English with primary accounts by those who experienced the war firsthand as combatants and noncombatants.[7] The claim to authenticity and, therefore, to truth made by the eyewitness is compelling. Who can contest the claim of someone who can say "I was there!"? The point, of course, is that many were there, and the "there" where they were was ten thousand different places. As the chapters by Merrel Clubb and Colonel Harry Summers, Jr. indicate, even the memories of those who were directly involved in combat vary widely depending upon time, place, proximity to the front lines, and the observer's own capacity to absorb and reflect upon experience. Different persons witnessed different things; memories diverge, and the multiplicity of voices contest one another's truths. The fault lines run not simply between friend and foe, but also between and among official and unofficial voices on the same side. This is true among Asian as well as American voices. As for secondhand memory, we have already noted that Maya Lin's vision, from wherever it may have derived, speaks to the Vietnam War in ways that cannot be denied simply because she was not of the generation that directly experienced the conflict.

Yet another familiar divide in the discussion of memory is that between individual and collective memory. (The idea of collective memory itself, as Linenthal reminds us, is a contested notion.) Here, too, the Vietnam Veterans Memorial both expresses and softens our analytic urge to divide. The full sweep of the memorial invites holistic contemplation of the collective action that was the Vietnam War. At the same time, visitors are invited to find—and to reproduce— the name of an individual, a friend, a family member, or a loved one, the personal memory of whom may be quite at variance with collective memory.

How, then, are we to proceed? First, we insist upon listening not only to the voices that dominate the memory of war but also to those that are often ignored, dismissed, or submerged in the din of memory. We do so in order to grasp the tangle of memory in Asia as well as in the United States. No less than war itself, the memory of war is a complex and messy phenomenon. As already noted, like war itself memory is always contested. On the battlefield of memory are an infinite number of paths and trajectories, entry and exit points, psychic wounds and traumas. It is easy to be overwhelmed by the din of memory, to lose one's way as a teacher or student.

Second, we insist upon the need to listen particularly attentively to the Asian voices from the wars that the United States fought on Asian soil. The implication of this is that, above all, we must listen to the voices of noncombatants. Rey Chow's chapter reminds us that the ethos and technology of modern warfare have blurred the distinction between combatants and noncombatants, but for us the distinction remains real nonetheless. Any claim to address the human dimensions of the United States and Asia at war must begin with the recognition that the largest sacrifice, wasted sacrifice for the most part, was that of noncombatants. Certainly we do not want to denigrate the traumas of Americans who lost loved ones in these wars or who themselves came back from foreign wars crippled in body or spirit. Nor should the sufferings of those who were prisoners of war (POWs) or missing in action (MIA) be forgotten. (Incidentally, the number of Japanese, Korean, Chinese, and Vietnamese MIAs dwarfs that of the American MIAs.) We would be remiss, however, did we not emphasize that the memories of the noncombatants are largely Asian memories. With the exception of Pearl Harbor, all three wars were fought on Asian soil. There were very few American civilian deaths and casualties as a result of these wars.

Cultural Approaches

We have no easy answer to the problems of complexity that we have touched upon, perhaps no answers at all that will satisfy the skeptical reader. Nevertheless, we are essaying in this volume what we call a *cultural approach*. We believe that the constant absorption and assimilation of the past into the present occurs in no small measure through cultural expression and the workings of memory. We suggest that a cultural approach can be an important means of learning about America's wars in Asia. The chapters in this volume are loosely configured around several themes that constitute what we intend by a cultural approach. Their individual perspectives and contents vary widely. We make no apology for this. It is our fundamental principle of design. Before looking at several variations of the cultural approach, let us first consider how this approach compares with conventional approaches to the study of war.

The wars that are the subject of this book were framed and fought as *conflicts between nations,* the interests they represent and the ideologies they profess. Historians and social scientists, too, usually conceptualize modern wars as clashes between nations that mobilize power in the pursuit of their interests within the arena of international politics. Most scholars focus on the "big picture"—the trends and incidents leading to the outbreak of war, the major campaigns and battles, the mobilization of national resources and deployment of military forces in pursuit of victory, and the outcome of war as reflected in its winners and losers. In the case of these wars in Asia, attention has also been focused on the political, economic, and cultural changes that war promoted in the countries of the Asia–Pacific region. Military and political leadership, strategy and tactics, and the role of modern technology in warfare are among the topics that dominate the conventional approach. These topics are also the stuff of the national myths that politicians and public opinion leaders create and that maintain such a tenacious hold on the human imagination.

We do not reject or dispute the importance of these approaches to the study of war. Yet we believe that such approaches often restrict and distort the realities of war. In particular, we believe that they often make it difficult to grasp the simple truth that nations are composed of individual human beings, people with family ties and connections to their villages and towns, their histories and their cultures. We seek an approach that enables us to transcend the abstraction of the international system as well as the fetishism of the nation-state with its attendant dichotomies of enemy and ally, friend and foes, hero and villain. We seek an approach that humanizes war, certainly not in the sense of softening its obscenities but, rather, in conveying its horrendous physical, emotional, and psychological impact upon peoples and cultures.[8]

Our cultural approach is diverse rather than singular. It is a river in which different currents flow, sometimes in parallel, sometimes in swirls and eddies. What integrates the various chapters in this volume is a concern, sometimes explicit, sometimes implicit, with the human dimensions of war as we have attempted to delineate them.

The main current is through the analysis of cultural artifacts or productions that in one way or another derive from or evoke the memories of war. These include, but are not limited to, novels, stories, poems, films, painting, and photography. Each of these "texts" can be read as a creative or artistic document that explores both the inner and outer experiences of war.[9] The increasing availability in the West of Asian literature in translation and of subtitled Asian feature and documentary films enables those without knowledge of Asian languages to explore the perspectives of the hitherto exoticized and demonized Asian Other. Let us introduce this approach by briefly considering two Asian texts.

Certainly one of the most disputed events of the Pacific War is the American atomic bombing of Hiroshima and Nagasaki. Historians have framed the debate over these actions in terms of what role they played in hastening the end of the war. Was the atomic bomb the instrument that forced Japan's surrender, or was it a senseless and unnecessary act of destruction?[10] The fiftieth anniversary of these events reopened old wounds. The Japanese government, for example, vehemently protested the U.S. Postal Service's issuance of a commemorative stamp depicting the famous mushroom cloud and bearing the caption "Atomic bombs hasten war's end, August 1945."[11] A planned exhibition at the National Air and Space Museum in Washington, DC, memorializing the ending of the Pacific War unleashed a torrent of controversy in the United States. (This is detailed in Edward Linenthal's chapter in this volume.) Fifty years after the fact, multiple perspectives, each one still deeply charged with emotion, continue to contend with each other.

Masuji Ibuse's poignant novel *Kuroi ame* (Black Rain, 1966) and the powerful film based upon that novel by filmmaker Shohei Imamura (1988) provide a very different perspective on the atomic bombing of Hiroshima. Black Rain is a personal story about the effects of the atomic bomb on an ordinary Japanese family, the Shizumas. Neither the film nor the novel are political works. At one point, a radio broadcast the Shizumas are listening to mentions the possibility that atomic weapons may be used in the Korean War that is then taking place. But this is a passing moment, very much in the background of the human relations that are at the heart of the story. The reader/viewer becomes intimately involved with the Shizumas, a family profoundly affected by the singular catastrophe of the Hiroshima bombing, who are struggling to make sense of precisely what happened while trying simultaneously to go on with their lives. Black Rain succeeds in conveying a deep and quiet sense of the horror of atomic warfare that no historical discussion of President Harry S. Truman's decision to use the bomb or even graphic pictures of the devastation wrought by the bomb can do. Black Rain does not take the place of a historical discussion, nor is it meant to do so, but reading the novel adds a dimension of understanding that no historical document provides.

A second example is Yun Heung-gil's short story "The Rainy Spell."[12] In a conventional sense, the arbitrary post–World War II division of Korea can be studied in the careers of the Korean leaders Kim Il Sung and Syngman Rhee, whose armies battled each other during the Korean War. But the human dimensions of the tragic consequences of division can be explored in "The Rainy

Spell." Narrated by a child unwittingly entangled in the web of the war, the short story describes the bitter conflict that arises between his grandmothers, each of whom has a son on opposing sides in the war. These Asian materials can be matched with and compared to the parallel American literary and other works to explore similarities and differences in the response of different peoples to war. They provide a way to consider both universal truths about the human condition and particular truths about cultures and individuals.

The examples of Black Rain and "The Rainy Spell" demonstrate the utility of focusing on the human dimensions of war. By studying cultural materials, we can transcend the polarizing rhetoric of diplomacy and official propaganda and shift our gaze from the political–strategic games played in capital cities by government leaders to the locales where ordinary people live, fight, and die. By so doing, we can restore the human face of the enemy, the soldier as well as the civilian and cease thinking about them as abstract "Others." An exploration of the human dimensions of war via a cultural approach decenters global strategy, military technology, and the political machinations that take place in capital cities. The unfamiliar names of countless provinces, towns, and villages eclipse Washington, Tokyo, Seoul, Pyongyang, and Hanoi. The names, lives, and concerns of ordinary Japanese, Korean, Chinese, and Vietnamese soldiers and civilians become the morphemes in our language of historical interpretation. In like fashion, through literature, film, and other media we can also better understand the experiences of Americans thrown into combat in distant and often terrifying places. In sum, the cultural approach shifts the analysis of war from the levels of international system and nation to the level of local place, family, and individual.

In a second but closely related sense, the cultural approach relocates these wars in the histories and cultures of the Asian countries themselves rather than seeing them merely as conflicts between the United States and Asian nations. Our own primary focus, to be sure, is on the United States and Asia at war, but it cannot be emphasized too often that during World War II Asia was primarily at war with itself and that Korea and Vietnam, too, were wracked by internal conflict before the involvement of other powers in their wars. Perhaps the most important example of this perspective is Bruce Cumings's controversial reading of the Korean War, which insists upon locating its origins in the social, economic, and political struggles of the Korean people themselves as they struggled to overcome the legacy of Japanese colonialism.[13] International involvement by outside powers like the United States transformed the character of these wars, but did not change the fact that they were rooted in native soil. Ultimately, whatever degree of outside force was brought to bear upon them, the peoples who originated these conflicts also had the primary responsibility of devising means to settle them.[14]

David McCann, following Cumings, insists in his chapter that the Korean War should be read mainly as a Korean narrative. His admittedly experimental reading of the Korean story "Potato," published in 1925, through the retrospective lenses of the Korean War, shows how a cultural approach can be used to illuminate literature from new perspectives. The chapters by Leslie Kennedy Adams and Jim Soular perform a similar task for the literature and poetry of the Vietnam War.

A third current in the cultural approach is the reaffirmation of the value of memory in narrating stories of the wars. Firsthand memories like those of Colonel Harry Summers, Jr. and Merrel Clubb are invaluable in conveying both the meaning and the texture of war. Who can forget Colonel Summers's recollection of the lines of careworn and weary Korean refugees trudging painfully south from the lines of battle or his terror in experiencing a Chinese "human wave" attack? Or Clubb, a young naval gunfire liaison officer, going into battle in the South Pacific with a book of poetry and Joseph Conrad's Lord Jim in his pack! Secondhand memories can be no less illuminating, as the chapters on Chinese memories of the Korean War by James Gao and Pingchao Zhu demonstrate. Here the silence of the fathers and the stories that are withheld as well as those that are told tell us much about the transmission of the Korean War experience to the next generation of Chinese.

As is so often the case, the story itself is stronger than any explanations or interpretations we can offer as historians. Stories provoke questions that are worth discussing with our students, and in this sense the cultural approach serves an important pedagogic purpose as well. Van Symons's chapter "Moral Judgment in War and Crimes Against Humanity" uses literature as a point of entry for considering a number of profound problems that war presents.

Yet another current in the cultural approach that we may call symbolic representation is represented by Rey Chow's chapter, "The Age of the World Target." Chow's meditations upon the imagery of the mushroom cloud lead her to a consideration of the role of the atomic bomb in transforming global culture in an era dominated by visual representation. Her pointed observations on issues of race, gender, and power constitute a brilliant and provocative stimulus to further dialogue.

Finally, even though the cultural approach concerns itself with the local and the particular rather than with the abstract and the universal, it is inherently comparative in spirit and inclination. G.L. Penrose's chapter links Asian wars with transcendent themes in world history. David Trask reminds us of the painful connections between U.S. wars against Native Americans (the "Indian Wars") and the U.S. involvement in Vietnam. Similar links could be drawn in the case of the Pacific and Korean Wars.

Conclusion

There is nothing new, of course, in the idea of studying war through a cultural approach. In the broadest sense, war itself is an intrinsic element of human society, and its cultural representations are among the oldest monuments of world literature, and a recurrent theme ever since. From one perspective, U.S. involvement in the three wars that are the subject of this book connect them backward in time to the nineteenth-century colonial wars pitting Western powers against non-Western peoples, except that in the case of Korea, Japan, an Asian country, was the colonial power. From another perspective, these three wars are quintessentially twentieth-century wars insofar as they manifest both the impact and the limits of modern technology on warfare. The unsatisfactory outcomes of the Korean and Vietnam Wars from the official American point of view challenge the conventional wisdom of technological determinists. The blurring of the distinction between combatants and noncombatants, caused partly by the advent of air power, and the enormous destructiveness of modern conventional warfare, to say nothing of nuclear war, have subverted the heroic readings of war that permeate national myths. To be sure, particularly in World War II, but in Korea and Vietnam as well, the U.S. and Asian governments continued to foster and propagate views of war as tests of national will sustained by the heroic efforts of inspired patriots, but the bibliographies and filmographies of these wars mostly point us in a different direction toward post-heroic, tragic, and cynical readings of the wartime experiences.

It would be comforting to suppose that the era of armed conflict between the United States and Asia is entirely a thing of the past and that growing economic interdependence is creating a transnational cultural comity that may function as a reliable prophylaxis against future wars. Be that as it may, past wars still make their claims upon us, Americans and Asians alike, in a variety of different ways. The cultural approaches limned in this Introduction and elaborated in the volume itself are among the ways we have to settle the claims of the past and transmit the memories and the meanings of these wars to our students and succeeding generations.

Notes

1. Frank Gibney, *The Pacific Century* (New York: Charles Scribner's Sons, 1992), p. 1.
2. Michael Kammen, *Mystic Chords of Memory: The Transformation of Tradition in American Culture* (New York: Alfred A. Knopf, 1991), pp. 3, 13.
3. Charles Hill, "Fighting Stories: The Political Culture of Memory in Northeast Asian Relations," in *Remembering and Forgetting: The Legacy of War and Peace in East Asia*, ed. Gerrit W. Gong (Washington, DC: Center for Strategic and International Studies, 1996), p. 3.
4. Lucian Pye, "Memory, Imagination, and National Myths," in *Gong, Remembering and Forgetting*, p. 21.
5. Herbert Butterfield, *History and Human Relations* (London: Collins, 1951), pp. 9–17.
6. Michael Schudson, *Watergate in American Memory: How We Remember, Forget, and Reconstruct the Past* (New York: Basic Books, 1992), pp. xii-xvi.
7. Haruko Taya Cook and Theodore F. Cook, *Japan at War* (New York: New Press,

1992); Donald Knox, *The Korean War: An Oral History*, 2 vols. (New York: Harcourt, Brace, Jovanovich, 1985, 1988); Larry Engelman, *Tears Before the Rain: An Oral History of the Fall of South Vietnam* (New York: Oxford University Press, 1990).

8. In his *Rites of Spring: The Great War and the Birth of the Modern Age* (New York: Anchor Books, 1989), Morris Eckstein makes this point with regard to historians' accounts of World War I.

9. In *The Great Cat Massacre and Other Episodes in French Cultural History* (New York: Random House, Inc., 1985), Robert Darnton emphasizes the importance of working "back and forth between text and context." His "history in the ethnographic vein" focuses on the texts of intellectuals and common people as a way to explore thinking in eighteenth-century France. Darnton admits that this process is "not much of a methodology," but it does have certain "advantages. It does not flatten out the idiosyncratic element in history, and it allows for consideration of the common ground of experience" (pp. 3–7, 262).

10. See the spring 1995 issue of *Diplomatic History* which is devoted to a consideration of this and related questions.

11. See, for example, "Japan Protests Postage Stamp," *Time,* November 12, 1994.

12. "The Rainy Spell" is one of several short stories in Suh Ji-moon, ed. and trans., *The Rainy Spell and Other Korean Stories* (Armonk, NY: M.E. Sharpe, 1997).

13. Bruce Cumings, *The Origins of the Korean War,* 2 vols. (Princeton: Princeton University Press, 1981, 1990).

14. For a more sophisticated reaffirmation of the Korean War as an international conflict, see William Stueck, *An International History of the Korean War* (Princeton: Princeton University Press, 1994).

Part I

Memorializing

1

Remembering Beginnings and Endings*

The Fiftieth Anniversary at Pearl Harbor and the *Enola Gay* Controversy at the National Air and Space Museum

Edward T. Linenthal

In December 1991, I had the opportunity to work as a volunteer for the National Park Service's History division at the fiftieth anniversary ceremonies at the USS *Arizona* Memorial at Pearl Harbor. I had written about fiftieth anniversary events at other battle sites, notably Lexington and Concord, Gettysburg, and the Little Bighorn, and I had been impressed and moved by the power of the intense remembering, the attraction so many people—participants and visitors alike—felt at being able to ritually "touch" events seen as crucial to the life of the nation. Fiftieth anniversaries, it was clear, were unlike any other. The thinning ranks of veterans, particularly, felt the passage of a half-century since the Minutemen fell on Lexington Green or near Concord Bridge, since the climactic Pickett–Pettigrew charge had been turned back at Cemetery Ridge at Gettysburg, or since Custer and his men fell to the Sioux and Cheyenne on the hills of the Little Bighorn. Subsequent generations, they feared, often grew up ignorant of the sacrifices that had shaped their lives and were seemingly unappreciative of the lessons and legacies of these events. Memory, it seemed, was not firmly entrenched, even though battlefields, monuments, reunions, and reenactments

*Parts of this chapter are adapted and reprinted from Edward T. Linenthal, *Sacred Ground: Americans and Their Battlefields,* 2nd ed. (Urbana: University of Illinois Press, 1993), and Edward T. Linenthal and Tom Engelhardt, eds., *History Wars: The Enola Gay Controversy and Other Battles for the American Past* (New York: Metropolitan Books, 1996).

located these events firmly in national memory. Forgetfulness threatened to consign to oblivion the death of so many.

As I wrote my "biographies" of these sacred sites it was clear, however, that the process of memorialization was anything but a single-minded expression of consensual feelings. There was intense disagreement over the nature and meaning of memorialization: who owned the "means of production" of such events, whether they were meant to function as acts of reconciliation or vehicles for more parochial nationalistic messages, and what were, exactly, the enduring messages of memorial expression. Such events do *not* express what is commonly conceived of as the "collective memory" of a people, but, as James E. Young notes in his study of diverse national memories of the Holocaust, they express "collected memory . . . an aggregate collection of [a society's] many, often competing memories."[1]

In the fall of 1993, Martin Harwit, director of the National Air and Space Museum (NASM), asked me to serve on an advisory committee for that museum's upcoming *Enola Gay* exhibit. By this time, I had published a book on the problems of memorializing American battlefields and had for more than a year been observing from within the volatile creation of the United States Holocaust Memorial Museum. In addition, as a historian I was aware of how uneasily the atomic bombings of Hiroshima and Nagasaki rested in the American consciousness. Nonetheless, nothing in my experience with memorial exhibits prepared me for what happened when the NASM tried to mount its *Enola Gay* exhibit to mark the fiftieth anniversary of the end of World War II.

These experiences have led me to formulate several working hypotheses about public memory: (1) the "finished product," a moving memorial service or tightly woven museum exhibit, for example, "hides" from our view the contentious nature of its construction, a process that tells us much more about the issues judged important by "memorial construction workers" (veterans, politicians, museum professionals, historians, opinion shapers of various kinds) than it does about the event being commemorated. For example, Geoffrey M. White, director of the East-West Center's Program for Cultural Studies, observes that commemorative events often occur when relations between previously warring nations have changed;[2] (2) processes of memorial construction will always be controversial because they involve issues in which people are deeply engaged. How, White asks, can nations "do justice to the memory of past wars without propagating the passions that motivated people to fight in the first place?" Arguing that they cannot, he declares that "the more policymakers struggle with diplomatic phrases that might neutralize the language of remembrance, the deeper they sink in the quagmire of moral indignations felt especially by those who fought the wars";[3] (3) controversy surrounding memorial activity does not mean, as many journalists would have it, that something is "wrong"; rather, it is indicative that volatile memory work is under way.

What follows, then, is an account of some of my experiences—and reflections on them—in the dramatic memorial events at Pearl Harbor and the memorial controversy at the National Air and Space Museum.

Beginnings: The Fiftieth at Pearl Harbor

In *Sacred Ground: Americans and Their Battlefields*—published several years before my involvement with the fiftieth anniversary at Pearl Harbor or my involvement with the *Enola Gay* controversy—I wrote, "It is largely through the ruins of the USS *Arizona* that Americans have been taught to think about the war, the Japanese, and the opening of the nuclear age. In doing so we have come to accept a patriotic orthodoxy that communicates the traditional lessons of the attack, namely, that the events at Pearl Harbor on that quiet Sunday morning were both tragic and fortuitous, for they propelled the nation into a 'good' war against the evil Nazis (in contrast to 'good' Germans) and the treacherous Japanese (the entire culture was so categorized). If America had been forced to invade Japan, it would have lost hundreds of thousands of men. Instead, thanks to modern science a weapon of benevolent destruction, the atomic bomb, had been created. Although it was unfortunate that two such bombs had to be dropped, they *did* end the war; and they also served as a final act of righteous vengeance for the 'Day of Infamy.' For many Americans the atomic bomb balanced the scales of justice."[4]

Not only did commemorative events at Pearl Harbor stress the link between the attack and the atomic bomb, but rhetoric called attention to the lessons of preparedness and the continued vulnerability of the nation—frightening in the age of atomic weapons; occasionally commemorative voices claimed the memorial as a place of reconciliation between former bitter enemies. The site was also sanctified by the presence of the USS *Arizona* herself, a unique relic in American life, functioning as historic site, shrine, and gravesite for those entombed in the ship. The presence of the USS *Arizona* established a "commemorative membrane" around the site—situated in the midst of a busy Navy base—within which any Japanese presence, cars and tourists, for example, were perceived by some visitors as a defiling intrusion into American sacred space. More significantly, these feelings complicated the National Park Service's (NPS) attempt to shape a historical narrative in the small museum at the visitor center.

In the late 1980s there was resistance to a plan to return to Pearl Harbor the *Ha. 119,* a Japanese midget submarine captured during the attack, the first American trophy of war. It was an artifact that could bring home to visitors the material reality of the attack. Some veterans' groups, under the mistaken impression that the submarine would be placed near the memorial rather than near the visitor center, complained bitterly, and the flames were fanned by journalists, ever eager to claim that the NPS was being unpatriotic in its stewardship of the memorial. The Park Service practiced effective damage control, but the midget submarine has yet to be returned to Pearl Harbor. Likewise, in 1987, there was opposition to a planned display of a Japanese airman's uniform. A New Jersey resident characterized the idea as an "atrocity" that would "defile the memory" of the men entombed in the ship. NPS Director William Penn Mott, Jr., responded that the display was designed to bring home the "awful reality" of the attack and to put a face on the former enemy.

Tensions mounted as the fiftieth anniversary drew near. In August 1991 the State Department settled a most sensitive issue: whether the Japanese would officially participate in the ceremonies. It announced that no representatives of *any* foreign government would attend. (Judged too controversial, for example, was a plan to have American and Japanese children meet at the memorial and throw commemorative wreaths around USS *Arizona*.) Accusations were made that the Park Service was not an appropriate guardian of the sacred memory of those Americans who died at Pearl Harbor. Critics complained that NPS interpretive programs and the film shown at the visitors center were too "soft" on the Japanese. (The film—since replaced—was, ironically, produced by the Navy and not the Park Service.) In response to claims that Japanese tourists clap at inappropriate times in the film, Superintendent Donald Magee remarked that he had never heard "any ethnic group laughing, clapping in glee, or in any way being disrespectful." He added, "I have also spoken to many of the park rangers, staff, and volunteers (that includes five Pearl Harbor survivors among their number) here at the Memorial. Three of the individuals, including the film projectionists, have been here since the facility opened in 1980 and they collectively have seen thousands and thousands of programs. They were unable to recall a single incident of Japanese visitors applauding, clapping, or cheering. If such behavior has happened, it must be very rare indeed."

Complaints about the irreverence of Japanese tourists intensified, however, and one angry tourist suggested in a letter to his congressman that "no visitors from areas of the Far East be allowed to visit this area during the first two weeks of December 1991." Park Service staff of Asian ethnicity but U.S. citizenship experienced tense moments with hostile visitors.

Just as various controversies seemed ready to burst into sustained public attack, the Park Service's moving four-day commemorative affair was judged a success by the overwhelming majority of veterans—particularly those belonging to the Pearl Harbor Survivors Association. Personal recollection dominated the events. The NPS was responsible for inviting the two surviving Medal of Honor recipients, and it also invited Franklin Van Valkenburgh, son of the USS *Arizona*'s captain, who had never been to the memorial.

Several moments stand out in my memory from these eventful days. December 6 was designated "Reflections of Pearl Harbor," and last to speak in the afternoon was the acclaimed author James Michener, himself a navy veteran, who told the audience, "I come before you today as one who was modified by our national experience in fighting Japan. For four long years I battled her empire with every shred of energy I had, and watched with pride as we slowly drove her from the oceans and assailed her on land. . . . For the next few years, I lived in Japan, studied her ways, grew to love her art, and wrote six books about things Japanese. From a dedicated enemy I slowly transformed myself into a devoted friend, with help from the Japanese themselves, who were becoming my friends." It was from this "devastation and cruelty," Michener said, "that a miraculous friendship developed, . . . and it is that triumph that we honor today."

After the ceremonies, on December 9–11, a number of American and Japanese survivors gathered with military, academic, and NPS historians, radar operators, nurses, pilots, NPS underwater archaeologists, and others in Honolulu's Blaisdell Center for the Performing Arts for "The Storm Unleashed," a symposium cosponsored by the Arizona Memorial Museum Association and the Navy Historical Institute. At the end of the conference, the Punahou School Chorale ascended the stage and sang the beautifully haunting Civil War song "Tenting on the Old Camp Ground." As the refrain "many are the hearts that are weary tonight, wishing for the war to cease; many are the hearts that are looking for the right, to see the dawn of peace" hung in the air, American and Japanese veterans met together in the front of the auditorium and joined the audience in singing "God Bless America." This utterly transfixing moment signified to me the power and promise of commemorative occasions. It was a moment beyond the politics of commemoration, beyond the great public commemorative occasions. The intimacy and authenticity of the moment was unforgettable. These men and women did not practice an insidious forgetfulness that often infects such occasions. They did not trivialize or sanitize the hatred and horror of the war. Rather, they acknowledged it and sought, fifty years later, to overcome it.

Endings: The *Enola Gay* Controversy at the National Air and Space Museum

Alfred Preis, designer of the USS *Arizona* Memorial, conceived of it as an architectural expression of American wars and the rhythm of World War II in particular. Pearl Harbor historian Michael Slackman observed that the architect "viewed the United States as an essentially pacifistic nation, one which inevitably would sustain the first blow in any war" and that he wanted to remind Americans of the "inevitability of sustaining the initial defeat, of the potential for victory, and the sacrifices necessary to make the painful journey from defeat to victory." The commemorative tensions at the USS *Arizona* Memorial at the fiftieth anniversary had little to do with the story itself, but, as we have seen, with the appropriate stewardship of a sacred place. Once the Park Service "proved" that it respected the commemorative sensibilities of veterans, there was an almost immediate cessation of hostilities from members of Congress, journalists, and a few disgruntled veterans who had fanned the flames of controversy.

The commemoration of endings was different, however, as from 1945 to the present, Americans have been divided on the wisdom or necessity of the use of the bomb. The National Air and Space Museum tried, in cultural commentator Tom Engelhardt's words, "to link the unlinkable: the burnished plane with the human suffering it caused and continues to cause; smiling shots of boisterous young airmen with unbearable images of seared victims; the consciousness of those who fought in World War II with the consciousness of those who grew up in the penumbra of World War III; the celebratory with the crematory; the just with the unjust; victory with defeat. . . . As an icon, the plane's gleaming fuse-lage would be both world redeemer and world destroyer."[5]

As a member of the exhibit's advisory committee, I was aware in the early spring of 1994 that controversy was brewing. My first reactions were to frame the issue entirely as one between those who refused to see the use of atomic weapons in anything but triumphalist terms or to peer beneath the mushroom cloud and those who wanted to tell a more complex story about the end of the war and the legacy of Hiroshima and Nagasaki. I still think that this is a large part of this story but, as the controversy grew, and I decided to write about it, it became clear that the story was more complicated. I have examined what seem to me three crucial components of this story: (1) the enduring ambivalence toward the *Enola Gay* itself and the impact of its presence in the exhibit; (2) the changing function of the National Air and Space Museum—from temple to forum to tribunal; and (3) the ways in which the controversy was framed in public and the consequences of the cancellation of the exhibit.

In 1946, New Mexico senator Carl Hatch proposed that the *Enola Gay* be housed in an "Atomic Bomb National Monument" at Alamagordo, New Mexico, under the stewardship of the National Park Service. The monument was not established, and in 1949 the *Enola Gay* came under the jurisdiction of the National Air Museum (the world "Space" would be added to its name in 1966). From 1953 until 1960, the airplane sat on a runway at Andrews Air Force Base in Maryland, in disrepair, until it was finally disassembled and moved to a Smithsonian preservation facility in Maryland in 1961. There was uneasiness about the Smithsonian displaying a restored *Enola Gay.* Even Arizona senator Barry Goldwater, who had been an Army Air Force pilot during World War II, stated during congressional hearings on the Smithsonian in 1970, "what we are interested in here [for the museum] is the truly historic aircraft. I wouldn't consider the one that dropped the bomb on Japan as belonging to that category." By the time Martin Harwit became the NASM's director in 1987, however, there was pressure from B-29 veterans to have a restored *Enola Gay* displayed, and Harwit agreed. There was long-standing concern, however, that the *Enola Gay,* by its overwhelming presence, would appear too celebratory, that it would, in fact, overwhelm the text and artifacts of *any* exhibit. Consequently, the script was shaped in part as an antidote to the presence of this powerful relic. What those of us involved in thinking about the exhibit did not fully appreciate, however, was that, like the USS *Arizona,* the *Enola Gay*'s presence in the exhibit established a commemorative membrane around it, within which the language of commemorative respect was expected to dominate. For many NASM visitors, the *Enola Gay* could not help but transform exhibit space into commemorative space, where unambiguous narratives recalling the sacrifices of Americans at war could be expected to prevail, especially on the fiftieth anniversary of the war's end. Consequently, when it was decided that the proposed exhibit would focus on the difficult story of the bomb as both savior and destroyer, some people saw this as an offense to the heroic memory of the war.

The construction of the exhibition took place in a museum that had traditionally been perceived as a temple, an aeronautical showcase for the aerospace industry and the military. Gleaming airplanes and missiles were often displayed with little regard to the historical context in which they functioned. Martin Harwit believed that the American public was ready for an exhibit on the atomic bomb and the end of the war because under his leadership there had been several successful exhibits through which the museum functioned as a forum, a place where public issues could be engaged. An old exhibit on the V-2 rocket—a Nazi weapon of mass destruction—had, for example, focused on the technological innovation of the V-2 and ignored the fact that concentration camp labor built it, that it killed and terrorized thousands, and that American space hero Wernher von Braun created the V-2 for Hitler's Germany. The new V-2 exhibit consciously jettisoned the technological celebratory, believing that a more important story was being ignored.

For those comfortable with the museum-as-temple, the NASM seemed to be moving beyond a forum, however, to a tribunal in which American air power was being put on trial. For example, critics pointed to the 1991 exhibit "Legends, Memory, and the Great War in the Air," which examined, in part, how the romantic mythology of air war could mask the brutal realities of combat in World War I. While the *Washington Post* characterized the exhibit as a "dose of reality," the *Wall Street Journal* called it a "sneering look at aerial combat in World War I."

Like the "Great War in the Air," the *Enola Gay* exhibit would become a lightning rod in a bitter contest over the relationship between memory and history as well as between celebratory and critical stances toward the American experience generally.

In the spring of 1994, the Air Force Association (AFA)—a lobbying organization for the Air Force—which had engaged in fruitless discussions with Harwit and the exhibit's curators over the script since the fall of 1993, released a stinging critique of the script in the pages of *Air Force Magazine*. The script was characterized as lacking attention to the context in which atomic weapons were used (the long and bloody march across the Pacific) and, on balance, as focusing too much attention to the Japanese-as-victims of the bomb and not nearly enough on the Japanese-as-aggressors and perpetrators. They were unhappy with the script's section on historically controversial questions—did the United States ignore Japanese peace initiatives, should the United States have guaranteed the

Japanese emperor's position, how important was the Soviet factor—for example. This section concluded that most scholars "believe that Truman and his advisors saw the bomb first and foremost as a way to shorten the war. . . . Still, virtually all now agree that the bomb's usefulness for 'atomic diplomacy' against the Soviets provided one more reason for Truman not to halt the dropping of the bomb."

The controversy escalated throughout the summer and fall of 1994, as journalists, ignorant of the fifty-year history of controversy about the atomic bomb, judged it a post-Vietnam product of disaffected left-wing historians. Apparently none of them knew that, in the immediate postwar years, conservatives had been some of the most vociferous critics of the use of atomic weapons. Rather, the public was informed that the sacrifice of Americans in the Pacific War was being demeaned, when in fact, even the Air Force Association, in its ringing denunciation of the first script, allowed that the men of the 509th (Composite Group) were treated "extensively, and with respect." Despite the fact that the NASM worked with military historians from, for example, the Office of the Secretary of Defense and various services, many of whom thought revisions of the script were acceptable, veterans' groups were up in arms, congressional critics clamored about "revisionist" history, Martin Harwit and the curators came under withering attack, and in January 1995, Smithsonian secretary I. Michael Heyman canceled the exhibit.

Ironically, the controversy over this exhibit exposed the American public to the scholarly debates over the use of atomic weapons. Newspapers carried contending opinion pieces, national and cable networks carried special programs on the issue, and new books appeared that ensured the debates a new public life.

The *Enola Gay* controversy is much more about the cultural climate of the 1990s than it is about events in 1945. Why is it that certain volatile stories can be told at some cultural moments and not others? In 1980, for example, Republican senator Mark Hatfield of Oregon helped bring an exhibition of artifacts and graphic photographs from the Hiroshima Peace Memorial Museum to the rotunda of the Old Senate Office Building in Washington, DC. Hatfield had been in Hiroshima a month after it was destroyed and recalled, "The bomb saved my life. . . . But to see the indiscriminate devastation and to think that now the world has one million times the nuclear explosive power of that one bomb—maybe this exhibit will give us pause."

The cultural climate of the 1990s, however, proved far less amenable to the telling of this darker narrative about atomic weapons. For many, even to allow mention of the ambiguities and darknesses in our country's history appeared a dangerous activity. It is telling, I think, that it was easier to raise questions about the use of atomic weapons in 1946 than it was in 1995.[6]

On May 18, 1995, I testified on the *Enola Gay* controversy before the Senate Committee on Rules and Administration. Besides offering my own interpretation of the controversy, I observed that, in calling the exhibit "revisionist," members of Congress were operating from a faulty understanding of history, namely, that history is a frozen set of facts to which we pay obeisance. The term had come to be linked with Holocaust denial (formerly called Holocaust "revision"). I argued that all historical writing is, in some way, a revision of our understanding of the past. We turn to *Glory* or Ken Burns's *The Civil War* series and not to *Birth of a Nation* or *Gone with the Wind* to understand the Civil War, for example. It came as no surprise that the senators were not interested and, in some cases, exhibited a naïveté about "doing history" that one would expect from a college freshman. California senator Diane Feinstein said, for example, that when she studied history it was "essentially a recitation of fact, leaving the reader to draw their own analysis. . . . I wonder about the wisdom in presenting any interpretation."

Near the end of my testimony, Alaska senator Ted Stevens—a long-standing opponent of Smithsonian exhibits that questioned heroic interpretations of American history—grew visibly angry and declared, "I do not want my grandson to walk out of that museum and ask me why I was one who was the aggressor, and why did I try to kill Japanese babies."[7] I said that I never would have read the script that way, and we moved on to other issues. With the benefit of hindsight, I would have liked to respond in this manner. "Senator, I do not think that the script was intended to portray the United States as an aggressor in the Pacific War. But the script certainly did show the horror of what the atomic bomb did to people, many of them innocent of the crimes of the fascist government of Japan. And perhaps you could have taken your grandson to this exhibit and spoken with him about these shocking photographs of dead Japanese, and also the horrific photographs of American casualties of war. Perhaps you could have imparted a wisdom born out of your experience in the war by telling him that in war sometimes innocent people are killed and that one of the great tragedies of World War II was that so many innocent people were killed. You could tell him that many people believe that the use of the atomic bomb was the only way to bring the war to an end, and that others disagree because the bomb killed so indiscriminately. You could tell him that, in your opinion, the bomb was necessary, but that while it offered relief that the killing would finally end, it also caused sadness and mourning for the innocent dead, not only in Hiroshima and Nagasaki, but for all innocents who died in the war. What a powerful commemorative message that would have been, Senator Stevens. It would have helped your grandson begin to appreciate the complexity and ambiguity of history, and that our memories can encompass this, while also paying homage to those who died. This, in my opinion, could have been the enduring legacy of the *Enola Gay* exhibition at the National Air and Space Museum."

Notes

1. James E. Young, *The Texture of Memory: Holocaust Memorials and Meaning* (New Haven: Yale University Press, 1993), p. xi.

2. Young, *The Texture of Memory*, p. 15; Geoffrey M. White, "Memory Wars: The Politics of Remembering the Asia-Pacific War," *East-West Center*, no. 21 (July 1995): 3.

3. White, "Memory Wars," p. 3.

4. For an examination of the history of the USS *Arizona* Memorial, and a description and analysis of fiftieth-anniversary ceremonies, see Edward T. Linenthal, *Sacred Ground: Americans and Their Battlefields,* 2nd ed. (Urbana: University of Illinois Press, 1993), pp. 173–212, 233–49. Unless otherwise noted, all quoted material in this section is from this chapter.

5. Tom Engelhardt, "Fifty Years Under a Cloud: The Uneasy Search for Our Atomic History," *Harper's Magazine* (January 1996): 72. Unless otherwise noted, quoted material in this section is from Edward T. Linenthal, "Anatomy of a Controversy," in *History Wars: The Enola Gay Controversy and Other Battles for the American Past,* ed. Edward T. Linenthal and Tom Engelhardt (New York: Metropolitan Books, 1996).

6. Likewise, changing cultural climates dictated what was remembered and forgotten at Pearl Harbor ceremonies. Roger Dingman notes in the early 1950s that Japan provided bases of support for American military efforts in Korea: "it would have been imprudent . . . for the president or his surrogate to have called attention to the Pearl Harbor attack." During the Vietnam War, commemorative ceremonies had "no intention of stirring up unpleasant memories about a nation that was once again providing bases essential for prosecution of an American war in Asia" ("Reflections on Pearl Harbor Anniversaries Past," *Journal of American–East Asian Relations* 3, no. 3 [fall 1994]: 283, 285).

7. Feinstein and Stevens quoted in *U.S. Congress Senate Committee on Rules and Administration, Hearings on the Smithsonian Institution Management Guidelines for the Future,* 104 Cong., 1st sess., May 11, 18, 1995, pp. 62, 64.

2

The Bombed

Hiroshimas and Nagasakis in Japanese Memory

John W. Dower

Hara Mieko, who was a youngster in Hiroshima when the city was bombed, later wrote of herself that the "Mieko of today is completely different from the Mieko of the past."[1] Most *hibakusha* (survivors of the atomic explosions) experienced this fracturing of identity, and for Japan as a whole the very meaning of time was altered by the atomic bombings of August 6 and 9, 1945.

Such a profound sense of disjuncture was, of course, not peculiar to Japan. For much of the world, the Holocaust in Europe and the nuclear genocide of Hiroshima/Nagasaki signified the closure of "modernity" as it had been known and dreamed about until then and the advent of a new world of terrible and awesome potentialities. In Japan, however, the situation was unique in two ways. Only the Japanese actually had experienced nuclear destruction. And in the years immediately following, only they were not allowed to publicly engage the nature and meaning of this new world. Beginning in mid-September 1945, U.S. authorities in occupied Japan censored virtually all discussion of the bombs.

Such censorship reflected both the general U.S. policy of secrecy concerning nuclear matters and, on a different plane, the broad agenda of media control pursued as part of U.S. occupation policy in defeated Japan itself. Where Hiroshima and Nagasaki specifically were concerned, the rationale for censorship within Japan was essentially twofold. American occupation authorities feared that unrestrained discussion of the effects of the bomb might incite "public unrest" against them (the most elastic and all-encompassing rationales of censors everywhere). More specifically, statements by Japanese politicians and the print media early in September conveyed the impression that the Allied policy of

Reprinted with permission from *Diplomatic History,* Volume 19, Number 2, Spring 1995.

publicizing Japanese war atrocities and conducting war-crimes trials might confront a Japanese countercampaign that called attention to the Allies' own atrocious policies, most graphically exemplified by the nuclear destruction of the two essentially civilian targets.[2]

Such a hypothetical countercampaign was plausible. Shigemitsu Mamoru, a once and future foreign minister (and future convicted war criminal in the interim), authored an early internal memorandum explicitly proposing that the Japanese use the atomic bombs as counterpropaganda to Allied accusations of Japanese war crimes. Hatoyama Ichirō, an ambitious conservative politician who aspired to the premiership (the occupation-period purge disrupted his timetable, but he did serve as prime minister from the end of 1954 to 1956), rashly voiced similar opinions in public.[3] In the opening weeks of occupation, the Dōmei news agency and leading newspapers, such as the *Asahi,* also naively attempted to balance the record of war behavior in this manner. With the advantage of hindsight, however, it can be said that the censorship of Japanese discussion of the bombs and their human consequences was misguided, perhaps counterproductive, certainly disdainful of the needs of survivors themselves.

Between August 6 and 9, when the bombs were dropped, and mid-September when censorship was imposed by the U.S. occupation forces, Japanese responses to the new weapon actually were varied and provocative. Until the American victors established their presence in defeated Japan, of course, the media was censored by Japan's own imperial government. Thus, the historian faces a biased public record both before and after the occupation commenced. Still, it is possible to recreate a kaleidoscope of responses beyond the overwhelming sense of horror and shock experienced by those who suffered the bombings directly, and apart from the political notion of playing Allied atrocities against Japanese ones.

Initially, rage was one such response. In Hiroshima immediately after the bombing, for example, survivors came upon uninjured American POWs (they had been confined in underground cells) and beat them to death.[4] In a makeshift Hiroshima medical facility, the rumor spread that Japan had retaliated by bombing the United States with its own secret weapon, causing comparable atrocious death and suffering—and that the Japanese survivors, it was reported, were pleased. The government and media naturally condemned the weapon as evidence of the enemy's barbaric and demonic nature. Early in September, before occupation censorship was imposed, *Asahi Shimbun* ran a vivid article about the hatred of Americans visible in the eyes of Hiroshima survivors. Later, in one of the countless unnoticed individual tragedies of the occupation period, a Nisei soldier affiliated with the U.S. forces visited relatives in Hiroshima, where his parents came from, and was so shattered by their hostility to him as an American "murderer" that he committed suicide soon afterward in his quarters in Tokyo.[5]

Perhaps surprisingly, however, at least at first glance, hatred against the Americans did not become a dominant sentiment in the weeks, months, and years that followed. The destructiveness of the bombs was so awesome that many Japanese initially regarded them—much like the calamitous losing war itself—almost as if they were a natural disaster. Then, as the man-made nature of the disaster sank in, what riveted attention was the realization that science and technology suddenly had leapt to hitherto unimagined levels. Such attitudes soon became conspicuous even in the two bombed cities themselves (although the Americans still took care to assign British and Australian forces to oversee local occupation administration in Hiroshima). Certainly they were prevalent throughout defeated Japan as a whole, where rage dissipated quickly in the face of the urgent challenges of recovery—and, indeed, simple daily survival.

The Japanese identified the new weapon as a nuclear bomb within a matter of days. Their own scientists had investigated the possibility of building such weapons after Pearl Harbor and had concluded that doing so was technically feasible but practically impossible for many decades to come.[6] Nishina Yoshio, an eminent physicist who had studied with Niels Bohr and supervised some of the wartime research on the military application of nuclear fission, was sent to Hiroshima right after the attack and immediately recognized that these long-term projections had been naive. (Nishina died of cancer in 1951, and it is popularly believed that his illness resulted from his exposure to residual radiation in Hiroshima.)

By August 15, when Japan capitulated, it was widely known throughout the country that a weapon of entirely new dimensions had devastated the two cities. The emperor himself, in his careful, self-serving address of this date announcing acceptance of the Potsdam Declaration, took care to emphasize this. "The enemy has for the first time used cruel bombs to kill and maim extremely large numbers of the innocent," Hirohito informed his subjects, "and the heavy casualties are beyond measure; if the war were continued, it would lead not only to the downfall of our nation but also to the destruction of all human civilization."[7] Japan's capitulation, in the official imperial rendering, thus became a magnanimous act that saved humanity itself from possible annihilation.

By the time the first contingent of U.S. occupation forces actually arrived in Japan at the very end of August, popular responses to the defeat and unconditional surrender had begun to assume complex configurations politically. The bombs quickly became a symbol of America's material might and scientific prowess—and this symbol was all the more stunning because it contrasted so sharply with Japan's relative material backwardness. While the Americans had been perfecting nuclear weapons, Japan's militaristic government had been exhorting the emperor's loyal subjects to take up bamboo spears and fight to the bitter end to defend the homeland. A year after all the surrender, Katō Etsurō, a famous cartoonist, perfectly captured this dichotomy in the opening pages of a little book of illustrations chronicling the first year of occupation. An exhausted Japanese man and woman lay on the ground on August 15, fire buckets discarded beside them, contemplating the absurdity of pitting bamboo spears and little pails against atomic bombs.[8]

Katō's juxtaposition of atomic bombs against bamboo spears captured a widespread and politically explosive sentiment. In sum, it amounted to this: Japan's ideologues and military spokesmen had deceived the people and led the country into a hopeless war against a vastly superior United States. Personally, they obviously were fools (thus there was not much popular Japan hand-wringing about the showcase Tokyo war crimes trials). More generally, one clearly could not trust military appeals or military solutions in the future (thus the "no war clause" of the new 1947 Japanese constitution, originally drafted by the Americans, found strong support among ordinary Japanese).[9]

The popular antimilitary sentiment that has influenced so much of postwar Japanese politics has its genesis in such visceral feelings. The "fifteen-year war" in general was devastating for Japan. Close to three million Japanese soldiers, sailors, and civilians were killed between the Manchurian Incident of 1931 and Japan's surrender in 1945, and a total of sixty-six cities, including Hiroshima and Nagasaki, were bombed. In the end, misery and humiliation were the only conspicuous legacies of the so-called holy war.[10] The atomic bombs quickly came to exemplify this tragic absurdity.

In these various ways, a complex symbolic field already had begun to resonate around the bomb by the time the victorious Americans arrived. The horror of a war brought home with unimagined destructiveness was one aspect of this, Japan's own backwardness another, the immense potentiality of science yet another. The Japanese did not place a negative construction on "science" in this context but, on the contrary, singled out deficiency in science and technology as an obvious explanation for their defeat and an immediately accessible means by which the country could be rebuilt.

Scarcely a day passed between Japan's capitulation and the imposition of censorship by the Americans in mid-September that did not see a statement by the government or press about the urgent necessity of promoting science. On August 16, in his first broadcast after being named prime minister, Prince Higashikuni Naruhiko declared that "science and technology" had been Japan's biggest shortcoming in the war. A day later, the outgoing minister of education thanked school children for their wartime efforts and urged them to dedicate themselves to the elevating Japan's "science power and spiritual power" to the highest possible levels. On August 19, the press reported that under the new minister of education, Maeda Tamon, the postwar school system would place "emphasis on basic science." "We lost to the enemy's science," the *Asahi* declared bluntly in an August 20 article, going on to observe that "this was made clear by a single bomb dropped on Hiroshima." The article was headlined "Toward a Country Built on Science."[11] In the years that followed, improving science education remained one of the country's foremost priorities.

In Japan, as elsewhere, the bomb thus became Janus: simultaneously a symbol of the terror of nuclear war and the promise of science. More than in other countries, however, the peculiar circumstances of the nuclear bombings, unconditional surrender, and, later, the new pacifist constitution created a postwar milieu in which "building a nation of science" almost invariably was coupled with an emotional emphasis on "peace" maintained through nonmilitary pursuits. Economically, the long-term consequences of this development were spectacular. Japan's emergence as an economic superpower by the 1980s resulted in considerable part from the fact that, after the surrender, the vast majority of talented Japanese scientists, businessmen, and bureaucrats devoted themselves to promoting *civilian* applications of science. Unlike the United States, where many scientists and engineers found the sweetest problems and most lucrative funding in weapons-related research, in Japan such work carried a social stigma.[12]

The immediate sanguine linkage between the tragedy of Hiroshima/Nagasaki and the promise of a "country built on science" had ramifications beyond just the material promotion of science and technology. Science itself became equated with the development of more "rational" modes of thinking in general. The disastrous folly of the lost war, that is, was attributed to a weakness in critical thought and "conceptual ability" throughout Japanese society. From this perspective, it was only a short but momentous step to linking promotion of science to promotion of democracy in a postwar Japan, on the grounds that scientific progress was possible only in a "rational" environment that encouraged genuinely free inquiry and expression. In this manner, a seemingly technological response to defeat contained within itself a political logic that contributed greatly to support for casting off the shackles of the imperial state and instituting progressive reforms.[13]

At the same time, the trauma of nuclear devastation and unconditional surrender also reinforced an abiding sense of Japan's peculiar vulnerability and victimization. As the bombs came to symbolize the tragic absurdity of war, the recent war itself became perceived as fundamentally a *Japanese* tragedy. Hiroshima and Nagasaki became icons of Japanese suffering—perverse national treasures, of a sort, capable of fixating Japanese memory of the war on what had happened to Japan and simultaneously blotting out recollection of the Japanese victimization of others. Remembering Hiroshima and Nagasaki, that is, easily became a way of forgetting Nanjing, Bataan, the Burma–Siam railway, Manila, and the countless Japanese atrocities these and other place names signified to non-Japanese.

"Victim-consciousness" (*higaisha ishiki*) is a popular euphemism in postwar and contemporary Japan, and the bombs occupy a central place in this consciousness. From this perspective, it can be observed that nuclear victimization spawned new forms of nationalism in postwar Japan—a neonationalism that coexists in complex ways with antimilitarism and even the "one-country pacifism" long espoused by many individuals and groups associated with the political Left.

II

Such considerations leave out the fate of the nuclear victims themselves; and, in fact, most Americans and Japanese at the time were happy to ignore those victims. Official U.S. reports about the two stricken cities tended to emphasize physical damage and minimize human loss and suffering. Prescient early journalistic accounts about the horrifying consequences of radiation sickness were repudiated or repressed by occupation authorities. Japanese film footage was confiscated. Accounts of fatalities were conservative.

The U.S. policy of prohibiting open reporting from Hiroshima and Nagasaki was made clear at an early date, in a celebrated incident involving the Australian journalist Wilfred Burchett. Burchett made his way to Hiroshima early in September and succeeded in dispatching a graphic description of victims of an "atomic plague" to the London *Daily Express*. This was the first Western account of the fatal effects of radiation, and occupation officials immediately mounted an attack on what Burchett had reported. He was temporarily stripped of his press accreditation, and his camera, containing film with yet undeveloped Hiroshima exposures, mysteriously "disappeared." A comparable early account by an American journalist in Nagasaki never cleared General Douglas MacArthur's press headquarters, and reports to the outside world thereafter were carefully controlled through complacent, officially approved mouthpieces, such as William Laurence, the science editor of the *New York Times*.[14] Some eleven thousand feet of movie film shot in the two cities between August and December by a thirty-man Japanese camera crew was confiscated by the U.S. authorities in February 1946 and not returned to Japan until two decades later, in 1966.[15]

Accurate estimates of atomic-bomb fatalities also have been difficult to come by over the years. In June 1946, the prestigious U.S. Strategic Bombing Survey placed the number of deaths at approximately seventy to eighty thousand individuals in Hiroshima and thirty-five to forty thousand in Nagasaki. An honest estimate at the time, these figures have been perpetrated in most subsequent commentary about the bombs, although they probably are conservative in themselves and obviously fail to take into account bomb-related deaths subsequent to mid-1946. For the usual political reasons, after 1946 neither the U.S. nor Japanese governments chose to revise the initial estimates or call attention to the ongoing toll of *hibakusha* deaths. It now appears that the total of immediate and longer-term deaths caused by the bombing of two cities may be as high as triple the familiar earlier estimates—in the neighborhood, that is, of three hundred thousand or more individuals.[16]

Disregard for the victims extended beyond sanitized reporting, suppressed film footage of the human aftermath, and disregard of the real death toll. Unsurprisingly, the United States extended no aid to survivors of the atomic bomb. Among other considerations, to do so could have been construed as acknowledging that use of the bombs had been improper. Aid to victims also might have opened the door to claims for compensation or special treatment by victims of conventional U.S. incendiary bombing. The well-known Atomic Bomb Casualty Commission (ABCC) established by the U.S. government in Japan at the beginning of 1947 was set up exclusively to collect scientific data on the long-term biological effects of the bombs. Whether fairly or not, to many Japanese the ABCC thereby earned the onus of simply treating the *hibakusha* residents of Hiroshima and Nagasaki as experimental subjects or guinea pigs a second time.[17]

More surprisingly, perhaps, the Japanese government began extending special assistance to the bomb victims only after the occupation ended in 1952. In the aftermath of the devastation of Hiroshima and Nagasaki, local treatment was largely dependent on local resources—and this from municipalities that had come close to annihilation. One of the several legacies of this callous early history of neglect has been to make identification of victims and precise quantification of the effects of the bombs even more problematic than might otherwise have been the case.[18]

In the localities themselves, suffering was compounded not merely by the unprecedented nature of the catastrophe, as well as by the absence of large-scale government assistance, but also by the fact that public struggle with this traumatic experience was *not permitted.* It is at the local level that U.S. censorship was most inhumane. With but rare exceptions, survivors of the bombs could not grieve publicly, could not share their experiences through the written word, could not be offered public counsel and support. Psychological traumas we now associate with the bomb experience—psychic numbing and the guilt of survivors, for example, along with simple coping with massive bereavement and mutilation and grotesque protracted deaths—could not be addressed in open media forums. Nor could Japanese medical researchers working with survivors publish their findings so that other doctors and scientists might make use of them in treating the *hibakusha.* U.S. occupation authorities began easing restrictions on the publication of personal accounts by survivors only after more than three years had passed since the bombings. And it was not until February 1952—two months before the occupation ended, and six and one-half years after the residents of Hiroshima and Nagasaki were bombed and irradiated—that Japanese academic associations were able to engage freely, openly, and independently in investigating atomic-bomb injuries.[19]

American isolation of the *hibakusha* was compounded by ostracism within Japanese society itself, for the bomb, of course, stigmatized its victims. Some were disfigured. Some were consigned to a slow death. Some, *in utero* on those fateful midsummer days, were mentally retarded. Many could not cope well with the so-called real world to which most other Japanese (including survivors of combat as well as conventional incendiary bombing) returned after the war. And all initially were presumed to carry the curse of the bombs in their blood. *Hibakusha* were not welcome compatriots in the new Japan. Psychologically if not physically, they were deformed reminders of a miserable past. Given the unknown genetic consequences of irradiation, they were shunned as marriage prospects. The great majority of Japanese, overwhelmed by their own struggles for daily survival, were happy to put them out of mind. So was the Japanese government, which did not even establish its own research council to conduct surveys of bomb survivors until November 1953.[20]

In this milieu, where time was so peculiarly warped, the Japanese as a whole did not begin to really *visualize* the human consequences of the bombs in concrete, vivid ways until three or four years after Hiroshima and Nagasaki had been destroyed. The first graphic depictions of victims seen in Japan were not photographs but drawings and paintings by the wife-and-husband artists Maruki Toshi and Maruki Iri, who had rushed to Hiroshima, where they had relatives, as soon as news of the bomb arrived. The Marukis published a booklet of black-and-white Hiroshima drawings in 1950 under the title *Pika-don* ("Flash-bang," a euphemism peculiar to the blinding flash and ensuing blast of the atomic bombs). In 1950 and 1951, they were permitted to exhibit five large murals of *hibakusha* entitled "Ghosts," "Fire," "Water," "Rainbow," and "Boys and Girls." This was the beginning, as it turned out, of a lifelong series of collaborative paintings addressing the human dimensions of World War II in Asia.[21]

As the Marukis later recalled, they began attempting to paint Hiroshima in 1948 not merely because they remained haunted by what they had witnessed but also because they believed that if they did not put brush to paper there might never be a visual eyewitness record of these events for Japanese to see. Actual photographs of the effects of the bombs in Hiroshima and Nagasaki were not published in Japan until after the occupation ended in the spring of 1952—and in theory never should have been available from Japanese sources to publish at all, since occupation policy forbade even possessing such negatives or prints.

In the print media, the easing of censorship in late 1948 finally paved the way for publication of reminiscences, poems, essays, and fictional recreations by *hibakusha*. A minor publishing boom developed in this area, led by a remarkable outpouring of writings by Nagai Takashi, a widowed young father dying of radiation sickness in Nagasaki. Nagai, ironically enough, had been a medical researcher specializing in radiology and was a devout Catholic. His wife had been killed outright in the Nagasaki blast. He lived in a tiny hut in the ruins of Nagasaki with his young son and daughter—reflecting on the meaning of his city's fate, writing furiously before death caught him (which it did on April 30, 1951, killing him with heart failure caused by leukemia). Nagai was extraordinarily charismatic in his prolonged death agony and captured popular imagination to a degree unsurpassed by any other Japanese writer about the bombs until the mid-1960s, when the distinguished elderly novelist Ibuse Masuji, a native son of Hiroshima prefecture, published *Kuroi ame* (Black Rain).

Nagai's interpretation of the nuclear holocaust was apocalyptically Christian. The bombs were part of God's providence, a divine act of suffering and death out of which world redemption would arise. And in his view, it was not mere happenstance that the second and last nuclear weapon fell on Nagasaki, a city with a long Christian tradition—exploded, indeed, above the great cathedral at Urakami. "Was not Nagasaki the chosen victim," Nagai wrote in a typically passionate passage, "the lamb without blemish, slain as a whole-burnt offering on an altar of sacrifice, atoning for the sins of all the nations during World War II?"

There is no evidence that the Japanese who flocked to buy Nagai's writings, or wrote him in great numbers, or made pilgrimages to his bedside, were fundamentally moved by his Christianity. More obviously, they were moved by his courage, his struggle to make sense of his fate, and the pathos of the two youngsters he soon would leave orphaned. And regardless of what one made of messianic Christian theology, Nagai's sermon that Japan had been divinely chosen to endure unique and world redemptive suffering clearly struck a resonant chord in the Japanese psyche. Even Emperor Hirohito, who had been formally recostumed as "the symbol of the State and the unity of the people" under the new constitution, undertook a pilgrimage to Nagai's bedside in 1949.[22]

In his own telling, Nagai conceived the idea for his famous book *Nagasaki no kane* (The Bells of Nagasaki) on Christmas eve of 1945 and completed the manuscript around August 9, 1946—the first anniversary of the Nagasaki bomb that had killed his beloved wife, also a Christian, and scores of medical coworkers. The book was not approved for publication until the beginning of 1949, however, and its handling at that time captured the lingering nervousness of U.S. occupation authorities on these matters. Between the same covers, the publisher was required to pair Nagai's abstract and emotional reflections with an extended graphic account of Japanese atrocities in the Philippines. This coupling was extremely ironic, for it unwittingly subverted the official U.S. position that use of the bombs had been necessary and just. Japanese readers, that is, could just as easily see the juxtaposition of the Hiroshima/Nagasaki bombs and the rape of Manila as suggesting an equivalence between American and Japanese atrocities. Despite this crude and revealing intervention, in any case, *Nagasaki no kane* not only became a best-seller but also soon was turned into a popular movie with an equally well-known theme song.[23]

Nagai's breakthrough essentially opened the door to the publication of books, articles, poems, and personal recollections by *hibakusha,* beginning in 1949.[24] By the time the occupation ended, a distinctive genre of atomic-bomb literature had begun to impress itself on the popular consciousness—often, as in Nagai's case, associated with a vivid sense of martyrdom. In 1951, two years after completing "Summer Flowers," one of the classic stories about Hiroshima, for example, Hara Tamiki committed suicide by laying down on a railway crossing near his Tokyo home. Toge Sankichi, by far the most esteemed poet of the atomic-bomb experience, wrote most of his verses in an extraordinary burst of creativity while hospitalized in 1951 for a chronic bronchial condition complicated by exposure to radiation in Hiroshima. Toge died on the operating table in March 1953, with friends from the Japan Communist Party clustered nearby, while a compatriot read the "Prelude" to his *Genbaku shishū* (Poems of the Atomic Bomb). Later engraved on a memorial in the peace park in Hiroshima, "Prelude" became the single best-known Japanese cry of protest against the bombs:

> Bring back the fathers! Bring back
>   the mothers!
> Bring back the old people!
> Bring back the children!
> Bring me back!
> Bring back the human beings
> I had contact with!
>
> For as long as there are human beings,
>   a world of human beings,
> bring back peace,
> unbroken peace.[25]

Among the many things that the paintings of the Marukis and the writings and reminiscences by *hibakusha* provided were a vocabulary and iconography of nuclear annihilation that soon became familiar to most Japanese. Textually and visually, the closest existing approximation to the experience of August 6 and 9, 1945, was to be found in medieval writings and pictorial scrolls depicting the horrors of the Buddhist hell. Phrases such as "it was like hell" and "hell could not be more terrible than this" were the most commonly heard refrain in recollections by survivors. The first detailed Japanese survey of the effects of the atomic bombs—made public on August 23, 1945, a week before the American victors arrived—described Hiroshima and Nagasaki as a "living hell."[26] In the Marukis' paintings, the fire that consumed men, women, and children in Hiroshima was painted in the same manner that medieval artists had used in rendering the flames of the underworld—and, indeed, the only real Japanese precedents for the naked, mutilated figures in the Marukis' depictions of atomic-bomb victims were the tormented sinners in these old Buddhist hell scrolls. Years later, in selecting a title for a collection of drawings by *hibakusha,* Japan's public television network turned naturally to the phrase "unforgettable fire."[27]

The "procession of ghosts" that was the subject of the Marukis' first, stark, India-ink mural—depicting naked, stunned, maimed *hibakusha* with hands outstretched, skin peeling from them—captured another enduring image of the bomb experience. In this instance, the nuclear reality resonated with traditional depictions of ghosts and ghouls, who also moved with eerie slowness, hands stretched before them (many bomb survivors had their hands severely burned when they covered their eyes against the blinding flash of the bombs and almost invariably walked holding their hands palms down in front of them because this eased the pain).

Benign images grotesquely transformed also emerged as unforgettable metaphors of the nuclear disaster. Water, for example, became a central fixation in several forms—the parching thirst that victims felt (the most often heard last words spoken by victims were *mizu kudasai* or "water, please"); the enduring guilt that survivors experienced because they did not heed these pleas (the Japanese had been told, as a matter of general principle, not to give water to injured people); the seven great rivers of Hiroshima, running out to the beautiful Inland Sea when the bomb fell, all clogged with corpses (people threw themselves into the rivers to escape the fires, and drowned or died there of their injuries).

Black rain fell after the bombs had transformed the clear-day atmosphere. The ominous rainfall stained skin and clothing and became in time an indelible metaphor of the unprecedented after-effects of the new weapons. Although subsequent research by the ABCC found no lethal connection between the black rain and radioactive fallout in Hiroshima and Nagasaki, in popular consciousness the rain became associated with the terrible radiation sickness that soon killed thousands of individuals who appeared to have survived the bombings. After a few hours or days, they experienced fever, nausea, vomiting, diarrhea, abnormal thirst, and sometime convulsions and delirium. Beginning in the second week after the bombs were dropped, apparent survivors found blood in their spit, urine, and stools; bruise-like discolorations (*purpura*) appeared on their bodies; their hair fell out in clumps. At the time no one knew what such grotesqueries portended. The Japanese government report made public on August 23, captured the local horror by describing what we now know to be radiation sickness as an "evil spirit."[28]

Other traditionally benign symbols also were transmogrified. Mother and infant, universal icons of love and life, were transposed into a symbol of the broken life bond—mothers attempting to nurse dead babies, infants attempting to suck at the breast of dead mothers. (Classic medieval texts such as the early thirteenth-century *Hōjōki* had offered such fractured images as evidence of *mappō,* the Buddhist apocalypse or "latter days of the Buddhist law"). Bizarre iconographies became commonplace in August 1945: monstrously mutilated people, of course, unrecognized by neighbors and loved ones—but also a man holding his eyeball in his hand; hopping birds with their wings burned off; live horses on fire; permanent white shadows on scorched walls (grass, ladders, people), where what had made the shadow no longer existed; people standing like black statues, burned to a crisp but still seemingly engaged in a last energetic act; legs standing upright, without bodies; survivors as well as corpses with their hair literally standing on end; maggots swarming in the wounds of the living.

All this, and much more, became familiar to most Japanese when those who witnessed Hiroshima'and Nagasaki belatedly began to express what they had experienced.

III

The delayed timing of these first intense Japanese encounters with the human tragedy of Hiroshima and Nagasaki had unanticipated consequences. For example, censorship began to be lifted at approximately the same time that the Tokyo war crimes trials ended (in December 1948). The culminating moment of the protracted Allied juridical campaign to impress Japanese with the enormity of their wartime transgressions thus coincided with the moment that many Japanese had their first encounters with detailed personal descriptions of the nuclear devastation that the Americans had visited upon them. While former Japanese leaders were being convicted of war crimes, sentenced to death, and hanged, the Japanese public simultaneously was beginning to learn the details of Hiroshima and Nagasaki for the first time. For many Japanese, there seemed an immoral equivalence here.

Of even greater political consequence, the Japanese really confronted the horrors of nuclear war three years or more after Americans and other unoccupied peoples did—at a time when China was being won by the communists, the Soviet Union was detonating its first bomb, hysteria in the United States had given rise to rhetoric about preventive and pre-emptive strikes, runways all over occupied Japan and Okinawa were being lengthened to accommodate America's biggest bombers, and, in a short time, war came to Korea. In effect, the Japanese confronted the bombs and the most intense and threatening moments of the Cold War simultaneously. They did so, moreover, at a level of intimate concern with the human consequences of nuclear weapons that ran deeper than the generally superficial American impressions of a large mushroom cloud, ruined cityscapes, and vague numbers of abstract "casualties."

The impact of John Hersey's classic text *Hiroshima* in the United States and Japan can be taken as a small example of the ramifications of this aberrant collapse of time. Hersey's tense portraits of six victims of the Hiroshima bomb stunned American readers when first published in 1946. His account originally was written for the urbane *New Yorker* magazine, however, and reached a rather narrow upper-level stratum of the American public. By 1949, moreover, when anticommunist hysteria had taken possession of the American media, the initial impact of the book had eroded. By this time, Hersey's masterpiece had no conspicuous hold on the American mind. A Japanese translation of *Hiroshima,* on the other hand, was not permitted until occupation censorship was terminated in 1949. The translation became a best-seller in 1950—four years after Hersey's account first appeared in the United States—and reinforced popular Japanese sentiment against active commitment to U.S. military policy in the Cold War.

It was in this context that the Japanese "peace movement" (*heiwa undō*) took shape between 1949 and the mid-1950s. Vivid recollections and recreations of the old war coincided with confrontation with new Cold War realities—including, beginning in July 1950, Japanese rearmament and, beginning in April 1952, the indefinite maintenance of U.S. military bases in sovereign Japan. In attempting to mobilize public support behind a more neutral position for their country, liberal and leftist intellectuals starting with the prestigious "Peace Problems Symposium" (*Heiwa mondai danwakai*) adopted a policy of promoting pacifism by appealing to the personal experiences of Japanese in the war just past—essentially appealing, that is, to the Japanese sense of victimization.

An internationalist peace consciousness, this liberal and left-wing argument went, was like the outermost ring in a series of concentric circles. To promote such a consciousness one had to begin at the center, with the intimate experience of suffering in the recent war, and strive to extend this aversion to war to the outer rings of a national and ultimately international outlook. The atomic-bomb literature contributed to this. So also did a complementary vogue of publications evoking the experiences of other Japanese who had suffered in the war. Conspicuous here were collections of the wartime letters of student conscripts killed in battle.[29] Even on the Left, in short, victim consciousness was seen as the essential core of a pacifist and ultimately internationalist consciousness.

By the early 1950s, fear of a nuclear World War III had become almost palpable in Japan. President Truman's threat to use nuclear weapons in the Korean conflict in November 1950 inflamed these fears; and even after a truce had been arranged on the battlegrounds next door, a great number of Japanese remained alarmed by the continued testing of nuclear weapons by the American and Soviet superpowers, extending now to hydrogen bombs. When fallout from a U.S. thermonuclear test on the Bikini atoll irradiated the crew of a Japanese fishing boat misnamed *Lucky Dragon 5* on March 1, 1954, the public was primed to respond with intense emotion to this concrete presentiment of a second cycle of nuclear victimization (one fisherman eventually died from exposure to these "ashes of death").

A campaign to ban all nuclear weapons, initiated by Japanese housewives in May 1954, for example, soon collected an astonishing thirty million signatures.[30] This same turbulent period also saw the birth, in November 1954, of *Godzilla,* Japan's enduring contribution to the cinematic world of mutant science-fiction monsters spawned by a nuclear explosion. In serious cinema, the director Kurosawa Akira followed his triumphant *Seven Samurai,* a 1954 production, with an almost incoherent 1955 film entitled *Record of a Living Being,* in which fear of atomic extinction drives an elderly man insane.

This was the milieu in which, in 1955, a memorial peace museum and peace park were opened in Hiroshima and the first national coalition against atomic and hydrogen bombs was established. The latter development gave temporary coherence to the antinuclear movement—and simultaneously delivered the movement into the hands of fractious political professionals and ideologues.[31] As a consequence, in the decades that followed, popular remembrance of Hiroshima and Nagasaki can be characterized as having gone through cycles of renewal— or, put differently, through cycles of rehumanization, in which individuals or grass-roots movements reacted against the ritualization and gross politicization of remembrance. While the professional peace advocates warred over whether socialist nuclear weapons were as objectionable as capitalist ones, and while the organizers of formal antinuclear observances negotiated the seating on the speakers' platforms, certain writers, artists, and projects succeeded in casting new perspectives on the human costs of the bomb.

Beginning in 1963, for example, the gifted young writer Ōe Kenzaburō began to use reports about the annual peace observances in Hiroshima as a vehicle for criticizing "the strong odor of politics" that hovered over the peace park and rediscovering "the true Hiroshima" in the ordinary citizens who lived with and died from the legacies of the bomb.[32] Ibuse Masuji's *Black Rain,* a masterful fictional reconstruction of death from radiation sickness based on the diary of a Hiroshima survivor plus interviews with some fifty *hibakusha,* was serialized in 1965–66 and enjoyed perennial strong sales in book form thereafter. Ibuse himself had been born in Hiroshima prefecture in 1898, and his evocation of the rhythms and rituals of ordinary life restored the human dimensions to the horror of nuclear destruction with immense dignity.[33]

In the early 1970s, Nakazawa Keiji, a cartoonist for children's publications who had been a seven-year-old in Hiroshima when the bomb was dropped, achieved improbable success with a graphic serial built on his family's own experiences as victims and survivors. Nakazawa's *Hadashi no Gen* (Barefoot Gen) was serialized in a boy's magazine with a circulation of over two million and ran to some one thousand pages before the series was terminated—surviving thereafter as both an animated film and a multivolume collection.[34] In a very different form of popular graphics, Japanese public television solicited visual representations by *hibakusha* in the mid-1970s and received several thousand drawings and paintings of scenes that had remained buried in the memories of the survivors. These intensely personal images became the basis of television broadcasts, traveling exhibitions, and publications.[35]

As time passed, popular perceptions of Hiroshima and Nagasaki were transformed in ways both predictable and unpredictable. Through painstaking demographic reconstructions—an immense task, since entire families and neighborhoods and all their records had been obliterated—higher estimates of nuclear fatalities became generally accepted. And with the passing of years, the "late effect" medical consequences of the bombs became apparent in higher incidences among survivors of leukemia, thyroid cancer, breast cancer, lung cancer, stomach cancer, malignant lymphoma, salivary gland tumors, hematological disorders, and cataracts.

Belated insensitivity to the enduring social and psychological legacies of the bomb introduced new euphemisms into the lexicon of nuclear victimization. One spoke not merely of "A-bomb orphans," such as the children Nagai Takashi left behind, but also of the "elderly orphaned," in reference to old people bereft of the children who ordinarily would have supported them in old age. The painful disfiguring scars known as keloids were said to have a spiritual counterpart in "keloids of the heart," just as the radiation-caused leukemia had its psychological counterpart in a "leukemia of the spirit" among survivors. In the cruel vernacular of everyday discourse, youngsters who were born mentally retarded due to exposure to radiation while in the womb became known as "*pika* babies," in reference to the blinding flash of the bombs.[36]

Such new information and perceptions gave ever greater concreteness to the victim consciousness that always had accompanied popular recollections of Hiroshima and Nagasaki. At the same time, however, the fixation on Japan's nuclear victimization proved unexpectedly subversive—for the closer the Japanese looked at Hiroshima and Nagasaki, the clearer it became that more nationalities than just the Japanese had been killed there. Hiroshima prefecture was one of the major areas from which Japanese emigrated to the United States. After Pearl Harbor, many second-generation Japanese Americans who had temporarily gone to Japan were stranded there—and it is estimated that around thirty-two hundred may have been in Hiroshima when the bomb was dropped. If that is true, then extrapolating from overall casualty rates it is probable that at least two thousand American citizens were killed by the Hiroshima bomb.[37]

While these American deaths in Hiroshima are of slight interest in Japan (and, involving ethnic Japanese, of negligible interest to most Americans), by the early 1970s the Japanese found themselves confronting a more troublesome question of victimization, for it had become apparent by then that thousands of Koreans also were killed in Hiroshima and Nagasaki. As a Japanese colony, Korea was a source of extensively conscripted and heavily abused labor in wartime Japan, and it was belatedly estimated that between five and eight thousand Koreans may have been killed in Hiroshima, and fifteen hundred to two thousand in Nagasaki.[38] Such laborers were, in effect, double victims—exploited by the Japanese and incinerated by the Americans. By the same token, the Japanese were revealed as being simultaneously victims and victimizers. Indeed, as the story unraveled, it was learned that even in the immediate aftermath of the nuclear holocaust, Korean survivors were discriminated against when it came to medical treatment and even cremation and burial.

A small number of Japanese read a large lesson in this, concerning the complexities of both victimization and responsibility. In 1972, for example—over two decades after they first started portraying the Japanese victims of the bombs in their collaborative paintings—the Marukis exhibited a stark mural entitled "Ravens," depicting the black scavengers descending on a mound of Korean dead, plucking out eyes. In the Hiroshima peace park itself, however, the guardians of memory thus far have succeeded in keeping a memorial to the Korean victims from violating the central, sacred ground. Even in the peace park, the Japanese unwittingly reveal themselves to be both victims and victimizers.

These tensions—racial and ethnic bias and dual identity as victims and victimizer—never will be entirely resolved in Japan. Since the 1970s, however, they have become more transparent and openly debated. Acknowledgment of the Korean victims of the atomic bombs in the early 1970s, for example, coincided with restoration of Japanese relations with the People's Republic of China—and, with this, renewed attention by liberal and left-wing writers to Japanese atrocities in China, beginning with the Rape of Nanjing. Until then, and despite the zealous didacticism associated with the war crimes trials conducted by the Allied victors during the occupation period, it seems fair to say that most Japanese regarded Hiroshima and Nagasaki as the preeminent moments of atrocity in World War II in Asia, towering above all acts of war just as the mushroom cloud had towered over Hiroshima on August 6, 1945.

Belatedly reencountering China changed this. Here, again, memory was reconstructed after an abnormal interlude of silence, during which defeat followed by Cold War politics isolated Japan from China and essentially smothered recollections of Japan's aggression and atrocious war behavior there.[39] The struggle to reshape memory of the war has become more intense since then—increasingly so as other Japanese atrocities have been exposed, such as the murderous medical experiments carried out in Unit 731 in Manchuria and the forced recruitment of Asian women to serve as prostitutes (*ianfu,* or "comfort women") for the emperor's loyal troops. To the extent that popular consciousness of victimization and atrocity has changed in contemporary Japan, this has entailed greater general acknowledgment of Japan's own war crimes vis-à-vis fellow Asians.[40]

Even this remains contested, of course, as the May 1994 resignation of the newly appointed minister of justice, Nagano Shigetso, attests. Nagano was forced to step down after calling the Nanjing massacre a "fabrication," characterizing the *ianfu* as "public prostitutes," and referring to the war in Asia by the patriotic old name "Great East Asia War" (*Dai Tōa sensō*).[41] In all this, he was repudiated by his government, which formally acknowledged that the war against Asia had been a war of aggression. That same month, however, in the face of considerable domestic pressure, the same conservative coalition government also canceled plans for the emperor, Hirohito's son, to visit Pearl Harbor while on a state visit to Hawaii. This, it was argued, was too great a concession—for, after all, no American head of state ever had visited Hiroshima or Nagasaki, or even expressed regrets for those terrible deaths.[42]

For most Japanese, the war against other Asians was different and more regrettable in a moral sense than the war against the Americans; and Hiroshima and Nagasaki account for much of this difference.[43]

Notes

1. Hara Mieko, untitled memoir in Publishing Committee for "Children of Hiroshima," ed., *Children of Hiroshima* (Tokyo: Publishing Committee for "Children of Hiroshima"), pp. 244–46, quoted in John Whittier Treat, *Writing Ground Zero: Japanese Literature and the Atomic Bomb* (Chicago: University of Chicago Press, 1995).

2. The first occupation forces did not arrive in Japan until the very end of August; the formal surrender ceremony took place on September 2; and the occupation headquarters in Tokyo did not become effectively operational until early September. Formal occupation censorship generally is dated from September 19, 1945, when a press code was announced. Beginning October 5, prepublication censorship was imposed on major newspapers and periodicals. For general accounts concerning nuclear-related censorship, see Matsuura Sōzō, *Senryōka no genron danatsu* [Suppression of speech under the occupation] (Tokyo: Gendai jyānarizumu kyōkai, 1969), especially pp. 167–212; Committee for

the Compilation of Materials on Damage Caused by the Atomic Bombs in Hiroshima and Nagasaki, comp., *Hiroshima and Nagasaki: The Physical, Medical, and Social Effects of the Atomic Bombings,* trans. Eisei Ishikawa and David L. Swain (New York: Basic Books, 1981), pp. 5, 503–13, 564, 585 [hereafter this basic source, originally published in Japanese in 1979, is cited as *Hiroshima and Nagasaki*]; Monica Braw, *The Atomic Bomb Suppressed: American Censorship in Occupied Japan* (Armonk, NY: M.E. Sharpe, 1991); Glenn D. Hook, "Censorship and Reportage of Atomic Damage and Casualties in Hiroshima and Nagasaki, *Bulletin of Concerned Asian Scholars,* 23, no. 1 (1991): 13–25.

3. Hatoyama's statement appeared in *Asahi Shimbun,* September 15, 1945. His account of this incident, and enduring contempt for the "recklessness" and hypocrisy exemplified in the U.S. use of the atomic bombs and punishment of him for criticizing this, emerges clearly in his memoirs: *Hatoyama Ichirō kaikoroku* [Hatoyama Ichirō memoirs] (Tokyo: Bungei shunjū shinsha, 1957), pp. 49–51.

4. On American POWs in Hiroshima, see "Nijsannin no beihei horyo mo bakushi shite ita" [Twenty-three American POWs Also Killed by Bombing], *Shūkan Yomiuri,* August 13, 1978, pp. 28–31; Barton J. Bernstein, "Unraveling a Mystery: American POWs Killed in Hiroshima," *Foreign Service Journal* (October 1979): 17ff; Robert Karl Manoff, "American Victims of Hiroshima," *The New York Times Magazine,* December 2, 1984, pp. 67ff. This became the theme of a 1971 mural by the painters Iri and Toshi Maruki, who are discussed below; see John W. Dower and John Junkerman, eds., *The Hiroshima Murals: The Art of Iri Maruki and Toshi Maruki* (New York: Kodansha International, 1985), pp. 21, 78–81.

5. *Asahi Shimbun,* September 7, 1945; Grant Goodman, *Amerika no Nihon—Gannen, 1945–1946* [America's Japan—the First Year, 1945–1946] (Tokyo: Otsuki shoten, 1986), pp. 120–23.

6. Japan's research on the possibility of making a nuclear weapon is described in "'NI' and 'F': Japan's Wartime Atomic Bomb Research," in John W. Dower, *Japan in War and Peace: Selected Essays* (New York: New Press, 1994), pp. 55–100.

7. *Hiroshima and Nagasaki,* p. 496.

8. Katō Etsurō, *Okurareta kakumei* [The Revolution That Was Given to Us] (Tokyo, 1946). A copy of this fascinating booklet, which is now almost impossible to find in Japan, is in the Gordon Prange Collection in McKeldin Library, University of Maryland.

9. The great majority of Japanese at the time exonerated the emperor from such criticism. Postsurrender propaganda by the Japanese elites, parroted by the U.S. occupation authorities, strongly emphasized that the emperor too had been misled by the military.

10. From the historian's viewpoint, we can now identify many ways in which Japan's fifteen-year mobilization for war created positive technological, technocratic, and institutional legacies for the postwar state, but these certainly were not apparent in the immediate postsurrender years. See "The Useful War," in Dower, *Japan in War and Peace,* pp. 9–32.

11. The quotations come from the *Asahi Shimbun* in the period immediately following capitulation, but such sentiments were ubiquitous.

12. The social stigma attached to weapons-related research was reinforced by institutional constraints. In the early reformist phase of the occupation, the imperial military establishment was eliminated. Although constitutional prohibition of the maintenance of military forces under the new "no war" charter was violated after the Korean War broke and Japan began to rearm (beginning in July 1950), the constitutional restraint did remain strong enough to prevent the creation of an industrialized militarism comparable to the Pentagon and military-academic-industrial complex in the United States. Preservation of bureaucratic turf helped to perpetuate this situation over the decades, for primary responsibility for budgetary allotments resided in the hands of the Ministry of Finance, which

remained largely committed to civilian-oriented policies. There is still no defense ministry per se in Japan. At the same time, public opinion, while tolerating incremental remilitarization, remained opposed to constitutional revision and the more blatant sort of all-out militarization this might permit. There is no question that the "no war" constitution is an anomaly in the 1990s, when Japan does in fact have a large military budget, has become a major producer of "dual-use" technologies, and has sent "peacekeeping forces" abroad under the United Nations auspices in response to immense U.S. pressure. Nonetheless, the persistence of popular opposition to constitutional revision for almost a half century to date has conspicuously influenced the nature and balance of Japan's economic and political policies in nonmilitary directions; and the most effective arguments against such revision consistently have played upon memories of Japan's "victimization" in World War II, of which Hiroshima always will remain the prime symbol. Contemporary political struggles over who will control the memory of the war (as seen in the Ministry of Education's notorious efforts to produce sanitized textbook coverage of this topic) are intimately linked to these issues of constitutional revision and whether or not Japan should become a more "normal" state with a bona-fide military. In this contest, Japanese liberals and leftists commonly are able to make more effective neonationalistic use of the bombs than their conservative and right-wing opponents. To encourage popular support for the constitutional revision and more "normal" militarization, the latter must perforce downplay the horrors of the old war—not only the suffering the imperial forces caused to others, but also the horrors brought home.

13. For early examples of this political logic equating "science" with a more "rational" democratic society generally, see the *Asahi Shimbun* of August 22, 1945; also Toyoshima Yoshio's comments in the September–October 1945 issue of *Bungei,* quoted in Honda Shūgo, *Monogatari: Sengo bungaku shi* [The story of postwar literary history] (Tokyo: a reprint of the 1966 Shinchōsha edition by Iwanami, 1992), vol. 1, p. 13.

14. See Wilfred Burchett, *Shadows of Hiroshima* (London: Verso, 1983), especially chapters 1–3. Burchett's story, essentially as published in the *Daily Express,* is reproduced on pp. 34–37. The counterpart scoop from Nagasaki, squelched by occupation headquarters, was by George Weller of the *Chicago Daily News* and totaled some 25,000 words (ibid., pp. 44–45).

15. Iwasaki Akira, *Nihon gendai taikei: Eiga shi* [Outline of Contemporary Japan: Film History] (Tokyo: Tōyō keizai shimpōsha, 1961), pp. 226–27; Matsuura, *Senryōka no gen ron danatsu,* pp. 192–95. Iwasaki was part of the project filming the aftermath of the bombs in Hiroshima and Nagasaki, which was conducted by the Nichiei studio.

16. The United States Strategic Bombing Survey, *The Effects of Atomic Bombs on Hiroshima and Nagasaki* (Washington, DC: U.S. Government Printing Office, June 1946), pp. 3–5. Accurate estimates of atomic-bomb–related deaths are made problematic by many factors: the demographic turmoil that prevailed in Japan at war's end, especially in urban areas; the extraordinary destructiveness of the bombs, which obliterated whole neighborhoods, along with the records pertaining to their residents; the chaos prevailing after the bombs were dropped, including hasty mass cremations of victims to prevent disease; and the absence of clear, coordinated, publicly accessible records of subsequent *hibakusha* illnesses and deaths. Useful data on fatalities, and the difficulty of calculating them, appears in the voluminous 1979 Japanese report translated into English as *Hiroshima and Nagasaki* (see note 2 above); see pp. 113–15, 367, 369, 406. Although conflicting figures are given here, the general conclusion is that total long-term *hibakusha* deaths were approximately double the 1946 figures for each city. In 1994, when the Japanese parliament belatedly debated legislation concerning death-benefits compensation to *hibakusha* families (see note 18 below), Ministry of Health and Welfare statistics commonly were cited indicating that between 300,000 and 350,000 *hibakusha* had died

prior to 1969, with all but 50,000 to 70,000 of these deaths occurring prior to 1958; see *Asahi Shimbun,* October 27, and November 3, 1994. Persistent replication of the outdated initial low estimates of fatalities has contributed to perpetuation of one of the enduring misleading statements in standard accounts of the war—namely, that more people were killed in the Tokyo air raid of March 9 and 10, 1945, than by the atomic bombs in each city. Official Japanese estimates for fatalities in the Tokyo raid are less than 100,000. Indeed, the Ministry of Health and Welfare estimates that *total* Japanese deaths from the conventional U.S. bombing of some sixty-four Japanese cities apart from the two nuclear targets was in the neighborhood of 300,000 persons—that is, equal to or less than the fatalities associated with Hiroshima and Nagasaki.

17. On the ABCC, see John Beatty, "Genetics in the Atomic Age: The Atomic Bomb Casualty Commission, 1946–1956," in *The Expansion of American Biology,* ed. Keith R. Benson, Jane Maienschein, and Ronald Rainger (New Brunswick: Rutgers University Press, 1991), pp. 284–324, and M. Susan Lindee's *Suffering Made Real: American Science and the Survivors at Hiroshima* (Chicago: University of Chicago Press, 1995).

18. Passage of a comprehensive *"hibakusha* relief law" remained a subject of parliamentary debate in the final months of 1994 and was widely covered in the Japanese press in November of that year. For a concise critical commentary on the national government's relative neglect of the *hibakusha,* see Shiina Masae, *hibakusha engoh* [Hibakusha Relief Law] (Tokyo: Iwanami Booklet 208, c. 1992).

19. The general U.S. policy of media censorship in occupied Japan began to be eased in late 1948 and was formally terminated in mid-1949. It was not until the February 1952 meeting of the Hiroshima Association of Medical Sciences, however, that academic societies were allowed to engage freely in investigation and discussion of the medical effects of the bomb; see *Hiroshima and Nagasaki,* p. 513. In 1949, some Americans, including several Nisei who had been involved in censorship at the local level, argued that they were sensitive to these matters and would have been lenient if the Japanese had submitted noninflammatory writings on their bomb experiences. Such writings, the ex-censors said, simply were not submitted; see *Asahi Shimbun,* May 16, 1994. Such claims are unpersuasive, however, given the clear top-level opposition to such writings, plus concrete examples of local suppression of such materials, plus the deplorable ban on scientific writings until the very end of the occupation (which involved bureaucratic complications in Washington, and not just Tokyo). In the three years from 1946 through 1948, a total of seven published books or articles, plus twenty-seven written testimonies, were recorded in Hiroshima, most of them appearing in 1946; *Hiroshima and Nagasaki,* p. 586. U.S. restrictions on scientific findings concerning the effects of the bombs were so severe that, even in the closing years of the occupation, American medical investigators working with Japanese *hibakusha* for the ABCC were uninformed of the existence of earlier studies pertinent to their own research; see James N. Yamazaki, M.D., and Louis B. Fleming, *Children of the Atomic Bombs: Nagasaki, Hiroshima, and the Marshall Islands* (Durham: Duke University Press, 1995).

20. *Hiroshima and Nagasaki,* pp. 512–13.

21. Maruki Iri and Akamatsu Toshiko [Maruki Toshi], *Pika-don* (Tokyo: Potsdam shoten, 1950). The Marukis' remarkable collaborative paintings, which eventually extended beyond the atomic bombs to deal with such subjects as the Rape of Nanjing and Auschwitz, are reproduced in John W. Dower and John Junkerman, eds. *The Hiroshima Murals: The Art of Iri Maruki and Toshi Maruki* (New York: Kodansha International, 1985). A documentary film of the artists' work by Junkerman and Dower, entitled *Hellfire: A Journey from Hiroshima,* is available from First Run Features, New York.

22. The Marist priest Paul Glynn published a book-length homage to Nagai in 1988 titled *A Song for Nagasaki* (Catholic Book Club, 3 Mary Street, Hunters Hill, NSW 2110,

Australia). In Nagai's eschatology, after singling out Nagasaki, God then inspired the emperor to issue the sacred proclamation ending the war. These views emerge vividly in Glynn, especially pp. 115–21, but the ideological logic of the connection between the patriotic Christian visionary and erstwhile Shintoist god-emperor, who had portrayed himself as intervening to prevent the apocalypse in the surrender proclamation of August 15, 1945, is generally overlooked. Nagai's radiation sickness, incidentally, apparently was contracted from his research prior to the bombing of Nagasaki, although his suffering from the bomb is beyond dispute.

23. For an English translation of this book, see Takashi Nagai, *The Bells of Nagasaki,* trans. William Johnston (New York: Kodansha International, 1984). Prior to *Nagasaki no kane,* Nagai had been permitted to publish a moving, sentimental account entitled *Kono ko o nokoshite* [Leaving These Children Behind], reflecting on the future of his soon-to-be-orphaned children. This became an immediate "top ten" best-seller in 1948 and remained on the top-ten list in 1949, where it was joined by *Nagasaki no kane;* see Shiozawa Minobu, *Shōwa besuto-serā sesō shi* [Social History of Shōwa Bestsellers] (Tokyo: Daisan bunmeisha, 1988), pp. 108–10.

24. According to records compiled in Hiroshima, atomic-bomb writings pertaining to that city alone totaled fifty-four books, essays, and stories plus 284 testimonials in 1949 through 1952. By 1971, the total was 500 published books and short pieces and 2,234 written testimonials; *Hiroshima and Nagasaki,* p. 586. In 1983, major literary writings on the atomic-bomb experience were collected in a fifteen-volume series entitled *Nihon no genbaku bungaku* [Japanese Atomic-Bomb Literature] (Tokyo: Horupu shuppan, 1983). See also the thirty-article series on atomic-bomb literature during the occupation published in *Chūgoku Shimbun,* the leading Hiroshima-area newspaper, between June 30, and August 12, 1986. For English translations of some of this extensive literature, see Ōe Kenzaburō, ed., *The Crazy Iris and Other Stories of the Atomic Aftermath* (New York: Grove Press, 1985); Kyoko and Mark Selden, eds., *The Atomic Bomb: Voices from Hiroshima and Nagasaki* (Armonk, NY: M.E. Sharpe, 1989); and Richard H. Minear, ed. and trans., *Hiroshima: Three Witnesses* (Princeton: Princeton University Press, 1990).

25. Minear, *Hiroshima,* p. 305. Hara's "Summer Flowers" and Tōge's "Poems of the Atomic Bomb" are translated in full by Minear, along with another early classic of atomic-bomb literature, Ota Yōko's 1950 narrative "City of Corpses." In his commentary, Minear calls attention to the implicit anti-Americanism in many of Tōge's poems (pp. 295–97).

26. *Asahi Shimbun,* August 23, 1945.

27. For the English version of this stunning collection, see Japan Broadcasting Corporation (NHK), comp., *Unforgettable Fire: Pictures Drawn by Atomic Bomb Survivors* (New York: Pantheon Books, 1977).

28. The nonlethal consequences of the "black rain" are noted in Yamazaki and Fleming, *Children of the Atomic Bombs,* and attributed to the relative high altitude at which the Hiroshima and Nagasaki bombs were detonated. This is in contrast to the conspicuously lethal fallout from the 1954 U.S. hydrogen-bomb test in the Marshall Islands.

29. For a broad annotated discussion of Cold War struggles within Japan in general, see John W. Dower, "Peace and Democracy in Two Systems: External Policy and Internal Conflict," in *Postwar Japan as History,* ed. Andrew Gordon (Berkeley: University of California Press, 1993), pp. 3–33. By far the most influential collection of student-conscript letters was Nihon senbotsu gakusei shuki henshū iinkai, ed., *Kike—Wadatsumi no koe: Nihon senbotsu gakusei no shuki* [Listen—the Voice of the Ocean: Testimonies of Conscripted Japanese Students] (Tokyo: Tōdai kyōdō kumiai shuppanbu, 1949). Like Nagai Takashi's *Bells of Nagasaki,* this also was quickly refashioned as a popular movie. This collection of student letters tapped not only an earlier postwar collection of wartime

letters by Tokyo Imperial University conscripts, but also a wartime series of such letters published in the Tokyo Imperial University student newspaper—a striking example indeed of war words becoming peace words. After Japan's defeat, such wartime writings often were reinterpreted as evidence of peaceful, idealistic, and even antiwar sentiments—as well, of course, as intimate examples of the tragic loss of talented and attractive young men in a foolhardy and misguided war.

30. The appeal is reproduced in Nihon Jyānarisumu Kenkyūkai, ed., *Shōwa 'hatsugen' no kiroku* [A Record of Shōwa Pronouncements] (Tokyo: Tokyo Agency, 1989), pp. 138–39.

31. Gensuikyō, short for *Gensuibaku Kinshi Nihon Kyōgikai* (Japan Council Against Atomic and Hydrogen Bombs) was founded in September 1955. Its domination by the Japan Communist Party led to the splintering off of rival organizations in the 1960s. In 1961, the centrist Democratic Socialist Party and conservative Liberal Democratic Party formed the National Council for Peace and Against Nuclear Weapons (Kakukin Kaigi, short for Kakuheiki Kinshi Heiwa Kansetsu Kokumin Kaigi), and in 1965 the Japan Socialist Party formed the Japan Congress Against Atomic and Hydrogen Bombs (Gensuikin, short for Gensuibaku Kinshi Nihon Kokumin Kaigi). Factionalism on the Left has continually plagued the antinuclear movement.

32. For an English translation of Ōe's early essays, which originally appeared in the monthly *Sekai*, see his *Hiroshima Notes,* translated by Toshi Yonezawa and edited by David Swain (Tokyo: YMCA Press, 1981).

33. For an English translation, see Ibuse Masuji, *Black Rain,* trans. John Bester (New York: Kodansha International, 1969). This is without question the classic Japanese literary reconstruction of the atomic-bomb experience. The Japanese film version of Black Rain, directed by Imamura Shōhei, did not appear until 1988.

34. Three volumes from the *Barefoot Gen* series (originally published in Japan by Shōbunsha, Tokyo) are available in English translation from New Society Publishers, Philadelphia.

35. See note 27 above for an English rendering of NHK's edited collection of *hibakusha* drawings.

36. These later developments in demographic, medical, and linguistic understandings are scattered throughout the chaotic but invaluable 1979 study *Hiroshima and Nagasaki* (note 2 above).

37. Sodei Rinjirō, *Watakushitachi wa teki datta no ka—Zaibei hibakusha no mokushiroku* [Were We the Enemy?—A Record of the *Hibakusha* in the United States] (Tokyo: Ushio shuppansha, 1978).

38. *Hiroshima and Nagasaki,* pp. 471, 474. Korean groups placed the figures of Korean casualties much higher. See ibid., p. 468. See also Kurt W. Tong, "Korea's Forgotten Atomic Bomb Victims," *Bulletin of Concerned Asian Scholars* 23, no. 1 (1991): 31–37. Apart from the previously mentioned American POWs killed in Hiroshima, the atomic bombs also killed small numbers of Chinese, Southeast Asian, and European individuals.

39. This reencounter with China, and with Japanese war atrocities there, began with nongovernmental contacts in the mid-1960s, before the formal restoration of relations in 1972. The key Japanese writer in bringing the Rape of Nanjing to public attention was the well-known progressive journalist Honda Katsuichi, whose influential writings from China were published in newspapers and magazines in 1971 and subsequently collected in a volume entitled *Chūgoku no tabi* [Travels in China] (Tokyo: Asahi shimbunsha, 1971). The ensuing contentious debates on this topic in Japan are concisely summarized in Daqing Yang, "A Sino-Japanese Controversy: The Nanjing Atrocity as History," *Sino-Japanese Studies,* 3, no. 1 (November 1990): 14–35.

40. In 1994, in anticipation of the fiftieth anniversary of the dropping of the atomic bombs, officials associated with the memorial museum in Hiroshima announced that they would expand their exhibitions beyond depictions of Japanese victimization to include reference to Hiroshima's military role since the Meiji period, Japanese aggression and atrocity in World War II, and the presence of Korean and Chinese forced laborers in Hiroshima at the time of the bombs.

41. Convenient compilations of Nagano's statements appear in *Asahi Shimbun,* May 7 and 19, 1994. Although the government officially repudiated Nagano's comments, his remarks accurately reflect a mainline conservative view in Japan.

42. *Asahi Shimbun,* May 20, 1994. There were other arguments against the state visit as well, including the liberal and left-wing criticism that this would involve repoliticizing the role of the emperor in significant ways. The nuances of these acts of symbolic politics are subtle and convoluted.

43. In the realm of popular symbolic "equations," the most extreme expression of Japanese victimization involves pairing the Holocaust in Europe and "nuclear holocaust" of Hiroshima/Nagasaki. In the more specifically Asian context, the most familiar equation pairs the Rape of Nanjing and nuclear destruction of the two Japanese cities. Americans are most likely to conjoin Pearl Harbor and Hiroshima/Nagasaki, but this is a view that has little credence in Japan. Here again, the issue is a contentious one. Whereas the U.S.-dominated Tokyo war crimes trials portrayed Pearl Harbor as a deep-seated "conspiracy" against peace, however, the more persuasive view in Japan is that the attack was an ill-conceived response to a collapsing world order—and best comprehended in the capitalistic, imperialistic, and colonial terms of the time. The Japanese also tend to place greater emphasis than Americans do on the fact that the imperial government had intended to break off formal relations with the United States at the eleventh hour, minutes prior to the Pearl Harbor attack, and only failed to do so because of a clerical breakdown in the Japanese embassy in Washington. In this construction, Pearl Harbor emerges more as a tactical and technical blunder than a treacherous and atrocious act.

Part II

Analyzing Literature and Films

3

Japanese Films about the Pacific War

Tadao Sato (translated by Kana Moll)

Kajiro Yamamoto's Three Treatments of Air Battles
and *Amerika Yōsoro*

Immediately after the Japanese naval forces attacked Pearl Harbor in December 1941, the Japanese Department of the Navy contacted the producer of the Toho movie company, requesting that a movie about the attack be created within a year. At that time, film for making movies was reserved for the military, and permits were required for its use. With the military controlling the key component of the film industry, the department's request was actually more of an order. Toho responded by producing *Hawaii-Marei Oki Kaisen* (The War at Sea from Hawaii to Malaya, 1942), released as requested on the first anniversary of the attack on Pearl Harbor. The movie became one of the most successful in the history of film in Japan.

Kajiro Yamamoto, who served as the film's director, was a gentle and talented person, often creating films with a humanistic flavor. Before the Toho project he had made no war films and had not been considered particularly right wing or militaristic. His wide-ranging directing skills made him the perfect choice for a film requiring a considerable number of special effects.

For the set design, Yamamoto needed to create models of Japanese aircraft carriers but was denied access to the necessary military documents. Instead, he turned to photos of American aircraft carriers as they appeared in magazines. When the film was released, the top brass in the navy reprimanded the director for having used these "American aircraft carriers." Nonetheless, the movie enjoyed wide popularity before wildly enthusiastic audiences.

One key to its success was the carefully detailed, near-documentary portrayal of the navy's young fighter pilots trained for the attack on Pearl Harbor. Personally, I was quite disappointed two and a half years after seeing the movie, when I joined the navy's air corps and found myself on the receiving end of many butt-whippings from deputies of the squadron. That aspect of training did not appear in the film.

A second reason for the film's popularity was the quality of the Pearl Harbor replicas. Realistic models of the American fleet and the Japanese fighter planes produced authentic battles on the screen. The techniques used for this film were later applied to the postwar series of monster movies that started with *Gojira* (Godzilla) in 1954 and made a significant contribution to the dissemination of Japanese movies around the world.

After the success of *The War at Sea from Hawaii to Malaya,* Kajiro Yamamoto directed two other war films, creatively using model airplanes. With these three films under his belt, he became the most successful director of war propaganda movies during the Pacific War. One of the films, *Kato's Falcon Fighters* (1944), portrayed a heroic squadron commander who dies at the battlefront in Burma. The other one, *Torpedo Attackers* (1944), featured the South Pacific battle in which Japanese pilots plunged to their deaths in crashes against American aircraft carriers.

Many filmmakers participated in creating war propaganda films during the Pacific War. However, Kajiro Yamamoto's case is particularly interesting. In an interview in 1964 with *Yomiuri Shimbun* he described his feelings about his wartime films:

> To tell the truth, with the gloomy, oppressive atmosphere carrying on day after day [before the beginning of the war], I felt a sort of relief when I heard the news that the war had broken out. I made movies such as *Kato's Falcon Fighters* and *Torpedo Attackers,* but the only movie that pains my heart is *The War at Sea from Hawaii to Malaya.* At that time, I was feeling confident that we could win, and so I focused on the training of young fighter pilots. There were probably young men who enlisted as fighter pilots after seeing the movie, or people thinking, "If only that movie hadn't been made, my son wouldn't have died." Had I been a writer, I would have thrown my pen away for life. In fact, I didn't make any movies for awhile.

That Yamamoto expressed "relief" at the beginning of the war is an important point. In another interview, he remarked, "The feelings within myself were released."

The Japanese attack on Pearl Harbor in December 1941 was not the only aggressive act of the recent past. Although Japan never declared war on China, fighting began there in 1931 with the so-called Manchurian Incident. Full hostilities broke out in 1937, four years before the United States was at war with the Axis powers, Germany and Japan. The war with China had no clear cause. The Japanese government and military announced that victory in the Pacific War would bring a new order in Asia with Japan as the leader, but the argument did little to justify an invasion of China. Many Japanese thought that the conflict with China would end quickly, but unexpected Chinese resistance prolonged the war, and there seemed to be no end in sight. This is the context for what Kajiro Yamamoto described as "the gloomy atmosphere carrying on day after day" before the beginning of the war against America. Perhaps he "felt a sort of relief" because the unexpectedly successful attack on Pearl Harbor created the illusion that Japan could win a war against America. The more plausible reason seems to be that the war was not only against America but also against her allies, Britain and Holland. For the first time there was clear justification for the war; Japan was fighting to free Asia from Western imperialism.

In the mid-nineteenth century, when Japan ended its seclusion and opened its ports to the American navy and other Western forces, the Japanese were surprised to learn that Western countries had already colonized many areas of Asia. To protect it from a similar colonization of its islands, Japan strengthened its armed forces by using Western technology and chose to become a colonial power much like other developed nations. Despite the self-serving motive, the actions were justified by an ideology enlisting Japan to free Asia from Western colonialism. Japan believed that it was the only Asian country with the power to oppose Western nations. While building an even more militant nation and assuming the leadership of the "Greater East Asian Co-Prosperity Sphere," Japan encouraged independence movements in each country, preaching that Western imperialism must be overcome.[1]

In battles against China, Japan always flourished the flag of ideology. Japan demanded that other countries join the "Asian Allied powers" in their fight to end Western imperialism. Those that refused and accused the Japanese of invasion were attacked and considered "foolish" for not recognizing Japan's honest intentions. However, China's resistance was difficult to overcome. The militaristic leaders of Japan explained that a weak nation like China would not surrender as long as it had support from the United States and Great Britain. The Japanese public gradually accepted the idea that the United States and Great Britain, not China, were the real enemies.

The "free Asia" ideology provided a convenient cover for Japan's motives in starting the Pacific War. More basic to Japanese interest and welfare was the threat from the United States to stop oil sales to Japan unless Japanese forces retreated from China. Without oil from the United States, Japan's army would be crippled, perhaps leading to defeat in China. The simple solution was a retreat from China as the United States demanded. However, a retreat was simply out of the question. Japan's involvement in China had been extensive and deep; a withdrawal would mean that the army's achievements over the years in China would be wasted and that the ideological link between military power and a free Asia would crumble. The government and military could not admit the failure of an ideology that had supported their actions for so long. Seeing no other choice, they decided to invade and seize oil from Indonesia, the Philippines, and Malaya. Strategy called first for attacks on the largest obstacles, America's Pacific fleet based at Hawaii's Pearl Harbor and Britain's Asian fleet in Singapore.

It is incredible that Japan's military and government intelligence could have calculated victory in such a large-scale war. Yet to have started that war, they must have believed that abandoning the "free Asia" ideology and retreating from China would have led to a more terrifying and humiliating collapse of power. Similarly, Japanese citizens balanced feelings of inferiority to modernized Western nations with feelings of superiority over the developing nations of Asia. The terror of admitting their mistaken pride as Asia's leader was greater than the terror of possibly losing a war against the Allied powers. Given these fears, it was thought better to reaffirm the "free Asia" ideology by challenging the "real enemy" than to continue with days of "gloomy, oppressive" fighting in China. Thus, even a gentle and nonmilitant man such as Kajiro Yamamoto "felt a sort of relief" when he learned that war broke out, and although he had never made a single war movie during the war against China, he became the most successful war propaganda filmmaker during the Pacific War.

In the film *The War at Sea from Hawaii to Malaya,* there is a scene where an officer tells the young fighter pilots he is training, "Someday soon, the time will come to fight the 'real enemy.' " Other than in this scene, the reason for attacking American and Britain is not explicitly addressed. The concept of the "real enemy" was suggested subtly in movies about war against China such as *Shanghai,* made early in the war in 1937, and *Nizhizumi senshacho-den* (The Story of Tank Commander Nishizumi) of 1940. Although Japan was not in open combat with the "real enemy" yet, references were subtle but revealing enough for Japanese audiences. Clear mention of the "real enemy" in *The War at Sea from Hawaii to Malaya* clarified the reasons for the war.

Japan started the Pacific War not because it expected victory against the Allied powers but because it could not accept the collapse of its ideology. I do not mean to argue that Japan logically thought it better to wage war and perish than fail in its attempt to lead Asia to a new world order. However, a similarly deranged state of mind seemed to prevail. Indeed, the attempt was suicidal.

In two successive films, *Kato's Fighters* and *Torpedo Attackers,* Kajiro Yamamoto characterized the psychology of the Japanese people at the time very well. As in *The War at Sea from Hawaii to Malaya,* these movies give little attention to the reasons for attacking U.S. and British forces. The Japanese pilots hardly seem to despise or scorn the enemy. Instead, the young men seem to meditate on a splendid, beautiful death. Especially in *Torpedo Attackers,* many Japanese airplanes are destroyed and many lives lost in constant battles with Americans in the South Pacific. Piecing together remaining scrap parts, the Japanese forces assemble planes that can fly well enough to carry out the final mission—direct crashes against enemy forces. Although this scene conveyed the message that there were not enough planes on the battlefront—and thus encouraged more production in factories at home—it foreshadowed defeat and provided no optimistic propaganda that the war could be won with more effort. In other words, the film did not reinforce any illusions of victory for the audience. Strangely, it might be said that this was an honest film if one accepted that the end sought in war was not victory but the glorious suicide of a people.

When the Japanese government surrendered to the Allied powers on August 15, 1945, Kajiro Yamamoto was filming a movie called *Amerika Yōsoro*. It was the story of a fishing village burdened by American air raids, but assisted in its work by a Japanese navy division training in the area. When the division must depart for battle, the commander leaves the villagers with the words, "Amerika yōsoro." The term *yōsoro* is a sailing command for steering. So, his parting words were a way of saying, "Steer your boats straight toward the incoming American ships." The climax of the film was intended to show a counterattack against the approaching U.S. armada by *kamikaze* aircraft, special marines, and motorboats loaded with explosives. The motorboats were to be captained by those men who had trained in the fishing villages. Unfortunately, filming ceased with the end of the war, and the existing scenes were destroyed. I should not evaluate an unfinished film, but here, too, we find not the illusion of victory but the climactic mass suicide of specially trained troops.

The mentality represented in *Amerika Yōsoro* reflects a kind of insanity. When insanity fades and is replaced with clarity, one cannot recall the source of such deranged thoughts. Kajiro Yamamoto made his war films enthusiastically, but after the war he became the unmilitaristic filmmaker of the prewar years. He repeatedly apologized to parents who might have lost sons who had enlisted for fighter pilot training after seeing *The War at Sea from Hawaii to Malaya*. However, only a handful of communists criticized him for his wartime film efforts. Generally, Yamamoto was recognized for his wide range of knowledge, and he became a popular celebrity guest on a radio quiz show under the control of the American occupation forces.

In his interview, Yamamoto admitted, "The only movie that pains my heart is *The War at Sea from Hawaii to Malaya*." Is it heartless to emphasize the words "the only movie"? One must assume that he suffered from thoughts that his film helped recruit young fighter pilots and often led them to an unfortunate death. In contrast, the movies *Kato's Falcon Fighters, Torpedo Attackers,* and the uncompleted *Amerika Yōsoro,* which were not propaganda films requested by the military, were films that he took seriously and personally and appeared not to have made against his conscience. Yamamoto never elaborated on these matters. Perhaps he thought that those movies were honest portrayals of the Japanese mentality of the period.

Concerning Honorable Sacrifice

Just as Kajiro Yamamoto returned to his gentle, peaceful self after the insanity of the war, many other filmmakers who had been making war movies suddenly reversed course and began producing movies dealing with the theme of pacifism. The American occupation forces removed presidents and several executives from movie companies but did not question the responsibility of film directors. Instead, they were called upon immediately to make films promoting democracy, and the Japanese filmmakers obediently answered that call. Complaints arose when American agents not pleased with a particular democracy-promoting film disallowed production of regular entertainment movies, or when an agent, usually an amateur, gave instructions on technical production. Those directors who ignored suggestions from the Americans would not be allowed to make movies. Frustration also greeted the prohibition—on the grounds that they were "feudalistic"—of samurai movies created for general entertainment. No one opposed the attempt of the occupation army to replace the ideas of militarism, war, and feudalism with the principles of democracy. Although initially stunned, filmmakers responded enthusiastically and soon produced films of high quality.

Many filmmakers completely changed their way of thinking only six months to a year after the war ended. This is quite embarrassing as it appears that they had no personal convictions but merely followed those in power like slaves. Clearly, films are difficult to produce if they do not enjoy the support of the authorities; so in a sense filmmakers are enslaved. There were filmmakers who opposed the war but had to make propaganda films in order to survive. Others openly supported the war but were forced to follow American directives after the war ended. Most filmmakers, like Kajiro Yamamoto, contributed to the war effort, believing in the goal of an Asia freed from Western imperialist powers. When Japan's policies were described after the war as militaristic aggression, the same filmmakers awoke as if from a dream and realized the mistakes that had been made. Perhaps the radical change in thinking is unconvincing and even disturbing, but it must be understood as the broken spell of an ideology and *not* the evolution of a philosophy. A false ideology based on misplaced fear and feelings of inferiority and superiority had arisen and imprisoned the filmmakers and, indeed, the majority of the Japanese people. For these reasons, filmmakers who had made propaganda movies during the war could then turn around and produce films that criticized and regretted war only a few months after its end.

During the war, Keisuke Kinoshita made a film called *Rikungun,* 1944 (Army) that portrayed a family that loyally served in the military. Then, in 1946, he produced *Osone-ke no asa* (A Morning with the Osone Family), the tragic story of an officer's horrible actions against a liberal family. In 1943 Tadashi Imai filmed *Boro no kesshitai* (The Suicide of the Watch Tower) honoring Japanese police and military forces who fought guerrillas in Korea during the war. In 1950 he filmed a beautiful romance, *Mata au hi made* (Until the Day We Meet Again), focusing on lovers who are separated by the war and die alone. In 1944 Akira Kurosawa honored the girls who labored in artillery factories during the war in the film, *Ichiban utsukushi-ku* (The Most Beautiful). In 1946 he filmed *Waga seishun ni kui nashi* (No Regrets for Our Youth), the story of an antiwar activist who dies in prison while his wife takes up his cause and boldly opposes militarism throughout the war. The list of examples is long, but if this were indeed a superficial transformation reflecting the vagaries of time, then the achievements of the 1950s "golden age" of Japanese films would not have occurred.

I was fourteen years old when the war ended. During the war, newspapers, radio broadcasts, and even school teachers recited the phrases "offer 100 million honorable lives" and "fight to the last man," as if it were natural behavior. After Japan's defeat, I was surprised that few of the adults committed *hara-kiri;* most were changing their attitudes. I was also amazed by the movies mentioned previously and found my thoughts changing as well. At the same time, however, I wondered if the Japanese ability to transform attitudes so easily could ever be trusted. This doubt lingered for years. However, as I observe the rapid changes following the collapse of ideologies in the former Soviet Union and in China, I think that such flexibility is not specific to the Japanese.

It is now widely accepted among the people of Japan that the Pacific War was a reckless and foolish venture and that the army and military supporters who led citizens into such a war lacked rationality. Even so, some individuals continue to believe that the Pacific War was waged to liberate Asia. They cite the many Asian countries that shook off Western colonialism and declared independence after the Pacific War. Clearly, Japan did not liberate them. Perhaps the war with Japan diverted Western attention, but Asian countries fought their own battles for independence when the opportunity arose. Many Japanese could not accept that the lives lost in the war were wasted foolishly. They cherished thinking of the war itself as reckless but of the soldiers who had shed blood as having made "honorable sacrifices." To this day, there are still people who openly argue that the Pacific War was fought for the liberation of Asia.[2] But they are an extreme minority, and there are hardly any films that represent them.

Commercial films must appeal to a broad cross-section of the general public. Since 1945 many Japanese movies have addressed the war in China and the Pacific War, but most often the war in China is but a backdrop for the debate among the central intelligence officials, military leaders, and the emperor over the merits of attacking Allied forces. Nearly all Japanese films dealing with World War II climax during the meeting with the emperor in which surrender is decided. There are several reasons why films focusing exclusively on the war in China are limited. Only ground forces were active in China, making it impossible to include spectacular air and sea combat scenes that appeal to general audiences. But there is a more fundamental reason. The campaign in China lacked the heroism of the Pacific War. Needless to say, heroism sells well in movies.

The war in China was a dirty invasion for which Japan has no excuse. Propaganda by the Japanese army produced a number of heroes from the 1936 Shanghai riot, for example, the Three Bomb Experts, Tank Commander Nishizumi, the Overseas Bomb Troop, Major Kuga, and the Shanghai Navy Troop. But after defeat they were forgotten. No one wanted to remember the heroes of a dirty war.

The Pacific War was also a war of invasion. However, most Japanese people have slightly different perspectives on the two wars. It is difficult to view the Pacific War as a war of aggression because the risks were so great. Upon reflection, it was really a suicidal conflict. Why, then, did Japan embark upon such a foolish, self-destructive path? In the minds of many Japanese—minds that had been severely controlled by the government and military—the American demand of retreat from China was an impossible condition. More recent great movies that recall the Pacific War such as *Gunbatsu,* 1971 (Factions in the Army), *Rengohkantai,* 1981 (The Combined Fleet), and *Dai Nippon teikoku,* 1982 (Imperial Japan) abbreviate the preliminary stages of the war in China and begin with the period in 1941 when the Japanese government considered the American demand. The films do not criticize or depict America as transgressor. On the other hand, the films do not suggest that the war could have been avoided if Japan had retreated from China. If the films had included the context of the war in China, America's demand would have been justified, and Japan should have accepted the request. By excluding the context of war in China, the idea that the Pacific War was impossible to avoid could linger. The desire to preserve the honor of the nation exerted a force so powerful that the Japanese chose a war that approached suicide. Although it may seem foolish, it was heroic to die for the preservation of honor.

The later films do not criticize the enemy, nor do they express that Japan's actions were justifiable. They reach the audience with grief and condolences for the souls of the thousands of Japanese soldiers who fought and died bravely. Although the characters are not explicitly identified as heroes in the films, their courageous roles imply such status, especially in the portrayals of the *kamikaze* pilots. If the Pacific War can be considered suicidal, then it is the *kamikaze* pilots falling to their deaths one after the other that best represents the mindset of the Japanese people during the war years.[3]

While Japanese films rarely spotlight the soldiers who died in the war with China, many are dedicated to those lost in the Pacific War, particularly *kamikaze* pilots. Kinya Naoi, a former member of this particular group of soldiers, wrote the screenplay for the 1953 film, *Kumoga nagaruru hateni* (Beyond the Clouds), the first of many postwar films dealing with these special forces. A similar movie is produced every few years, all sharing a common fixed theme. A young college student is recruited, goes through training, and becomes a pilot. He fears being called a coward if he does not join the special forces and is haunted by the necessity of his death. The young corp members do not talk of a war to free Asia or even express hatred of the enemy. In fact, they suffer by trying to make sense of their efforts. When the time for combat approaches, they vow to die on behalf of their families and fellow countrymen, realizing that they may not return from their missions. The stories make no logical connection between their suicidal actions and any benefits that would accrue to their families or the people of Japan. If not fighting for some just cause or out of hatred for an enemy, the only remaining justification would be patriotism or pride in eluding cowardice. In postwar Japan, patriotism had become one of the most unpopular themes in film, and personal pride was an embarrassing public admission. "Dying for the sake of family and fellow countrymen" was a different way of describing loyalty and pride. Director Kihachi Okamoto explored deeply this theme in his film, *Nikudan*, 1968 (Human Bullet), and produced a parody of the kamikaze pilots as amiable and somewhat pitiful men who had no choice but to think the way they did.

In Kazuo Kasahara's 1974 film, *Aah kessen kohkuutai* (The Final Air Corps), popular movie star and former attack pilot Koji Tsuruta plays Takajiro Ohnishi, the supreme commander of the *kamikaze* pilots. In the film Commander Ohnishi recognizes toward the end of the war that nothing can save Japan from defeat. Why, then, did he begin the brutal suicidal attacks with no hope of victory? To close friends, he explains that if Japan must lose, it must do so only after an exhausting battle. Had they admitted defeat when still able to fight, then defeat would have been not only material but also psychological. A defeat that followed a final suicidal defense would at least maintain the pride of the Japanese people. The logic that holds pride and patriotism above all other virtues is akin to fascism. The preeminence of pride in Japanese nationalism was the underlying theme in Kajiro's *Amerika Yōsuro,* the unfinished film destroyed at the war's end.

In proudly refusing to withdraw from China, the Japanese government and military embarked on a suicidal conflict and asked as much of its people under a call for "one hundred million honorable deaths." Although such a slogan was never actually *implemented*, the notion was embodied on a small scale by the *kamikaze* pilots sent to their death at the war's end. *Kigasumanai* ("I'm not satisfied") and *kigasumu* ("I'm satisfied") are commonly used phrases among the Japanese people. They reflect the assumption and resolution of a psychological burden. Unable to critique itself and recognize the injustice of its aggression in China, Japan took the American demands for withdrawal as an insult that only reinforced existing fears and feelings of inferiority before Western nations. For Japanese people, who upheld emotional responses over realistic beliefs, the suicidal entrance into war and the actual suicide of the special forces were at least a display before the West of the code of the samurai warriors, and in that the people could take some satisfaction. *Kigasumu.* Then, with the end of the war, the same Japanese people moved quickly to praise Western ways and pursue the American way.

In this manner, the souls of men who died in the war are recognized for their "honorable sacrifices." Still, some are hostile to this interpretation. Pacifists decry the pointless loss of life, while other individuals and conservative politicians describe the fallen pilots as *eirei* or "war heroes." The argument continues to this day.

Retrospections on War

With the outbreak of the Korean War in 1950, General Douglas MacArthur ordered the creation of a reserve police corps to replace the American troops that would leave Japan. The police corps was the predecessor of today's Self-Defense Forces. Although the new postwar constitution explicitly limited military build-up, the reserve police corps was really the resurrection of the armed forces. I was nineteen at the time and feared that the draft would return to gather an army that would be sent to battle under American command. My fears were shared by many others and were reflected in a number of openly antiwar films such as Keisuke Kinoshita's *Karumen junjosu,* 1952 (Carmen's Pure Love), Minoru Shibuya's *Kunsho Award* (1953), and Kon Ichikawa's *Pooh-san.* The mood and tone for each of these movies was serious and threatening. The plots involved former military leaders rejoicing that they might reclaim positions of power and munitions factories as the only businesses flourishing in a poor country. However, these movies did not succeed commercially. Two films that did succeed were Masashi Imai's *Himeyuri no To* (The Towers of Lilies) in 1953 and Keisuke Kinoshita's *Nijushi no Hitomi* (Twenty-Four Eyes) in 1955. In both of these retrospectives on World War II, the Korean War figures very peripherally, but their releases were related to the threatening atmosphere of the times.

The Tower of Lilies dramatizes the true story of schoolgirls in Okinawa, recruited near the end of the war to form a nurses unit. While American troops advance on the island, the girls tirelessly care for injured soldiers and carried ammunition. Showing no doubts about their government or their teachers, they loyally follow orders. Tragically, none of them survive the war, caught at the end in a cave where they are unable to overcome their hesitation at answering the American demand for surrender. The tragedy was in their loyalty. In the film, the U.S. forces hardly appear. Japanese army officers led the innocent girls to the battlefield without guidance on survival. Obviously, the movie opposes the resurrection of the Japanese armed forces.

Twenty-Four Eyes depicts a female teacher and her twelve elementary school students living between 1928 and 1946 on an island in Japan's picturesque Seto Inland Sea. The angelic schoolteacher and her adoring students lead lives full of love in moving, beautifully portrayed scenes. With the onset of military rule and the requirement that students be taught to honor members of the armed forces, the teacher decides she cannot continue to teach and resigns. After the war, she returns to teach at the school, having lost her husband in combat. Some of the students are children of her former students, but she learns that many of them also died as soldiers in the war. She cries before the graves of her students. There is not a single tragic battle scene in the film, taking place as it did in a rural area. It does reflect on some of the hardships of life during wartime, but overall it is a touching, beautiful, poetic picture. As such, it was very popular among women, who often couldn't care less for brutal scenes of battle and could relate, perhaps, to the feelings of a schoolteacher, a woman who cursed the war.

Few Japanese films have moved general audiences to tears as did *Twenty-Four Eyes.* The simple but sensational film had merit beyond its sentimentality and eye-catching scenes. It was renowned for its artistic quality that attracted a wide cross-section of viewers, from academics to coarse men who claimed to dislike sentimental movies. *Twenty-Four Eyes* evolved to represent Japanese regrets over the wars in China and the Pacific and stood in symbolic opposition to the impending return to militarism. However, in my opinion, as a reconsideration of a war of aggression, the film does not go far enough. The movie beautifully dramatizes the love between the schoolteacher and her students but does not address their later actions as soldiers. As the teacher recalls the childhoods of the earlier students and cries before their graves, the audience cries with her over the thought of such adorable children dying on the battlefield. But this is one form of delusion. They did not die as cute children; they died as Japanese soldiers—soldiers who could have been merciless in combat. Tears would not have been shed had such thoughts entered the minds of the audience. Without any scenes suggesting determined soldiers, moviegoers can cry with peaceful assurance.

Twenty-Four Eyes implies that the honest citizens of Japan were only victims of trauma and sorrow and fundamentally innocent of any culpability for the war.[4] Most likely because questions of aggression and responsibility were not addressed, the film became a symbol of Japanese opposition to the return of militarism. Had the movie assigned responsibility for the war to all Japanese people, opposition would have arisen, and it might not have become such a box-office hit.

A common thread among many successful retrospective war films appears in their treatment of antiwar sentiment and antimilitarism. Often as in *The Tower of Lilies* and *Twenty-Four Eyes,* the plot revolves around the hardships borne by honest Japanese civilians without laying blame on them.

There are several films describing crimes committed by Japanese forces during the wars in China and the Pacific. First among these is the six-film series by Masaki Kobayashi called *Ningen no joken* (The Human Condition) that appeared between 1960 and 1961.[5] The films portray the brutal treatment of Chinese prisoners of war watched over by Japanese military police in Manchuria near the end of the Pacific War. The screenplay author, Junpei Gomi, also produced a best-selling novel that Rikuo Yamamoto released as a three-part melodrama between 1970 and 1973. This series, *War and People,* exposed the conspiracy among the Japanese military capitalists seeking to control the Chinese in Manchuria during the 1930s.

Nagisa Oshima's film of 1983, *Merry Christmas Mr. Lawrence,* presents the conditions in a prison camp maintained by the Japanese army in Java during the Pacific War. The atrocities of the Japanese soldiers against the British, Dutch,

Australian, and New Zealander prisoners compel the viewer to cringe in horror. The film proposes that the brutality originates from Japan's history of admiring Westerners and the subsequent feelings of inferiority. The commander of the prison camp is a young Japanese officer as stoic and solemn as the legendary *samurai* that he forces the prisoners to imitate. Beneath his nationalist shell, however, the commander harbors an enthusiastic admiration for Western culture, released in his love for a prisoner from New Zealand, played by the British rock star David Bowie. Torn between loyalty for his country and admiration of the West, the polite and honest commander becomes deranged and brutally violent. The film is among the best explorations of the psychology of the Japanese during the war in the Pacific.

Although some retrospective movies have criticized Japanese behavior during the war, most, like *The Tower of Lilies* and *Twenty-Four Eyes,* emphasize the tragic penalties paid by the Japanese people while overlooking their own responsibility. In most cases, the experience of the atomic bomb takes center stage. The bombings of Hiroshima and Nagasaki represent the greatest penalty Japan paid for its aggression in Asia. The Japanese people are keenly aware of this experience, which dominates reflections on the Pacific War.

During the American occupation from 1945 to 1952, Japanese films were scrutinized, strictly at first and, gradually, with more lenience. Treatments of damage caused by the atomic bombs, though, always received special attention. When the news film company Nihon Eiga, sent a production crew to Hiroshima and Nagasaki to record the damage, the American army assumed control of its management and had the film completed in American facilities as a lengthy documentary. When completed, the film was sent to the United States and not even released in Japan.[6]

Takashi Nagai, a Catholic doctor conducting research on radioactivity, died from leukemia following his exposure to the Nagasaki explosion. Before his death, a series of books he wrote became best-sellers. Writing from his bed, Nagai viewed the bomb as a trial from God. He did not describe the tragic details of the impact of the bomb but wrote sentimental stories reflecting thoughts of his lost wife and his soon-to-be orphaned children. One of his novels was given special permission to be made into a movie. Adapted by Kaneto Shindo and directed by Hideo Ohba, it became the 1950 movie, *Nagasaki no kane* (The Bells of Nagasaki). The bombing itself remains mostly in the background; it appears in only one scene where young children, removed to the countryside for safety, wonder about the small mushroom-like cloud they see rising far away above Nagasaki city. During the American occupation, concrete descriptions and portraits of the aftermath of the bombings were severely restricted not only in film but in any media. As a result, many Japanese knew little about the damage until after the end of the occupation. Only in the week following the signing of the peace treaty did Japanese theater audiences finally see news reports of the impact of the bomb.

Kaneto Shindo, the screenwriter for *The Bells of Nagasaki*, had lived in Hiroshima and was well informed about the disastrous effects of the bomb. He had planned to make a movie thoroughly covering the bomb. After the occupation ended, his film, *Genbaku no ko* (Children of the Atom Bomb) was released in 1952. Only a general description of the bomb's immediate impact was featured, while the focus of the movie drew attention to the phenomenon of people who died seven years after exposure to the radiation. Even since the release of Shindo's film, many Japanese films have explored the bombings of Hiroshima and Nagasaki. Some emphasize the disaster of the explosion, but most present the long and tragic side effects from radiation poisoning; most Japanese today are aware of the lingering dangers of nuclear fallout. One can understand, then, the collective horror of the Japanese when news reports showing American soldiers entering recently bombed test areas and workers mopping up after the Chernobyl disaster were broadcast. The Japanese wonder whether individuals would have taken such risks if they had seen Japanese films on Hiroshima and Nagasaki.

Interestingly enough, these films have not attracted international interest. A partial explanation seems apparent in the media response to Akira Kurosawa's film of 1991, *Hachigatsu no kyoshikyoku* (Rhapsody in August). At the film's premiere, the journalists who gathered, mostly American, were clearly uneasy about his depiction of the Nagasaki bombing. Afterward, Kurosawa was greeted with comments that he should consider the attack on Pearl Harbor before portraying Nagasaki and also with questions regarding his position on militarism.

I mentioned above that few Japanese films examine the responsibility of the Japanese people for the war, while many depict the price they paid. Japan must clearly reflect upon and come to terms with its role in the Pacific War. At the same time, Americans often react defensively to Japanese discussions of the bombings of Hiroshima and Nagasaki, feeling that anti-American sentiment underlies the retrospection. In truth, very few of the many atomic bomb films made since 1952 could be considered anti-American. Most movies warn of the possible dangers of future nuclear wars. Some Americans appear to firmly believe that Japanese discussions of Hiroshima and Nagasaki reflect a grudge against the United States and an attempt to even the score with their responsibility for starting the war. When news of the media criticism leveled at Kurosawa's *Rhapsody in August* reached Japan, many Japanese who hold no such feelings were stunned by the depth of misunderstanding between the two countries. The lack of international recognition for Japanese films focusing on the atomic bombings demonstrates that many countries around the world, not only the United States, consider it improper for Japan to condemn the damaging impact of the atomic bomb. The Japanese people feel that they have reflected sufficiently on the war, but the world does not agree. The Japanese do not understand this difference in perception.

Notes

1. See chapter 14, "Controversies Surrounding the Pacific War: The Tokyo War Crimes Trials," by Kentaro Awaya, for more information on the Greater East Asian Co-Prosperity Sphere.

2. See chapter 14 for an extended discussion of this group.

3. For a brilliant portrait of the Japanese *kamikaze* fighter pilots, see "If Only They Should Fall," in Ivan Morris, *The Nobility of Failure: Tragic Heroes in the History of Japan* (New York: Holt, Rinehart, and Winston, 1975).

4. See chapters 2 and 14.

5. In chapter 7, "Moral Judgment in War and Crimes Against Humanity," in this volume, Van Symons discusses *The Human Condition* in detail.

6. See chapter 2 by John Dower, "The Bombed: Hiroshimas and Nagasakis in Japanese Memory," for an extended discussion on the American suppression of information on the atomic bombings in Japan.

4

Our Forgotten War

The Korean War in Korean and American Popular Culture

David R. McCann

Popular conceptions about war make it out to be a natural if unfortunate occurrence; an interruption, a breakdown in the smoothly connecting narrative of civilization. Popular rhetoric about war and those who die in it also makes it seem as though remembering war were the most natural occurrence. But rhetoric about war and remembering the dead in war demand a reordering of emotions and a sequence of ceremonial events that are not natural. This chapter concerns the question of how Korean and American popular culture reacted to that demand as it was imposed by the events and complex circumstances of the Korean War. In particular, how the processes of forgetting and remembering are intertwined in Korean and American literature related to the war.

First, this chapter considers how the Korean War has been dealt with in Korean literature; primarily, how the war is treated as a civil war in Korean literature. The perspective presented here draws on Bruce Cumings's two-volume history of the origins of the Korean War, which proposes that the social and economic structures, dislocations, and unresolved oppositions that were created, set in motion, and then left suspended by the Japanese colonial occupation of Korea—followed by Japan's defeat and withdrawal from Korea at the end of World War II—created conditions that led to a civil war.[1] Cumings argues that this civil war drew the United

My thanks, first of all, to participants in the NEH Summer Institute, "American Wars in Asia: A Cultural Approach," and the Maureen and Mike Mansfield Center at the University of Montana. I am grateful to Jackie Hiltz of the Center staff, for her thoughtful comments and suggestions. Finally, I am pleased to acknowledge the able assistance of my son Max for his help on the chapter and particularly for his discovery of *Time*'s "Man of the Year."

States, the Soviet Union, the People's Republic of China, and other countries, in their various, early Cold War alignments, into its whirlpool. If the Korean War was a civil war with indigenous origins, then it should be possible to discover in Korean literature from the 1920s or 1930s—there being little to speak of from the 1940s—traces of the structures, the dislocations, and the unresolved oppositions that Cumings describes as the origins of the Korean civil war. Conversely, if the principle features of the ideological and political terrain modulate from dislocation and opposition toward political participation, broader, more equitable distribution of wealth, and a sense of ownership vis-à-vis government, then the landscape of Korean literature on the Korean War might be expected to reflect those changes as well. Because such changes are said to have taken place in the period before and after the 1987 election of Roh Tae Woo, the first relatively open presidential election in South Korea, the 1980s furnish the second benchmark for this examination of (South) Korean literature on the Korean civil war.

Second, this chapter explores the impact of the Korean War on American popular culture. The starting point for this discussion is the Korean War's reputation as the forgotten war. Not much has been produced about the Korean War; nothing like the fiction and films of World War II and Vietnam. Even the long-running television series *M.A.S.H.* seemed in most of its episodes to deploy only bits and pieces of a stereotyped "Korea" as a situational background for its comedy routines. The forgetting persisted for forty years, as the national Korean War monument was dedicated in Washington only in July 1995.

What accounts for the avoidance of the Korean War in American history? Two explanations are put forth here. The process of literary forgetting of war can be traced historically to the poems of Wilfred Owen and others and to the realization that the rhetoric of war—of combat, and particularly of death and of mourning—with which Europe went cheerfully off to war in 1914–15, could not provide a meaningful account of what happened. A tradition of literature going back to the time of Pericles's "Funeral Oration" in ancient Athens, a tradition that had articulated the meaningfulness of death in combat, in war for a state cause, lost its capacity for persuading anyone that the massive horror of death in World War I had any meaning.

The Spanish civil war (1936–39) demonstrated that both sides in an ideologically defined war could be equally inhuman. World War II blurred political and racial causes, within which only huge numbers—of military casualties, tons of bombs or shells dropped or fired, cities destroyed and civilians killed—conveyed meaning and about which, in turn, irony seemed the only reasonable response.[2]

Beginning five years after the end of World War II, the Korean War would test the capacity of Western discourse about war to respond. The relationship of the Korean War to a Western literary and rhetorical tradition of memorializing death in war provides the starting point for this discussion.

If forgetting war were all, or if the war alone were the only forgotten subject, then the rhetorical history of its forgetting would provide a sufficient explanation of the Korean War's noteworthy invisibility in American popular culture. But the Korean War is also entangled in a complex American story of struggle, repression, and social and ideological change taking place after World War II. Two expressions of this other story, explored here, suggest, in turn, a parallel between the selective remembering of the war in Korea and the persistent forgetting of it in America; whereas the Korean War is now viewed at least in part as a civil war, there are signs of a similar civil struggle in domestic American politics during the same period.

The Korean Civil War

Geopolitical and temporal perspectives are significant in determining such ostensibly objective matters as the question of when the Korean War began. To most Americans in 1950 and to the Cold War historians afterward, it seemed to begin on June 25 with the North Korean invasion. To revisionist historians in the 1970s and later, the Korean War began to look more and more like a civil war that had been triggered soon after the Allied liberation and the American division of Korea in 1945 and grew from the increasingly violent struggles within Korea between the political Left and Right into the conflict that broke out on a massive scale in 1950.[3] Some contemporary Korean scholars and others locate the starting point for the civil war more pointedly in the year 1941, as a Korean narrative that began when Korean males conscripted into the Japanese Imperial Army refused to join, went up into the hills instead, and from there, or from bases in Manchuria, engaged directly in a struggle against the Japanese occupation.

The present search for early literary signs of Korean civil war seeks its Korean origins through three well-known Korean short stories: "Potato," published in 1925, "Cranes," in 1953, and "Land of Exile" in 1981. These particular stories were chosen, first, because their qualities as works of literature are widely recognized in Korea as well as elsewhere through their translations; and, second, because they sharply illustrate the conflicted Korean attitudes about remembering and forgetting the war. As an experiment this chapter uses the basic idea of Bruce Cumings's study on the origins of the war to explore whether there are signs in the 1920s of the dislocations and tensions that he located at the root of conditions leading to the war's outbreak in 1950. This line of inquiry will then lead to an examination of "Cranes," which famously typifies those literary works that ignore the politics or ideology of the war to focus, instead, on the distinctive Korean national culture, which was disrupted and torn by the war but still salvageable. This well-known story bespeaks the Korean literary response to the war up to the 1980s. After the dramatic mobilization of the democratic movement in South Korea in the wake of the 1980 Kwangju uprising and massacre, ideological division, class conflict, and their significance in the war became subjects that forcefully engaged Korean writers. How these themes played out in the fiction of Cho Chŏngnae, in his story "Land of Exile," concludes this section.

On the assumption that readers are likely to be less familiar with Korean works than with the American ones, or at least have readier access to them, a lengthier summary and excerpted materials are provided in this section than in the following section on American popular culture.

"Potato"

Kim Tongin, the author of the short story "Potato," was born in 1900 in P'yŏngyang.[4] He died in Seoul, during the Korean War, in January 1951. Kim Tongin was a leading practitioner of "naturalism," which in Korean literary circles meant the use of literature to present case studies, fictional situations in which the reactions of the characters in a story might be tested, pursued, and studied. Many of Kim's stories read like case studies in modern madness, and "Potato" is one of his most accomplished. The story follows the brief life of a woman named Pongnyŏ, who marries a worthless local and struggles to keep herself and her husband going by trying one job after another. She finally becomes a prostitute and then dies at the hands of one of her customers, whom she attacked in a jealous rage. The story is full of violently pointed dialogue between the woman and her husband, which even the most accomplished English translation would be hard-pressed to convey. Even so, it is worth reading in full, even in translation.

The following series of passages from the story describe Pongnyŏ's background and circumstances, but they can also be read as pieces of a naturalist analysis not of the character Pongnyŏ, but of the Korean nation. The beginning signs of the Korean War can be found in this work, which was published in 1925.

The story begins with a brief description of the Seven-Star Gate in P'yŏngyang:

> Strife, adultery, murder, thievery, begging, imprisonment—the slums outside the Ch'ilsŏng Gate of P'yŏngyang were a breeding ground for all the tragedy and the violence of this world. Until Pongnyŏ and her husband moved there they had been farmers, the second of the four classes (scholars, farmers, artisans, and merchants of society).[5]

The setting of the story is the world between a rural way of life, based upon centuries-old farming traditions, and the new, money-based economy of the growing cities of Korea. Why did the couple leave their land and move to the slum, a place that was neither countryside nor city?: "Her bridegroom was twenty years her senior, and originally, in his father's time, the family had been farmers of considerable means and owned several plots of land. But by the groom's generation they were sinking and began losing their possessions one by one."

The groom's family had possessed land, but lost it. Pongnyŏ's family had also possessed a certain amount of wealth, but they too had been losing ground and sold her into marriage for 80 wŏn. Unable to survive in the village, largely because of the husband's shiftless ways, they decide to move to the city and try to make a living as day laborers. Again they fail, for the same reason. Begging does not work either, because Pongnyŏ, who is nineteen years old, looks too healthy.

Through a series of introductory steps, Pongnyŏ learns, first, about working as a day laborer, picking caterpillars off the trees in a city park, and then about sexual work, first with the supervisor of the work site and then as a streetwalker. In a key passage, the author reflects on the questionable morality of Pongnyŏ's success and her sudden accession to personal autonomy:

> As for Pongnyŏ's sense of morality or her view of life, from that day they changed. Until then, she had never considered having sexual relations with a man other than her husband. She had considered such as not human behavior but as that of beasts, and she was certain that if she did such a thing, she would be struck dead.
>
> But how can one account for what had come to pass? Since she herself, who was certainly human, had had this experience, it was by no means out of the range of human possibility. Besides, though she need not work, she got more money; there was a certain guilty thrill in it; and it was a lot more dignified than begging for a living. . . . If I were to describe this in other terms, it was a "waltz through life" . . . nothing could match this enjoyable experience. Was this not, then, the secret to human existence? Moreover, from the time this happened, she acquired, for the first time in her life, the self-confidence of a real individual human being.
>
> From that time on, she began to powder her face.

Pongnyŏ eventually develops a regular arrangement with Wang, a Chinese landowner from whose field she had tried to steal sweet potatoes. When he marries, she goes to his room on his wedding night to confront him. An argument ensues, and when Pongnyŏ threatens him with a sickle, she is killed in the struggle that follows. Pongnyŏ's husband negotiates with Wang, and the two of them, in turn, with an herbalist. The outcome of their negotiations is that for 20 wŏn the herbalist records the cause of death as a cerebral hemorrhage. Pongnyŏ's husband receives a 30-wŏn settlement, and she is buried in the potter's field.

Several elements in this story seem remarkably prescient as indicators of a Korean civil war. The first concerns the social, cultural, and moral dislocations caused by the loss of title to land. Pongnyŏ and her husband are, in effect, uprooted and sent on a long slide down into the slum life of P'yŏngyang. The cause of their dislocation is an undefined process of loss, which nevertheless would coincide with the period following the Japanese land survey and registration project from 1910 to 1918. The cadastral survey had the effect either of expanding the holdings of existing Korean landowners who knew how to work with the Japanese colonial system or of transferring the land title to Japanese owners from tenant farmers or others who did not. At the hands of either type of landowners, Japanese or Korean, peasant farmers were cut adrift in the Korean colony as the lands that they might have occupied for generations became absorbed into an economic system in which land itself had become a cash crop.

A second element, perhaps even more telling, is the sudden and extreme violence that accompanies Pongnyŏ's confrontation with Wang:

> The strange laugh that had been flowing from Pongnyŏ's lips suddenly evaporated into silence.
> "You low-life bitch." She raised her foot and kicked at the finely attired bride.
> "Come on, let's go, let's go." Wang was shaking all over. He shook free from her grip.
> Pongnyŏ fell, but she got right up again, and when she rose, she was brandishing a glittering sickle in her hand.
> "You Chink bastard, I'll kill you. You son of a bitch, you hit me, you bastard, you're killing me!"
> Screaming at him, she brandished the sickle. A violent scene ensued, its setting the house of Wang, that house standing alone in the desolate fields outside the Ch'ilsŏng Gate. However, even this violent scene soon stilled. The sickle that had been in Pongnyŏ's hand somehow got into Wang's and, blood, gushing from her throat, Pongnyŏ fell dead on the spot.

The battle that breaks out between Pongnyŏ and Wang comprises a battle between laborer and owner. Her rage overwhelms her when the revolution of Pongnyŏ's rising expectations, the sudden discovery of personal, individual control of her life, breaks down in confrontation with Wang's far weightier, institutionalized autonomy as an owner of land, as a member of the moneyed class, as *foreign* and Other—a coded reference to the Japanese occupants of the colony. To carry the class and social analysis to its end point, one should note that Pongnyŏ is lacking in one notable particular, a sense of her identity as a member of the exploited lower class and of Wang as her ideological opponent. Kim Tongin was not a member of the just-developing socialist movement in Korea, so we should not expect class consciousness or other elements of socialist realism in his work. Even so, his experiment in literary naturalism concludes with a situation remarkably like Korea's at the conclusion of the Korean War. Pongyŏ's marital state had been divided between her shiftless, lazy husband and the Chinese patron. When she cannot abide the formalization through Wang's marriage of her divided state, she tries to invade and conquer the other, Chinese, half by force. Her personal civil war ends with her death, following which the two powers, husband and former lover, negotiate their lack of responsibility for the death and then bury her.

To be sure, this reading of the origins of a civil war that started in the 1940s into a story published in 1925 is an experimental procedure. Kim Tongin was not anticipating the war, or his own death in it, when he published "Potato," yet the experimental nature of the naturalist story itself makes it an exceptionally useful data field for exploration. Clearly visible in the story are the severe social, cultural, and moral dislocations caused by the loss of land, as well as the extremely violent nature of Pongnyŏ's relationships with her husband and her lover. Stories published in the period after the war seem strangely muted in contrast. The social–cultural dislocations, the class differences and antagonisms, both immediate and historical, are largely absent, and in their place is the state of war. The violence that does occur in the stories seems in a sense to take place off-stage, out of sight, in the past, or the near or immediate future—not, in any event, directly in front of the reader's eyes, as with Pongnyŏ's death.

"Cranes"

One of the best-known of the postwar stories, "Cranes," by Hwang Sunwŏn, first published in 1953, tells about two friends from a village, separated by the division and the war, and then reconciled at the end.[6] The story is told from the point of view of Sŏngsam, a member of the South Korean forces, who discovers that a Communist League prisoner, flushed out from his hideout, is his old chum Tŏkchae. Sŏngsam volunteers to take the prisoner to the jail in the next town for eventual execution. Because the reader's perception is, perforce, Sŏngsam's, we understand his anger at the guerrilla when he asks Tŏkchae "So how many have you killed?" Gradually it emerges that Tŏkchae is just a farmer: "the only thing I'm good at is digging in the soil." Tŏkchae stayed behind in the village to take care of the land and his old father, who was ill. Sŏngsam, on the other hand, ran away from his home, being more of an opportunist. At the end of the story, Sŏngsam finds a way to let Tŏkchae escape. The final sentence captures the transcendent reconciliation in the image of two cranes that "soared high into the clear blue autumn sky, fluttering their huge wings."

Hwang Sunwŏn has been criticized for what is viewed as an overly optimistic hope for the reconciliation of human differences or, phrased somewhat differently, for his failure to confront the reality of the division and the after-effects of the war.[7] However, security laws in place during the interval of American military government (1945–48), the Syngman Rhee regime (1948–60), and the authoritarian government of Park Chung Hee (1961–79) made serious, sustained engagement with the political and ideological issues that underlay the Korean civil war impossible. Hwang's story might be read, therefore, as negotiating an accommodation with existing legal limits. Yet it is also a subtly subversive campaign against the established ideology: the apparent communist partisan, Tŏkchae, turns out to be a decent, simple fellow, while the protagonist, Sŏngsam, is a slippery economic animal. This O'Henry-like plot reversal suggests, at least, that not all characterizations of the communists—including official government ones—as murdering villains are correct.

Two events mark the beginning and end points in a drastic decline in the level of tolerance for authoritarianism and the monolithic anticommunist political line in South Korea. The first was the Kwangju uprising of May 1980. South Korean troops, at the direction of Chun Doo Hwan's government but under the command of Roh Tae Woo, Chun's military academy classmate and successor as head of state, were sent into the southwestern city of Kwangju to put down a demonstration-turned-uprising. The number of citizens killed is estimated at 2,000, though government figures report two hundred or fewer. The uprising itself, and the brutal actions of the troops sent to quell it, marked a turning point in South Korean state–society relations. The U.S. government was widely thought to have permitted the dispatch of South Korean troops, then under the ultimate command authority of the United Nations commander, an American general. In response to later South Korean investigations of the uprising, the State Department prepared a statement denying American government involvement in the dispatching of troops. The failure of the United States government to intercede—even though President Jimmy Carter had made human rights one of the key themes of his administration—also led to resentment and to criticism of American responsibility for the original, 1945 division of Korea and its prolongation.

In addition, the Kwangju uprising marked the point at which the Korean government's antidemocratic, dictatorial actions were widely and explicitly identified. Chun Doo Hwan's legitimacy as head of state was deeply compromised, while a general feeling grew that Kwangju had been the last time that such government action against Korean citizens would be tolerated. One indication of changing attitudes, widely noticed at the time, was a poll conducted at one of the major universities in Seoul on the "worst disaster" to befall Korea in the twentieth century. The customary answer had always been the Korean War, and the course would then go on to study it, but that time, in the mid-1980s, the overwhelming majority of responses named the Kwangju uprising.

The history of the 1980s is itself complex. The change in student perceptions about the war is reflected in the development of an independent organization of primary and secondary school teachers, the Korean Teachers Union, which until now has had to remain an illegal organization. In 1985, the union published a compendium of materials titled *Popular (Minjung) Education*. Although the book was banned by the Korean government, it sold some eighty-five thousand copies. The leadership of the union was arrested, and approximately two thousand teachers affiliated with the union were fired. The growth of the teachers' union was part of the larger *Minjung* movement, a congeries of labor groups, student activist groups, and religious, educational, and other associations, which worked to refocus popular attention on the identity and history of the Korean people, as contrasted with the ruling elites, and to pursue an extremely broad array of social, cultural, economic, and political reforms. One of the movement's primary goals was economic justice and the equitable distribution of wealth, an issue woven into the class and other conflicts that the Japanese occupation had instigated.[8]

Whatever the particulars of the social analysis, the changes associated with the growth of the *Minjung* movement in the 1980s reached a culmination in 1987, when the then-president Chun Doo Hwan attempted to name Roh Tae Woo as his successor. Protests spread throughout Korea. In part because South Korea was planning the 1988 Olympics and was therefore very much in the world's eye, the government's response to the demonstrations was measured. When Roh announced his desire to proceed with an open and direct election instead of the closeted succession that Chun had proposed, both Koreans and non-Koreans were completely surprised. The election took place, Roh won, and a new constitution was passed in 1988 that permitted a much freer range of expression in literary works, film, and other media.

Throughout the 1980s, literary works and literary movements pushed back the limits on what could be written and published. "Labor literature" (*nodong munhak*) gave way to "literature by laborers" (*nodongja munhak*). Both of these were inconceivable under the prior strict interpretation of anticommunist and antiunion laws. Though technically hidden by the insertion of blank spaces for place names, references to the Kwangju uprising appeared in works such as "A Shared Journey" by Im Ch'oru in a 1984 collection entitled *You and I Know*.[9] The poet Ko Un published poems on the subject of Kwangju, most notably including "When May Is Gone" (*Owŏri kamyŏn,* 1986), with one section a particularly strong echo of the final scene in "Potato:"

> . . . we were carried away like so many dead dogs,
> carried off somewhere in fast army trucks.
> Ah, Mangwoldong [The graveyard]! Not only there!
>   Not only there!
> Still they lie in unknown places,
> buried there. Seven hundred? Eight hundred?
> Two thousand of us?[10]

"Land of Exile"

One of the most controversial and successful writers of the decade is the novelist Cho Chŏngnae. His story "Land of Exile," published in 1981, and his ten-novel *Taebaek Mountain Range,* published between 1983 and 1989, grapple respectively with the intense self-hatred that lay behind the Korean War and the indigenous origins of the leftist/communist movement in South Korea in the period following the 1945 division.

The short story describes the wanderings of the character Mansŏk, a member of the peasant group in a village, who took advantage of a communist takeover in the course of the war to settle bitter grievances against the Ch'oes, the family that had controlled the village for generations.[11] The story begins with Mansŏk trying to return to his home, unable to do so because of the terrible things he had done during the war. One passage epitomizes the horror: Mansŏk is remembering the period when the village was under the control of the people's army. He and his comrades have just captured the Ch'oes' grandson, whose father had been executed a few days before:

> At the commander's word, Mansŏk winked a signal to his subordinates. The three men hoisted their bamboo spears and lunged at Elder Ch'oe's grandson, who was tied to the trunk of the pine. Screams, long screams, spread forth—screams that seemed to tear through the mountains, rend the skies, rip open the very earth. Sugil stood rigid as a post, eyes tightly closed. You ass, you don't deserve to be chairman, thought Mansŏk, watching him with a mocking sneer.
>
> Quite unlike Sugil, Mansŏk listened to the drawn-out screams with a pleasure that thrilled every joint in his body. The sense of pleasure was, in fact, one of sweet revenge.
>
> All the sorrow and pain and mortification they had all known over generations of slavery, and that he himself had endured for twenty-five years, were slowly, slowly washed away by that thrilling pleasure. ("Land of Exile," p. 211)

This is not an easy scene to encounter, even in an English translation that distances the event.

The title of the story clearly invokes the idea of Korea itself, that Korea will remain divided and filled with self-hatred until it begins to confront the actual horrors of the war. In a perceptive review-article on Korean films since 1987–88, Isolde Standish observes that, in many of today's films and literary works, the common suffering of all Koreans because of the war, and as a result of the continued division of the country, is a theme that could serve to reunite the Korean people.[12] One can certainly respect the hope while hesitating to endorse what seems at the same time to be an exploitation of the violence. For example, the narrative in "Land of Exile" continues as follows:

> For Mansŏk, this feeling amounted to an exhilaration even more intense and passionate than what he felt on top of his wife, Chŏmnye. That sensation was also maddening in its way, but it was too short-lived, and it was followed by a sudden, precipitous hollowness. But the pleasure he took from the screaming lasted as long as the time it took for the unforgettable memories to float up one after the other and then vanish. ("Land of Exile," pp. 211–12)

Such extreme, sadistic pleasure in violence, especially when directed against women as it is in many examples of Korean modern fiction and film, is more disturbing than the divided, anguished portrait of Korea during the war. Brutality toward women that ranges from mere contempt and dismissal to pathological sexual violence permeates a recent anthology of exemplary postwar Korean fiction. The anger and self-contempt that modern Korean literature is steeped in seems to derive in part from the Japanese occupation and the sense of prolonged violation that it caused. The unresolved class conflicts stirred up by the occupation and the division, as well as the division itself, have also fastened upon the image of the woman as object and source of an obsessive anger.[13] More recent work seems at last to be engaging the sources of the rage, in such novels as Cho Chŏngnae's *T'aebaek Mountain Range,* while avoiding the scapegoating or objectification of women as substitutes for both cause and locus of the dispossession. As Standish concludes:

> The films of the "new wave" are infused with an overpowering humanism and depict the shared *han* of the whole Korean race. Despite the fact that they fail to offer tangible solutions to the social and political problems they depict, these films, through their adoption of social realistic cinematic conventions, do offer a dark exposé of contemporary Korean society which is motivated by a humanistic concern for the plight of ordinary Korean citizens . . . at the cultural level, they work to mitigate entrenched fears of North Korea as a threat through images of the Korean people as a whole—both North and South—as victims of foreign imperialist policies and their own governments.[14]

The Korean War has been constantly remembered and even prefigured in Korean literature and film but, until the 1980s, the remembrance of the war remained partial and incomplete. The sundering of the Korean people and their nation, the pathos of the violence reflected in that community of people—that is, the symbolic significance of the war as it affected ideas about the idea of the national culture—seemed more powerfully to engage the attention of literature than did the violence of the war itself or the political and social struggles that immediately preceded it.

The Korean literary history of the war falls into three general stages. First, the Japanese colonial occupation initiated a massive sea-change in Korean society and culture, one that set loose a cascade of upheaval and change while at the same time implicating in that process the Korean nation and people who lived through it. This combined process of dislocation and implication furnished the plot of "Potato" and other representative works from the colonial era.

When World War II ended and the Japanese were sent home, the repressive regimes established north and south of the dividing line did not permit the dislocations to mend; rather, their repressive policies increased the tensions and levels of anger across a fractured society and polity. Where the story of social and political upheaval had been suppressed during the colonial period by the Japanese because it was at least implicitly a nationalist, Korean story of resistance against Japanese rule, the same story was repressed even more thoroughly in the period after the Korean War. In the South the story represented an empathetic reading of the leftist position, and in the North, a retrograde, rightist sympathy for the ruling class landowners and industrialists. The result of these mirror-image, hegemonic misreadings was that the serious ideological conflicts of the war and its origins were erased from the national histories. In their place in South Korean literature, one finds variations on the story "Cranes," Hwang Sunwŏn's evocation, touched with dramatic irony of the ineradicable, national spirit of the Korean people.

This second stage in the history of Korean literary and more general cultural responses to the war have been followed by the current, third stage: empathetic, engaged readings and representations of the complex, thoroughly conflicted ideological and political origins of the war; acknowledgment of the brutality visited by both sides in the conflict upon each other (rather than the much more common, earlier representations of the foreign troops—especially the Americans—as the agents of all atrocities); and recognition of the need for unflinching engagement with the whole story, rather than just its more convenient, ideological parts. All these conditions must be met if the two sides in the conflict, the people of North and South Korea—who had, after all, existed as a *divided* nation for only five years when the war broke out—are to achieve reunification.

The Korean War in American Popular Culture

A recent study of American literature, *Restrained Response: American Novels of the Cold War and Korea, 1945–1962,* repeatedly cites the "forgotten war" theme in literature on the Korean War. For example:

> That Korea so soon lost its warlike and ominous association is most likely connected with its status . . . as a "forgotten," officially unrecognized and publicly unpopular war. This aspect is also taken up by almost all writers of Korean War novels, and the collected testimony of American military narratives strongly suggests that, to Americans in general, the Korean conflict was, or had better be, forgotten.[15]

Why the forgotten status? This section seeks answers to the question in two areas. The first, a broad review of the rhetorical dimensions of war literature of Western civilization, sketches the process of literary deconstruction of the meaningfulness of death in war. This section begins with reflections on the classical funeral oration as exemplified by Pericles's speech to the Athenians during the Peloponnesian War and ends with Dylan Thomas's poem "A Refusal to Mourn the Death, by Fire, of a Child in London," from World War II. The American popular response to the Korean War was partially shaped by this process of rhetorical, literary deconstruction, a process that had left irony, reportage, or silence as the only acceptable responses to war.

In the American popular response to the Korean War, silence has abounded. For a dose of irony, American popular culture provides the example of *M A.S.H.,* the book, the movie, and the long-running TV series. For reportage, there is the example of *Time* magazine's feature on the 1950 Man of the Year, the American fighting-man (sic) in Korea. In retrospect, the article has a visibly patched-together quality as rhetoric that, by downplaying the heroic, seeks to reinstate it. The second area will observe two other representations of the American popular response to the war, the movie *The Manchurian Candidate* and the play "The Crucible."

Toward the Post-Rhetorical

The rhetorical tradition of Western responses to war and its meaning begins with the funeral oration by the Athenian statesman Pericles, who spoke at a *public* funeral for the Athenian dead in the war against Sparta, known as the Peloponnesian War. Pericles's oration constitutes a prolonged argument to postpone, circumscribe, and defuse the most natural impulse of citizens receiving home again the remains of those who had died in war. The first 274 lines of his oration recall the Athenians' ancestors, enumerate the unique characteristics of the Athenian state and people, declare the meaningfulness of the battle deaths in defense of such histories, institutions, and accomplishments, and acknowledge the difficulties that will attend the living when they must confront the heroic example of the dead. The last two lines of the oration state: "now, when you have mourned for your dear ones, you must depart."[16]

According to the oration, all the mourning can and must be completed at the ceremony of the funeral. There must be no extension of the mourning into the continuing lives of the Athenian citizens, no prolonged lamentation. Why this circumscription of lamentation and expressions of grief? A compelling study of women's laments and Greek literature argues that the development of the funeral oration, the Epitaphios Logos, as a public ceremony and display of private grief, coincided with the origination of the standing army for the conduct of the Athenian wars and with the banning of women's laments in the Solonic Code. The ban on laments and the imposition of careful legal controls on expressions of *private* grief accomplished two things: By limiting laments, the Athenian city-state forestalled the cycles of revenge that had followed battle or other deaths prior to the fifth century B.C.; and because such vendettas required the settling of accounts—determining responsibility for the deaths, and then punishing those found to be responsible—the state was able to forestall the wrath of citizens who were repeatedly being sent into war.[17]

Pericles's "Funeral Oration" strains to mediate the conflicting needs and demands of the individual and the state: for the individual, the need to grieve, to lament, to blame, to seek retribution, and, for the state, the need to carry on with its business of imperial expansion and war without interruption:

> The (male) funeral oration for those who die in battle makes a virtue of death, provided it is death in the service of the state. This is in direct opposition to the

lament of the female relatives, who, if we are to take the folk laments of Greece and other modern cultures as representative, mourn their personal loss in terms of emotional, economic and social deprivation, and look on death as an enemy. The tension between public and private burial can only be resolved when the state, as it has done many times in modern European history, convinces the families, particularly the mothers of the soldiers, that the glory of dying for the fatherland outweighs private grief, and compensates them for their loss.[18]

The same difficult, strained balance, weighted heavily in favor of the state and mediated through a romanticized vision of death in battle—as for example in poems like Rupert Brooke's, repeatedly quoted in Sunday sermons in England[19]—persisted into the early years of World War I. But as the Great War continued, the experience of modern, technological, industrial warfare destroyed the assumptions upon which the rhetorical gambit and tradition relied, leaving only a "modernist" irony as the characteristic tone of war literature.

The rhetorical claim of the public funeral oration is both the subject and the object of Wilfred Owen's poem "Dulce et Decorum Est," written in the last few weeks of the war, just days before Owen was killed in action in France. The poem is well enough known not to require citation in full; those who have read it will remember the deliberately soothing rhymes and line rhythms of the first stanza, as the patrol is returning from action. The soothing cadences obscure the gas shells that fall behind the tired marchers in the last few words of the stanza:

> All went lame; all blind;
> Drunk with fatigue; deaf even to the hoots
>   Of tired, outstripped Five-Nines that
> dropped behind.[20]

Even the gas shells are tired and quiet in this scene; "outstripped"—a deliberately ambiguous term in this context—they simply "dropped behind." When the shells explode in the second stanza, one soldier, too late to fumble on his helmet, is caught in the gas, where he flounders, drowning. The final stanza describes the horror of the man's prolonged death agony, "eyes writhing in his face," the blood "Gargling from froth-corrupted lungs." Against that image, the reader is left to confront "the old lie," the schoolboy-Latin paraphrase of Pericles's argument that it is sweet and proper to die for one's country.

Having lost the classical rhetorical base upon which it had been constructed, what could the modern literature of war take as its subject? If not the nobility of sacrifice *pro patria,* then might ideology establish a justification for the horror? The disenchanting experience of World War I was briefly swept aside by the ideological enthusiasms of the Spanish civil war. Politically committed volunteers journeyed to Spain to join the international battalions, but soon enough discovered that both sides, Left as well as Right, pursued their aims with equally appalling brutality. German and Soviet participation only added to the carnage and waste. George Orwell's *Homage to Catalonia* recounts the disillusionment of one leftist in the civil war, who counted himself lucky at the end just to get out of it. The significance of the war, which had at first seemed tied to ideological positions, is captured most strikingly in Picasso's *Guernica*. What shapes the painting is the cry of grief and horror at the meaningless deaths of the village people slaughtered in the German air attack. The painting returns to the subject of private or personal lamentation in place of public ceremonials.

The vast literature of World War II also refuses in large part to attempt the oratorical and monumental ceremonials on the theme of some greater meaning to death in war. Dylan Thomas's representative poem, "A Refusal to Mourn the Death, by Fire, of a Child in London," echoes Owen in its angered tone and its refusal to engage in public mourning. At a greater distance, with the mention of parents, the city, and the forgetting of the first dead, the poem's final two stanzas echo and then close the book on Pericles:

> I shall not murder
> The mankind of her going with a grave truth
> Nor blaspheme down the stations of her breath
> With any further
> Elegy of innocence and youth.

> Deep with the first dead lies London's daughter,
> Robed in the long friends,
> The grains beyond age, the dark veins of her mother,
> Secret by the unmourning water
> Of the riding Thames.
> After the first death, there is no other.[21]

Mourning is not the same as remembering or lamenting; it seems to be the opposite, the submersion of the private individual in the public collective, the singular in the numerous, the first death in the deaths of *all* the others.[22] Thomas's poem refuses public mourning, grief multiplied, in its argument against the forgetting of the particulars of life and death that the public gesture requires. In place of such public, "classical" ceremonial, the final stanza of the poem insists upon the return to private grieving among friends and relatives.

The Korean War began at the start of the Cold War, as has often been noted, but it was also the first war of the "postrhetorical" age. The poets of the Korean War would turn out to be photographers like David Duncan and Margaret Bourke-White; the novelists, ironists like Richard Condon (*The Manchurian Candidate*) or Joseph Heller (*Catch-22*). The silence, irony, and reportage were conditioned by the literary reaction to World War II, as a predisposition not to seek literary heroism in connection with the war in Korea.

This rhetorical devolution may account for one part of the silence on the Korean War. The specific events of the war and its surrounding moment in American history also played a role in suppressing the desire to remember it. During the first six months of the Korean War, particularly in the aftermath of the astonishing success of MacArthur's landing at Inch'ŏn, American popular opinion supported the war as a necessary effort to contain the expansion of international communism. President Harry S. Truman made that larger objective of the Korean intervention explicit when he announced his intention to commit American troops to the defense of South Korea; at the same time, he stated his plans to place naval forces in the Taiwan Strait and to support the French in Indochina against the Vietminh and the Philippine government against the Huk insurgency.

In the brief period of heady success that followed the September landing at Inch'ŏn, *Time* assembled the materials for its portrait of the Man of the Year.[23] Making a virtue of necessity, the article extolled the workmanlike approach of the troops to their assignment and their uncomplicated belief that communism somehow lay behind what was happening in Korea. There was no mention of Korea, the Korean people—except in macabre descriptions of what happened when they blew up—or of the brief, intense history of the 1945 division of Korea. A few phrases capture the tone of the piece. The American fighting man was "comfort-loving," "hated war," and "much preferred riding to walking." As *Time* summarized, he was "called soft and tough, resourceful and unskilled, unbelievably brave and unbelievably timid, thoroughly disciplined and scornful of discipline." The article doubles back on itself to say, "Nobody could find a typical U.S. Soldier of 1950. There was no one type; there were as many types as there were men. Here are some of the men." There follow thirteen profiles, from the brief sketch of Private Kenneth Shadrick, "cut down by machine gun fire," to substantially longer accounts about Private Stanley Popko, Ensign David Tatum, and Sergeant Robert Ward.

From their comments, we learn that Popko originally thought that "if Koreans wanted to fight among themselves, let them fight. It was like that revolution in China. It was nothing to do with us." Tatum volunteered for the navy in 1946. His political outlook was elementally clear. His "seventh-grade teacher taught him some current affairs-something about isms. Nazism to him was the swastika, and evil because it was against the underdog. Fascism to him was a fat man on a balcony. Communism? Today he says without hesitation and with deep seriousness: 'I will not live under Communism.' "

The article has a rather cobbled-together quality; its contradictory and unstable narrative rapidly fell apart. Just two weeks later, *Time* reported the imminent capture of Seoul under the Chinese counterattack that had commenced in late November. South Korean president Syngman Rhee and his cabinet once again fled to Pusan, while the Allied evacuation proceeded, for a time, quite efficiently, since, said a U.S. officer bitterly, "we've had a lot of practice."

Support for the war effort dissipated as the war continued past the beginnings of the armistice negotiations in July 1951, then into 1952, and still on into 1953. Public attention shifted from the news reports of distant combat around stalemated positions to live television coverage of Senator Joseph McCarthy's increasingly ominous pronouncements about communist infiltration throughout American life and institutions. The domestic tragi-comedy that eventually led to the Army–McCarthy hearings brought the Wisconsin senator, the lawyer Joseph Welch holding his head in sad despair, and other props and actors into American living rooms. Amid the buffoonery and tragedy of McCarthyism, the witch hunts, the hearings before the House Un-American Activities Committee, black-lists, and all the rest of that dramatic passage in American history, the political Left was wiped out.[24]

Two quite different literary expressions seem to have resonated with the public sentiments of this period. One, the 1962 movie version of a 1959 novel by Richard Condon, *The Manchurian Candidate,* played to the anxieties of the American people with the melodramatic story of a brainwashed assassin pro-grammed to kill a presidential candidate. The running mate, the dimwitted stooge of the conspiracy, was then to ride a wave of popular sympathy and revulsion into the White House. The image of repellently sinister foreign agents who constructed the scheme and prepared the assassin resonated with the stories of the brainwashing of prisoners of war by North Koreans and Chinese.[25] It also echoed the by-then decades-old American distrust of immigrants and foreign ideas so neatly summarized in David Tatum's comments in *Time* about a fat man on a balcony and those "isms." It reflected a deep-seated fear of the colonies or what became known as the Third World.[26] The film's ironic, bitter sweep ex-tended to the Right as well, in its portrayal of Senator Johnny Iselin, the vice-presidential candidate, a mockery of McCarthyism and the senator from Wisconsin, famous for drunkenness, wild, unsubstantiated claims and lists such as those the candidate promises to reveal in the movie. The movie captured and played to a mood of national paranoia.

Arthur Miller's play "The Crucible," though set in early colonial America, en-gaged even more directly that mixture of prejudice, local jealousy, and ideological fervor that characterized the mid-1950s. The play was first presented on January 22, 1953, and two of the lead actors, E.G. Marshall and Beatrice Straight, were closed out of television contracts the next year as a result.[27] A few years later, in his Introduction to *Arthur Miller's Collected Plays,* the playwright reflected:

> It was not only the rise of "McCarthyism" that moved me, but something much more weird and mysterious. It was the fact that a political, objective, knowl-edgeable campaign from the far Right was capable of creating not only a terror, but a new subjective reality. . . . It was as though the whole country had been born anew, without a memory even of certain elemental decencies which a year or two earlier no one would have imagined could be altered, let alone

forgotten. Astounded, I watched men pass me by without a nod whom I had known rather well for years; and again, my astonishment was produced by my knowledge . . . that the terror in these people was being knowingly planned and consciously engineered, and yet all they knew was terror. That so interior and subjective an emotion could have been so manifestly created from without was a marvel to me. It underlies every word in "The Crucible."[28]

The Korean War has been a forgotten, invisible war in American popular culture, to be sure, just as the Korean War has also been misremembered in Korea until only relatively recently. The explanation for its invisibility seems to involve at least two factors: the final deterioration of a literary and rhetorical tradition that glorified war and a process of domestic American social and ideological change that eventuated in the erasure of the political Left. The forgotten, misremembered, invisible elements in both stories, Korean and American, were the struggles between the institutions of government and business power and those groups or sectors in the society perceived as critical or hostile to them. Some of that perception was well founded, but much of it was not. Violence, hatred, self-loathing, class conflict, and local jealousies pursued in the name of self-righteousness: the story of the turmoil registered in Miller's historically distanced play, as also in Cho Chŏngnae's excruciating projection of the Korean War into the interior spaces of Korea's class and gender conflicts, could be rewritten and called *Our Forgotten War*.

Notes

1. Bruce Cumings, *The Origins of the Korean War: Liberation and the Emergence of Separate Regimes 1945–1947* (Princeton: Princeton University Press, 1981), pp. xx–xxi.

2. See Paul Fussell, *The Norton Book of Modern War* (New York: Norton, 1991), pp. 307–8 et passim.

3. See John Merrill, *Korea: The Peninsular Origins of the War* (Newark: University of Delaware Press, 1989), passim.

4. Peter H. Lee, *Flowers of Fire* (Honolulu: University of Hawaii Press, 1974) pp. 10–18. "Potato" was published as "Kamja" in the journal *Chosŏn mundan* (Korean Literary World), published in Seoul, 1925.

5. Ibid., pp. 10–18.

6. Ibid., pp. 108–14.

7. Marshall R. Pihl and Bruce and Ju-Chan Fulton, *Land of Exile: Contemporary Korean Fiction* (Armonk, NY: M.E. Sharpe, 1993), p. 35: "Despite critics' quibbles about the social relevance of his fiction . . ."

8. See various references in Hagen Koo, ed. *State and Society in Contemporary Korea* (Ithaca: Cornell University Press, 1993), including "The State, *Minjung*, and the Working Class in South Korea," pp. 131–62.

9. Pihl and Fulton, *Land of Exile,* pp. 265–84.

10. Ko Un, *The Sound of My Waves* (Ithaca: Cornell University Press, 1993), p. 65.

11. Pihl and Fulton, *Land of Exile,* pp. 201–43.

12. Isolde Standish, "United in Han: Korean Cinema and the 'New Wave,'" *Korea Journal* (Winter 1992), pp. 109–18.

13. See David McCann, "Land of Exile: Contemporary Korean Fiction," *Korean Studies* 19 (1995).

14. Standish, "United in Han," pp. 109–10.

15. Arne Axelsson, *Restrained Response: American Novels of the Cold War and Korea, 1945–1962* (Westport: Greenwood, 1990), p. 54. See also Paul Fussell, *The Norton Book of Modern Warfare,* p. 651: "But if it [the Korean War] resembled the Vietnam War in these ways, in another way it is unique; it generated virtually no literature, perhaps one reason it seems to be . . . The Forgotten War."

16. Thucydides, *The Peloponnesian War* (New York: Penguin Books, 1988), p. 151.

17. Aeschylus's *Eumenides* cauterizes the wound of war, the endlessly unraveling tale of revenge, by turning the witches who hunt, the Furies or Erinnyes, into the domesticated "Gracious Ones," the *Eumenides.* The transformation is accomplished by Athena's rhetoric: "Nay, if Persuasion's holy majesty, The sweet enchantment of these lips divine, Is aught to thee, why, then reside with me . . ." See *Eumenides* in Dudley Fitts, ed., *Greek Plays in Modern Translation* (New York: Dial Press, 1961), p. 138.

18. Gail Holst-Warhaft, *Dangerous Voices: Women's Laments and Greek Literature* (London: Routledge, 1992), p. 5.

19. See *The Collected Poems of Rupert Brooke* (New York: Dodd, Mead and Company, 1929), p. 111. Brooke's sonnet "Peace," the first in the sequence of five entitled "1914," presents death in battle as a vision of a romantic encounter, filled with such Whitmanesque enthusiasms as youth, cleanness, leaping, release, and in the end, a meeting with the romanticized Other: "And the worst friend and enemy is but Death."

20. *The Collected Poems of Wilfred Owen* (New York: Chatto and Windus, 1963), p. 55.

21. Gerald Dewit Sanders, ed., *Chief Modern Poets of England and America* (New York: Macmillan, 1964), p. 416.

22. R.W. Burchfield, *The Compact Edition of the Oxford English Dictionary* (New York: Oxford University Press, 1971), p. 1864. Under mourn: "To exhibit the conventional signs of grief for a period following the death of a person."

23. *Time,* January 1, 1951.

24. See Barton J. Bernstein, "The Truman Administration and the Korean War," in *The Truman Presidency,* ed. Michael J. Lacey (Cambridge: Cambridge University Press, 1989), pp. 411 et passim.

25. See Stephen J. Whitfield, *The Culture of the Korean War* (Baltimore: John Hopkins University Press), pp. 211–13.

26. Note the implied epidemiological link between immigrants and radically unsettling ideas in, for example, Walter LaFeber's *The American Age: United States Foreign Policy at Home and Abroad Since 1750* (New York: Norton, 1989), pp. 122–23: "Between 1820 and 1840, about 700,000 newcomers entered the country; but between 1840 and 1860, some 4.2 million flooded over eastern cities and western lands. In Europe, communism first began to appear as a movement to be reckoned with; in the United States, the first important labor unions emerged. The United States could not escape the crosscurrents that racked the Western world."

27. Whitfield, *The Culture of the Korean War,* p. 119.

28. Arthur Miller, *Arthur Miller's Collected Plays* (New York: Viking Press, 1957), pp. 39–40.

5

Fragmentation in American and Vietnamese War Fiction

Leslie Kennedy Adams

> "Vietnam [will] always be a place with no real point of reference, then *or* now."
>
> —Philip D. Beidler, *American Literature and the Experience of Vietnam,* p. 16

By most accounts, the Vietnam War was a disaster—a military disaster, a political disaster, an economic disaster, an ecological disaster, and a personal disaster for many of the people involved. It literally blasted some people's lives into tiny, irretrievable fragments. Some people died as their bodies were blown to pieces, some too small to be accounted for or collected and placed in the body bag that would carry them home; others had their minds blown, the result of drugs, combat trauma, or some combination of the two. Others lost their homes, their families, and their identity. This was especially true for the Vietnamese people. It could be argued that some of the Vietnamese even had their genes fragmented by the tons of pesticides and defoliants sprayed on their fields, their homes, and their bodies.[1]

It is easy to see why "Vietnam histories have one thing in common: they are all, to some extent, fragmentary"(Meyers 1988, p. 547). Both American and Vietnamese authors have tried to recreate this chaos, or fragmentation, in their novels about the Vietnam War. They physically break, or fragment, the narrative structure of the story in a variety of ways in order to mimic or recreate the atmosphere of the war and the experience of the soldiers who fought in Vietnam. For example, in fiction about Vietnam, memories of events or specific scenes are often presented out of sequence or in fragments. The reader is presented with a memory or part of a story; then, suddenly the narrative shifts to a different character's memory or a different place or time. The effect of this narrative fragmentation is similar in some respects to a badly cut film or to trying to watch television with someone who keeps switching from one channel to another. Some of these authors employ dramatic "shifts in time, mood, [and] tone," mix "understatement . . . with overstatement," and juxtapose "catalog[s] of events" with "the heightened realism of minute details and focused description"(Anisfield 1988, p. 57) in order to " 'defamiliarize' reality or make it seem strange" since these sections differ so sharply from usual ways of speaking and seeing (Victor Shklovsky, quoted in Martin 1986, pp. 47–48). As Nancy Anisfield explains, the "reader learns to adapt to quick change"(1988, p. 57) as these authors perform a variety of tricks in trying to recreate the unreal atmosphere of the Vietnam War. This fragmentation forces the reader to "piece together information in the same manner that the characters [in these novels] must piece together the reality of the war" (Calloway 1995, p. 254). This narrative technique also helps the reader to experience, to some degree, the frustration and confusion of the soldiers and families on both sides who tried to make sense out of the war and its effects.

Some of the novels offer a chronological backbone, or structure, but the narrative constructed upon this framework is internally fragmented. That is, the backbone is a deceptive facade. This structure mimics the experience of the American soldier who served a twelve-month tour of duty (thirteen months if he was a Marine) but whose experiences within that temporal structure were chaotic and often surreal. Michael Herr's *Dispatches,* Tim O'Brien's *Going After Cacciato,* and Larry Heinemann's *Paco's Story* employ this structure.

Other novels use a more fragmented structure. These novels make no attempt to impose order on their character's experiences; instead, they offer a series of narrative fragments including war stories, journal entries, menus, song lyrics, graffiti, and metafictional discussion of the writing process. Tim O'Brien's *The Things They Carried,* Bao Ninh's *The Sorrow of War,* and Duong Thu Huong's *Novel Without a Name* are representative of this more fragmented format.

Michael Herr's *Dispatches*

On first glance, *Dispatches* appears to be a well-ordered, traditional novel. It is organized into six clearly demarcated chapters whose titles represent a different period of time in Herr's "tour of duty" in Vietnam. The reader soon discovers, however, that this novel is instead a chaotic tour de force, a "freewheeling collage" (Ringnalda 1994, p. 81). In fact, it is fair to say that *Dispatches* is the most fragmented of the American novels about the war. This is perhaps due in part to Michael Herr's difficulty in writing the book. In an interview with Eric Schroeder, Herr says he "wrote the book inside out" (Schroeder 1991, p. 41), meaning that he wrote the various sections of the book out of order: "Chronologically, the first piece I wrote is the second chapter of the book; the next piece I wrote is the Khe Sanh piece, followed by 'Illumination Rounds,' and then I wrote 'Colleagues' "(ibid.). The book is as Herr describes it—a loosely connected group of war stories that the narrator remembers from his time in Vietnam. The deceptive chronological framework of the chapters is the only controlling factor in this novel.

Dispatches opens with "Breathing In," a chapter that begins with a scene similar to the opening scene of *Apocalypse Now*.[2] The narrator, reminiscing, describes the old Vietnamese map on the wall in his apartment, the map he used to stare at for hours at the end of the day. He concludes this opening section with the story of an information officer he met "at the end of [his] first week in country" (Herr 1978, p. 2); the officer showed him a similar map on the wall, explaining what ground had been taken to date and about the various operations: "It had been part of his job for nearly a year now to tell people about that operation; correspondents, touring congressmen, movie stars, corporation presidents, staff officers. . . and he still couldn't get over it" (ibid.). This memory sets the tone for the rest of the book because, like the information officer, Herr's narrator seems bound to go over and over the terrain he covered in Vietnam, recounting the stories he gathered in each place, describing each operation for the reader.

What follows is a mixture of these different stories, loosely connected by place names and chapter headings. The memories the narrator recounts are sometimes printed in italics, as if he wants to emphasize that these sections have fallen into the narrative as memories drop into people's stories when they mention other specific events or tales for an audience. The chapter titles Herr provides offer a map of sorts for readers and offer clues as to what type of memories each section will contain.

For example, the first chapter is entitled "Breathing In," a title that could represent the start of the journey or the start of a drug trip. It is followed by "Hell Sucks," which includes the narrator's memories and stories of the Tet offensive. The next chapter, "Khe Sanh," recounts the narrator's experiences and observations from the battle for Khe Sanh. The fourth chapter title, "Illumination Rounds," refers to the ammunition that was used to light the battlefield for better marksmanship and clarity of vision. The war stories in this chapter offer insight into the journalist's understanding of his relationship with his subject: "It took me a month to lose that feeling of being a spectator to something that was part game, part show," he writes (p. 178).

"Illumination Rounds" is followed by "Colleagues." In this chapter, the narrator introduces the cast of characters, the Vietnam press corps. Here, he offers war stories about the famous correspondents he worked with in Vietnam, including Sean Flynn and Tim Page, instead of focusing on the stories of the soldiers he met. In fact, it is in this section that he refers to his time in Vietnam as his "movie," a movie that, ironically, never would have been made because people would not have paid to see it, fed up as they were with the war: "So we have all been compelled to make our own movies, as many movies as there are correspondents, and this one is mine. . . . My movie, my friends, my colleagues. But meet them in context . . ." (pp. 200–201).[3]

The title of the final chapter, "Breathing Out," represents Herr's attempt to use cyclical imagery to draw the novel to a close. This chapter opens with three epigraphs, "release graffiti on the walls at Tan Son Nhut airport" (p. 267):

> I am going home. I have seen a lot of Vietnam in 18 months. May Lord help this place.
>
> DEROS 10 Sept 68.[4]
>
> Mendoza was here. 12 Sept 68. Texas.
> Color me gone. (Mendoza is my buddy.) (p. 267)

These graffiti express the soldiers' emotional relief in finally being physically released from duty in Vietnam. In a way, this chapter is the narrator's release graffiti, in that it symbolizes his feelings of relief and freedom from the oppressive and hellish environment of Vietnam. He begins by describing his long journey home—aided on his way by "a small ball of opium" (p. 267)—and, between the last few stories, reflects on his need to write about Vietnam: "They were always telling you that you mustn't forget the dead, and they were always telling you that you shouldn't let yourself think about them too much. . . . 'You'll get used to it,' people would say, but I never did, actually it got too personal and went the other way" (p. 270). The chapter closes with the most often quoted words in the book: "Vietnam Vietnam Vietnam, we've all been there" (p. 278).

Tim O'Brien's *Going After Cacciato*

In this novel, Tim O'Brien presents a war story of a day in the life of Specialist 4 Paul Berlin, who takes a fantastic journey of the mind similar to that taken by Alice in Lewis Carroll's *Alice in Wonderland* and *Through the Looking Glass.* Like Alice, Berlin dreams that he is on an imaginary journey through foreign lands. Like Alice, he pursues someone, meets people from different cultures in faraway lands, and is threatened with execution at one point before he escapes. This complex novel can also be compared to Kurt Vonnegut's *Slaughterhouse Five,* which combines remembered events from the war with fantasy. Like Billy Pilgrim, Paul Berlin tries to escape from his horrific memories of combat by imagining a better life for himself, by imagining he is somewhere else. Specifically, Berlin's dream trip takes place while he is on duty one night in an observation post on a beach in Vietnam. Earlier in the day, Berlin and his fellow soldiers had been in pursuit of Cacciato, a Forrest Gump–like character who went AWOL. It is this pursuit that becomes the fantastic journey. Like Orr in Joseph Heller's *Catch-22,* Cacciato had often talked of quitting the war and walking to Paris. In his dream, Berlin and his friends follow Cacciato through Laos, Turkey, Iran, and France, where they finally find their man in Paris.

The novel is composed of "three narrative strands—randomly juxtaposed and roughly equal to past, present and future" (Herzog 1983, p. 88). The story unfolds in the six or so hours Berlin stands watch. During this time, he recalls the start of his tour, the deaths of several members of this squad and his lieutenant, and imagines that he and his buddies follow Cacciato to Paris. Berlin's memories are mixed together in a jumbled disarray with the "real time" story line of the imagined journey. Clues are provided throughout this journey, however, to remind the reader that the trip to Paris is, in fact, imagined. These blatant clues appear in ten chapters throughout the novel. Tobey Herzog sees these chapters as "the fulcrum of the book: the point at which 'what happened' extends into 'what might have happened' " (Herzog 1903, p. 92).

Denis Vannata has divided the forty-six chapters of the book into three types: "observation post chapters, recollected war chapters, and the going-after-Cacciato chapters" (1982, p. 243). Critics of this novel agree that the observation post sections constitute the narrative present, the point from which Berlin moves back into the remembered past and forward into the imagined future; the war stories are chaotic, reflecting the trauma of war on Berlin's psyche; and the Cacciato sections are pure fantasy, representing Berlin's flight from that trauma (McWilliams 1988, p. 245).[5] Much of O'Brien's work, including *If I Die in a Combat Zone, The Things They Carried,* and *In the Lake of the Woods,* focuses on the importance of the relationship between memory and imagination. He uses fragmentation to explore this relationship and to recreate the sudden shifts his characters experience in "space and time, memory, and imagination" (Ringnalda 1994, p. 36). By fragmenting the standard forward progression of the story with imagined sequences or flashbacks, O'Brien is able to create a world in which his characters (and readers) experience "multiplicities of truth." After all, he explains, "that's the way the world is" (McNerney 1994, p. 13). "In any war story," he writes, "it's difficult to separate what happened from what seemed to happen" (O'Brien 1991, p. 78). Consequently, "What seems to happen becomes its own happening and has to be told that way. . . . The pictures get jumbled; you tend to miss a lot" (1991, p. 78). O'Brien's fragmented novels recreate the veteran's experience, both in war and in storytelling, for the reader.[6]

Larry Heinemann's *Paco's Story*

Heinemann employs a narrative framework similar to that used by Joseph Conrad in *Heart of Darkness* and Francis Ford Coppola's film adaptation of that novel, *Apocalypse Now.* He allows a narrator to set up or introduce and then recount the events of the central story, events in which he is both participant and witness. Heinemann adds a twist, however: his narrator is dead—the voice speaking to the reader represents the collective ghost, if you will, of Paco's fellow soldiers in Alpha Company. Everyone but Paco was killed in a horrific friendly fire bombing raid. The central story is Paco's story.

The ghost narrator introduces himself and briefly lectures his listener, "James" (and the reader), on the art of telling war stories. He then explains the demise of Alpha Company and Paco's near death and rescue. He moves the story along quickly to the current point on Paco's Odyssean journey; he is a rider on a bus headed through the Midwest. He gets off the bus only when he has run out of money and is forced to disembark. He lands in Boone, USA. The ghost invites the reader to witness Paco's experiences in Boone—we watch with him as Paco struggles to find a job and make friends—major obstacles for this physically and emotionally crippled Vietnam veteran. The people Paco encounters summarily despise him; the one exception is Ernest Monroe, a World War II veteran who hires Paco to work in his diner, the Texas Lunch. Paco stays on in Boone for only a short time. One evening he returns to his motel room and finds that it has been searched by Cathy, a young woman who lives next door. The ghost gleefully informs us that, in Vietnam, Paco was known as "the Sneak"; he was especially skilled at setting booby traps. Paco sneaks into Cathy's room and proceeds to search it, eventually finding her diary. Her diary reveals the true feelings of the people in town: "he's a dingy, dreary, smelly, shabby, shabby, little man. . . . He gives me the creeps. . . . He gets this set look on his face. . . . Unc says he wonders if the guy knows where he is half the time" (Heinemann 1989, p. 205–206). When Paco is finished reading the diary, he abruptly packs his things and leaves town on the next bus.

The ghost fragments, or cuts, the central story of Paco's time in Boone with a series of war stories—the ghost's recounting of events that occurred to Paco and his fellow soldiers in Vietnam. When Paco is at his most vulnerable, while he sleeps, the ghosts haunt him. They assault his subconscious with special nightmares composed of memories of the war his conscious mind has buried. These visits are Paco's punishment; the ghosts torture him because he has survived. The ghost's description of these nightmares allows the reader to find out about Paco's past. The ghost describes how he and the other members of Alpha Company died, he provides information about the type of soldier Paco was, and he tells several war stories, including a description of the company's brutal gang rape and murder of a female Viet Cong sniper.

The ghost narrator does not limit himself to Paco's experiences, however. He also recounts some of his own escapades as well, both past (while he and his friends were alive in Vietnam) and present (the various ways in which he and his ghostly comrades haunt Paco). "And when Paco is most beguiled," he says, "most rested and trusting, at that moment of most luxurious rest, when Paco is all but asleep, *that* is the moment we whisper in his ear, and give him something to think about" (p. 138).

The ghost also allows the reader into other characters' minds. For example, he allows us to intrude on the thoughts of the bus driver who leaves Paco in Boone before he shifts to his discussion of Paco's attempt to make a new start in this new place: "Shit, take it all around, he ain't got it so bad—if this was Korea,

1953, he'd be pushing up daisies; if this was summer, 1945, he'd have been long gone" (p. 39). Later, after recounting Paco's rescue, the ghost tells the story of the medic who found him that day in the ash-covered jungle clearing; this man is tormented even now, years later, by his memory of that day. He repeats his story at the local bar, day after day, about the day he found Paco, "the guy not dead, but should have been" (p. 33).

These two story lines, Paco's experiences in Boone and the ghost's war stories, are further fragmented by the insertion of other narrative fragments—headlines, lullabies, marching ditties, want ads, signs, menus, and entries from a young woman's diary. These fragments "establish rapport with the [reader]"(Lanser 1981, p. 125), "establish a relationship between the story and history" (ibid.), and allow Heinemann to convey subtle and often disturbing information about Paco's situation and experiences.

Tim O'Brien's *The Things They Carried*

Like *Dispatches* and *Going After Cacciato, The Things They Carried* relies heavily on fragmentation to convey the sense of dislocation and chaos of the war. Some of the stories take place in Vietnam; others take place in the United States both before and after the characters went to Vietnam. Some of the stories in this novel are self-reflexive and refer forward or back to some of the other stories included in the book; others include additional "war stories" within them. Toward the end of the novel, in "The Lives of the Dead," the narrator says, "We kept the dead alive with stories" (O'Brien 1991, p. 267); these characters are the link that holds the twenty-two "stories" together in this novel. While the characters are "consistent," however, their "performance times vary wildly . . . swirl[ing] back and forth across the borders of time and space" (Ringnalda 1994, p. 110). O'Brien adds an extra feature in this novel that *Going After Cacciato* lacks, but it is this twist that connects *The Things They Carried* with the other novels discussed in this section. In *The Things They Carried,* he goes beyond having a character fantasize about how endings and outcomes can be changed. In this novel, O'Brien steps in as a character (the narrator) and demonstrates how the writing process can accomplish this. This technique, notes Catherine Calloway, "actively engages the reader in the process of technical creation" (1995, p. 253). By explaining "how to tell a true war story," O'Brien explores the relationship between creating fiction in prose and creating fictional memories, what he refers to as the difference between "story truth" and "happening truth." Writing fiction, he explains, helps "manufacture a system that is coherent and meaningful and moving without having to wade through layers of competing versions of fact" (McNerney 1994, p. 9).

The collection begins with "The Things They Carried," a story about the group of soldiers who shared time in Vietnam with the narrator. This story introduces the various characters who will be mentioned in the stories that follow. The narrator uses a description of the items the various men carried as a way of introducing them to the reader:

> First Lieutenant Jimmy Cross carried letters from a girl named Martha. . . . Henry Dobbins, who was a big man, carried extra rations. . . . Dave Jensen, who practiced field hygiene, carried a toothbrush, dental floss, and several hotel-sized bars of soap. . . . Ted Lavender, who was scared, carried tranquilizers . . . and six or seven ounces of premium dope, which for him was a necessity. Mitchell Sanders, the RTO [radio telephone operator], carried condoms. Norman Bowker carried a diary. Rat Kiley carried comic books. Kiowa, a devout Baptist, carried an illustrated New Testament. (pp. 3–4)

The description of the items each man carried gives the reader some initial impression of the character's personality, but the items also represent the private anxieties of each soldier.

The structure of this first story sets up the structure of the entire novel. The descriptions of the things each man carried are interrupted by the insertion of short narrative fragments describing events from various times in the characters' tour. Each of the stories in this book is fragmented in some way by references to previous stories or references to the deaths or actions of the various characters or by the narrator's intrusive discussion of the writing process.[7]

For example, the story of Jimmy Cross (who, the reader is told in "The Things They Carried," carries letters from Martha) is continued in "Love," the second story, which is set stateside, after the war. Stories four and five, "Enemies" and "Friends," are companion pieces. Each tells the story of the conflict and ensuing friendship between Dave Jensen and Lee Strunk. Norman Bowker also crops up in a pair of stories: "Speaking of Courage," the fifteenth story, and "Notes," the sixteenth story. Henry Dobbins figures prominently in three stories: "Stockings," the tenth story; "Church," the eleventh story; and "Style," the fourteenth story. "Stockings" describes Henry's superstitious nature; he wears a pair of his girlfriend's stockings throughout his tour, even though his girlfriend broke off the relationship well before his tour ended.

Ted Lavender dies shortly after he is mentioned in "The Things They Carried," but his death is repeatedly mentioned in the same story and later in "Style." Like Ted Lavender, Kiowa is killed in Vietnam; the night of his death is described in "In the Field," the seventeenth story, and the narrator refers back to that night in "Field Trip," two stories later. The narrator retells Rat Kiley's "war story" in "Sweetheart of the Song Tra Bong," the ninth story, and describes Kiley's wounding in "Night Life," the twenty-first story.

Ironically, Curt Lemon, who is not mentioned in "The Things They Carried" is featured in two stories, "How to Tell a War Story," the seventh story in the collection, and "The Dentist," the eighth story. Mitchell Sanders appears in several stories in the book, but there is not a story specifically devoted to him.

The intertwining of these stories can best be deconstructed by taking apart one story and tracing the fragmentation of the narrative. The best example of this is "Spin," a loosely connected set of disjointed fragments of memories. "Spin" is really a set of three distinct narrative strands that repeat themselves. The story begins with a string of bad memories, followed by a string of good memories, broken by an editorial intrusion. This pattern is then repeated.

"Spin" offers a mixture of fragments representing various representative activities and events of the characters' time in Vietnam. It begins with a brief, paragraph-long memory—the narrator's recollection of a crippled Vietnamese boy begging for a chocolate bar. It moves next to the narrator's memory of Mitchell Sanders mailing an envelope of body lice to his draft board, then to a mention of Norman Bowker and Henry Dobbins's habit of playing checkers "every evening before dark" (p. 36). This narrative string of memories is broken by a series of intrusions by the narrator, who says, "I'm forty-three years old, and a writer now, and the war has been over for a long while. Much of it is hard to remember" (ibid.). He then mentions the deaths of Kiowa and Curt Lemon before moving on to happier memories of the war. These happier memories include mention of Ted Lavender on a good day ("'How's the war today?' somebody would say, and Ted Lavender would give a soft, spacey smile and say, 'Mellow, man'" [ibid.]) and the memory of the time an elderly Vietnamese man led the group safely through a minefield. The story then moves to a description of the boredom of combat before the narrator breaks in again with an editorial comment: "I feel guilty sometimes. Forty-three years old and I'm still writing war stories. . . . That's the real obsession. All those stories " (p. 38).

The stories themselves are repetitive, too. "Ambush" and "Good Form," for example, refer back to "The Man I Killed"; "Notes" refers back to "Speaking of Courage"; "Field Trip," which is set after the war, refers back to "In the Field"; and "The Lives of the Dead," the last story in the set, repeats the story of the death of Ted Lavender and thus refers back to the first story in the set, "The Things They Carried."[8]

This pattern of advance and retreat, of forward progression interrupted by narrative intrusion, repeats throughout the rest of the story. The effect is unsettling; just as the reader begins to orient himself and impose order on the story, O'Brien changes the map, mimicking the experience of the American soldier who could not find his place in Vietnam and the experience of the American veteran and civilians who try to make sense of their memories of the war.

Bao Ninh's *The Sorrow of War*

This complex Vietnamese novel, like Michael Herr's *Dispatches* and Tim O'Brien's *The Things They Carried,* offers a series of war stories and tributes to the dead. The protagonist of these stories, Kien, is one of only ten survivors of the Lost Battalion, the Twenty-Seventh Battalion of the North Vietnamese Army. As in *The Things They Carried,* the stories are presented by a Marlowlike narrator, an unidentified speaker, and portions of the book address the writing process.

Like the American novels about the war, *The Sorrow of War* relies heavily on fragmentation to convey the chaos of the war and the havoc it wreaked on the lives of everyone involved. This novel is by far the most fragmented of those discussed here. Like the lives of the narrator and his friends, the stories in this novel have been blown apart, separated into more than forty story fragments. Little attempt has been made to impose order. The fragments are separated from one another only by additional space between the paragraphs. And, at four points in the novel, the text is broken by a set of ellipses in the center of the page. Some of these stories refer forward or back to other stories in the book; some of the stories include other "war stories" within them; some of the stories, like those in *The Things They Carried,* discuss the writer's attempt to come to terms with his wartime experiences and feelings of alienation and loss.

The opening story in the novel finds Kien in the Jungle of the Screaming Souls. He and his fellow soldiers have returned to the scene of a terrible battle to collect the bodies of the dead. Kien falls asleep in the back of the truck and begins to recall the events of "times long, long ago" (Ninh 1993, p. 4). In the next fragment he recalls the "end of the dry season of 1969, . . . [when] his 27th Battalion was surrounded and almost totally wiped out. Ten men survived." (p. 5). This allusion to the battle leads to an explanation of the clearing's name—it alludes to the wandering souls of the dead. This scene will be returned to again and again as the novel progresses—instead of recounting Kien's time in the area in one, chapter-long story, the story is fragmented, scattered throughout the novel, and the reader is asked to pull it together.

The deaths of Kien's friends are also mentioned early in this first section of the novel. In the fourth story fragment, Kien remembers a happier time in the Jungle of Screaming Souls: "They were really happy days. . . . The entire platoon of thirteen was safe. Even Lofty Thinh spent a happy month here before being killed. Can hadn't yet deserted. His friends Vinh, 'Big' Thinh, Cu, Oanh, and 'Elephant' Tac were all still alive" (p. 9). Then, at the end of this fragment, the deaths of Van, Thanh, and Tu are briefly mentioned, without emotion: "Before an hour was up Van was burned alive in a tank together with the tank crew. . . . Only Tu had fought, together with Kien, to Gate 5 of Saigon's Tan Son Nhat airport. Then Tu was killed" (p. 11). The specific stories of each of these deaths appear later, in various sections of the novel.

As in *The Things They Carried,* one of the subplots in this war novel involves a love story, the story of Kien and Phuong, Kien's "childhood sweetheart, his classmate, his female lead in one of the strangest opening nights of the war theater, and his self-created ikon [sic] for salvation in peacetime" (p. 69). Phuong is first mentioned in the fourteenth story fragment, but fragments of their experiences together before, during, and after the war appear throughout the novel. In the first fragment, Phuong has left Kien "again." This time, the reader is told, she "had probably decided never to return" (ibid.). This information is provided well before the reader learns of the development of this relationship and the cataclysmic event that forced a chasm between them, Phuong's rape during an air raid.

Portions of the book describe the writer's struggle to transform his experiences into fiction and further blur the distinction between the character of Kien and the character of the writer. For example, just before readers learn of Phuong's departure, they are told that "He [the writer] started by writing about the MIA Remains-Gathering Team, those about-to-be-demobilized soldiers on the verge of returning to ordinary civilian life. But relentlessly his pen disobeyed him" (p. 57). This thread is picked up several stories later, when readers are told that "the flames of memory led *Kien* [emphasis added] deep into a labyrinth, through circuitous paths, and back out again into primitive jungles of the past. . . . Then the novel drifted towards the MIA team gathering the remains, making a long trail linking the soldiers' graves scattered all over the mountains of the North and Central Highlands" (p. 89). (These metaphors aptly describe the experience of reading this novel as well.)

The writer also compares the flow of his memories (again, it is possible that he is describing the character of Kien's memories) to a stream: "The flow of his life focused and refocused and each moment of that stream was recalled, each event, each memory was a drop of water in his nameless, ageless river" (p. 117). A little later, the writer describes his life as a "stretch of river, full of fire. War" (p. 119). These contrasting metaphors represent the writer's conflicting feelings about the war. Water imagery is used in literature to represent absolution and the cleansing away of guilt. The fire imagery here is used to represent the destructive and hellish effects of war. The writer's life is a combination of these two opposing forces—fire and water do not exist together in nature; water, after all, is used to extinguish fires. Thus, this description of the writer's life represents his struggle to deal with his memories of his war experiences. It also suggests that this struggle will ultimately end with the destruction of some part of himself.

These contrasting images also represent the two story lines of the novel: the story of the writer's experiences in the war and the story of the love affair of Kien and Phuong. Portions of the novel describing the war are filled with scenes of death, destruction, and, literally, fire. Portions of the novel describing the love affair represent Kien's attempts to redeem himself. He believes that he can return to a more innocent state if he recaptures the purity of the love they shared before her rape, which occurs during an American air raid that sets on fire the train in which they are riding.

Finally, these contrasting images also represent the twisting together of the narrative voices in the novel. Some sections of the novel are written in the first person and others in the third person. But because the stories in the novel are related through a mediated consciousness, it is never clear how much tinkering with the works has taken place. In the last few pages of the book, the narrator describes how he found the writer's manuscript and tried to impose order on it as he read through the various pages. The narrator's voice could be that of the reader: "While copying the pages and rereading them," he says, "I was astounded to recognize that inside his story were ideas and feelings and even situations of mine. It seemed that by some coincidence of words and plot my own life and the author's had unexpectedly become entwined, enmeshed in each other" (p. 231).[9] Once it is difficult to be certain who is telling the story; it is impossible to determine the speaker's bias or motivation. And, since the novel is loosely subdivided by spacing and ellipses only, it is difficult to determine which portions represent the narrator's words and which portions represent the writer's words (those portions of the novel that the narrator "found").

Duong Thu Huong's *Novel Without a Name*

Novel Without a Name is remarkably similar to *The Sorrow of War*. It too deals with the sorrows and loss associated with the long war with the United States, and it too offers a look at the war from a uniquely Vietnamese perspective. Like *The Sorrow of War*, the stories in the novel appear as entries in a journal—there are no formal divisions between chapters, only a series of ellipses to indicate separate "entries." As in *Dispatches* and *The Sorrow of War*, there are no dates to guide the reader; however, the narrator's experiences, memories, and dreams are presented within a chronological narrative framework. Clues are provided throughout the book to indicate how much time has passed.

This novel takes a more traditional forward narrative pattern than *The Sorrow of War*. When the novel opens, the North Vietnamese are still at war with the South Vietnamese and their American allies. The narrator, a North Vietnamese soldier named Quan, provides a running commentary of his experiences as he travels on a special mission for the division commander's deputy—one of their childhood friends, named Bien, allegedly has gone mad and Quan must go and rescue him—and as he fights in a series of battles as the war comes to a close. His account is fragmented, with war stories from the earlier years of the war mixed with memories of his childhood and life before the war with the Americans. For example, in the opening pages of the novel, one of Quan's fellow soldiers convinces him to go hunting for orangutan with him, a mission that Quan finds particularly distasteful. Quan recalls the first time that he was forced to try orangutan stew. The sight of the small hands of the ape floating in the pot reminds him of the birth of his younger brother, Quang, and the sight of Quang's tiny feet splashing in a basin of water as the midwife washed him: "Once more I felt the nausea, the desire to vomit up the orangutan hand. I took another drag on my cigarette and tried to reason with myself: *It has nothing to do with that . . . nothing to do with. . . .* But again I saw my brother's tiny feet kicking at the air" (p. 15). This memory reappears when Quan returns on leave to his native village. He recalls the day of his brother's birth and his mother's cries for his father, who was away fighting the French. This section of the novel includes many memory fragments: the memory of his father's return from the war; his parent's subsequent breakup; and the development over the years of his relationship with Hoa, the woman he had promised to marry as he prepared to go off to war ten years earlier.

Like Kien and Phuong, the young lovers in *The Sorrow of War,* Quan and his intended had postponed consummating their relationship until they could marry. Quan and Hoa are separated by the war. Quan returns to find Hoa pregnant, rejected by her family because she has refused to reveal the identity of the father of her child: "Ten years had passed. *I'll wait for you.* It was just the murmuring of a wave at the bottom of the sea. Now I walked toward the hillside. In the end, the girl I had loved had been cast out, but not for having loved me." (p. 143). Like Kien, Quan is haunted by dreams of his beloved; these dreams are dispersed throughout the remainder of the novel.

The soldier's tales are also cut with thinly disguised criticism of the war and the communist regime. Quan is summoned by the division commander but is received instead by his childhood friend, Luong, the division commander's deputy. The account of their meeting is undercut by Quan's memory of the day they enlisted, and the following section of the novel exposes Quan's bitterness over the war and its effects:

> The deeper we plunged into the war, the more the memory of that first day haunted us. The more we were tortured by the consciousness of our appalling indifference, the more searing the memory of our mothers' tears. We had renounced everything for glory. It was this guilt that bound us to one another as tightly as the memory of our days tending water buffalo together. (pp. 31–32)

Luong cuts short Quan's "reverie," ordering him to investigate Bien's case. The novel shifts to Quan's account of his journey to find Bien. Later, when Quan prepares to leave the special unit to which Bien was reassigned after Quan's intervention, he muses again about the waste and misery of war: "Me, my friends, we had lived this war for too long, steeped ourselves for too long in the beauty of all its moments of fire and blood. Would it still be possible, one day, for us to go back, to rediscover our roots, the beauty of creation, the rapture of a peaceful life?" (p. 193). The book ends on this sorrowful note. As Quan sits in the abandoned office of an American base, he reminisces about his experiences in the war:

> I thought about the spiderwebs that hung in the wind, about this strange game of hide-and-seek we called war. How many times had I seen corpses hanging from branches, eyes gouged out, men's bodies split into two, ligaments cut at the knee, legs folded back like those of grasshoppers? An endless settling of scores. Even as the cannons announced our victory, crows shriek in circles above our cemeteries, violating corpses we didn't have time to bury.... A dizzying stench of carrion and gunpowder. (p. 286)

The novel ends abruptly, in much the same way it begins. Quan, joined by a fellow soldier, continues to think back on his experiences and recalls a chant he and the others had recited during the war.

***

While it is not restricted to postmodern fiction and criticism, the fragmentation of the narrative structure of the text in Vietnam fiction is certainly an effective stylistic device when used by these authors to represent and recreate the experience of the Vietnam conflict. The physical disruption of the text and the use of carefully placed fragments of outside texts allow these authors to recreate the atmosphere and experience of the war and the experience of having one's life and memories blown apart. This fragmentation also helps the authors to present the reader with a disorienting maze; a confusing and sometimes frightening mental landscape where nothing is certain, a place where the path is never clear, where stories are constantly changed, and where people die only to rise and walk again—alive and as ghosts. In short, these novelists present the reader with a map much like that described by Michael Herr in the opening pages of *Dispatches:*

> the most detailed maps didn't reveal much anymore; reading them was like trying to read the faces of the Vietnamese, and that was like trying to read the wind. We knew that the uses of most information were flexible, different pieces of ground told different stories to different people. We also knew that for years now there had been no country here but the war. (p. 1)

Many of the American novels written about the Vietnam War are like Herr's map; that is, they don't "reveal much." Others, like the work of Tim O'Brien, Larry Heinemann, Michael Herr, and Stephen Wright offer a constantly shifting landscape that mimics the physical and mental terrain of the war. The Vietnamese novels are only now being translated into English. It remains to be seen whether or not the rest, like the work of Bao Ninh and Duong Thu Huong, will be structured in a similar fashion. For now, readers can only read and reread the work that is available in their attempt to understand the complexity and horror that was the war in Vietnam.

Notes

1. Lady Borton provides a moving description of the horrific Vietnamese birth defects in her recent novel *After Sorrow: An American Among the Vietnamese.* Bobbie Ann Mason refers to American birth defects in her novel *In Country.*

2. This is not surprising since Michael Herr assisted Francis Ford Coppola with the script for *Apocalypse Now.*

3. The portrayal of the Vietnam War as a film or movie is a common image in American fiction about the war. Stephen Wright uses this motif in *Meditations in Green.*

4. DEROS stands for Date Eligible to Return Overseas; this acronym is often used in

Vietnam fiction to refer to the soldier's designated time to return home to the United States or "the world."

5. Dean McWilliams (1988) provides a detailed chronology of the important events in the novel in "Time in O'Brien's *Going After Cacciato,*" and Steven Kaplan (1994) discusses the novel at length in *Understanding Tim O'Brien.*

6. Numerous studies have examined the fragmentation in this novel. See, for example, Mark Busby (1982), G. Thomas Couser (1983), Dale W. Jones (1982), Steven Kaplan (1994), Dean McWilliams (1988), Edward Palm (1995), Donald Ringnalda (1994), and Dennis Vannata (1982).

7. Catherine Calloway discusses this metafictional technique in " 'How to Tell a True War Story': Metafiction in *The Things They Carried*" (1995).

8. Steven Kaplan also discusses the fragmentation of *The Things They Carried* in *Understanding Tim O'Brien* (1994); his discussion offers a different perspective on the use of fragmentation in this novel.

9. This structure is a brilliant masking device for the author, an understandable ruse when one considers that the novel presents an unpalatable picture of the war and its effects and was written and published in a country that exercises censorship over dissidents, including Bao Ninh and Duong Thu Huong (author of *Paradise of the Blind* and *Novel Without a Name*). It should be noted here that Huong uses fragmentation in both of her novels as well.

References

Anisfield, Nancy. 1988. "Words and Fragments: Narrative Style in Vietnam Novels." In *Search and Clear,* ed. William J. Searle, 56–61. Bowling Green: Bowling Green State University Popular Press.

Beidler, Philip D. 1982. *American Literature and the Experience of Vietnam.* Athens: University of Georgia Press.

Borton, Lady. 1995. *After Sorrow: An American Among the Vietnamese.* New York: Viking.

Busby, Mark. 1982. "Tim O'Brien's *Going After Cacciato*: Finding the End of the Vision." *CCTE* (Conference of College Teachers of English) 47: 63–69.

Calloway, Catherine. 1995. " 'How to Tell a True War Story': Metafiction in *The Things They Carried.*" *Critique* 36, no. 4: 249–56.

Carroll, Lewis. *Alice in Wonderland.* 1929/1991. Rutland, VT: Charles E. Tuttle.

———. *Through the Looking Glass.* 1872/1984. New York: Penguin Books.

Conrad, Joseph. 1950. *Heart of Darkness and the Secret Sharer.* New York: New American Library.

Coppola, Francis Ford. 1979. *Apocalypse Now.* Zoetrope Studios.

Couser, G. Thomas. 1983. "*Going After Cacciato*: The Romance and the Real War." *Journal of Narrative Technique* 13 (Spring): 1–10

Heinemann, Larry. 1989. *Paco's Story.* New York: Penguin Books.

Heller, Joseph. 1985. *Catch-22.* New York: Dell.

Herr, Michael. 1978. *Dispatches.* New York: Avon.

Herzog, Tobey. 1983. "*Going After Cacciato*; The Soldier-Author-Character Seeking Control." *Critique* 24, no. 2: 88–96.

Huong, Duong Thu. 1995. *Novel Without a Name.* Trans. Phan Huy Duong and Nina McPherson. New York: William Morrow.

———. 1994. *Paradise of the Blind.* Trans. Phan Huy Duong and Nina McPherson. New York: Penguin Books.

Kaplan, Steven. 1994. *Understanding Tim O'Brien.* Columbia: University of South Carolina Press.

Jones, Dale W. 1982. "The Vietnams of Michael Herr and Tim O'Brien: Tales of Disintegration and Integration." *Canadian Review of American Studies* 13 (Winter): 309–20.

Lanser, Susan Sniader. 1981. *The Narrative Act: Point of View in Prose Fiction.* Princeton: Princeton University Press.

Martin, Andrew. 1993. *Receptions of War: Vietnam in American Culture.* Norman: University of Oklahoma Press.

Martin, Wallace. 1986. *Recent Theories of Narrative.* Ithaca: Cornell University Press.

Mason, Bobby Ann. 1985. *In Country.* New York: Harper and Row.

McNerney, Brian. 1994. "Responsibly Inventing History: An Interview with Tim O'Brien." *War, Literature, and the Arts* 6, no. 2: 1–26.

McWilliams, Dean. 1988. "Time in Tim O'Brien's *Going After Cacciato.*" *Critique* 29, no. 4: 245–55.

Meyers, Kate Beaird. 1988. "Fragmentary Mosaics: Vietnam War 'Histories' and Postmodern Epistemology." *Genre* 21 (Winter): 535–52.

Ninh, Bao. 1993. *The Sorrow of War.* Trans. Phan Thanh Hao and ed. Frank Palmos. New York: Pantheon.

O'Brien, Tim. 1992. *Going After Cacciato.* New York: Dell Publishing.

———. 1973. *If I Die in a Combat Zone.* New York: Delacrote Press/Seymour Lawrence.

———. 1994. *In the Lake of the Woods.* New York: Houghton Mifflin.

———. 1994. Personal communication with the author.

———. 1991. *The Things They Carried.* New York: Penguin Books.

Palm, Edward. 1995. "Falling In and Out: Military Metaphor as Metaphoric Motif in *Going After Cacciato.*" *Notes on Contemporary Literature* 22, no. 5: 8.

Ringnalda, Donald. 1994. *Fighting and Writing the Vietnam War.* Jackson: University Press of Mississippi.

Schroeder, Eric James. 1992. *Vietnam, We've All Been There: Interviews with American Writers.* Westport: Praeger.

Vannata, Dennis. 1982. "Theme and Structure in Tim O'Brien's *Going After Cacciato.*" *Modern Fiction Studies* 28 (Summer): 242–46.

Vonnegut, Kurt. 1968. *Slaughterhouse Five.* New York: Dell.

Wright, Stephen. 1983. *Meditations in Green.* New York: Charles Scribner's Sons.

6

American and Vietnamese Poetry of Witness
Bridge over Troubled Waters

James Soular

> "Here is one of our customs," Uncle Firmness explained. "During a thousand years, whenever we beat the Chinese, we sent a delegation to China to apologize. You see, the Chinese had lost face in the defeat. We should have apologized to the French and the Americans after their defeats. After we break our heads against each other, we must recognize we are family."
>
> —Lady Borton, *After Sorrow*

Twenty years have gone by since the images were flashed to the world: the American official punching the face of a panic-stricken Vietnamese attempting to board one of the last aircraft out of Da Nang, the helicopters perched on the rooftop of the U.S. embassy annex in Saigon as people climbed ladders to board the last evacuation flights, euphemistically called "retrograde movements," Vietnamese pilots desperately ditching their helicopters in the South China Sea near American ships lying offshore of South Vietnam, and the victorious North Vietnamese Army tank crashing through the gates of the presidential palace in Saigon.

As those gates clattered to the ground and the existence of South Vietnam dissipated as quickly as the tank's diesel fumes did in the celebratory air of April 30, 1975, the Vietnam War officially ended. So too ended a conflict whose cost in human life and resources is still uncertain. In Washington, DC, a black wall with 58,196 engraved names reminds us of the cost of our intrusion into Vietnam. For the Vietnamese, the costs are more difficult to calculate. Some estimates place the loss of life at three million. More than ten million Vietnamese were made refugees.[1] It is believed that nearly 300,000 soldiers and civilians are still missing.[2] The war's spillover into Laos and Cambodia resulted in additional tragedy and incalculable loss of human life. Why it all happened, no one seems to know or to agree upon, but few can deny that it was one of history's great tragedies. As with all wars, a great deal of energy and emotion has been expended trying to make sense of the madness of this one. Some of that sense-making has manifested itself in the form of "poetry of witness," a synthesis of experience and creativity that is an attempt to wend one's way through the labyrinth of the Vietnam War.

Poetry of Witness

For the survivors, the war's horrors, its tremendous costs, were, as veteran and poet Bruce Weigl has written, "burned behind [their] eyes" (1988, p. 35). It is those many grim images, those mean memories of the darkness that were visited upon them, that the war's survivors, both Vietnamese and American, both men and women, continue to struggle with. That struggle is no more palpable than in their poetry, which Carolyn Forché calls "poetry of witness," which arises out of "the impress of extremity upon the poetic imagination" (Forché 1993, p. 9).

Poetry of witness is a record, documentation, that an event, usually dramatic or traumatic, has occurred. In fact, poetry of witness may be the sole evidence or trace of that event; its objectivity, its "truth," cannot usually be verified through independent means. These poems are as much experiential as imaginative; the authors cannot be separated from the events described.

To distinguish poetry of witness from either political or personal poetry, Forché defines for it a space between the two that she calls "the social" (ibid.). "[T]he social is a place of resistance and struggle," she writes, "where books are published, poems read, and protest disseminated. It is the sphere in which claims against the political order are made in the name of justice" (ibid.). Poetry of witness is not, however, a call to arms against the state; rather, it is a *documentation* of experience and an *exhortation* against forgetfulness. It does not appeal to immediate political rectification so much as it appeals to a sense of communal conscience or spirit. Most poetry by Vietnam War survivors (or those who wrote poetry before they perished in the war) falls into this "social space."

Poetry of witness is very similar to what Kali Tal describes as the "literature of trauma," and, like Forché, she sees in it three common elements: "the experience of trauma, the urge to bear witness, and a sense of community" (1991, pp. 217–18). Survivors of a terrible and at times ruthless conflagration, the poets to be studied here have found it necessary to testify to the events they experienced during the course of the Vietnam conflict. The war continues to play itself out upon the battered landscapes of their minds, and it is upon this battlefield where the war's final resolution must take place. Tal sees in the literature of American Vietnam War veterans (and, as will be shown, their Vietnamese counterparts) a connection to literature by other trauma survivors, including literature written about the Holocaust, the atomic bombings of Hiroshima and Nagasaki, and rape or incest (p. 217).

The urge to bear witness is a common characteristic of survivors of trauma. Usually, but certainly not always, occurring a decade or more after the experience, a process of *re*-visioning of the event begins to take shape in the survivor's mind. Along with this re-visioning is a need or desire to share the trauma with others. It is the collective cry rising out of the ashes of the Holocaust that shouts "Never again!" (a slogan adopted by many American Vietnam War veterans). Terence Des Pres has written of the Holocaust:

> The testimony of survivors is rooted in a strong need to make the truth known, and the fact that this literature exists, that survivors produced these documents—there are many thousands of these—is evidence of a profoundly human process. Survival is a specific kind of experience, and "to survive as a witness" is one of its forms. (1976, p. 30)

Survivors of trauma are transformed by their experience, and this transformation is, in a sense, a loss of innocence that can never be fully restored. The meat grinder of the Vietnam War assaulted repeatedly the innermost assumptions, the personal myths, that many of the war's participants, both Vietnamese and American, had formed about the way life is supposed to be lived and what war actually entailed. Unable to forget and driven by a desire, a *need,* to bear witness to the pain, guilt, or sorrow of what for many was the most traumatic and defining period of their lives, they turned to poetry. Forced onto the page in a badly needed *de*-compression, their poems are forthright and emotionally unconstrained. Written principally by the "ordinary" individual, who was not university-trained, and often written with gut-level, concrete images, poetry of witness has often borne the criticism that it is not *real* poetry, that it is not stylistically and technically mature. Perhaps what is most important about this poetry is not so much its ordination as poetry befitting the traditional canon, but, rather what this poetry arose out of and what it *says*. After all, very little about the Vietnam War was conventional.

Although personal and intimate, these poems are also very public. Witness poems are like letters, postcards, or news reports, "ways of writing that stress the interpersonal aspects of poetry, the public side of literature. They underline the collective urgency that propels a literature of the social" (Forché 1993, p. 12). These poets attempt to awaken their respective societies to the realities they endured in Vietnam as a result of the war; their hope that maybe we will learn from them. Vietnamese Buddhist monk Thich Nhat Hanh writes: "We who have experienced the war directly have a responsibility to share our insight and experience concerning the truth of war. We are the light at the tip of the candle. It is very hot, but it has the power of shining and illuminating" (1993a, p. 92). Poetry of witness drives a wedge between the oblivion of forgetfulness and the living reality.

Fragments of memory, these poems are snapshots of experience in a war that was the quintessential snapshot. It was, after all, the first media war, and America was bombarded daily with images of it. Most soldiers carried cameras and were forever taking pictures of the country, of its people, and of the war that engulfed them all. Vietnam was the sudden flash of a tripped booby trap, the pockmarked countryside that looked like a moonscape in places, the adrenaline rush of a firefight that could be over in thirty seconds, and the long line of corpses stretched out in the hundred-degree heat, the "body count."[3] People, even entire villages, were always on the move, forever at the mercy of that relentless war. There were no lines, and there was never any progress; there were just places with names like Khe Sanh, Ia Drang, the Pineapple Plantation, the Ho Bo Woods, Cu Chi, and Hué, fragments or splinters of a larger, unstructured whole. Poetry of witness, the "postcard," was the perfect form for the fragmented nature of the Vietnam War.

These works describe, in an overall sense, a violent invasion of the personal by the political. They explode upon the page and reopen wounds, laying the corpses out once again for a final body count. Their language inscribes upon our consciousness the environment of extremity, and, through their individual and collective impacts, these poets erode our ability to forget, to deny, and to replace truth with myth. Even if nothing can be done directly about the traumatic experiences portrayed, it is essential for these poets that their stories be told and recorded. Since war is, for the most part, a universal human condition, these poems know no geopolitical boundaries; they are written for all mankind and for all generations, including the unborn.

Songs of Napalm: Voices from the War

> Again, thanks for the dud
> hand grenade tossed at my feet
> outside Chu Lai. I'm still
> falling through its silence.
> —Yusef Komunyakaa, "Thanks"

Bruce Weigl, who served with the First Air Cavalry in Vietnam during 1967–68 and currently teaches in the writing program at Pennsylvania State University, is "considered one of the consummate poets" (Smith 1991, p. 57) to come out of the Vietnam War. Weigl's *Song of Napalm* (1988) moves back and forth between Vietnam and the United States, between then and now, a montage of the horror of war and its sometimes indefinable and irredeemable costs.

In part because of the many casualties who never saw the enemy, which generated deep frustration and a desire for revenge, in part because of an inherent racism, and in part because of the dehumanizing character of war, atrocities were committed by American soldiers against the civilian population of Vietnam in the thousands. In Weigl's "Surrounding Blues on the Way Down," the speaker witnesses an atrocity shortly after arriving in Vietnam. Riding in a jeep "under the rain-black clouds" (1988, p. 13) with another soldier who is taking him "into the jungle" and to "the beautiful war" he "did not yet hate" (ibid.), the two soldiers come upon a Vietnamese peasant:

> We flew past her but he hit the brakes hard,
> he spun the tires backward in the mud.
> He did not hate the war either
> but other reasons made him cry out to her
> so she stopped,
> she smiled her beetle-black teeth at us,
> in the air she raised her arms.
>
> I have no excuse for myself.
> I sat in that man's jeep in the rain
> and watched him slam her to her knees,
> the plastic butt of his M16
> crashing down on her.
> I was barely in country, the clouds
> hung like huge flowers, black
> like her teeth.[4] (pp. 13–14)

For no obvious reason, this woman is brutally attacked, and the speaker's complicity in the act is evinced by his inaction, his silence. Looking back now in remorse, he offers no excuse for his inaction. The imagery Weigl uses in framing the poem, "the rain-black clouds" and the woman's black teeth (possibly lacquered, a Vietnamese custom, or from chewing betel, which turns saliva purplish black and dyes the mouth and teeth), enhances the darkness of the poem and the darkness of the deed. It presages what this war is going to be like. New to the country and not yet hating the "beautiful war," this act might have planted the seeds of Weigl's eventual disillusionment with the war.

Even back home, years later, he cannot escape the war and its signifiers, those powerful pieces or fragments that evoke the whole, and which now rear up in front of him unexpectedly. In the title poem, "Song of Napalm," the speaker and his wife watch horses from the doorway of their home after a hard rain:

> The grass was never more blue in that light, more
> scarlet; beyond the pasture
> trees scraped their voices into the wind, branches
> crisscrossed the sky like barbed wire
> but you said they were only branches.[5] (p. 33)

The crisscrossed branches remind the speaker of barbed wire, one of the signifiers of the war. It kept Charles (the Viet Cong, Victor Charles, VC) away; it helped ward off the elephant coming to crush you. Concertina wire, spiraling in all directions, could entangle you, cut you, leave you hanging helplessly, an easy target. But Charles was also uncanny in his ability to infiltrate, greasing himself up and sliding through the deadly coils of wire like a snake, armed with his satchel charges to blow you up while you slept. Like the enemy slipping through the barbed wire in Vietnam, the wire, the war, slips into the speaker's consciousness where and when he least expects it.

Trying to regain his equilibrium after the pounding storm, the speaker attempts to convince his wife (and himself) that he is all right, that he has "turned [his] back on the old curses" (p. 34). It is not that easy, though. The branches, finally, are still wire, and the storm's thunder is the pounding of artillery. Experiencing a flashback, he sees again a Vietnamese girl, caught in a napalm strike, running, burning, "napalm / stuck to her dress like jelly" (p. 34). He continues:

> So I can keep on living,
> so I can stay here beside you,
> I try to imagine she runs down the road and wings
> beat inside her until she rises
> above the stinking jungle and her pain
> eases, and your pain, and mine.
>
> . . .
>
> The lie works only as long as it takes to speak
> and the girl runs only as far
> as the napalm allows
> until her burning tendons and crackling
> muscles draw her up
> into that final position
> burning bodies so perfectly assume. Nothing
> can change that, she is burned behind my eyes
> and not your good love and not the rain-swept air
> and not the jungle-green
> pasture unfolding before us can deny it.[6] (pp. 34–35)

Although the speaker tries to convince himself, "to imagine," that she rose like an angel away from "the stinking jungle and her pain," the lie will not, cannot, hold. The image is too strong, the atrocity too horrible. He sees the girl, an innocent victim of war, caught in the middle of a napalm strike, one of the deadliest technologies of the war. It conjures up the memory of the Pulitzer Prize–winning 1972 photograph of nine-year-old Kim Phuc running naked, screaming in agony from third-degree burns inflicted over much of her body during a napalm bombing attack by U.S. jets. If you were too close the heat would suck the air right out of your lungs. If you were *really* close and got some splashed on you, you burned and burned until it burned itself out.

Through harsh imagery, Weigl shows us the war and what it could do, not only to the immediate target of its ferocity but also to its survivors many years later. Tormented by his memories, the speaker is desperately clinging to his sanity and his marriage and, perhaps, his life. The final image of the girl dying, drawing up "into that final position," is almost a denigration of life. The "final position" that burning bodies assume is the fetal position, similar to the one spent *in utero* for nine months. Here, Weigl's pain becomes his wife's pain, our pain. Although we tell ourselves lies to escape the reality, survivors of the war deny us that escape.

Dien Cai Dau

Yusef Komunyakaa like Weigl, is trying to make sense of the "beautiful war" and its many reverberations. Komunyakaa, awarded a Bronze Star in Vietnam, served as a combat correspondent with the Americal Division from 1969 to 1970 and now teaches English at Indiana University. *Dien Cai Dau* is his fourth book of poems and the first that deals solely with the war. The long wait has given Komunyakaa distance from his subject and time to hone his craft. His poetry weaves through Vietnam, forming connections with the land, other soldiers, the Vietnamese people, and even the enemy, connections that do not end with the war. Komunyakaa does not mortar the reader like many veteran-poets; rather, he informs us with illumination rounds (flares), poetry at times almost surreal, that punches a "white fist" (1988, p. 32) through the black night of Vietnam instead of detonating around us and leaving dogtags hanging in the trees.

One must bear in mind that the title of his Pulitzer Prize–winning book, *Dien Cai Dau* (American servicemen pronounced it "dinky dow"), means "crazy" or "crazy in the head" in Vietnamese. It was one of the most-used Vietnamese phrases during the Vietnam War. The Vietnamese often used it to refer to Americans, and Americans in turn used it to refer to everything in Vietnam: the war, the people, one another, the military. It was one of the catchall Vietnamese phrases, and it is no accident that Komunyakaa used it for the title of his book. In passing from civilian life to military life to Vietnam, there was a loss of identity, a loss of the invisible link to cultural sustenance and *restraint*, and Vietnam was the place where everything that constituted a person's makeup could all break down in one blinding flash. Vietnam was a *crazy* place, he is saying, and he's going to tell us about some crazy things that happened there, which, as in Weigl's case, included acts of atrocity.

In "Re-creating the Scene," Komunyakaa describes a rape that takes place inside an armored personnel carrier (APC):

> The Confederate flag
> flaps from the radio antenna,
> & the woman's clothes
> come apart in their hands.
> Their mouths find hers
> in the titanic darkness
> of the steel grotto,
> as she counts the names of dead
> ancestors, shielding a baby
> in her arms. The three men
> ride her breath, grunting
> over lovers back in Mississippi.[7] (p. 19)

The very title of the poem is not just Komunyakaa's "re-creation" of an event from memory; he is also indicating that this will be the "re-creation" of a *crime* scene. Having abducted the Vietnamese woman and her baby, the men take turns raping her, "inside a machine/where men are gods" (ibid.), finally throwing her out and driving off. The woman goes to a U.S. base to report the crime, and a captain "accosts her with candy kisses" (p. 20). The speaker, however, informs a newspaper, and the publicity results in a trial, a trial that never sees a resolution:

> on the trial's second day
> she turns into mist—
> someone says money
> changed hands,
> & someone else swears
> she's buried at LZ Gator.[8] (p. 20)

The complementary elements of misogyny and atrocity tear like a jackal into the hindquarters of American myth: that its soldiers were humane, civilized.[9] This woman and her child were abducted, and she was raped, trying all the while to protect the child she carried in her arms. Attempting to seek justice, we are led to believe that she was bought off or, even worse, killed.

This poem also raises the issue of racism, symbolized by the Confederate flag on the APC and the three soldiers from Mississippi. Komunyakaa never bludgeons the reader with this element, though he deftly insinuates it into his poetry, as shown here.

Komunyakaa writes in free verse, applying his skill through the use of varying line lengths, skillful enjambment, figurative language, and attention to detail. Even in his description of a brutal event, his artistry is evident in phrases like "She floats on their rage / like a torn water flower" (p. 19), or "They hold her down / with their eyes, / taking turns, piling stones / on her father's grave" (ibid.). These rapists hold this woman down with their *eyes,* indicative of their complete control over her and her life. They destroy her virtue, her sense of *self* and *honor*—very important to the Vietnamese—and in doing so they pile "stones / on her father's grave." These are brutes that Komunyakaa describes, not human beings, not the young and innocent sons of America.

The armored personnel carrier in the poem is a technological symbol of America and what it tried to do in Vietnam. Its metal door closes "like an ancient turtle / that won't let go / of a finger till it thunders" (ibid.). The APC rolls over the land, "crushing trees & grass, / droning like a constellation / of locusts eating through bamboo" (ibid.). This is what the American war machine was like: a swarm of locusts trying to consume Vietnam with its technology, trying to trample the land and its people under the treads of its tanks or to burn it up with its napalm.

"You and I Are Disappearing" echoes Weigl's "Song of Napalm" with its central figure of a girl burning after a napalm strike. Weigl's "burned behind my eyes" is mirrored by Komunyakaa's "still burning inside my head" (p. 17). While Weigl graphically, concretely, describes what happens to a burning person, Komunyakaa struggles vainly for a simile to describe the horror he is witnessing:

> We stand with our hands
> hanging at our sides,
> while she burns
> like a sack of dry ice.
> She burns like oil on water.
> She burns like a cattail torch
> dipped in gasoline.
>
> . . .
>
> She burns like a shot glass of vodka.
> She burns like a field of poppies
> at the edge of a rain forest.
> She rises like dragonsmoke
> to my nostrils.
> She burns like a burning bush
> driven by a godawful wind.[10] (p. 17)

The poet finally runs out of comparisons, out of *language*. The collective "we" includes us, the readers, in witnessing this terrible vision, and the "hands hanging at our sides" indicates *our* frustration, *our* helplessness and lack of control. What the speaker has witnessed goes beyond language, almost beyond comprehension. The use of the anaphora "she burns" makes it almost a lament, with the men standing in awe of this terrible vision, and though the poet finally relents, the imagery has succeeded. It is so horrible that it can only be compared to an act of

God, a "burning bush," another unknowable. Perhaps it is an "awful God" that allows atrocities of this nature to occur or perhaps this is an act that is too godlike for man to commit or even to contemplate committing. It is an excruciating way to die, and Komunyakaa has tried to burn this behind *our* eyes.

These are the acts many American sons committed in Vietnam, Komunyakaa is saying. It was far from a noble or even a just cause. Like Weigl before him, the poet is saying that we are guilty of atrocity and nothing can change that reality. "[I]f he's dead and Vietnamese, he's VC" (Caputo 1986, 69), said the military in Vietnam and added each "dead VC" (which actually might have been, and often was, a civilian) to its grotesque method of measuring the war, the "body count." Robert Jay Lifton called it "the perfect symbol of America's descent into evil" (1971, 25). What it came down to, finally, is that the war itself reached critical mass, resulting in a partial moral meltdown that led to a failure of leadership and to the perpetration of atrocity after atrocity against both the human body and the spirit of the Vietnamese people, though many would prefer to deny that they occurred.

Komunyakaa (and many other American veteran-poets) constantly challenges that self-deception, calling our attention to the realities still out there, even extending his vision back to Vietnam, to the Vietnamese child "with American eyes / who keeps singing / rat-a-tat-tat, hugging / a broken machine gun" ("Toys in a Field," in 1988, p. 56), or to boat people clinging to each other, seasick, and daydreaming of "Jade Mountain / a whole world away, half-drunk / on what they hunger to become" ("Boat People," in 1988, p. 57). In "To Have Danced with Death," he speaks of a black sergeant first class and "[t]he empty left leg / of his trousers," rocking "on his good leg / like a bleak & soundless bell" (p. 46). There are still many empty trouser-legs, still many refugees and exiles, still much pain, confusion, and denial left over from the "beautiful" war.

In the last poem of the book, "Facing It," Komunyakaa confronts his own ghosts when he visits the Vietnam Veterans Memorial in Washington, DC:

> My black face fades,
> hiding inside the black granite.
> I said I wouldn't,
> dammit: No tears.
> I'm stone. I'm flesh.
> My clouded reflection eyes me
> like a bird of prey, the profile of night
> slanted against the morning. I turn
> this way—the stone lets me go.
> I turn that way—I'm inside
> the Vietnam Veterans Memorial
> again, depending on the light
> to make a difference.

> I go down the 58,022 names,
> half-expecting to find
> my own in letters like smoke.
> I touch the name of Andrew Johnson;
> I see the booby trap's white flash.
> Names shimmer on a woman's blouse
> but when she walks away
> the names stay on the wall.
> Brushstrokes flash, a red bird's
> wings cutting across my stare.
> The sky. A plane in the sky.
> A white vet's image floats
> closer to me, then his pale eyes
> look through mine. I'm a window.
> He's lost his right arm
> inside the stone. In the black mirror
> a woman's trying to erase names:
> No, she's brushing a boy's hair.[11] (p. 63)

The poet faces the ultimate poem of the war, the ultimate text. He finds that he is still one with the dead, his blackness blending into the black granite. At the same time, he realizes that he is not stone but flesh, and flesh weeps, even when it is determined not to. Confronted by the power and the cumulative weight of 58,000 names, still questioning his own survival, he half expects to find his own name engraved "in letters like smoke."

He presents a series of images, juxtapositions, that almost seem to contradict one another. Things are not as they seem—it depends "on the light / to make a difference," the *point of view.* Touching a name summons a "white flash," a memory of sudden death. "Names shimmer on a woman's blouse" but "stay on the wall" when she leaves. The names are permanent; the lives they represent were not. Although the world goes on living, these voices have been silenced forever, and it is the poet's "brushstrokes" that will keep the memories, the truths, alive. Like the wall, the poet is a window through which we look to discover truths, to learn the stories of the tribe, to read the names.

One thing Komunyakaa sees reflected in the polished black granite is the potential for history to repeat itself. First, there is the sky, then the plane in the sky, a symbol of the power used extensively in Vietnam. Next comes the white veteran, missing an arm, followed by a woman, a widow, perhaps, trying to "erase" her dead husband's name, accompanied by a young boy who might never have known his father. Komunyakaa leaves us with that final image of the boy, a representative of the next generation, inviting, with the suggested image of the absent father, the possibility that it will be *his* name carved on the next wall. Lost arm, lost husband, lost father, lost son? Or is it the image of rebirth, of hope in the ability of the next generation to avoid the mistakes of this one? It all depends on the light, on the point of view.

Komunyakaa, as a "survivor" of war, is testifying to that experience and challenging America's myths about the Vietnam War and the soldiers who fought it. He is one of the most skilled poets to come out of the war, and with *Dien Cai Dau,* he has made a significant contribution to the genre of war poetry in general and to Vietnam War literature in particular. Although poetic form and technique are certainly very important to Komunyakaa, *what* he says is unquestionably the fulcrum of his art.

Thich Nhat Hanh

A poet who was trying to make sense of the conflict while it was happening is the Vietnamese Buddhist monk Thich Nhat Hanh, an eyewitness to much of the destruction of his beloved Vietnam. In 1967, his poem "Condemnation" described a village that was bombed merely because six Vietcong had passed through it. "Every soul was killed," the monk writes. "When I returned to the village the next day, / there was nothing but clouds of dust" (1993a, p. 37). He goes on to denounce the war, "this murder of brothers by brothers!" (ibid.). He asks that we face the "real enemies—/ ambition, violence, hatred, and greed. / Humans are not our enemies—even those called 'Vietcong.' / If we kill our brothers and sisters, what will we have left? / With whom then shall we live?"[12] (ibid.).

Another poem written in 1967, "The Sun of the Future," asks additional questions. The speaker of the poem, a black American soldier, waits in ambush for "Victor, / Victor Charlie, / the yellow-skinned Vietcong" (ibid.). The soldier notices "[h]ow sorrowful is the cry of the monkey / in this Asian mountain. / How sorrowful is this country called Vietnam" (ibid.). He goes on to ask questions: "Why do I have to hate you, / Victor Charlie? . . . Why are we in Vietnam, / the forests and mountains of Asia? . . . Victor Charlie, / when did we sow the first seed of hatred and anger?" (1993a, pp. 38–39). There really are no answers, of course, just the sad reality of the sorrow of war, the sad reality that "[t]o support half a million immigrant families, / education, / children's programs, / housing, / and health care, / to meet the yearly budget for all of that, / we only need to stop the war for eight hours"[13] (1993a, p. 39). That was the tragic reality of the war, the unconscionable expenditure of human life and resources when so much *good* could have been accomplished. Thich went on to be labeled an antiwar poet and even a procommunist propagandist, eventually leaving Vietnam and taking up residence in France, where his "torch of poetry is still shining"(1993a, p. 52).

Visions of War, Dreams of Peace

A long-ignored "torch of poetry" illuminates another landscape—the battered terrain upon which women who witnessed firsthand the consequences of the war struggle to come to terms with, to endure the heavy weight of, "life-altering experience[s]" (Van Devanter and Furey, 1991, p. xxii). Their poetry has been gathered in a stirring collection called *Visions of War, Dreams of Peace.* These women, both American and Vietnamese, testify to the brutality of war and what their exposure to it did to them and to others.

The war reached out and touched, hurt, everyone in different ways. In her poem "A Boom, A Billow," Lady Borton, who worked for the American Friends Service Committee in Quang Ngai during the war, describes the consequences, the gruesome reality, that can follow an American air strike. Waiting for a plane in Da Nang, she watches the bombers go about their business some distance away:

> The uninvolved objectivity with which
> I stared at the sleek jets,
> their wings sloping back in fiercely
>   powerful lines,
> confused and disturbed me.
> The jets swooped down,
> then up quickly,
> to circle and swoop once more.
> A boom.
> A billow of dark gray smoke.
> Napalm.
>
> That afternoon I met a boy at the Helgoland
>   hospital ship.
> He sought me out because I came from
>   Quang Ngai,
> his ancestral home.
> He had no nose,
> only two holes in the middle of his face.
> His mouth was off to the side.
> One eye was gone;
> There was a hollow in his forehead above
> the other.
>
>   . . .
>
> One hand was partly usable,
> the fingers of the other,
> soldered to his wrist.
> Napalm.[14]

Here, the speaker has watched American bombers in a somewhat detached manner, and that "uninvolved objectivity" bothers her. It is the distance, of course, a distance that allows one to view the activities of war without seeing the up-close consequences. Later, however, the speaker encounters firsthand the results of a napalm bombing and what it can do to the human body. Napalm was used widely and indiscriminately in Vietnam, and it caused tremendous damage to the land and its people. Lady Borton knows whereof she speaks. She worked in a Friends Service rehabilitation center for civilian amputees in South Vietnam from 1969 to 1971.

The internal costs of the war are readily apparent in the following poem written by a former American nurse known only as "Dusty": "I went to Vietnam to heal / and came home silently wounded. / I went to Vietnam to heal / and still awaken from nightmares / about those we couldn't save. / ... I went to Vietnam to heal / and discovered I am not God" (p. 117). Here, all the illusions, all the ideals, have been stripped away, and in their place lie nightmares and disillusionment.

The disillusionment, the nightmares, the terrible memories, are common themes that run throughout the poetry of these women. It is echoed again in "Some Days," written by another American nurse, Joan Furey, who served in Pleiku:

> Some days
> I can't help but remember
> Who knows what triggers it today,
> 18 years later.
> The game was war,
> the prize survival.
> The toys were guns and tanks,
> mortars and grenades.
>
> . . .
>
> Some days
> I can't help but remember,
> when these very young men,
> without their arms or legs or
> half their faces,
> looked to me for hope, encouragement
> strength or peace.
> When hidden behind my smile of,
> "It'll be OK"
> was the burden of the lie,
> that knew that it wouldn't.[15]

That heavy weight, that "burden" again. The speaker continues, describing the anger generated "at the death / the anger at the carnage / the anger at the demands" (p. 90) and the frustration brought on by the lack of time, lack of resources, and that "there never seemed to be / enough me / to respond to the cries / and the sighs" (pp. 90–91). So she does what many in that situation did—she "numbed out," turned herself off to the tragedy thrown at her day after day after day. The costs were constant, their burden cumulative: "So I went on knowing / a part of my youth died every day / a part of my soul was lost. / Learning so clearly, without a doubt / There's no such thing / as a respite from war" (p. 91). She goes on to describe coming home "to a life / that no longer was real" and the great difficulties encountered and frustration generated trying to explain the war to those who "didn't seem to care" (pp. 90–91). And she learned that coming home did not necessarily mean *being* home: "They seemed to think I should / be glad to be home, / when much to my surprise / I found that I wasn't" (p. 93). This is one of the sorrows of war, that loss of innocence, that transformation of self that forever alters one's balance, one's perception of the world, and how one fits into it.

Trying to communicate the horror of war to those who never experienced it is another frustration recorded in these women's poetry. In "My Dead Are Not Silent," Dana Shuster grapples with her memories and how to make others understand: "My dead are not silent. / They scream in my dreams. / My dead are not still. / They reach for their mothers. / . . . Their blood yet drips through my soul / Their moans still echo through my heart" (p. 168). The dead, the speaker says, demand remembrance and honor, and they "demand that lessons be learned" (p. 169). Although the speaker hears these dead loud and clear and has learned these lessons well, she asks the reader a plaintive question at the end, "How can I make you hear?"[16] (ibid.).

In "Camouflage," written by Joan Furey, the speaker notes a similar penchant for forgetfulness or indifference to the lessons of the past. The speaker is talking about the proliferation of camouflage fatigues she seems to be noticing everywhere: "The children, / I've seen them so often / at the malls and in the halls / and most recently / at the Wall. / In their green fatigues and camouflage shorts / with matching shirts and hats and socks" (p. 184). For the speaker, the camouflage clothing is "a uniform of war / soiled by blood and mud / and dirt and death" (ibid.). She herself has one piece of this clothing that she can no longer wear or discard; it's "a last reminder / of the devastation / encountered by a youthful mind / who now shuns / thoughts of war / and dreams of peace" (p. 185). She sees the unknowing and unaware children, dressed in their "camouflage sunsuits," reflected in the black granite of the wall and shudders "at thoughts / of lessons left unlearned"[17] (ibid.). Like the speaker in the previous poem, she fears that the harsh realities, the hard lessons of Vietnam, are not being taught, or learned.

The sorrow of war, of course, was not limited to Americans. *Visions of War, Dreams of Peace* includes six poems by Vietnamese women. One of them, "The Vietnamese Mother," written by Huong Tram, portrays emotions that are timeless and know no borders. The poem opens with a Vietnamese mother receiving a letter from her son on the battlefield describing his experiences in battle: "He'd seen a young American soldier / Agonizing / As he let out his last sigh. / 'Oh Mama!' the American had cried. / Tears filled the Vietnamese mother's eyes" (p. 41). In the second stanza, seven years have passed when she receives a letter from a friend of her son, informing her of her own son's death: " 'Oh Mama!' he cried before he died / Bathed in moonlight" (ibid.). The mother reads and re-reads the few letters she received from her son, the agony of her loss extending 10,000 miles to another mother: "Again and again she cries / For her lost son / And for an unknown American mother / Who lost her beloved child" (ibid.). The poem is primarily straight narrative and straight from the heart.

This deep sense of loss, along with a strong undercurrent of bitterness, pervades another poem, "The Gift in Wartime," written by Tran Mong Tu. The speaker is a young Vietnamese woman addressing her betrothed, now a casualty of war:

> I offer you roses
> Buried in your new grave
> I offer you my wedding gown
> To cover your tomb still green with grass
>
> . . .
>
> I offer you my youth
> The days we were still in love
>
> . . .
>
> You give me the smell of blood
> From your war dress
> Your blood and the enemy's
> So that I may be moved
>
> I offer you clouds
> That linger on my eyes on summer days
> I offer you cold winters
> Amid my springtime of life
>
> . . .
>
> Seriously, I apologize to you
> I promise to meet you in our next life
> I will hold this shrapnel as a token
> By which we will recognize each other[19] (pp. 80–81)

The anaphora "I offer" becomes a lament to wasted youth, to unfulfilled dreams, to destroyed futures. Even in the midst of summer, clouds cover her eyes, and the springtime of her life is like a cold winter. Her tone ironic, bitter, her dead lover now can offer her only "lips with no smile / . . . arms without tenderness / . . . eyes with no sight" (p. 80). Left with just a piece of shrapnel, she apologizes and promises to meet him in their next life, after, we can be assured, she lives out the wintertime of this one.

Similar feelings are expressed by Minh Duc Hoai Trinh in "Poem Without Name," written in 1974 after American combat troops had withdrawn and only Vietnamese were fighting Vietnamese. The speaker describes the sights and sounds of battle just over the horizon and mentions a soldier she had seen the day before. She wonders now, after the soldier's death, why they hadn't talked, why they had not learned about each other. From this arises the tougher questions: "Why do you shoot each other? / Why lay those mines? / How many have died! And what for? / Who doesn't have a heart? / Who doesn't dream to be a bird?" (p. 174). The speaker prays for the fighting to stop, even importuning the heavens to make the weather so bad that the soldiers cannot fight. Returning to earth, she pleads: "Think of our beautiful native land. / Turn your face and look / Before you destroy everything. / The land can be green everywhere, / With a girl's light-flying blouse over yonder."[20]

Her pleas, of course, were not to be answered until a year and many thousand deaths later. The poem exemplifies the weariness with the war, which for the Vietnamese had really been going on since the French attack at Da Nang in 1858. She wonders why the war continues and why the killing goes on and makes a plea for compassion, for the war's participants to look beyond the baseness of the war to the potential of the human spirit, to "dream to be a bird."

The poems in *Visions of War, Dreams of Peace* are exactly what the title indicates. They are visions and dreams, but they are also more than that. These women writers, American and Vietnamese, allow us to view the war through another prism, from another perspective. They also give us a view, if only a protracted one, of Vietnamese feelings on the war, a war that took place, literally, in their living rooms. The inclusion of the Vietnamese in the equation of the Vietnam War is an aspect sorely neglected in American literature of the era. In fact, they are almost totally absent, save for occasional appearances (often of a derogatory nature) as characters along the periphery of American involvement.

Poems from Captured Documents

This long-overdue exploration of the Vietnamese literary arena can only reap great benefits in our understanding of that tragedy and in our continuing efforts at some kind of closure. That closure cannot take place without encompassing and understanding the people around which the tragedy fully revolved. The recent publication of a collection of poetry derived from captured "enemy" documents can only serve, in the words of one of its compilers, "as a bridge to such an understanding" (Thanh and Weigl 1994, p. vii). *Poems from Captured Documents* is a bilingual edition of twenty-three poems gathered from documents captured by the U.S. military during the Vietnam War. These works humanize an enemy who was stereotyped by the U.S. military and the media as barbaric, ignorant, and unfeeling. Rather, we find moving poems written under extreme conditions, portraying love, loneliness, fear, sadness, and determination, evincing emotions often strikingly similar to those felt by their American counterparts.

Like many of the poems in this collection, "Night of the Moon" speaks beautifully of love and of the separation caused by war:

> Murmuring water stirs the moon's gold in the stream.
> Whose lamp glimmers in the deepening night?
> When I held your hands, my heart seemed to stop.
> The fragrance of the flower is the fragrance of love.
>
> . . .
>
> Separated from you, my heart is dead.
> When will we find the love we had?
> How long until the day we return
> To the place we promised to meet?[21] (Ibid. p. 9)

For many soldiers of the National Liberation Front (established in 1960 as the formal organization of the South Vietnamese revolutionary forces, consisting of nationalists, communists, and ideologues; the PLAF or People's Liberation Armed Forces, was its fighting arm) or the North Vietnamese Army, service was for the duration, which for many exceeded ten years. Many soldiers did not see their families or friends for years and years because the logistics of returning home were too difficult and too dangerous.

When one returned home after a long absence, there was no guarantee that things would be as they were when one left. This is vividly portrayed in Vu Cao's poem "The Couple of the Mountains," a poem copied and carried by many North Vietnamese soldiers:[22]

> Seven years ago you were seventeen,
> I had just turned twenty.
> Two villages, Xuan-Duc and Doai-Dong, two rice fields.
> One day you would come to me,
> And one day I would come to you.[23] (p. 57)

During one of the periodic cease-fires during the war, the speaker, seven years away at war, eagerly heads home to his family and his fiancée. While visiting his parents, he hears the news that his betrothed was the only casualty during an enemy attack. He looks up at the two mountains called "Lovers Mountains" by the villagers and laments: "The mountains stay together but I lost you" (p. 59). He continues:

From the mountains to the river the road is blocked.
Xuan-Duc and Doai-Dong are thick with wild grass.
Bomb-cratered yards have become ponds, houses burn,
Destroyed in the dust and broken tile.

. . .

On the way to the market I heard someone say
The next harvest would bring much rice.
The mountains remain side by side
And I remember our love.
As long as the enemy is here, I will fight.

. . .

Red star on my hat
Always guiding my way,
I joined the troops.
You are the flower on top of the mountain.
In all seasons you send out your fragrance.[24]
       (ibid., pp. 57–61)

It is little wonder that the speaker vows to fight as long as the enemy is present, the enemy, in this case, presumably American and South Vietnamese forces. The speaker moves off with his troops, and the poem ends with a lovely tribute to his lost love.

The enemy, in the form of American troops, was, of course, soon driven from the land, and the "other" enemy, South Vietnam, was defeated shortly thereafter. The terrible tragedy of Vietnam had reached its final cease-fire, at least temporarily. Further challenges were massing on the horizon: an eventual incursion into Cambodia against the Khmer Rouge and an invasion of Vietnam by China. But on April 30, 1975, there was reason to celebrate—the "American War" was over, and Vietnam was now one country.

For the survivors, it was time to pick up the pieces, to try to fit them together into some meaningful shape, some cohesive pattern, a task that proved daunting and almost impossible. Many, like the refugees or "boat people," burned their bridges behind them, escaping to the West in search of the freedom they perceived as having lost in Vietnam, becoming the world's new homeless, the new exiles. For others, like American veterans, both men and women, came the difficult process of assimilating their individual "Vietnam experiences" in a country that seemed to have turned its back on them. Returning home, they had been met with silence, and, in some instances, outright resentment and condemnation. In the end, they were all, Vietnamese and Americans, survivors of a firestorm that had consumed millions. It would take years but finally would come the opening of lines of communication between the two estranged nations, the tentative beginnings of bridge building in a mutual effort toward sense-making and rapprochement.

Building Bridges—A Collaboration of Voices

> It is either the beginning or the end
> of the world, and the choice is ourselves
> or nothing.
> —Carolyn Forché, "Ourselves or Nothing"

Many participants in the war chose poetry as the means to share their experiences with the world. Through poetry of witness, these poets have grappled with the war's complexity in an attempt to arrive at meaning and understanding. They may not have always succeeded in their endeavors, but they have left us with a body of literature whose worth, though largely unheralded, is invaluable. Although not often considered "great literature" because it is unpolished, it is nonetheless always honest and straight from the heart. These poets confront the brutal side of man's nature and dare to ask "why?" without always expecting an answer or, sometimes, not living to hear the answer.

Robert Pinsky has written that one of the responsibilities of poets "is to mediate between the dead and the unborn: we must feel ready to answer, as if asked by the dead if we have handed on what they gave us, or asked by the unborn what we have for them" (Pinsky 1987, p. 424). We, the living, in keeping alive the art of poetry, an art passed on to us, must in turn pass it on to those who follow us, so that they may accept or change it if they like or not accept it at all. Pinsky bestows upon poets an additional trust defined by Carolyn Forché as a "poetry of witness": "we must use the art to behold the actual evidence before us. We must answer for what we see" (Pinsky 1987, p. 425).

The poets of witness studied here have not flinched from either of those responsibilities. They have passed on what the dead gave them, not only from the many poets before them but also from the dead, on *both* sides, who fell in places like the A Shau Valley, Khe Sanh, or Hamburger Hill. They have borne witness *for* those dead, testifying to the horror of war and its realities, rather than to jingoistic or spurious myths. By doing so, they have made their anguish humanity's, and they have warned us of what grim possibilities lie in war.

"Poetry makes nothing happen," said Auden, but he also said in almost the same breath that "it survives." This poetry will survive. The undaunted commitment to the act of remembering, and testifying to that remembrance, may just make "something happen."

Forché writes: "The resistance to terror is what makes the world habitable: the protest against violence will not be forgotten and this insistent memory renders life possible in communal situations" (Forché 1993, p. 16). These poets "protest against violence," and they will not let us forget what it did to them, nor will they let us forget what *they* did to *others,* during that madness. "There is nothing one man will not do to another," Forché insists in her poem "The Visitor" (Forché 1981, p. 15), and these poets, through their "songs of napalm," are witnesses to the truth of her claim, whether it is watching an American soldier cruelly beating a Vietnamese woman for no reason or it is as a witness to the use of napalm and its horrifying consequences. For understanding and resolution to take place, the truth must be known.

Through poetry, through literature, bridges can be built across troubled waters, as evidenced by the publication of *Poems from Captured Documents,* discussed in this study. Bruce Weigl, co-editor of the volume, worked closely with his Vietnamese counterpart, Thanh T. Nguyen, and in 1992 he traveled to Hanoi, where he worked with two leading translators to ensure "an accurate representation of the Vietnamese version that maintains its integrity in translation" (Thanh and Weigl 1994, p. xiii). More recently, 1995 saw the publication of an anthology of postwar fiction, *The Other Side of Heaven: Postwar Fiction by American and Vietnamese Writers,* which was a collaborative effort by Vietnamese and American writers. Meetings between American and Vietnamese writers have been taking place since 1988, and following one such meeting in 1993 came the idea for the anthology. Bridges are being built.

We need these Vietnam War survivor-poets to continue building bridges. We need them to speak out, to testify to the brute reality of war and what it costs humanity to undertake it. We need them, most of all, to speak the truth, to help correct and rewrite the myths all nations live under, and, most important, to help keep our children alive. It *is* ourselves or nothing.

> "Time for Americans and Vietnamese to drink tea together,"
> Uncle Firmness said.
>
> —Lady Borton, *After Sorrow*

Notes

1. Douglas Allen, and Ngô Vinh Long, eds., *Coming to Terms: Indochina, the United States, and the War* (Boulder: Westview Press, 1991), p. 308.

2. As of July 21, 1995, the Pentagon listed 2,202 cases of U.S. troops missing in Vietnam, Laos, and Cambodia ("Pentagon Drops 567 MIA Cases," *Missoulian,* November 14, 1995, Sec. A-7), a number that pales by comparison to the number of Vietnamese missing. Lady Borton writes in *After Sorrow: An American Among the Vietnamese* (1995): "Vietnamese tend an ancestor's grave on the anniversary of the person's death. The Fifteenth Day of the Seventh Lunar Month is reserved for those souls whose graves and death days are unknown. Since these souls cannot be properly tended, they wander, forever restless. For years I'd been hearing about the twenty-four hundred missing Americans; now I began to consider the one hundred thousand to three hundred thousand Vietnamese who are missing. They are Viet Nam's wandering souls" (p. 16). Lady Borton's numbers are substantiated in a December 30, 1994 story in the *Missoulian* ("Let's Close the Book on MIAs") by Mark Wilson, who writes: "The Vietnamese government conservatively estimates there are more than 300,000 Vietnamese MIAs—nearly 200 times as many U.S. servicemen still unaccounted for from that war."

3. The success of military units, and thus of their commanders, was measured by how many "enemy" bodies they could count among the dead. This often led to the blurring of

lines between civilian and combatant. The Vietnam War was a time whose horrors were so great that new terminology, new descriptors, had to be invented to encompass and to blunt the harsh, everyday reality of the tremendous damage caused by the war: "train wreck," for someone who had suffered multiple traumatic injuries; "gork," for a patient who was severely neurologically impaired and comatose; "crispy critters," for those casualties who were severely burned; and "mix 'n match," for mass casualty situations in which numerous patients had sustained multiple amputations (Van Devanter and Furey, 1991, pp. 206–7). Here, the term "wasted" emerged, not only meaning dead but also symbolizing another life "wasted" for no perceivable reason, another loss of life in a war no one understood, least of all the soldiers doing the dying. For North Vietnamese troops, bullets became bronze "candy" (Bao, 1993, p. 37). B-52 bomber strikes became "music from Thailand" (Borton, 1995, p. 96), named after the country from which many of the flights originated.

The uniqueness of the war, its sheer craziness, could be told only in its own language, and that language was not restricted to the euphemistic obfuscations of the upper echelons ("aggressive defense," "peace offensive"). The common soldier, the "grunt," appropriated or created his own nomenclature for the fantasy-world of Vietnam. "There it is" became the major cliché of the war. It was a catchall referent for the myriad events that occurred in Vietnam and might indicate one's insight into the *why* of those events. Or it might indicate one's complete *lack* of understanding why something happened, a realization that war was just that way, that mysterious forces were at work here and thinking about it too much could make you *dien cai dau,* or crazy.

It was also *the* signifier of irony, an understanding that "shit happens," and sometimes there is not any logic to the event. It was what two GIs would say to each other as the smoke of battle cleared, and the GI who had been fighting between them lay dead at their feet. It is what they would say to each other when a mortar round exploded and only one man was killed, maybe because his flak vest had not been zipped shut allowing one little piece of shrapnel to penetrate. "There it is," they would say. It says it all; no need to say more. That was also a sort of buffer, a euphemism, between them and the big "it," *death.* It is what the grunts would say to one another when a man with only a few days left on his tour would get killed in a random rocket attack. It was an acknowledgment that as soldiers they understood certain things implicitly, a form of communal understanding and sharing. "There it is," one would say, and the rest would nod their heads in agreement. There it is: the Nam. The war generated so many terms of its own that many authors feel the need to include glossaries in their books.

4. Used with permission of Atlantic Monthly Press.

5. Used with permission of Atlantic Monthly Press.

6. Used with permission of Atlantic Monthly Press.

7. Copyright 1988 by Yusef Komunyakaa, Wesleyan University Press. Used with permission of University Press of New England.

8. Copyright 1988 by Yusef Komunyakaa, Wesleyan University Press. Used with permission of University Press of New England.

9. Crimes against humanity are not uncommon in war, and the Vietnam War was no exception. The Vietnam War was different from other wars in many ways, and this difference extends into certain categories of atrocious acts, the most notorious being crimes against women. Jacqueline K. Lawson notes: "What distinguishes the war in Vietnam from other wars is the number of atrocities committed against women (Vietnam was our longest war and involved more men) and the fact that these atrocities are copiously documented in the memoirs and oral histories produced by Vietnam veterans. These non-fiction narratives, the veterans' own accounts, are replete with misogynistic allusions to the women of Vietnam: acts of rape, gang rape, assaults on women, torture, mutilation,

and murder crowd the pages of these texts, raising disturbing questions about this nation's combatants and the culture they sought to defend" (from "The Misogyny of the Vietnam War," in *Fourteen Landing Zones,* ed. Philip K. Jason [Iowa City: University of Iowa Press, 1991], p. 19). Lawson goes on to attribute the high incidence of atrocities against women to racism, to the highly misogynistic character of men in general and the military in particular, and to a fear of emasculation, with its resultant adoption of the Rambo or John Wayne persona.

10. Copyright 1988 by Yusef Komunyakaa, Wesleyan University Press. Used with permission of University Press of New England.

11. Copyright 1988 by Yusef Komunyakaa, Wesleyan University Press. Used with permission of University Press of New England.

12. Reprinted with permission of Parallax Press, Berkeley, California.

13. Reprinted with permission of Parallax Press, Berkeley, California.

14. Borton, Lady, *After Sorrow: An American Among the Vietnamese* (New York, Viking, 1995) p. 13.

15. Van Devanter, Lynda and Joan A. Furey, eds., *Visions of War, Dreams of Peace* (New York, Warner Books, 1991), pp. 89–90.

16. Ibid., pp. 166–69.

17. Ibid., pp. 184–85.

18. Ibid.

19. Ibid, pp. 80–81.

20. Ibid., pp. 174–75.

21. Copyright 1994 by the University of Massachusetts Press. Used with permission.

22. Little is known of Vu Cao, other than that his poem "was a particular favorite among soldiers" (Thanh and Weigl 1994, p. xiii).

23. Copyright 1994 by the University of Massachusetts Press. Used with permission.

24. Copyright 1994 by the University of Massachusetts Press. Used with permission.

References

Allen, Douglas, and Ngô Vinh Long, eds. 1991. *Coming to Terms: Indochina, the United States, and the War.* Boulder: Westview Press.

Bao Ninh. 1993. *The Sorrow of War.* Trans. Phan Thanh Hao. New York: Pantheon.

Borton, Lady. 1995. *After Sorrow: An American Among the Vietnamese.* New York: Viking.

Caputo, Philip. 1986. *A Rumor of War.* 24th ed. New York: Ballantine.

Des Pres, Terence. 1976. *The Survivor: An Anatomy of Life in the Death Camps.* New York: Oxford University Press, 1976.

Forché, Carolyn. 1981. *The Country Between Us.* New York: Harper & Row.

———. 1993. "Twentieth-Century Poetry of Witness." *American Poetry Review* 22, no. 2 (March/April): 9–16.

Karlin, Wayne, Le Minh Khue, and Truany, Vu, ed. 1995. *The Other Side of Heaven: Post-War Fiction by Vietnamese and American Writers* (Willimantic, CT: Curbstone Press.

Komunyakaa, Yusef. 1988. *Dien Cai Dau.* Middletown, CT: Wesleyan University Press.

Lawson, Jacqueline K. 1991. "The Misogyny of the Vietnam War." In *Fourteen Landing Zones,* ed. Philip K. Jason, 15–37. Iowa City: University of Iowa Press.

Lifton, Robert Jay. 1971. "Beyond Atrocity." In *Crimes of War,* ed. Richard A. Falk, Gabriel Kolko, and Robert Jay Lifton, 17–27. New York: Random House.

Pinsky, Robert. 1987. "Responsibilities of the Poet." *Critical Inquiry* 13, no. 3 (Spring): 421–33.

Smith, Lorrie. 1991. "Resistance and Revision in Poetry of Vietnam Veterans." In *Fourteen Landing Zones,* ed. Jason, 49–66.

Tal, Kali. "Speaking the Language of Pain." In *Fourteen Landing Zones,* ed. Jason, 217–50.

Thanh T. Nguyen, and Bruce Weigl, ed. and trans. 1994. *Poems from Captured Documents.* Amherst: University of Massachusetts Press.

Thich Nhat Hanh. 1993a. *Call Me by My True Names.* Berkeley: Parallax Press.

————. 1993b. *Love in Action.* Berkeley: Parallax Press.

Van Devanter, Lynda, and Joan A. Furey, ed. 1991. *Visions of War, Dreams of Peace.* New York: Warner Books.

Weigl, Bruce. 1988. *Song of Napalm.* New York: Atlantic Monthly Press.

Selected Bibliography

Balaban, John, ed. and trans. *Ca Dao Vietnam: A Bilingual Anthology of Vietnamese Folk Poetry.* Greensboro, NC: Unicorn Press, 1980.

Barry, Jan, and W. D. Ehrhart, eds. *Demilitarized Zones.* Perkasie, PA: East River Anthology, 1976.

Durand, Maurice M., and Nguyen Tran Huan. *An Introduction to Vietnamese Literature.* Trans. D. M. Hawke. New York: Columbia University Press, 1985.

Ehrhart, W. D., ed. *Carrying the Darkness, American Indochina: The Poetry of the Vietnam War.* New York: Avon Books, 1985.

————. *Unaccustomed Mercy: Soldier-Poets of the Vietnam War.* Lubbock: Texas Tech University Press, 1989.

Emerson, Gloria. 1986. "The Children in the Field." *TriQuarterly* 67 (Winter): 221–28.

Forché, Carolyn, ed. *Against Forgetting: Twentieth-Century Poetry of Witness.* New York: W.W. Norton, 1993.

Hu'u Ngoc, and Françoise Corrèze, comps. *Anthology of Vietnamese Literature.* Trans. Peggie Preston, Dang The Binh, and Hoang Tuy. Hanoi: Foreign Languages Publishing House, 1984.

Huynh Sanh Thông, ed. and trans. *The Heritage of Vietnamese Poetry.* New Haven: Yale University Press, 1979.

Jamieson, Neil L. *Understanding Vietnam.* Berkeley: University of California Press, 1993.

Larsen, Wendy Wilder, and Tran Thi Nga. *Shallow Graves: Two Women and Vietnam.* New York: Harper & Row, 1986.

Raffel, Burton, ed. and trans. *From the Vietnamese: Ten Centuries of Poetry.* New York: October House, 1968.

Rottmann, Larry, Jan Barry, and Basil T. Paquet, eds. *Winning Hearts and Minds: War Poems by Vietnam Veterans.* New York: McGraw-Hill, 1972.

7

Moral Judgment in War and Crimes against Humanity

Van Jay Symons

In the novel *War and Peace,* shortly before the encounter of Russian armies with those of Napoleon at Borodino in 1812, Prince Andrew expresses Leo Tolstoy's views on war:

> But what is war? What is needed for success in warfare? What are the habits of the military? The aim of war is murder; the methods of war are spying, treachery, and their encouragement, the ruin of a country's inhabitants, robbing them or stealing to provision the army, and fraud and falsehood termed military craft. . . . They (the military) meet, as we shall meet tomorrow, to murder one another; they kill and maim tens of thousands, and then have thanksgiving services for having killed so many people (they even exaggerate the number), and they announce a victory, supposing that the more people they have killed the greater their achievement.[1]

In this classic work of literature, Tolstoy asks questions frequently left unaddressed by those who study war only from a political, diplomatic, or military perspective or who glorify it for any number of reasons. Works of literature and film can provide a corrective for teachers and their students who become preoccupied with tracing the origins of conflicts, the reasons why one side proves victorious over another, or the impact of a struggle on the broader world community. Such approaches analyze war from a distance, and, although the carnage of war and particularly the terrible loss of life may be quantitatively noted, little effort is made (perhaps it is too painful to do so) to explore as fully as one might the impact of war on the individual, be he or she a combatant in the conflict or merely a civilian maligned by it. In addition, questions about the morality or immorality of war or how the individual may struggle to remain moral in the often immoral environment of war are sometimes left unasked.

In his work entitled *Just and Unjust Wars,* Michael Walzer observes, "War is so awful that it makes us cynical about the possibility of restraint, and then it is so much worse that it makes us indignant at the absence of restraint."[2] Given the horrors of war, all belligerents create elaborate rationalizations for their participation in them and for the actions they sometimes take in conducting them. Although conventions of war have been established to define how wars should be conducted, to constrain war excesses, and to hold individuals morally responsible for their actions in war, we have failed abysmally to limit carnage. Again, as suggested in another passage from Tolstoy in which Prince Andrew conjectures about the next day's battle at Borodino, good literature is an effective vehicle to consider war's excesses and why there is often little restraint shown by its participants:

> One thing I would do if I had power . . . I would not take prisoners. Why take prisoners?
>
> It's chivalry! The French have destroyed my home and are on their way to destroy Moscow, they have outraged and are outraging me every moment. They are my enemies.
>
> In my opinion they are all criminals. And so thinks Timokhin and the whole army. They should be executed![3]

This chapter analyzes a film and two novels to show how film and literature can be used in the classroom to deepen our understanding of the impact of war on its participants. The works are produced by Asians and are about the Pacific War, the Korean War, and the Vietnam War. Recently, as Asian film and Asian literature in translation have become more available, those who study and teach about the wars fought in Asia during the past half-century are discovering the usefulness of these resources. Consequently, students become more fully aware of the horror of war, the difficulty faced by soldiers seeking to exercise moral judgment, and the importance of considering which actions, particularly those waged against noncombatants, should be viewed as crimes against humanity.

Each of the three works considered here introduces the viewer/reader to a fundamental issue related to war sometimes overlooked by political, diplomatic, or military historians. The first work is the Japanese film *Ningen no joken,* titled *The Human Condition* when released in the West, which deals with the Pacific War and explores the efforts of a young Japanese man to avoid becoming involved in what was, to him, a morally reprehensible war. The film boldly addresses the question of whether an individual can remain moral in the often immoral environment of warfare. The second, a novel written by Ahn Junghyo about the Korean War titled *Silver Stallion,* considers the impact of war on the civilian inhabitants of a small, remote village. The rape of a Korean woman by soldiers of the "liberating" armies of the United Nations and the establishment of a complex of whorehouses near the village to service UN forces provides the context for this examination. The third, also a novel, is about the Vietnam War.

Duong Thu Huong's *Novel Without a Name* reveals the gradual stripping away of the innocence and of the ideals of the Vietnamese during their protracted struggle with the United States, its allies, and South Vietnam and considers the way the state mobilized an increasingly disillusioned populace for an increasingly desperate conflict. All three works enable the viewer/reader to understand more fully the horrors of war at a personal level, the loss of innocence of combatants and noncombatants who become embroiled in the struggle, and the seriousness of addressing questions of moral responsibility and crimes against humanity within the context of warfare.

The Human Condition

The Human Condition, set during the last few years of the Pacific War, is a nine-and-a-half-hour long, three-film series, released between 1959 and 1961 and re-released in 1969. Based on a six-volume novel written by Jumpei Gomikawa and directed by Masaki Kobayashi, the film clearly addresses one of Kobayashi's recurrent themes, the question of how the individual loses his/her voice for humanity in a larger, often malevolent, society.[4]

The film chronicles the struggle of one man, Kaji, to remain humane in the most abject of conditions, first as a supervisor of Chinese prisoners of war in a Japanese forced labor camp in Manchuria (film 1, entitled *No Greater Love*), then as a soldier drafted into the Japanese army (film 2, entitled *Road to Eternity*), and finally as a soldier in a defeated army fleeing first Soviet forces and then increasingly hostile local Chinese (film 3, entitled *A Soldier's Prayer*). In the last segment, Kaji surrenders to Soviet forces and is sent to a POW camp. He manages to escape but ultimately dies alone in the freezing cold of Siberia. The tragedy in the story is not just that Kaji dies, but that, despite his best intentions, in his struggle to survive he is forced to commit immoral acts. Moreover, even Kaji's acts of humanity prove meaningless since they were undertaken in the violent arena of warfare.

The film begins by introducing us to Kaji, a recent college graduate, now working for the South Manchuria Steel Company, who is deeply in love with his girlfriend, Michiko, but unwilling to marry her because he is certain that in a matter of weeks he will be inducted into the military. It is 1943 and Kaji, who is somewhat sympathetic to socialist ideals, has become a silent critic of the war, but he perceives that he has no alternative but to fight in it. Miraculously, Kaji's boss proposes that he accept a position as supervisor of labor in a bleak and remote Manchurian coal mining operation owned by the company. Because coal production is essential to the war effort, this offer enables Kaji to avoid conscription as well as to marry Michiko.

Once Kaji reaches the mining site he is immediately struck by the poor food and living conditions offered impressed Chinese workers and the brutal way that the Japanese treat them. Most pit bosses assert that the way to ensure increased productivity is "to lash and beat and kill if need be," and Kaji's superiors at the camp remind him that although they are not at the front fighting the enemy they are "at war here. . . at war in the name of final victory." They also inform him that unless there is a 20 percent increase in production during the year they will all be replaced, which for Kaji means sure induction into the army. Nonetheless, Kaji seeks to create more humane conditions for the workers by persuading his jaded colleagues that profits for the company, and therefore promotions for the bosses and foremen at the camp, are more likely if workers are better treated because laborers would then be more eager to report for work and more capable of completing it.

Kaji's job is made more difficult almost immediately when Japanese security forces (the Kempeitai) offer labor camp officials six hundred additional workers, Chinese prisoners of war transported to the north from China, if the company is willing to accept the responsibility of isolating them from regular laborers by enclosing them in an electrified barbed wire impoundment and guaranteeing that they will not escape. Because the company desperately needs more workers, it accepts the offer, but Kaji is left to deal with this volatile workforce.

When Kaji arrives at the train station to take charge of the newly arriving prisoners of war, he finds some already dead from starvation and abuse and others in such a weakened condition that they are unfit for labor. As the surviving prisoners pour out of the train cars, they spot a grain wagon nearby and rush to it seeking food. The challenge faced by Kaji, to practice humanity in the often inhumane environs of war, becomes starkly apparent because Kaji has no choice but to mount the wagon to beat the prisoners back not only in order to quell the unrest but also to protect these men from the danger of consuming too much grain in their weakened condition.

From these beginnings, the first film in the trilogy explores Kaji's ongoing struggle with his hardened coworkers who believe that brutality and force are the most effective ways to keep men working in the mines; Chinese collaborators with the Japanese who benefit at the expense of conscripted Chinese workers by acting as middlemen; the Chinese prisoners of war in the camp, who naturally mistrust Kaji because he is Japanese, and who have their own agenda, including escape, even though their escape attempts undermine Kaji's efforts to see that they are better treated; and the Kempeitai, who are particularly abusive toward prisoners of war and constantly warn Kaji what will befall the prisoners and Kaji himself should there be any escape attempts.

Although Kaji never lets go of his intention to remain moral in this immoral environment, he is forced to make compromises. For example, a coworker persuades Kaji that a man will work harder and be less inclined to escape if his needs are met, by insisting that "Man is not a poem! Nor is he morality! He is a mere mass of matter formed of lust and greed." In an effort to win favor with the Chinese prisoners of war, Kaji, therefore, pays a local prostitute to send thirty of her "comfort women" to the compound on a regular basis to service his six hundred men. When they arrive, one of the women accosts Kaji, saying, "I didn't come of my own free will" any more than the laborers did. Despite his good intentions, Kaji has become an accomplice in sordid dealings and admits to his wife he is running a whorehouse.

Kaji's efforts to discourage the Chinese prisoners of war from attempting to escape fail, with disastrous consequences for both the prisoners and Kaji. Initially, a small group of eleven men escapes. Once they are recaptured, in order to assure that they are not harshly treated, Kaji accepts full responsibility for them and promises no future incidents. When a second escape occurs, involving eighteen men, Kaji does not report it. Finally the Chinese prisoners botch a third escape attempt, which the Kempeitai discover. Kaji is told that seven prisoners of war involved in the attempted escape will be executed as a deterrent to further escapes and that he and the other prisoners of war must witness this. At great risk to himself, Kaji tries to intervene to prevent the executions from being held, but he fails. When forced to witness the beheadings, he finds that he can bear it no longer. As the fourth prisoner is being prepared for execution, Kaji begins to argue with the executioner. This incites into action the Chinese witnessing the beheadings, and they begin in unison to chant "sha ren, sha ren" ("murderers, murderers"). Because of the unrest, the Kempeitai are forced to make a hasty retreat and call off the executions. The humiliated Kempeitai hold Kaji responsible. He is arrested, tortured, and forced to confess that he covered up the second escape. Ultimately he is released by the Kempeitai, but fired by his company. Shortly thereafter, the Kempeitai orchestrate the drafting of Kaji into the military; he is eventually sent off to the front.

No Greater Love exposes the brutal way in which the Japanese exploited people in their colonies to provide for their armies. Before Kaji leaves for the front, a friend of his at the camp ironically congratulates Kaji for having caught "the humanism train." Despite this, however, *No Greater Love* shows how Kaji's efforts to limit these excesses had only a minor impact in righting the wrongs being perpetrated in the forced labor camps of Manchuria by Japanese civilians, the Kempeitai and the Japanese military, and their Chinese collaborators.

Films 2 and 3 of *The Human Condition* are primarily exposés on the harsh life lived by soldiers in the Japanese military during the Pacific War, the inhumane treatment of recruits by veteran soldiers, and the disarray of the Japanese military near the end of the war.

Kaji is again the focal point in these films. He has been dispatched through the machinations of the hated Kempeitai northward in Manchuria to the Japanese front with the Soviet Union, and, although his mental and physical abilities place Kaji at the forefront of new recruits, his clash with the Kempeitai causes the officers and veterans in his company to discriminate against him. Although Kaji is labeled a pacifist and perhaps even a socialist, he still finds a natural ally in Shinjo, whose brother had been arrested as a communist sympathizer. Shinjo has therefore been branded as a "red" and is, like Kaji, ostracized.

Shinjo, a three-year veteran of the army, dreams of fleeing to Soviet Siberia, only a short distance from where their Japanese unit is located. Although angered at the harsh and repressive treatment he suffers in the Japanese military and, like Shinjo, hopeful that life would be better in a socialist utopia where "men are treated as human beings," Kaji determines that he will not join Shinjo in an escape attempt for fear that he might lose contact with his wife, Michiko. There is nothing left for him to do but make the best of a difficult situation in the military.

The Japanese army portrayed in films 2 and 3 of this trilogy is a brutal one that tolerated the mistreatment of new conscripts by officers and veteran soldiers. Soldiers were expected to be willing to die for their country, and they and their families were to devote themselves fully to the war effort. Just as Kaji found it necessary to protect laborers while working for the South Manchuria Steel Company, once in the army he could not resist befriending new recruits susceptible to abuse by the military.

Kaji's charity toward fellow soldiers becomes especially evident as he seeks to help the new recruit Obara. Obara is a weak, bespectacled inductee who is always the brunt of abuse by the veterans because he does not have the physical or mental stamina to keep up with the unit. When Obara receives a letter from his wife in which she reveals ongoing problems with her mother-in-law, he is told by the unit to demand that she stop whining because it is adversely affecting his morale. She also must sacrifice for the country. Nonetheless, Obara still struggles, and even though Kaji assists him by carrying some of his gear during one horrific forced march, Obara cannot keep up. Obara's failure is regarded as a unit failure, and after he is transported back to camp, he is beaten and disgraced by the veterans. Obara, devastated by this experience, withdraws to the lavatory and shoots himself.

In considering Obara's suicide, Kaji insists that "the fault lies with the military," which tolerates the bullying of new recruits by veteran soldiers and officers. Nonetheless, when Obara's wife comes to claim his ashes, Kaji does not incriminate the military and, in fact, encourages her not to probe too deeply into the reasons for his suicide. He even suggests that her problems with her mother-in-law had proved unsettling to her husband and that he too was at fault for not seeing that Obara completed his march with the unit, causing him to bring disgrace to his outfit as well as himself. Nonetheless, unbeknownst to Obara's wife, Kaji confronts the senior officer of the company demanding that the veterans who had beaten Obara be punished. Unsurprisingly, the senior officer proves unwilling to do anything. Again, Kaji has little impact on institutionalized Japan, and, though solicitous of the needs of his fellow soldiers, he failed to save Obara.

The third film in this trilogy, *A Soldier's Prayer,* chronicles the overwhelming defeat of the Japanese army when the armored divisions of the Soviet Union entered Manchuria. The Soviet forces find the Japanese woefully unprepared. Short of rifles, the Japanese soldiers are told to lash bayonets to birch branches and go to the fight. Tank pits are being dug by hand, but there is inadequate time to finish them. Each soldier is then instructed to dig a foxhole and stand his ground.

Once the battle breaks out, Kaji, for the first time, is forced to become a murderer and experience "the guilt of killing people," with each killing graphically depicted on the screen. First, he shoots an enemy soldier advancing behind Soviet tanks, then he kills an insane Japanese soldier threatening the ranks, and finally he is forced to stab to death a Soviet sentry to facilitate his retreat from the battle scene and his survival.

The remainder of this film focuses on Kaji's flight southward away from the battlefront and, he hopes, toward his wife. The Soviet onslaught has destroyed any semblance of order in the Japanese military, and soldiers, now totally devoid of formal ties to their military units, are forced to scavenge for food in the countryside, which the Chinese are protecting with force of arms. Kaji discovers that he must kill and steal in order to survive.[5] Nonetheless, at some risk to himself, he befriends a group of civilians, including two whores, who are also fleeing the Soviet advance. Ultimately, Kaji surrenders to the Soviet forces only to observe that the Red Army is no different from the Japanese one: "They rape women, and any woman will do." He discovers that the utopia he had hoped to find in the Soviet Union does not exist. In the end, Kaji manages to escape from detention only to wander alone in the desolate wastelands of Siberia. There he quietly succumbs to hunger and the cold.

To Masaki Kobayashi the Pacific War "was the culmination of human evil," and he directed *The Human Condition* to explore this dark side of human nature.[6] Kobayashi attributes this evil in man to "emotional rigidity, the negation of common feeling with one's fellow man,"[7] and he believes this negation occurred in Japan, particularly in the military, primarily because of the corrosive effect of a harsh and authoritarian social structure.[8] For Kaji, the assault against his compassion toward others comes from numerous quarters, especially Japanese capitalists, the Kempeitai, and the military in the name of protecting the fatherland and winning the war. Remarkably, Kaji never loses his charitability toward others and remains determined to act justly even though his actions endanger himself and even his wife.

Having seen this film, students may ask who is responsible for the mistreatment of conscripted laborers and military recruits described in these films or for the carnage and slaughter on the field of battle. Michael Walzer provides an answer by arguing that "wars are not self-starting . . . [they have] human agents as well as human victims."[9] These agents he calls criminals, and their crime is called aggression. It is they who are responsible. Students will agree that Kaji is not the criminal, for he has been dragged into the Asia–Pacific conflict against his will first as a provisioner of coal for the military and then as a soldier, and throughout the struggle Kaji remains moral as well as he can. Viewers of the film will also come to realize that despite the hellishness of war it is possible to recognize the just deeds of some participants as well as criminal acts of others.[10]

The theme of the abuse of individuals by structured authoritarian power so evident in Kaji's struggle in *The Human Condition* was explored by Kobayashi in other films, notably *Seppuku* (also titled *Harakiri*). However, another film directed by Kobayashi in 1957 entitled *Kuroi kawa* or (Black River), about the American military presence in Japan and the insidious spread of prostitution at the end of the Pacific War, more directly addresses one of the chief concerns evident in a Korean book entitled *Silver Stallion* written by Ahn Junghyo.[11]

The Silver Stallion

Silver Stallion considers the assault on traditional values posed by war and the men who fight in them, evidenced particularly by the rape of a village woman and then the establishment of a complex of brothels near a rustic village during the Korean War. The work is a study of the loss of innocence not only of Korean women but also of Korean youngsters exposed to the lewd conduct of servicemen. It also unflinchingly reveals the inability of tradition-bound village elders to adapt to the chaotic conditions of war and the adjustments demanded by it. Finally, *Silver Stallion* forces one to consider questions of command responsibility. Who is ultimately responsible for the failure of the allied forces to protect Korean women from the nightly attacks against Korean women by UN soldiers?

The story is set in Kumsan, a village so remote and so poor that previous invaders, whether pirates, thirteenth-century Mongols, or sixteenth-century Japanese, did not bother to cross the mountains to plunder the place. Even while Korea was a Japanese colony, not a single Japanese soldier or police officer bothered to come to the village. Consequently, as war breaks out on the Korean peninsula, the villagers of Kumsan hope that once again they will be ignored.[12]

The story revolves around three individuals who live in Kumsan. One is the village elder and county chief, named Old Hwang, who has been ill-prepared by his conservative Confucian background to respond effectively to the war, a condition shared by many of the village men around him whom he broadly represents. Old Hwang's authority has never been questioned because the Hwang family has been the wealthiest and most educated in the county for eight generations. He lives in Paulownia House, the only place in the county where one could find books, ink slabs, writing brushes and other scholarly objects handed down by Confucian ancestors through the ages (4–5, 25).[13]

As war erupts on the peninsula, Old Hwang seems unable to formulate a response to the growing uncertainty around him over which he has no control (5). When the "UN soldiers" of *Megado* (MacArthur) begin to cross the river adjacent to Kumsan as they march to meet the communist armies, Old Hwang leads a small group of dignitaries to meet them. Nonetheless, this first encounter with the Westerners proves disastrous, in part because no one from the village speaks a Western language, and although the UN armies are made up from soldiers of sixteen different countries, no *bengko* ("big nose") arriving at the village on this occasion speaks Korean or reads Chinese characters. Clearly, this war would challenge the status quo and prove hard to Old Hwang and other village notables (45–49).

Another incident occurs shortly thereafter that again reveals the inadaptability of these Confucian gentlemen. When fighting broke out in the nearby town of Chunchon, which had been controlled by the communists, the National Grange storehouse in Chunchon was bombed and tons of confiscated communist grain lay in the streets just for the taking. What were Confucian gentlemen to do given that "a proud man would not do certain things, such as begging or stealing, even if he starved to death?" (31). What most Kumsan men did was quietly to encourage their wives to rush to town to collect the bounty for "women did not care about pride or dignity, because only men were supposed to possess these qualities. Women could not afford to starve to death on account of anything as absurd as honor" (32).

The problem of maintaining morality, in Old Hwang's view a proper Confucian order, in the increasingly immoral environment created by war, reaches a critical point in the *Silver Stallion* when two UN soldiers enter the village at night and rape one of its women, a young widow named Ollye. This incident, the awkward response to it by Old Hwang, and Ollye's subsequent decision, once abandoned by the villagers, to open a house of prostitution on the edge of Kumsan, in order to provide for her two children, tear the village apart.

Rape is almost always a constant in any war. After Ollye is raped one villager observes, "That's what the Japanese did to our women when they invaded this country, and that's what the Mongols and the Chinese did when they were here. They raped every woman in sight—virgins, widows, housewives—every living thing with a skirt on. I don't think the Occidentals are any different" (58). "Rape is a crime, in war as in peace,"[14] and one that in time of war women are powerless to defend themselves against.

Ollye's rape occurred in front of her nine-year-old son, Mansik, and her infant daughter, and there was nothing she could do to protect herself against the two armed soldiers. Also chilling was the response of the villagers. Old Hwang did not know what to do, for no woman in the county had ever been raped before. Although he knew that Ollye was a victim and had done nothing wrong, "victim or not, she was a dirty woman. Loss of feminine virtue, under any circumstance, was the most profound shame for a woman—so profound a shame, in fact, that in the old days, a disgraced woman did not hesitate to drink a bowl of lye to terminate her life. The act of taking her own life symbolically restored the chastity of the defiled woman."[15] Not knowing what to do, Old Hwang did nothing, and because he stayed away from Ollye, so did the other villagers. Consequently, she was left alone "confined in her home, dead, while the world, ignoring her existence was busy living" (125).

Ollye's existence before she was raped had been precarious, but now it was nearly impossible. Because her husband had drowned before the war broke out, she had been forced to turn to Old Hwang for help. Initially, he offered her work doing domestic chores around his house, but she barely earned enough to feed herself and her children (22–28). However, now that Old Hwang and the villagers were ignoring her, Ollye found herself in an impossible situation, one that forced her to accept the offer of two prostitutes to join them in business, first at "Texas Town," a collection of makeshift whorehouses erected on an island in the middle of the river directly in front of Kumsan, and then at the edge of the village, by adding on to her small hut and inviting GIs to visit them there.

Naturally, Old Hwang and the men of the village were upset by Ollye's activities but there was nothing they could do to stop them. Ollye had been driven to these extremes by the neglect of the villagers as much as by the UN soldiers who raped her. Her growing hate for the people of Kumsan coupled with her determination to survive to feed and care for her children enabled her to practice a trade that she loathed while suffering the continuing censure of her neighbors (120–125).

The other key figure in this story is Mansik, the nine-year-old son of Ollye. Ahn Junghyo admits that the story of Mansik and his friends is, to some degree, influenced by his having read *Lord of the Flies,* William Golding's book about a group of young choirboys who lost their innocence after surviving a plane crash on a deserted island. Ahn's study of Mansik and his friends parallels Golding's in that both are concerned about each boy's struggle with good and evil. Golding asks whether it is possible for young boys to remain moral in what seems initially to be an ideal environment, while Ahn asks whether young boys can remain moral in the increasingly immoral environment of warfare. In the end, despite the harsh environment Ahn's boys are in, he seems more optimistic than Golding.[16]

In *Silver Stallion,* there are five boys, all from Kumsan village. Before the war breaks out they often play together, enjoying most taking long hikes to Phoenix Hill to search for the cave in which a mythical seven-foot-tall warrior resides in hopes of seeing him rush forth on a silver stallion with a crystal mane to rescue Korea from the growing turbulence. Unity among the Kumsan boys is broken, however, by the rape of Mansik's mother and her decision to become a prostitute. This is evidenced by the following words spoken to Mansik by Chandol, the biggest boy in the group, when Mansik approaches the other boys to play some time after his mother is raped: "I guess you came here to play with us, but we can't play with you. . . . We all know that your mother fucked a nigger. And you still expect us to play with you? . . . I heard your mother is whoring in Texas. Think, boy, think. How can you expect us to play with a whore's son?" (144).

From this point on, two Kumsan boys, Kijun, who is nicknamed "Toad," and the six-year-old Bong, follow Chandol, and quickly drift toward evil, but one boy, Kangho, the quiet son of the wealthy miller, chooses not to. Originally, he was Mansik's close friend, and although he cannot associate with the son of a whore, Chandol's abuse of Mansik and his discovery that Chandol and Kijun are frequenting the brothels to watch the whores and soldiers engaged in sex offends him. Consequently, Kangho seeks friends in a neighboring village and drifts away from the Kumsan group (190–91).

Mansik, like Ollye, is shunned by his former friends, but, even more disconcerting, Mansik eventually discovers that Chandol and Kijun intend to watch Ollye having sex with her customers. The voyeurism of Chandol and Kijun developed as they frequented the army dumps near the military base and "Texas Town" searching for discarded c-rations, canned fruit, powdered milk, candy, and other assorted goods to eat or share with their families. Eventually they are drawn to "Texas Town," where in the dark of the night they peep through holes in the walls of the flimsy houses to watch whores and their customers at play. When autumn comes, and the river between their village of Kumsan and "Texas Town" is too cold to swim across, they decide to sneak over to Ollye's house and watch what is going on there. Mansik's determination to prevent Chandol and Kijun from peeping on his mother leads to a dramatic finale, when Mansik armed with a makeshift gun confronts a bigger and stronger Chandol and also Kijun in the dead of night as they watch through the cracks of his mother's house. When Chandol attempts to take the gun away, Mansik pulls the trigger, but the gun blows up in his hand, severing his index and middle fingers. Hearing the sound of the gunfire, two soldiers rush out of the house. One cares for Mansik and the other chases after and catches Kijun. Kijun then implicates Chandol (243–50).

Mansik's mother, angered by what has happened, marches to the village, and although it is the middle of the night, wakes the whole town up as she confronts Chandol in the open square. Villagers begin to mumble, "When the Communists come back, they'll kill everybody in West County because we didn't do anything to stop these women from offering themselves to the Yankees" (258). Encouraged by his mother, Chandol denies having been outside Ollye's house, and then Ollye's friend says, "Sure, we—Ollye and me—are dirty whoring bitches as you and your angelic child said, but I see a lot more stinking characters around here who are worse—much worse—than Mansik's mother or any other whore" (260–61). As things heat up, Old Hwang arrives to put an end to the argument, saying, "Go back home Ollye. . . . Don't you think this war has brought enough hate and fighting among us? We have had enough of ill feelings for one generation. Now everybody go home" (262).

Silver Stallion ends on this sad note. The war has divided the village and left many villagers helpless and forced to struggle on their own. Nonetheless, in the final chapter, as Ollye joins the procession southward to avoid the returning communist armies, she is comforted in knowing that she is carrying American goods and a handful of bank bills that will enable her and her two children to survive the arduous trek. In the south, her business friends, who departed before she did, have already promised to help her even though she has told them that she is looking for another kind of work (264–69).

The paradox is that Ollye, through her experiences, has become empowered. Ironically, just the opposite fate has befallen Old Hwang, who was forced to flee the village using the guise of fleeing the communists to hide the fact that he lost all of his family's money speculating in a gold mine. The Hwang family's dominance of Kumsan village has ended, and Old Hwang will have to seek a livelihood in the south, perhaps selling goods in a shop, even though "the most humiliating degradation for a man of knowledge was to become a merchant" (205–6, 243).

Through Old Hwang, Ollye, and Mansik, *Silver Stallion* allows students the opportunity to see the impact of war on three generations of Koreans and explore the loss of innocence among them all. It shows how war assails traditional values and forces individuals confronted by it to adapt or perish. This proves liberating to some, but their new-found freedom seems fraught with danger, and devastating to others, who prove incapable of adjusting to the demise of the old order ravaged by the carnage of warfare.

An equally important issue made evident in Ahn's work worth considering with students in the classroom is the destructive power of marauding armies and armies of occupation on a civilian population. On a grand scale this is most evident in the bombing of the town of Chunchon mentioned earlier, but on a more insidious level it is represented by the raping of Korean women and the establishment of brothels for the soldiers.

A British journalist in Korea during the war observed that UN forces answered any threat posed to them by North Korean or Chinese communist forces with intense artillery or bombing attacks. He then suggested that,

> though these barrages were designed to save the lives of U.N. soldiers and made possible by the incredible productive and material might of the United States, it is certain that they killed civilian men, women, and children indiscriminately and in great numbers, and destroyed all that they had.[17]

Such was the case in the bombing of Chunchon. Consequently, students might ask whether or not there was a less destructive way of forcing a communist withdrawal from this town. Michael Walzer admits that "war necessarily places civilians in danger, that is another aspect of its hellishness,"[18] but soldiers must still seek to minimize the dangers to noncombatants even if it means accepting some personal risks rather than kill innocent people.[19]

The question of rape is equally troubling. As suggested by Ahn in his essay included in this volume (see chapter 10), Ollye's experience was not untypical. *Bengko* soldiers frequently terrorized women in the villages, forcing them nightly to leave their homes to hide from would-be rapists. When the Japanese general Tomoyuki Yamashita was censured by an American military commission for the massive breakdown of discipline among his forces in the Philippines near the end of the war, Douglas MacArthur reproved him by saying: "The soldier, be he friend or foe, is charged with the protection of the weak and unarmed. It is the very essence and reason of his being . . . (a) sacred trust."[20] Ironically, a short time later, General MacArthur struggled to maintain discipline among his own soldiers.

Military commanders are accountable for the actions of their subordinates and must see that standards are set and that everything possible is done to maintain them. Rape is a crime whether or not a war is being fought. Officers in the military must make this clear to their men and ensure that those who violate these standards are punished.[21]

Novel Without a Name

The third work considered here, was written by Duong Thu Huong, and is entitled *Novel Without a Name.* It is based on observations made by the author, who at twenty-one joined a communist youth brigade as a theatrical performer and journeyed to the front to boost the morale of North Vietnamese soldiers. She spent the next seven years there and was one of only three survivors from her group of forty. All four novels completed by Duong depict Vietnamese society in bitter terms. Like Bao Ninh's *The Sorrow of War* (discussed in this volume by Leslie Adams in chapter 6), *Novel Without a Name* reveals the growing despair and disillusionment of North Vietnamese with the war and the terrible toll the war took on combatants and noncombatants alike. Duong's book also seems preoccupied with why individuals joined the military to fight in the Vietnam War and with the methods used by a state to mobilize a populace for battle, two issues that deserve serious consideration by students in the context of any struggle.

The novel is a first-person account of the Vietnam War as witnessed by a North Vietnamese soldier named Quan, who joined the army at eighteen, with his village friends Bien and Luong, full of idealism and eagerness to serve his country. However, the retelling of Quan's story begins ten years later. Luong, who because of his unquestioning loyalty to his superiors and his discipline has risen through the ranks to become a staff officer, takes Quan, now a captain, off the front lines and sends him back to the north to search for their mutual friend, the war-crazed Bian.[22] As he makes his way north, Quan is forced to reflect upon how much he has lost in this struggle, concluding that he is as much a casualty of war as are the war dead.

In his journey Quan encounters other casualties of the war, including an ugly female soldier charged with burying the dead (34–50). Ultimately, Quan manages to find Bien. For six years the young soldier has been locked up in a small cell surrounded by piles of his own excrement and pools of rancid urine, feigning insanity to avoid having to fight in the war. Quan manages to have Bien released into his custody, and afterward, he tries to persuade Bien to return to the village. Although Quan assures Bien that he can secure a medical certificate for him that would discharge him from military service on the grounds of psychological instability, Bien refuses his offer because "the rumors would be awful . . . (and) somewhere in his young peasant's heart he still dreamed of glory" (109). Bien wants to hide somewhere in the vast theater of battle to await the war's end so that he can return to his village with the other survivors and decorate "his obscure, colorless life with trophies of victory" (109). Tragically, although assigned by Quan to a relatively safe duty station, Bien inadvertently steps on a piece of shrapnel. The wound becomes infected, and Bien dies of tetanus (261).

What Quan discovers upon his arrival in his native village before he returns to the front is equally disquieting. The war has taken a terrible toll on those individuals closest to him. His father has grown feeble and spends his time wandering aimlessly in the cemetery, his younger brother has been killed in the war, and his girlfriend, Miss Hoa, who promised to remain faithful to him as he left to join the patriotic struggle, has become pregnant out of wedlock. Because she refused to divulge who the father is, she has been thrown out by her parents and is struggling to survive on her own (116–53).

The members of Quan's family have experienced war as an almost integral part of their lives. Quan's father had joined the war against the French to liberate the country. Although he was engaged in a patriotic struggle, Quan's mother, with a young son and pregnant with another, had felt abandoned by him, while he unjustifiably suspected her of infidelity. His constant quarreling with his wife after his return from war led the young Quan to view him as "a brute, a cruel, hateful presence" (113). Although his mother died of typhoid fever shortly after the return of her husband, Quan believed that her death was due to his father's mistreatment and neglect of her.

After their mother's death, Quan and his younger brother, Quang, were raised by their father, who remained distant from them as did they from him. This breech between Quan and his father becomes irreparable when Quan discovers that his father had been instrumental in coercing Quang to join the army. Quang was brilliant and had placed second in the provincial mathematics competition. When the younger son told his father that he wished to study computer science rather than fight in the war, the war veteran had responded that "in times of war, the future belongs to the combatants" (123).

After learning of his brother's death, Quan confronts his father and tells him that he should have helped Quang avoid having to serve in the war. After all, Quan was risking his life for his country just as his father had. Hadn't their family shed enough blood for the Resistance? He discovers that Quang's fate was sealed by his father at a Party cell meeting when fathers had promised to convince their boys to enlist. Quan's "father's ambition had overcome him: He too had wanted to reserve his place at the victory banquet . . . (and consequently) the whole family (was) thrown into the game of war!" (124).

As already suggested, *Novel Without a Name* considers a range of reasons why North Vietnamese men and women went to war and continued to fight in it. One has already been suggested. For Quang, the reason for enlisting was filial, a response to a plea made by his father; likewise, Bian's decision to continue to fight was to avoid bringing embarrassment to his family. However, *Novel Without a Name* explores other plausible explanations for why North Vietnamese youth marched off to war, all of which Quan ultimately rejects.

It is clear that Quan, Luong, and Bien joined the conflict because of the patriotism and enthusiasm of the moment. On the day they were mobilized, the village committee raised banners praising the young recruits for upholding the traditions of the village ancestors and proclaimed long life to the new combatants for the country and to Marxism-Leninism. Drums were banged, the girls of the village dressed up to honor the departing soldiers, and the families who remained behind swore to hold "a plow in one hand, a rifle in the other" to be worthy of the young ones heading to the front (30).

Vietnamese soldiers also believed that they had an historical mission to protect the country against foreign invaders. They were aware that various ancestors had chosen this same course: "straw hat on his head, a musket slung over his shoulder, a saber in hand, belting out a song of glory" (72). "We joined the army as soon as we reached the age to do our patriotic duty. The blood in our veins is Vietnamese. As long as a foreign invader remains on our soil, we'll fight. That's the way it was for the Tran dynasty against the Mongols, and the same for the Le dynasty against the Ming Chinese invaders" (75). None had forgotten that it was the Vietnamese who had expelled the army of Genghis Khan from Vietnam territory (264).

Perhaps most disturbing to Quan is his realization that after he became calloused by the horrors of war he increasingly marched off to battle motivated only by hatred and a desire to kill. He proclaims that originally he and his friends joined the military seeking solely "to sing songs of glory," but now "we pulled the trigger, we shot, we hacked away, intoxicated by hatred" (72). At times, even when not in battle, Quan finds himself angry and "greedy for carnage. To snap a neck, to plunge a bayonet into flesh, to turn a hail of machine-gun fire on someone" (152).

As Quan loses his own sense of humanity, he becomes more cynical about war and begins to question the forces driving it forward. His cynicism deepens when he overhears a conversation between two high government officials as he journeys by train back toward the front. They casually chat about the Marxist revolution and their recognition that, like love, it is beginning to fade. Consequently, it is essential that there be ideological rectification campaigns to destroy alternative religions and that there be deeper efforts made to erect in their place Marxism as a force that can be used to manipulate the people. These two clearly enjoy their new-found power and view the ordinary Vietnamese as nothing more that puppets to be orchestrated for their personal advantage (153–67). Quan comes to believe that they and their associates are not above creating lies to generate continued patriotism (83–84) or even having relatives spy on relatives to ensure the stability of the state mobilized for war (138).

Quan's views about war are clarified when he interrogates a captured South Vietnamese soldier and seeks to discover why he has joined the enemy's war effort. He is offered a range of answers little different from those that he has come to recognize as the motivating factors behind his and his friends' enlistment. He is told by the soldier that he joined "Out of . . . duty." He "joined . . . for the nationalist ideal." When asked if he joined "For an ideal . . . to defend the beloved motherland," "To fulfill the patriot's duties. . . ,," "To serve the country, swearing to spill the last drop of your blood," he answered yes on all three occasions. When asked who this god is that he is ultimately dying for, the captured soldier professes to have no god in particular. This amuses Quan, who tells him that the North Vietnamese god is Marx. "He's got a pug nose, blue eyes, and a shaggy beard." Perhaps, suggests Quan, we could bring an end to war simply by agreeing to worship one god and it would be best if he was one of no real significance. Then nobody would think of killing someone over such a lousy god (238–46).

Quan survives the war, but he and the world he once knew have been cruelly transformed by it. His brother, Quang, and close friend, Bien, are dead. He has grown to despise his father and his one-time friend Luong because both were too willing to sacrifice others for the glory of war, and there is no possibility of reconciliation with Miss Hoa. More important, having witnessed and participated in so much bloodshed, he wonders whether he has retained any innate humanity.

Of all the works considered here in this paper, Huong's *Novel Without a Name* is clearly the most disjointed. It seems to lack a beginning, a middle, or an end, and the novel wanders as does Quan between fighting pitched battles on the front and launching guerrilla attacks in the rear. One struggles to differentiate the Vietnam at war from the Vietnam supposedly immune from it.

Perhaps it is appropriate to end with such a work because during the Vietnam conflict the normal rules of warfare were tested as they never had been before, as were the commitments of combatants to practice moral judgment when engaging the enemy. This was inevitable given the heavy reliance of the North Vietnamese and Vietcong on guerrilla warfare, which made it increasingly difficult to define the battlefield and to differentiate the combatant from the noncombatant.

One would need to go beyond the parameters of this chapter to explore the reasons for and justification of the escalation of violence directed against civilians during the Vietnam War by all participants in the conflict.[23] Nonetheless, the sheer carnage of this struggle and its all too frequent misdirection toward the civilian populace leads one to hope that through the thoughtful study of literature and film, such as those discussed here, students will become more engaged in reflecting upon the impact of war on individuals and the need to use moral judgment in war time and consider wartime crimes against humanity.

Notes

1. Leo Tolstoy, *War and Peace,* trans. Louise and Aylmer Maude (New York: Simon and Schuster, 1942), p. 865.

2. Michael Walzer, *Just and Unjust Wars,* 2nd ed. (New York: Basic Books, 1977), p. 46.

3. Tolstoy, *War and Peace,* p. 864.

4. The director Kobayashi's experiences during the war in many ways parallel those of the key figure, Kaji, in the film. As a young intellectual who in 1941 completed a college education focused on philosophy and Oriental art at Waseda University, Kobayashi, though critical of the war, was drafted in January 1942. He served first in Manchuria and then, in 1944, was transferred to the Ryukyu Islands until the war ended. He remained in a detention camp in Okinawa for a full year before being allowed in November 1946 to return to Japan. In a later interview with Joan Mellen, Kobayashi stated:

> I should add that I was in the army for six years. This experience heightened my social consciousness. During those six years I never became an officer. In fact I withheld myself from becoming an officer. I was really a rank-and-file soldier. I had a strong conviction that I must resist authoritarian pressure. I was wholly against the power which bore down on us and I was against the war itself. I still think that I was able to make *Ningen no Joken* because I had voluntarily refused to become an officer. I was the protagonist and I felt this identification very strongly. The life the hero leads was much the same life I lived as a soldier.

See Joan Mellen, *Voices from the Japanese Cinema* (New York: Liveright, 1975), p. 138, and Audie Bock, *Japanese Film Directors* (Tokyo: Kodansha, 1978), p. 248.

5. The parallels with Shohei Ooka's depiction in his book *Fires on the Plain* (Tokyo: Charles E. Tuttle, 1967) of the Japanese army in disarray in the Philippines at the end of the Pacific War are striking.

6. Mellen, *Voices from the Japanese Cinema,* p. 138.

7. Bock, *Japanese Film Directors,* p. 252.

8. Mellen, *Voices from the Japanese Cinema,* p. 148.

9. Walzer, *Just and Unjust Wars,* p. 31.

10. Ibid., pp. 29–33.

11. In lectures presented to participants of the NEH Summer Institute "American Wars in Asia: A Cultural Approach" at the University of Montana on July 6–7, 1995, Ahn Junghyo reflected upon his personal experience during the Korean War. When the war erupted in June 1950, Ahn's family sought refuge in the town of Sosa, fifty miles southwest of Seoul. At the time, he was only nine years old, and the novel *Silver Stallion* is, in part, drawn from his boyhood recollections. Ahn drafted his book in English and completed it during his third year of college at Sogang Jesuit University. However, it was not accepted for publication until twenty-seven years later, when he produced a Korean translation from the English text. In 1990, *Silver Stallion* was finally published in English and afterward was made into a popular Korean movie. This analysis focuses on the book rather than the film, which takes quite a few liberties with the text.

12. Junghyo Ahn, *Silver Stallion* (New York: Soho, 1990), pp. 5–6.

13. Numbers in parentheses in the section below refer to page numbers in Ahn, *Silver Stallion,* unless otherwise indicated.

14. Walzer, *Just and Unjust Wars,* p. 134.

15. Ahn lecture, July 6–7, 1995; Ahn, *Silver Stallion,* pp. 67–68.

16. See William Golding, *Lord of the Flies* (Jackson Heights, NY: Aeonian Press, 1954).

17. Cited in Walzer, *Just and Unjust Wars,* p. 54.

18. Ibid., p. 156.

19. Ibid., pp. 304–6, 316–17.

20. Quoted in ibid., p. 317, from A. J. Barker, *Yamashita* (New York, 1973), pp. 157–58.

21. Walzer, *Just and Unjust Wars,* pp. 316–317.

22. Duong Thu Huong, *Novel Without a Name*, trans. Phan Huy Duong and Nina McPherson (New York: William Morrow, 1995), pp. 27–29. Numbers in parentheses in this section refer to page numbers in this book, unless otherwise indicated.

23. A good place to start such an inquiry is Walzer, *Just and Unjust Wars,* pp. 188–96, 319–22.

Part III

Remembering

8

My Pacific War Revisited*

Merrel Clubb

Every war is unique for one who experiences its battles at first hand, and for me that war took place far out in the Pacific Ocean beginning December 7, 1941, and ending, at least officially, August 14, 1945. All other wars are history or history in the making. I knew at the time a "war" was going on in Europe, but it was irrelevant and of no consequence to me. Out in the Pacific somewhere, I heard vaguely of V-E Day celebrations back in the States, but they signified nothing. My war was still going on. And my war is still going on more than fifty years later.

I recorded my wartime experiences in over 150 letters to my parents in Stillwater, Oklahoma, the first on January 31, 1943, the day I left home on the train to enter a U.S. Naval Reserve Midshipman School, the last on April 20, 1946, a few days before I left a hospital at a Naval Separation Center in Memphis, Tennessee. I knew that my mother had saved the letters for me, but for some reason I ignored them for over forty years.

A year or so before I retired from the academic world in 1986, I came across the small round top trunk containing my war letters and read them for the first time. As I read and re-read, I took a long journey back into a past I had almost completely forgotten, and I began to recall the young man who went to war and wrote the letters.

I remembered the day the Japanese bombs exploded in Stillwater. Sunday, December 7, 1941, was a cold, cloudy day, when shouts outside the house of "EXTRA, EXTRA, READ ALL ABOUT IT," sent us all to the radio in the dining room of the large white house on Duck Street where we could listen to the

---

*This chapter is adapted from *A Life Disturbed: My Pacific War Revisited.* I have resisted all impulses to edit the letters significantly; therefore they appear for the most part—a few are shortened for inclusion here—just as I wrote them more than fifty years ago.

news about the bombing of Pearl Harbor: my mother and father, my two younger brothers, my grandmother, and my grandfather.

Our three-story house, formerly a sorority house with a big screened-in sleeping porch, a rabbit warren of bedrooms, two parlors, formal dining room, had been for me a home overflowing with books, with music, Caruso singing from old 78–speed records, my father playing Beethoven, Chopin, Mozart on the grand piano far into the night, my brother Will practicing the violin or oboe, Roger learning the cello, and I the piano.

At the time the Japanese bombed Pearl Harbor, I had been attending Oklahoma A & M College for almost three and a half years, at first majoring in English, later changing to mathematics and philosophy. My father had hoped I could attend Yale, but the Depression had put that out of the question. A & M, however, was a surprisingly good college, with a strong liberal arts program and many first rate, mostly young teachers with degrees from the best graduate schools in the country, who taught a wide variety of often yearlong courses in the arts, literature, philosophy, mathematics, and the sciences. And since my father was a member of the faculty, I came to know many of the college faculty in a social way, and some became personal friends.

All in all, I had been living a happy, stimulating intellectual and artistic life, now interrupted on that "day of infamy," gray and raw in Stillwater. I knew that the progression of my life was irrevocably changed.

Soon after the attack on Pearl Harbor the draft and patriotism began to take their toll in Stillwater, most of my acquaintances and friends drafted or "joining up" and leaving for military camps and bases scattered throughout the country. My father, an ardent pacifist and against all wars, including this one, which he blamed President Roosevelt for getting us into, hoped I would become a conscientious objector, though he never really pressured me. However, I could not see myself in a conscientious objectors' camp for the duration, because, as I put it at the time, I was really a coward at heart—I valued the good feelings of my peers too much.

So, on April 23, 1942, in Oklahoma City, I joined the navy—the navy because I had read *All Quiet on the Western Front* and wanted no part of trench warfare. "No muddy foxholes for me," I remember writing my closest friend at Quantico.

I signed up for the navy's V-7 Officer Training Program, which meant that after graduating from college in January 1943, I would attend a midshipman school for four months on the campus of Notre Dame University, and then become an ensign—a ninety-day wonder, I learned later.

On the train to Chicago and South Bend, I remember thinking, "What am I doing here? Where am I going?" I could hardly believe what was happening. I had not joined the navy out of any feeling of patriotism. I had no sense of what I would be fighting for. I did not hate the Germans; I did not hate the Japanese; I did not believe in war; it simply made no sense to me. What was it to me after I was killed? I wondered how I could go against everything society and my parents had taught me. How would I react to combat? To fear? To death? Would I really be able to kill?

After receiving my commission at the end of April and after a short tour of duty in San Francisco's International Settlement as a Shore Patrol Officer, I received orders in July assigning me to the Ninth A.T.C. [amphibious training core] as a Naval Gunfire Liaison Officer (NGLO.) I had no idea then of what a naval gunfire liaison officer was, but it was not long before I moved from San Francisco to Fort Ord where I became attached to the Second Battalion of the Eighty-seventh Mountain Infantry. There I found that I was apprenticed to an "experienced" battalion NGLO recently returned from the Attu campaign and that I would learn the rudiments of a shore fire control officer's duties while under fire in the battle for Kiska in the Aleutian Islands.

I remember wondering at the great wisdom of the military. It had gone to huge expense to train me in naval warfare (seamanship, naval gunnery, navigation) only to send me into battle with an army combat unit with no training in shore fire control procedures and no preparation whatsoever for land warfare, that is, into a situation where training and preparation could make the difference between life and death. And it was assumed at the time that one in five of us in the assault waves going ashore on Kiska would be dead by the end of the fight.

Fortunately, the battle for Kiska turned out to be a fiasco. Thirty-five thousand American and Canadian troops, supported by hundreds of ships, stormed ashore on Kiska only to discover that some 6,500 Japanese (not the 10,000 we had expected) had been evacuated about three weeks earlier.

Nevertheless, for me, that initial battle experience was as real as any I endured later on Makin, Guam, or Iwo Jima. I *believed* the Japanese defenders were there—all 10,000 of them—and they were there, for a time. And, too, the battle was a real one for the soldiers in the platoons who fired upon each other in the fog, and for those who became casualties, the twenty-four soldiers who were killed by their own fire and the four killed by booby traps or mines, as well as the fifty wounded by both.

Eventually, in the course of preparations for landing with the army on Butaritari in the Makin Atoll, a hundred miles north of Tarawa in the Gilbert Islands, I did learn what the job of a naval gunfire liaison officer was all about: In a nutshell—and oversimplified—the members of a naval gunfire liaison team went ashore with the troops in an early assault wave, set up radio contact with a destroyer or cruiser lying off shore, and called down and spotted naval gunfire onto targets designated by the battalion commander. But again I received no systematic training in land-warfare—though I must say I hardly needed training in digging foxholes; the skill just seemed to come naturally. Still, I landed on Makin under fairly heavy fire knowing nothing of battle tactics and having never fired anything but a .22 rifle and a beebee gun.

By the time the battle for Guam came around, however, I had learned too much about land warfare. For that operation, I was attached to the Second Battalion, Fourth Marines which along with the Twenty-second Marines formed the new First Provisional Marine Brigade on Guadalcanal, our staging area for Guam. We landed on Guam the morning of July 21, 1944, and I wrote my parents from aboard an LST [landing ship tank] the night before:

July 20, 1944

Tomorrow is the day! There are so many things I want to say, and I can't think of a thing. This one, [the battle] I fear, will be full sized and I should have plenty of time for thought amidst bursting shells. In my pack are: a book of poetry, a Galsworthy novel, one of Jane Austins's, and Conrad's *Lord Jim.*

I see in the news that Arne Anderson ran the mile in 4:01.6! That is going!

The show is within sight now—the flashes of gunfire over the horizon.

I asked a man today what he was fighting for. He didn't know, being a professional marine. Then I asked him why he hates the Japs. "Because they are a different color, speak a different language, and because I can't understand them." He's honest anyway.

I'm about ready to give it all up and come home. The usual small signs of nervousness and anticipation before battle are becoming evident in everyone now. The night before is of particular interest to me. One person reads, one sleeps, another worries about the heat, another walks around drinking coffee; some talk, pick up this, drop that; and my mind wanders so I can hardly write words, much less anything sensible. My usual reaction is to get sleepy and then not be able to sleep, but here's to try anyway.

[Back on Oahu]
August 15, 1944

Now the full story can be told. The morning of the landing I got up about 5:00, ate a good breakfast and went outside to look at the Island. The sun was coming up in a red haze over an island covered with smoke and dust. Ships were pounding away at it from all around us, but there was no fire coming from the island. It looked peaceful and beautiful amidst everything.

About 7:15 word came to get into our tractors (amphibious) and at 7:30 we were milling around out in the water. I was calm and felt little fear at first. Things moved pretty fast then. The naval gunfire became heavier, and we moved in closer to the beach where the Brigade was to land about 2000 yards south of the Orote Peninsula, near the town of Agat. I sat on a cartridge case in the bottom of the tractor, and fear took more and more hold of me. Then I heard we were receiving fire from the beach, and I thought of the slaughter that had taken place on the beaches of Saipan. Mortars made direct hits on some of the tractors both to the right and left of us while others were riddled with bullets. However, my whole battalion was lucky, for we got onto the beach with almost no tractor casualties—we had hit a blind spot in the fire. We were supposed to go quite a ways inland before disembarking, but the wreckage on the beach was so dense that we had to get out just at the water's edge. You have no doubt seen pictures of the tractors and know that one must climb from inside up onto the side and jump down in order to get out of them. Well, you have never seen anyone get out faster than I did. I literally rolled out and fell flat on my belly behind a coconut tree expecting any minute a grenade to go off in the tractor or a burst of bullets. A good friend of mine was killed when he stood up to get out. I started looking around for someone I knew and saw no one. My men were in the boat wave behind me and I had to find them and the Command Post. Finally, I spotted one of the C.P. officers and eventually found the C.P., which was about 50 yards from the beach. My men turned up there, too. The next hour I spent hugging a coconut tree scared to death. I seemed to become more and more afraid and could not seem to get control of myself. There was sporadic fire going on around us, and then mortar shells started dropping in the water. I watched the splashes hunting back and forth and creeping nearer. But the thought of them didn't bother me much. I was in the grip of some unreasoning fear which I couldn't shake off. Finally, the order came for us to move forward, and I had to lead my men in two columns across an open rice paddy, a small river (or creek) and across another open field before reaching the next C.P., a distance of less than a mile. I stood at the edge of the rice paddy frozen: I could hear, I could *feel* the bullets swish, swishing through the waist-tall grass. I was terribly alone facing that field, perhaps a test of who I was. And only I, somehow, could make the decision to move my feet rooted into the ground. I wondered how the bullet would feel, how it would feel to die. Dying seemed so futile. Finally, after what seemed like hours, but I am sure was only seconds, with a tremendous effort I moved my feet and stepped forward into the paths of the bullets, my skin tensing all over my body as I could almost feel the bullets splatting against me. At first I ran a little, turned and ducked, zig-zagged, but was so exhausted I finally just staggered along and "to hell with it." I remember as I stumbled on (there is nothing worse for walking, much less running, than a dry, fissured rice paddy) thinking, with no little shame, of Storm, my Sergeant, a tall, strong, twenty-year-old, blonde Texan, struggling along, sweating, with the bulky 85 pound radio wobbling on his back—I, with my 35 pound pack barely able to walk. The last 200 yards I stumbled and fell down every few feet—even crawled on my hands and knees. In less than a mile, I have never been so exhausted in my life. I finally fell headfirst into a small shell hole near the C.P., unable to move a step farther.

By this time, wounded were coming back from the front lines only a short distance ahead of us, walking or carried. Boy! did I envy them. I saw one boy, the one who did that cartoon I sent you, going back to the beach with a shell fragment in his leg. He wasn't hurt too badly, and the whole lousy business was over for him in less than two hours.

All hell was breaking loose by the time my radio was set up. We were near a tree in the complete open and in full view of the mountains and ridges rising above us. We could watch one of our companies trying to take the top of a ridge not more than 5 or 600 yards away from us. Mortars shells were falling all around us and clouds of bullets were in the air. I could see the mortars and grenades falling on the boys on the ridge bouncing them around. They would make a dive for the spot where a mortar shell had just fallen in order to get out of the path of the next one as it searched. You could actually see grenades being tossed back and forth over the ridge. After about an hour and a half a series of *banzai* attacks took place in plain view. Five or six Japanese at a time would run over the ridge heading straight for our C.P., waving their swords and shouting. Of course they were mowed down, but there were a lot of people hacked up. Practically every one in the C.P. was shooting—even my own men, and I had given explicit orders not to shoot except in self-defense. It was about this time that I finally gained control over my fear. I've never had such an experience.

That afternoon we were able to move quite a way up the mountain and to dig in for the night. During the night there was a lot of shooting and a tank attack which was stopped. And then I pulled about my most foolish trick. Bullets were flying thick and fast all through the C.P. when I got a call that I was wanted on a telephone about 50 yards away. Well, I went, but God helps drunks and fools. In the front line situations everything that moves is fair game.

Every C.P. I've ever had was under more or less constant fire of some sort even though we might be in a rest area. That meant foxholes every night. And it rained every night. And it poured every day. One evening at 6:30 *dark*, we received orders to move up to help another battalion. That meant moving through hundreds of our own men who, would shoot at anything at night, and meant digging in after dark with a counter-attack threatening to break any second. In single column the entire battalion moved up through large areas of Marines without being detected. What an experience: the only sound as we started out was the cocking of rifles up and down the line, the smell of rotting dead, and then up on a hill a thousand men silently digging holes in the middle of the night, now and then the clatter of a shovel and a muffled curse. We sweat, we dug with shovels, helmets, even our hands, while the moon looked quietly down on us.

It was the brigade which took Orote Peninsula and my battalion met much of the resistance. For *three days* I hugged a tree, rain and sun intermittently pouring down. First nearly frozen, next almost passing out from the heat! Men were hit right next to me. Bullets, explosive bullets, were everywhere. Now and then there would be a lull, but just as we would start to cook coffee, they would start again. During one of these lulls, the Executive Officer of our regiment, Lt. Colonel Puller, the brother of Chesty Puller of Guadalcanal fame, was killed by a stray bullet, leaving no doubt in our minds that everyone is vulnerable. I watched truck loads of dead Americans piled up like cord wood pass by every day, and when we finally moved up I saw piles of dead and rotting Japanese. We use good psychology there. The Japs are allowed to lie and rot for 5 or 6 days in the hot sun. It makes them horrible, stinking, rotten; and the feeling is easily transferred to the living; while our dead are immediately covered up with something and are taken to the cemetery as soon as possible. Thus, we never see how rotten we ourselves could be when allowed to rot. I can think of only a few instances where I've come across really "ripe" Americans.

After a few days of being pinned down, the C.P. was able to move up farther forward. As we walked along the littered road, we came under artillery fire, and we all dived into the ditches beside the road each of us struggling to get under someone else and thus have the shelter of another's body. It is sickening what one will do out of fear and to stay alive. Later we stopped at what had been the front lines the night before. Battle aftermath has always fascinated me and it was particularly interesting that morning, for there had been a terrific fight and heavy casualties, and the company that had caught most of it had remained there to be in reserve. There was no shade, and two-man foxholes about a foot and a half deep had been uniformly dug side by side in the blood-red ground: broiling heat, men covered with red dirt sitting, staring dumbly, or lying down sick at their stomachs, and silence. I felt ashamed to look them in their faces. A few covered dead were waiting to be picked up, and now and then a little machine gun fire or artillery could be heard in the distance.

From there we moved toward the end of the peninsula with no resistance except snipers. Beside one blockhouse I came upon 11 dead Japanese: one without a head, another with his guts spilled out in his hands, another with a foot and an arm blown off, another with an empty skull, another with no marks except a small hole just over his ear. All of their clothes had been blown off. I stood looking at that heap of clay when the thought came to me that I should be sick at my stomach, but I pushed it out of my mind and started imprinting the picture indelibly in my mind. Then the thought came to my mind: Am I responsible for this carnage? I had been spotting fire from the cruiser onto these blockhouses.

I walked farther past the bodies and looked down upon a leg, still with legging and two-toed shoe, lying there in the middle of the trail—nothing else. What a strange sight! It had been blown off just above the knee, and the owner was nowhere around.

* * *

As I think back on Guam, I remember the anger I felt when, my support ship having departed for parts unknown after we took Orote Peninsula, I realized there was no one to detach me from my unit. My function as NGLO was over, but I continued on with my battalion as the brigade joined with the Third Marine Division to fight our way for days to the northern tip of the island. I had nothing to do except try to stay dry, and alive. Yet, as I think back, I can see I had feelings on Guam that even if I had been detached I could not have deserted my unit or my battalion commander while the battle was still going on, whatever use I might not have been. Oddly, perhaps not so oddly, when I am asked today if I am a veteran and of what service, I think of myself as having been more a marine than a navy officer during the war. This feeling, which developed during maneuvers with the Fourth Marines in the Solomon Islands and the fighting on Guam, was reinforced by my experiences with the Ninth Marines of the Third Division on Iwo Jima. I wrote to my parents:

February 19, 1945

Here it is again as you will have guessed by the time this reaches you. The last three letters of this sort have completely drained me and I have practically nothing to say.

We land on Iwo Jima, probably day after tomorrow. This time I have no feelings at all. I know what to expect and have only an intense fear, disgust, and hate for the next few days. Never in my life have I hated so much the thought of something I knew that I would have to do. It is an entirely new emotion, although the beginnings of it were apparent in the last operation. The only bright spot, if it may be termed bright, is that the tremendous slaughter will take place in only a *few* days. Also, since I am a regimental gunfire officer this time, I should be well back behind the front lines instead of virtually in them as was often the case when I was attached to a battalion.

The food on this ship is of the best, but living conditions are pretty bad—some 80 of us in a hold below the main deck. It is hot as Hades, and water is rationed, though I suppose I shouldn't complain on that score. I do bathe every day.

I'm about half way through my book on psychoanalysis. It is a good one, and I think I'll take it ashore so that I may sit in my foxhole and watch for the immediate beginnings of a neurosis.

Heigh-ho! and they say the weather will be just about cool enough for pig-sticking. My love to you all and may we see each other soon.

February 28, 1945

As you have probably guessed by now, I am on Iwo Jima and damn sick of it. It is by far the worst fight of the Pacific war. They've run into everything in the book, and a lot of people are being hurt. It shouldn't last much longer, and we may not even be in the lines again, being in reserve now.

My Regiment didn't land until after the 4th or 5th day, so we were spared a lot of hell. Also being with a regimental headquarters, I'm much farther back from the front lines; so the odds are better anyway. We went ashore in landing craft as usual, but this time not under fire. The beach became steep almost immediately, rising up above us. The sand, or ash, was so loose we sank in over our ankles and had to claw our way up, sliding back almost as far as we moved forward. It must have been absolute hell on D-Day under the horrendous fire. Thank God I missed that.

The first night I spent in a deserted bunker near the first airfield with a few of the regimental officers, bouncing to an occasional artillery or mortar explosion, and a flood of memories came back. In the morning my Regiment, the 9th, moved into the lines between the Fifth and the Fourth Divisions to assault airfield #2. Things were pretty rough for a while, but now we are getting a little rest.

I'll write again as soon as I'm off the island, though the letters I write later on will reach you before this in all probability.

March 4, 1945

Nine days of hell! And when will it end? Such a well-planned and perfect defense has never been run into in this war. According to war correspondents who have been also in the European Theater, the various defense lines in Europe were child's play compared to this. Iwo is six square miles of pill boxes, block-houses, and caves.

I am well enough, though horribly tired of everything and particularly of artillery fire popping around close day in and night out. My helmet saved me the other day when a shell fragment hit me and dented it way in—and that was when I was back visiting *Division* Headquarters. There are Japanese within 10 yards of us right now in caves, but they won't come out. The other day in a different C.P. an interpreter tried to coax some out of a hole in a hill nearby, but they, some 30, refused, saying that at 11:00 that night they would *banzai*. Of course everyone took it as a joke, but at 11:10 P.M. the whole side of the hill 20 feet away blew up and came down on us when they tried to make an opening. Some ran out but were mowed down by guards. Boulders four feet in diameter flew through the air, 50 gallon drums of water appeared a hundred yards away, and our tent was blown down and half buried. I still don't understand how all of us in the tent got out alive, much less uninjured. I was asleep at the time and I remember that the first thing that passed through my mind was what I had read about the shock of being blown up and buried as a cause for hysteria neurosis. A terrific bedlam was all around, cries for help, moans of the hurt, commands, "get your gun," "where's my helmet?" went up. Some 25 or 30 were casualties though no one was killed. And then the artillery shells started falling—

This is Peleliu, Tarawa, and Saipan all rolled into one and ten times worse, 60-80,000 men on six square miles of land bent on slaughtering each other. At any rate, those who know rate the Japanese commander as a great military genius. A few more days should see me back aboard ship and a couple of months should see me in Pearl.

March 8, 1945

One of the things I have dreaded most smote me full in the face the other night. There are six officers (3 naval, 3 marine) and some 40 men attached to three battalions and under my indirect command. It fell to my lot (I was ordered by Division) to *order* one of the naval officers up to the front to actually spot fire while another would take his place at the battalion C.P. The particular Ensign who was to go was a puppy dog sort of a boy and had come to rely pretty much on me to keep him from falling apart—a sort of Freudian transference of the superego. It was horrible telling him, after taking an hour to get up my courage, and the way he took it was heartbreaking. He was practically begging for his life (in reality he was, too, for three spotters had been hit just ahead of him, two dead); I couldn't stand it and finally told him to forget it and to hell with Division. I finally managed to patch things up without directly disobeying orders—a serious offense, by the way.

March 11, 1945

. . . The island should be secured today or tomorrow. Our C.P. has not been under fire for a couple of days, and as a result reassurance and relief is so gratifying that I find myself feeling (not thinking!) that I could go through another operation with ease. However, one close air burst (artillery) completely flattens me, and the whole range of associations flash upon me, and I am as weak as though I had gone through the initial phases of a landing all over again. . .

March 18, 1945

The battle is over! Two days ago the "Admurl" said the island was secured, but men still die, are still maimed, and will continue to die for months to come. The formal battle is over, but in this most perfect of defenses, the Japanese have cave networks that reach the proportions of mines, different levels and every thing, from which they can issue forth at any time. Can you imagine that several hundred Japanese can still hide in six square miles, and in those six miles there are some 100,000 troops?

This has been by far the easiest operation on me I have been through. I have been scared at times when artillery was dropping around, but Regimental Head-quarters is pretty far behind the lines, even though there was one time when our Regimental C.P. was *ahead* of the Battalion C.P.'s and there weren't any front lines as such at all. Our C.P. that was blown up was rimmed with cliffs a few hundred yards away and we were under intermittent gunfire most of the time, but one gets used to a few bullets, even to 300mm mortar shells chugging through the air like locomotives. There's a saying about artillery and mortar shells: if you hear them, don't worry; if you don't, there's no worry—or something like that.

For toilet facilities at that C.P. there were several 50 gallon oil drums set up in a row with boards across them for seats. For several days, every time I would get settled to let nature take its course, zip, zip, the snipers in the cliffs (i.e., in the caves) would fire away; then the mad scramble of all of us there to foxholes as we pulled up our pants. The snipers must have had a few laughs.

Mainly though, the whole business is just a dull, boring job.

March 22, 1945

The fighting is over except for patrolling and mopping up. I am just being lazy waiting to get off the island, reading a few Saki short stories (they are fun) and some Houseman poems. The latter bring up emotions of by-gone cleanliness and happiness. Right now all I want to do is sun by the side of the road and watch the world go by. I have an intense craving to hear birds sing, bees buzzing, and to smell flowers and fresh-cut grass. I am hatefully tired of islands, airplanes, Marine camps, masses of men.

Up behind the front lines a bird used to chirp its mating call at sundown for several evenings. And his call was answered from amidst the desolation. It was beautiful, a sign maybe that there still remained a God somewhere. Only one evening, there was no answering chirp. Bullets and shrapnel were thick in the air. We gathered up hands full of shrapnel out of our foxholes in the morning where it had fallen spent during the night.

Incidentally, ask me, when I'm back, about sending unprepared boys to the front! One example for now. Our casualties have been terrible, some companies almost a hundred percent. Recently, our replacements haven't even finished boot camp. One of my spotters told me that when a young boy was handed a flame thrower and told to get on to that pillbox, he exclaimed, "But, Sarge, how do I work this thing?"

* * *

Reading my letters from the war so long after I wrote them has forced me to think about my personal war, and war, from many different perspectives. Sometimes I have had the strange feeling that I went to war without going to war. I never saw a Japanese soldier face to face in the heat of battle; I was never wounded. On Guam, on Iwo Jima, I learned a tremendous respect for the men, and boys, Japanese as well as Americans, who met in the front lines, bent on killing.

The First Provisional Marine Brigade received the Navy Unit Commendation "For outstanding heroism in action against enemy Japanese forces during the invasion of Guam," especially for its actions in taking heavily defended Orote Peninsula. And the Fifth Amphibious Corps received the Presidential Unit Citation "For extraordinary heroism in action during the seizure of enemy Japanese-held Iwo Jima." The latter citation continues: "By their individual acts of heroism and their unfailing teamwork, these gallant officers and men fought against their own battle-fatigue and shock to advance in the face of the enemy's fanatical resistance; they charged each strong point, one by one, blasting out the hidden Japanese troops or sealing them in. . ."

Again I am reminded of what I think of as "relativity" in war: For me, Kiska (with no Japanese defenders) had been a real battle, Makin (with its several hundred American and Japanese dead) as gut wrenching as Tarawa (with its many thousands). And when I look back on Guam and Iwo Jima, I know it was not the Brigade or the Fifth Corps that really won the Navy and Presidential citations. Although the upper echelons served their important functions, it was primarily the officers and men at the company and platoon level, the men in direct contact with the enemy, who really won those citations. Now well into my seventies, I have two long-time friends, both veterans of World War II: Bernie, once an army major, and Andy, a front-line marine corporal who was wounded on Guam and later landed with the Twenty-first Regiment of the Third Marine Division on Iwo Jima. I met Bernie in Honolulu during the war shortly after I returned from Makin and Andy sometime in the 1960s at a Modern Language Association meeting. Over the years the three of us have corresponded and met off and on at national and regional MLA meetings, in the course of which we eventually end up together drinking and talking in one of our hotel rooms. Inevitably, we engage in boozy wartime reminiscences, usually old songs and stories it would be better to forget. In these and other war contexts, Bernie speaking to me, or to Andy, or to both of us has frequently made remarks to the effect that people don't know what war really is like "as WE do." —And this when the closest Bernie ever came to the war was keeping track of Japanese Americans on Oahu and one short tour of duty on Guam after it was retaken from the Japanese.

Of course, Bernie *is* a veteran and spent some four years in the army most of the time out of the States, and he knows wartime in ways no serviceman or woman who never left the States during the war can possibly know it. Yet he has no notion of what war really is like in the same way I do. Nor do I know what war really is like in the same way as our friend Andy who was regularly in the true front lines in personal contact with the enemy. At various times I was under heavy, sometimes, constant artillery and mortar barrages, as well as machine gun, and rifle fire. I underwent *banzai* and counter-attacks, I was virtually blown up on Iwo Jima. But my war experience cannot compare with that of the individual front-line platoon or squad leader and rifleman, blowing up bunkers, flame throwing pill boxes, killing in close proximity, often in hand-to-hand fighting. Killing at a distance, as when calling fire down from a destroyer or a cruiser on pill boxes or concentrations of men is not killing up close where you see, even feel the man or men you kill. I was lucky. I remember the captain of the Canon Company the morning after he knifed to death one of his own men in hand-to-hand fighting during the *banzai* attack on Makin—he was no more than thirty yards or so away from me, but that distance may as well have been a mile in terms of our individual experiences that night. And I will never forget the first day on Guam hearing the bullets whispering by as I lay safely in a crater at the battalion C.P. and watched the Japanese *banzai* over the ridge five hundred yards or so away, some waving swords, others stabbing with bayonets, others tossing grenades—and the marines engaging them in hand-to-hand fighting, killing them as they themselves were being killed on the side of that ridge. So close, yet so far away from those of us in the C.P.

There is nothing novel in the observation that only a very small minority of the men in uniform during World War II ever saw combat and that even a smaller minority ever saw it in its essence, at the cutting edge of the front lines. But veterans and civilians often forget that the experiences of war are relative: a few yards behind the front lines is not the same as *in* the front lines, and the difference increases exponentially, echelon after echelon, from company C.P. to battalion, to regimental, to division, to corps headquarters on a ship, and on to Hawaii, and finally to the mainland United States.

After reading and re-reading my letters from the war, after reliving the war, and after reflecting on my wartime experiences, I find that my memories of the war, both those I have retained over the years and those that have come back to me as a result of reading my letters are strangely selective. I remember very few details of my leaves at home during the war—it is almost as though I never went home. And in spite of my struggles to recall all the details, there are huge blanks in the chronology of my experiences during the battles of Makin, Guam, Iwo Jima. Some details I remember vividly, but others simply are not there.

For reasons I do not understand, I can barely remember reports of the bombs dropping on Hiroshima and Nagasaki ending the war while I was in San Diego, events which, I thought at the time, almost certainly saved my life, as well as the lives of thousand upon thousands of the other young men destined to land on the main islands of Japan—and, ironically, the lives of thousands upon thousands of the Japanese destined to oppose those landings. I have only the vaguest memory of V-J Day, and none of any celebrations or parades in San Diego.

My views about war are essentially the same as they were when I went to war, only reinforced by my own experiences in the war and now by a lifetime observing latter-day wars. I still see no sense in war—although I am aware of complexities such a statement seems to ignore. There may be, and probably are, valid reasons for fighting a war, but there are few wars that have been fought for those reasons. Most wars are fought for wrong reasons, are unnecessary and a terrible waste of human life: World War I, World War II, the Korean War, the Viet Nam War, the Persian Gulf war, and other recent "wars" in the Falkland Islands, in Grenada, in Panama. I am not particularly proud of participating in World War II; it was something I could not escape.

Perhaps my views about war now, as then, are overly simplistic, but certainly no more simplistic than those of the average veteran of World War II today—only different.

I was amused some time ago when I read a statement by a prominent writer in a popular national magazine (*Newsweek* 11 January 1993, 26): "Not once in the years 1941–1945 did I hear a single American inveigh against the war." And five pages later another well-known writer: "I heard no soldier express a patriotic sentiment, rather the reverse . . ."

Both statements may represent their authors' beliefs, but neither is fully accurate. There was, of course, a sizable minority of servicemen (not to mention civilians) in the United States, perhaps even a small majority overseas in the Pacific, who at the time were not particularly patriotic, who cursed the war, who wondered what the hell they were doing on those godforsaken islands out there—I was one, and I knew many, as my letters show. Nevertheless, probably most veterans now would agree with the first statement.

For those veterans who look back, often through rose-colored glasses, to the "good old days," on TV or in oral histories, in Sunday supplements, in magazines, in books, World War II was the "good war," the last good war we can all be proud of—and this in spite of the experiences of many to the contrary and of books documenting its evils, that WWII was not a good war.

Many veterans who lived the horrors of the war felt sustained by their faith in the validity of the war, that the war was a just war. What sustained others was a sense of belonging, a sense of family, of comradeship, of esprit de corps. But I had no faith in the justness of the war, no notion of what I was fighting for. And my wartime job as naval gunfire liaison officer did not allow me a "family"—though I wish it had. When I was assigned to an army or marine unit for amphibious landings and joined one of those units, all the officers and men had been training together for months, even years, had become comrades, members of a family. I was an outsider, a guest, joining them for the occasion—I barely knew any of my associates when I landed on the beaches, even the members of my own radio teams. I was alone.

Many veterans of the war in the Pacific when they write and talk about the war seem to have a vested interest in justifying their participation in the war. They continue to romanticize, to sentimentalize, to glorify the war and their war experiences: Everyone "believed" in the war. It was a "transcendent experience." It was "the high point" of one's life and everything after "anticlimactic." It was a "test" of oneself, a rite of passage from childhood to adulthood, an "end to innocence."

But the war was not a transcendent experience for me. Although I sometimes romanticize my wartime experiences, I cannot sentimentalize the war, or glorify it. It was not the high point of my life; it was only one high point among many: the feel of Yale University library during my first days in graduate school; the moment I looked into the wide blue eyes of my first child minutes after his birth; the two years I lived in Italy when the Renaissance I had known only through literature and photographs in art books came to glorious life; the first time I saw Michelangelo's Moses in the marble flesh in Rome; the year I spent living among the Burmese people; a year in Colombia; the birth of my first grandchild; and many others.

For most veterans and Americans, even today, the Japanese bombing of our military bases on Oahu in December 1941 was a surprise attack, a sneak attack, "unprovoked and dastardly," an attack that for many justified dropping atomic bombs on the civilian populations of Hiroshima and Nagasaki in August 1945. But expressions such as "sneak attack" and "that day of infamy," and so on, are but the rhetoric of propaganda. There are no "rules" of war—though I hope there are "rules" of humanity. Surprise is part of the war game. Moreover, there is considerable evidence in many books to show that the attack on Pearl Harbor was not a surprise attack at all, that the Japanese in effect were pushed to attack, that it was well known in Washington the Japanese might attack without warning, that the United States toward the end wanted the Japanese to "commit the first act," that the question was how to "maneuver" the Japanese into making the first move, that the United States knew a Japanese attack was imminent, if, perhaps, it did not know exactly when or where.

Even more, for most veterans and Americans today, the bombing of Hiroshima and Nagasaki was justified because it saved a "million" American lives, lives of soldiers and marines who, as it was planned, would land on Japan later in 1945 and in the spring of 1946. But documents released over the years make clear that the war in the Pacific would have ended by early December 1945 even if the bombs had not been dropped, even if the Russians had never entered the war against Japan as they did just before the second bomb fell, and even without an American landing on Japan. The Japanese were ready to surrender weeks before the bombs were dropped. A million (an outlandish figure anyway) American lives were not saved by the bomb because the landings were not needed, would never have taken place. And many major military leaders involved in the highest level military decisions are on record as saying the bombs should not have been dropped.

But my seventy-two year old ex-marine friend Andy, who landed on Iwo Jima a couple of days before I did and whom I respect and admire, still believes the myth that the bomb saved his life and says he will continue to believe so whatever he hears or reads. Although I believed once that the bomb saved American lives, as well as my own, I no longer believe now that it saved mine. We in the United States seem to have a vested interest in maintaining the belief that the bomb saved lives; thus, we need not recognize our moral culpability and acknowledge we committed two of the major atrocities of World War II in dropping the atomic bombs—not to mention the atrocities of firebombing Tokyo and other major cities in Japan and Germany during the war. And recognizing this in no way would condone the many beastly atrocities committed by the Japanese both before and during the war, nor of course the atrocity of the Holocaust committed by the Germans. War itself is an atrocity.

As I attempt to sort through my thoughts about the war, I am faced with ambiguities I find, at times, difficult to understand. On the one hand I see the war as a horror of unmitigated evil. Yet, since I survived it, and unmutilated, I know that I am glad I participated in the war, that I saw it with many of its terrors at firsthand and at close quarters. In retrospect, I see that I took pleasure in many, if not most, of my wartime experiences—in part because as a naval gunfire liaison officer, I was relatively free of the regulations and rules that normally bound naval, marine, and army officers and men. But more than that, war is a time of vivid living, a time of intense personal experiences, with death daily and constantly close. In a perverse kind of way, I enjoyed the landings, the sounds of battle, the daily life during a campaign, the danger, even the fear at times. War is a time of freedom from the constraints of civilized society, freedom to lie, cheat, steal, kill. When I was attached to the Ninth Marines waiting for Iwo, I "scrounged," stole for my marine companions a jeep load of beer from a navy dispensing center on the beach, and lied to the clerk that I was attached to a navy outfit down the road. My corporal on Guam stole a BAR (a Browning automatic rifle) and lied to me that he had found it. I "scrounged" the .45 automatic I carried through Guam and Iwo. And though I try not to believe it, I killed.

9

A Double Exposure of the War

Ahn Junghyo

I was born in Seoul, South Korea, on the second day of December 1941, one week before the Japanese attack on Pearl Harbor. Supposedly, I was a Japanese, the enemy of Americans, at the time of the surprise attack because Korea was a Japanese colony. Many of the Japanese soldiers who fought against Americans in Southeast Asian countries and the Pacific islands were actually Koreans conscripted in the name of the Japanese Imperial Army. And so my life began as an enemy of the Americans when the world was at war. I had to wait for ten years, however, to have my first encounter with the Americans, the theoretical enemy.

The Pacific War ended when I was four years old, and another war began when I was eight, a second-grader. On Monday, June 26, 1950, my classmates and I went to school as usual only to have the teacher tell us to go home, saying that school would be closed until further notice; North and South Korea were at war. It was a very sunny day, I remember, and I was as happy as the weather at the news of war, which gave us an unexpected vacation.

We went home, a happy flock liberated from school. Several boys in my neighborhood gathered by the bicycle shop across the street to exchange any knowledge we had of the war. We shared the little information we had overheard from the worried conversations of our parents and neighbors. All of the tales about war sounded enticing and dramatic. It was the beginning of our lost childhood, a childhood of military marches and bomb drills instead of nursery rhymes and fairy tales. For us children, it was the first lesson in the study of war. Somebody said that North Koreans were coming with tanks. We had never heard of tanks and wondered if we could attack a tank with a kitchen knife. We were boys too young and innocent to know much about the tools of war. We were excited simply because everybody around us was. Our parents were fearful because they were uncertain about their future, while we boys were exhilarated because we expected some sort of adventure.

My own personal experiences of the Korean War as a child who tried in vain to comprehend the complexities of war is the theme of my second novel in English, *Silver Stallion*. Naturally, the five boys in the novel are reflections of myself and my childhood friends. In the novel these children are confused by the many contradictions and paradoxes of war.

Three days after the outbreak of the Korean War, the communist North Koreans arrived in Seoul. They occupied the South Korean capital so quickly that most of its population was trapped in its own city by the demolition of the Han river bridge. President Syngman Rhee had ordered the destruction as a way to stop the North Korean troops from crossing the river and chasing the fleeing president and his government. My family was also trapped in Seoul and waited for the war to come to our door. When the communists did arrive, other children and I went out into the streets to cheer and hail the conquerors, who called themselves "liberators." Our young eyes and minds were fascinated and overwhelmed by the dramatic scenes of rolling jeeps and tanks loaded with armed soldiers in impressive uniforms. We had never seen anything like it, and we enthusiastically welcomed the northern soldiers marching and parading into our city like a Roman phalanx.

We admired the heroic "Red" soldiers and were puzzled to find that the Reds were not red at all. They looked as yellow as ourselves, and we wondered why they were called Reds. Before their arrival, our parents had described the communists as devils with horns and fangs. Cheering at the communist soldiers because all the grown-ups did, we learned the sad truth that our parents could tell lies.

Confused and overwhelmed, we continued to watch the unfolding drama of war. There were rallies, arrests, street trials, and executions on the spot. We did not know what those big words really meant, but every single day of the three-month occupation was a succession of excitement. Supposedly, we had turned communist, but we could not see the difference. Then, we heard about our new enemy, the United Nations. We listened as the adults talked about the big-nosed Yankee Americans and the American general with the strange name of *Megado* (MacArthur).

Although my generation was born as Japanese colonials, we grew up with the simplified generalization that Japan was bad and America was good. After the national liberation in 1945, our elders and teachers told us time and again about the countless atrocities committed by the Japanese colonists until the mere mention of the word Japan instantly and automatically triggered hatred in our minds. American movies also trained us to despise the Japanese. As I described in my recent novel, *Life and Death of the Hollywood Kid,* Hollywood movies were such a powerful tool in shaping our young and impressionable minds that we were easily indoctrinated by their message of white supremacy. We came to believe that Indians and Japanese were evil, while everything white and American was good.

The mentality of my generation was strongly supported by Korea's historical experience with the United States and Japan. At least in the southern half of the peninsula, Korea was liberated from Japanese colonial rule by the Americans. The liberation of Korea, as well as the subsequent division, was indisputably a by-product of American victory in the Pacific. Americanism and the popularity of Americans in South Korea were already widespread when the giant Americans, General *Megado* and his soldiers, came to rescue South Koreans from the North Korean aggressors. Admiration for the United States in Korea grew to such fanaticism during the war and for three decades afterward that a common self-deprecating saying among Koreans described human feces as good if made in the USA.

In the opening scenes of *Silver Stallion,* five children of a remote village under communist occupation ponder over the fantastic tales they have heard about *bengko,* or "Big Nose." This was exactly how the children in my neighborhood and I first heard about and came to know the World Army, or the UN forces, and their commander, General Douglas MacArthur. The American general made his famous landing at Inchon, and the village children waited with great anticipation for the arrival of the World Army, hoping that General *Megado* would be the legendary general galloping on a silver stallion who would come back to rescue the Korean nation in time of distress.

Koreans were not ready for the arrival of the Americans, however. Certainly, they were eager to go out into the streets and cheer for the triumphant big-nosed soldiers of the daylight hours, but they were unprepared for those same liberators in the darkness of night. At night, the *bengko* soldiers came to the villages to sexually assault Korean women.

The Korean War

When the UN forces came to liberate us from the Reds, I was a small boy like Mansik in *Silver Stallion.*[1] I had found refuge in the town of Sosa, fifty miles southwest of Seoul. It was in this town, much like Silk Mountain Village in my novel, that I experienced my first significant double exposure of the phenomenon of war, particularly of the character of the American soldier. For us, the grass roots people of the hermit kingdom, the American liberators were like Santa Clauses. They were Santa Clauses during the day in every respect, handing out chocolate bars, Chuckles candy, and c-ration cans, sacrificing their own lives to fight the Reds for us, showering us with DDT to save us from the infesting army of lice, and teaching us how run a democratic government.

The American big brothers called themselves liberators as the Reds had, and we went out to hail them in the same way that we had welcomed the communist liberators. But it did not take long for us to realize how the big-nosed liberators behaved after nightfall. They terrorized the villagers with nightly visits to molest our mothers, aunts, and sisters. Every night my mother and other village women had to run and hide in the bushes, in rice boxes,* and under the floor to escape

---

*Storage for uncooked grains.

the UN forces of the night. In early evening, I watched my mother slip out of the house to hide, her face smeared with charcoal soot to make herself look ugly and dirty, in hopes of discouraging the sexual urges of American or Turkish soldiers if she were ever caught by one of them. At first, I thought that she was playing a game of hide-and-seek. I could not quite understand why she had to run away every night, especially because we had not experienced such nocturnal raids when the North Koreans or Chinese came to our village. The South Koreans who experienced the war still believe that the communists had been strongly indoctrinated not to include rape in their war efforts. It was too much for an eight-year-old boy to understand, but it certainly left me with a strong and powerful impression to mull over for many years to come.

Korean women, I believe, accepted this nocturnal reality of war stoically, as a natural part of life or some sort of evil they had to endure. It took a long time and another experience of war, in Vietnam, for me to accept it with the same stoicism as my mother did. In Vietnam, Koreans did everything Americans had done in Korea, including rape—though much less often. In *Silver Stallion* I wanted to present the sacrifice of women who, through no choice of their own, become swept away in the momentum and wake of war itself and its accompanying evils. But I also wanted to present the sacrifice from the viewpoint of young children who vainly try to cope with the violence of war in puzzlement and subdued anger. I tried to express these same feelings in my Vietnam War novel, *White Badge,* from an adult's point of view, which was more mature, openly sarcastic, and consciously disillusioned. I had grown up, if not matured.

The Vietnam War

I was twenty-four when I was sent to Vietnam to serve my compulsory thirty-month military term in the Ninth Army "White Horse" Division.[2] Before my combat experience, I had graduated from a Jesuit college and completed six months as a reporter for an English-language newspaper published in Seoul. Like most Vietnam-bound soldiers, I went to Vietnam with a misconception about myself and my war mission. I fantasized that I was a hero going on a romantic adventure befitting a "crusader of justice and peace," as the Korean government had officially dubbed us. In contrast to the United States, where many people disdained American involvement in Vietnam, the Korean government launched a national project glorifying the Korean soldiers' experience in Indochina. The state propaganda inspired most Koreans to the point of euphoria and fervor. We romanticized the war in Vietnam for many good reasons.

It may be necessary to provide some information about the collective psychology of the Korean people at the time to understand why Korean veterans of the Vietnam War have developed narrow and arrogant attitudes, which many of them still maintain today.[3] The administration of Park Chung Hee badly needed Korean participation in Vietnam to boost the country's economy. Many generals who later became politicians still boast of their Vietnam experience as not only a great military feat but also an epoch-making political achievement. This became especially apparent when they talked about what kinds of benefits the Koreans were showered with by the American government as a reward for joining the U.S. war efforts in Vietnam.

Although Americans may find it difficult to understand, most Korean soldiers who went to Vietnam, including me, were zealous volunteers. In fact, there were too many volunteers and competition to go to war was so high, especially in the first several years, that many soldiers cut their fingers to write petitions in blood to the president, the defense minister, the army chief of staff, and other high-ranking military officers, begging to allow them to go to war.

The Korean soldiers went to war believing that they were going to have an adventure of a lifetime—and they would be paid for it too. Under the government campaign of making heroes out of the soldiers going to Vietnam, the whole nation glorified and romanticized the warriors on their way to "battlegrounds in the 'land of palm trees and the southern cross.' " They believed that the war in Vietnam was all fun and no blood. The soldiers leaving for Vietnam enjoyed parades and fanfare, and soldiers returning from Vietnam received a hero's welcome. Proud Vietnam War veterans told tall tales to their families and friends when they were released from the army and returned to their home towns in the country. They flaunted what they had brought home from the war—National-brand Japanese refrigerators, RCA television sets, Akai tape recorders, and other choice items from the post exchange (PX) list. The veterans could make money by selling those items back home; that, too, was an advantage gained from their Vietnam duty.

Korean War veterans, as well as the soldiers returning home from Vietnam, claimed that the war in Vietnam was child's play compared to what the Korean nation had endured during the Korean War. They scorned the Viet Cong as cowardly weaklings. In combat photographs released to the press by the Defense Ministry, the enemy prisoners *did* look diminutive, starved, and defeated. While thus disparaging the enemy, the Korean military presented overblown images of their own victorious and invincible troops.

The media often described exaggerated military accomplishments. For instance, when the White Horse Division finished a search-and-destroy mission over a sixty-mile stretch between Nha Trang and Tuy Hoa, the Korean newspapers reported that the division had "opened Highway 1," the road that extends from Saigon (now called Ho Chi Minh City) all the way to Hanoi. Actually, the piece of road had been cleared earlier by the Americans, and then again by the Korean marines. Sometimes, Koreans talked as if they were winning the whole war all by themselves, while American, Vietnamese, and Australian troops kept bungling everything. Believe it or not, most Koreans still refuse to believe that they lost the Vietnam War; Americans, not Koreans, lost it. According to their own analysis, Koreans were officially never defeated; they won their share of the war and also greatly contributed to the development of the national economy. That is their firm and unchallenged belief.

Korean casualties were rarely, if ever, reported. War reports always emphasized how many Viet Cong were killed and how many enemy weapons seized. I do not remember reading any reports of friendly losses, except the special attempts to honor officers killed in and out of action by calling them "military deities." On March 6, 1991, fifteen long years after the end of the Vietnam War, the Korean Defense Ministry reluctantly disclosed the number of Korean casualties for the first time. The report was issued only to contradict the claim from the American Vietnam War Veterans Association that three South Korean prisoners were being held alive in Hanoi. The ministry had insisted that not a single South Korean prisoner was in the hands of the North Vietnamese. From September 1964 to April 1975, a total of 312,853 Korean soldiers fought in Vietnam; 4,687 were killed, and 8,000 wounded. These figures had been classified as military secrets under the administrations of Park Chung Hee and Chun Doo Hwan and never released to the public.

The Korean government obviously had a policy to keep negative information about the Vietnam War out of public reach. For example, the Defense Ministry forced all war correspondents from Korea to sign a written pledge before leaving for Vietnam. Originally drawn up in February 1965, the pledge specified three conditions. First, all articles reporting war activities in Vietnam would be censored by the ministry before public release. Second, war correspondents should abide by national security regulations, observe military laws, and obey the orders of commanding officers. Finally, in case of death or injury during coverage of combat, war correspondents could not make any demand for compensation from the government. The Korean government, dominated by strongman Park Chung Hee, never allowed any open discussion of Korean military involvement in Vietnam. Needless to say, direct opposition by politicians as well as the press and intellectuals was entirely out of the question. The media could not print any editorials criticizing policy. Writers could not write any novels reflecting defeatism or revealing friendly casualties. The suppression of free speech affected me personally when I first tried to publish *White Badge* in Korea in 1983. Publishers did not want to risk a trip to prison by supporting my work.

White Badge

White Badge, my first novel published in both Korean and English, focuses on a young man who goes to the war in Vietnam inspired by a fantasy or misconception created by the state. In Vietnam he discovers for himself the appalling reality of war. Like the gullible young boys in *White Badge,* many men of my generation went to war for a romantic adventure in a foreign land, believing the Vietnam War to be child's play and believing in the myth of the immortality and invincibility of brave Korean heroes. And they went to war for the money paid to them by the American government. Yes, the money.

When I was a corporal, the Korean army paid me about five dollars a month, barely enough for one haircut and a movie at the base. The Korean government did not feel obliged to pay a decent salary to the draftees, who were legally bound to serve their country for thirty months, with or without pay. Compulsory army service of two and a half years is still required of all eligible Korean males because the threat to South Korea from communist North Korea continues. On the other hand, in addition to the meager five dollars from the Korean government, a volunteer was paid about forty dollars by the American government under the terms agreed upon by the two governments for deployment of South Korean troops to Vietnam. Incidentally, the combat pay per diem for Korean soldiers paid by the Americans was approximately one-third of the pay received by their American counterparts serving in Vietnam. In the case of helicopter pilots, Korean colonels were paid six hundred dollars, while their American counterparts received twelve hundred dollars.

There is a theory that the American government paid the Korean officers and soldiers more, but that the Korean government took a chunk of it to build the expressway from Seoul to Pusan. Most Koreans do not know or care much about this possibility because the matter has never been discussed openly. If it really occurred, the unconfirmed state embezzlement could prove how unethical the Korean government has been; consider, too, the ethics of selling Korean lives at a discounted rate. Perhaps the concessions for discounted Korean lives had been made under other compensatory terms of agreement between the two governments, for example, terms relating to the transfer of weapons. According to the agreements, modern weapons, including M-16 rifles that were provided by the Americans to Korean soldiers fighting in Vietnam, were permanently transferred to the arsenal of the Republic of Korea's army. Or, perhaps the discounted rate was justified, because it was not the Korean soldiers' main pay but a supplement to their military income. Most of the soldiers and many of the officers who served in Vietnam never noticed or suspected the discrimination in combat pay. They are still unaware because they were not exposed to the information. Even if they knew, they would not have cared. They would have gone anyway. *I* would have gone any way. We all needed the American money.

For many soldiers, going to Vietnam meant an opportunity to earn and save enough money to celebrate in their adulthood or buy something they wanted after discharge from the army. With the money I received from the American government, I bought my first typewriter, a Smith-Corona, from the PX of the division headquarters. Korean soldiers were forced by their commanders to send more than 80 percent of their pay to Korea so that the government could accumulate precious dollars to build up the economy. Ironically, the mandatory regulation helped the soldiers gain a solid start in life. For instance, with savings from Vietnam one could purchase a cow, a very important asset for a farming family.

While it is true that economic necessity motivated young soldiers far more than the state propaganda campaign or patriotism, Koreans had a moral justification for going to Vietnam. They believed that they were indeed the vanguard of world peace, warriors fighting to protect freedom and democracy for a threatened Southeast Asian nation. They called themselves the "crusaders" and were naïve enough to believe themselves as such. But some, including Sergeant Han Kiju, who is the narrator and main character of *White Badge,* began to see the other side of the fantasy created by military pomp and tall tales.

Less than an hour after his arrival in Vietnam, Sergeant Han Kiju experiences his first confusion or double take. Sergeant Han and other Korean soldiers were told—and believed—that they were going to Vietnam to protect and preserve world peace and to pay back what they owed to the UN forces, especially the Americans, during the three years of the Korean War. They believed that they were doing to and for Vietnam what Americans had done in Korea during the previous war. Personally, I often had the impression that many Korean soldiers were imitating American GIs who fought in Korea in the 1950s. In a sense, they *were* Americans. Dressed in American uniforms, armed with American weapons, eating American c-rations, and even paid by the American government, they were indeed acting as Americans.

The Korean soldiers fighting in Vietnam held a common misconception. They pretended to be or truly believed that they were saviors or Santa Clauses. But the image of the giant they held in their mind's eye, the image of an American with an Oriental face, was a distorted one. Certainly, the Vietnamese intellectuals had a quite different impression of us. I often wondered, and still do sometimes, how ridiculous the Koreans swaggering around in American costume with their false identities must have looked to the Vietnamese. How Lilliputian we impostors must have seemed. Perhaps Koreans were performing a war circus as clowns in American uniforms. We were there for the our own personal and national interests in the first place, and we were there for Americans rather than for the Vietnamese. Indeed, many of us did not even know it.

Perhaps we overdid our performance as Americans in Vietnam. In Vietnam, Koreans did everything Americans had done in Korea—including what the *bengko* soldiers had done to the women in *Silver Stallion.* When you are fighting a war, ethics do not count too much—that was one of the more basic lessons I learned.

Largely unaware of the political realities of the conflict, Sergeant Han Kiju of *White Badge* endures in war one of the most intense experiences of his life. Through his adventures, he grows up but sacrifices his spiritual innocence, a phenomenon that is a common theme of all war literature. War makes innocent young boys become killers, a truth that is masked by the delusion that they are patriotic heroes. After all, the history of humankind is filled with wars and conquests, which ultimately mean massacre of a weaker group by a stronger one. War is a killing business—and a very serious one at that. After all the euphemistic slogans and propaganda eulogizing the noble spirit of self-sacrifice, bravery, and patriotism are put aside, the bottom line of war is merciless killing, an act of mass murder in the name of justice and, ironically, of peace.

In Vietnam, I learned that people act in illogical and unlikely ways, ways in which they would not think of acting under normal conditions at home. I saw how the military profession and uniforms could turn ordinary human beings into extraordinary killing beasts. The dramatic metamorphosis seemed only natural over there in the Vietnamese jungle, just as it must be during all wars. Koreans in Vietnam were famous, and infamous, for bravery and brutality—one and the same quality in the end.

I returned home after one year of what I believed was a traumatic experience. Years passed, twenty-five years. For thirteen years I wrote my Vietnam novel and kept thinking about the war. Ten more years passed as I kept talking and thinking about the war and my book. Then I returned to Vietnam.

Return to Vietnam

In 1992 I returned to Vietnam with a film crew for location shooting of *White Badge,* the movie. We shot the scenes that took place in Vietnam in and around the small town of Long Hai, or the Dragon Bay, near Vung Tau. It was there at Long Hai that I went through one of the most unsettling experiences of my life. The moment we touched down at Tan Son Nhut Airport, the same spot where I had been under Viet Cong attack at 4:00 A.M. on December 4, 1966, I felt uncomfortable. The nagging fear remained with me whenever I came across such signs as the Viet Cong Bank or any other indications of my old enemy while traveling on the chartered bus weaving through the familiar heavy traffic of bicycles and Suzuki motorcycles in Saigon.

It was scary to remind myself that I was back in the country now controlled by the communists who had been my enemy. For over a month while staying at Long Hai, I never ventured out alone to explore the town—especially at night. I was afraid of the back alleys. The actors, too young to have experienced the Vietnam War but well aware of the Korean display of bravery there, often went out at night, seeking adventure in a foreign land, just like the Korean soldiers of twenty-five years earlier. I was afraid whenever I went out to the beach for a stroll or for a shot of vodka with a small group. It made me nervous to go to the open café in front of the Rang Dong Hotel when I found out that it was run by a man who used to be a Viet Cong fighter. He had been awarded a medal of honor for his valor in fighting against us. In my eyes, the whole town was populated with former Viet Cong warriors and messenger boys. They could attack me at any time they wanted if they spotted me loitering alone in a back alley; they would accuse me, "You were here once as our enemy. You were here to kill us." It was a very realistic and tangible fear for me.

But they were no longer my enemy. *They* did not think they were. In the past two decades, the wounds of war had healed much in their hearts and minds as they were busy struggling to fight another war of poverty. They seemed to have forgotten, or stoically accepted, what the Koreans had done to them. Perhaps they have really forgotten. But I have not. I did not have an opportunity for spiritual reconciliation with the Vietnamese. When I returned to Vietnam, the gap of twenty-five years was gone; my mind and feelings jumped immediately back to wartime. You do not suddenly become a friend with your enemy on the first day of reunion, I thought. That was unnatural. It was embarrassing to find the Vietnamese villagers so friendly to us. When we were shooting the film in town, the popular troops, who were dressed in calico noir exactly like the Viet Cong during the war, came to protect us from the milling crowd and spectators. These modern Viet Cong were armed with M-16s looted from the Americans at the end of the war!

Was I their friend or foe? The confusing sense of identity was epitomized by a party I was invited to one evening. It was the celebration of the birthday of a Korean businessman based in Ho Chi Minh City. Among the guests at the party that night were a young hard-core communist from Hanoi, a former South Vietnamese army colonel who used to spy for the North Vietnamese during the war, and a former member of the Viet Cong who proudly claimed to have worked for the construction of the famous Cu Chi underground tunnel, which has turned into a popular tourist spot.

That night, I drank with these guests and sang "Happy Birthday" for the businessman, who ironically was enjoying the outcome of the war most. During the war, about 50,000 Korean soldiers were stationed in Vietnam for combat mission; this military presence paved the way for as many as 20,000 Korean civilians to go there and pursue their noncombat mission of making money at construction sites and PX installations run by American or Korean companies. I even encountered Korean photographers and traveling showgirls I had met during my tour of duty; they had been in Vietnam during the war making money. The photographers had been given privileges, under certain illegal contracts with some high-ranking officers, to visit combat units and take snapshots of the soldiers who wanted to have records of the romantic war liaisons of their youth. Most soldiers could not afford to buy a camera after sending most of their pay home. As for the showgirls, I gave some attention to them in *White Badge*. And now, twenty-five years later, when the war is over and the soldiers long forgotten, civilians were still there busy making money, apparently without any feelings of guilt.

I experienced guilt at the party, however. I had very mixed feelings, sitting side by side with my former enemies and celebrating the birthday of a prosperous Korean businessman. Twenty-five years ago my mission in Vietnam had been to kill these men. The same government that sent soldiers there to kill the Vietnamese is now sending Korean businessmen to Vietnam; the same government claims that the Vietnamese and Koreans are now friends. In the course of twenty-five years what has changed to make this remarkable difference? What, after all, is the true definition of the enemy? Why did we fight so hard to kill the Vietnamese? Did we fight the war to open markets? If so, we should have been told honestly, not betrayed by ideological rhetoric and false patriotism.

At the factory run by Korean businessmen, I saw Vietnamese working with high hopes for their future, earning thirty dollars a month. They reminded me of myself twenty-five years earlier, a hired gun at forty-five dollars a month fighting the war for the Americans and filled with an illusion of heroism and a misguided appetite for adventure.

* * *

I learned my first lesson of war in childhood as a boy watching strangers come to town, observing the Reds who did not look red at all and American Santa Clauses who did not behave like Santa Clauses at night. My second experience of war occurred in a land of strangers. In Vietnam I experienced the war as a soldier with a dubious sense of identity, fighting in a foreign country for another foreign country. My return to Vietnam echoed more loudly and boldly the sentiments I had felt earlier. War is futile; the enemy of yesterday does not remain an enemy forever. War is not flags of glory but waste filled with suffering and pain. It is fundamentally a human sickness camouflaged by the intricate workings of international interests and a beguiling rhetoric of abstract concepts. I hope that the world will spare me from a third experience of war.

Notes

1. In chapter 8 in this volume, Van Symons devotes a large portion of his discussion to a reflection on *Silver Stallion.*
2. Whereas military service in the Korean army was mandatory, participation in the Vietnam mission was voluntary.
3. That is, the veterans refused to admit that the war they participated in was an immoral one. They believed and behaved as if they were the most patriotic people in the world.

10

Through American Eyes

Combat Experiences and Memories of Korea and Vietnam

Colonel Harry Summers, Jr.

Although war is what the military is all about, I never quite expected it to happen to me. It came without warning while I was at the 118th Station Hospital in Fukuoka, Japan, recovering from a major operation. One day we were at peace, enjoying the good life of occupation duty in Japan; the next day we were at war with Korea. When I returned to my unit, the 24th Infantry Division's Company "A," 78th Heavy Tank Battalion, the company was already beginning to move to the port of Shimonoseki to board ship for movement to Korea.

Like Mike Mansfield, who in 1922 as a nineteen-year-old Marine landed in Tianjin to protect American interests there, I arrived in Pusan in 1950 as an eighteen-year-old corporal ready for a grand adventure. The older World War II veterans had another view. As we sailed across the Korea Strait, we young soldiers crowded at the bow trying to get our first look at land and anxious that the war might be over before we got there. But those who had "seen the elephant" were at the fantail looking pensively out to sea. They knew all too well what we were getting into.

Within weeks, I would witness and experience some of the most tragic events of my life: the loss of our company commander and two of my garrison roommates; countless South Koreans slaughtered by North Koreans; a million North Koreans—women with infants, children, and old men and women carrying everything they could load on their backs—fleeing south; Chinese "human wave" attacks. In Vietnam a decade and a half later, initially I would be insulated from combat and the Vietnamese. Soon, I would find myself in the midst of military action, witnessing unparalleled bravery and courage as well as the horrors of war.

"America's" Wars in Asia?

In considerations of war, individual experience and perspective usually yield to a discussion of politics, diplomacy, and military strategy. After all, modern warfare engages nation-states. Some years ago, a British diplomat commented that the conflicts in East Asia during the latter part of the twentieth century represented the clash of two of the most self-centered, ethnocentric civilizations in the history of mankind, the United States and China. The title of the NEH Summer Institute, American Wars in Asia, reveals this bias, a bias so profound that most are not even aware of it.

American ethnocentrism is suggested by the conventional wisdom accepted by supporters and protesters of the war alike: the wars in Korea and Vietnam were "our" wars. In both cases, America is seen as the prime protagonist, and China, officially at least, as the main adversary. In Korea it was the United States against North Korea and the Chinese communist forces; in Vietnam it was the United States against North Vietnam, from the start viewed as a Chinese proxy. In actuality, during both wars the United States was merely a partner and, in human terms, a junior partner at that.

Some background information will provide support for this reality. The war in Korea began in June 1950 with a North Korean invasion of South Korea. At the time, President Harry S. Truman viewed the aggression as a scheme by monolithic world communism, with Moscow at the helm, to spread its ideology by armed force. New evidence has concluded, however, that North Korea's Kim Il Sung instigated the invasion to reunify the country under his control, with the Soviet Union and China as somewhat reluctant partners. Far from attempting to engage the United States in global conflict, the plan was to avoid American involvement by overrunning the south with a lightning blitzkrieg. That strategy was thwarted by the unexpected resistance of the South Korean army, which paid dearly while waiting for a response from its American ally in nearby Japan. Under the facade of the United Nations, the United States entered the war not so much for the sake of South Korea as because its loss would threaten the vital economic interests of America in Japan.

The United States shouldered the majority of the material costs, but the human costs—deaths, casualties, and suffering—were paid overwhelmingly by South Korea. When the war ended on July 27, 1953, the United Nations Command ground forces stood at 932,539. Of those, 302,483 were U.S. forces and 39,145 were from other UN members. South Korea, with 590,911 men under arms, had almost double that number in the field. That disparity is reflected in the casualty figures as well. U.S. battle deaths totaled some 33,651, while other UN members lost 3,063 troops killed in action. An estimated 59,000 South Korean soldiers and marines lost their lives in the war, while South Korean civilian casualties are believed to have run into the millions.

Likewise, the war in Vietnam was not an American one. According to the communist government of Vietnam, the war began in January 1959, when Resolution 15 of the Central Executive Committee of the North Vietnamese Communist Party changed its strategy for reunifying the country under its control from "political struggle" to "armed struggle." For the next six years the war was fought mainly by South Vietnamese forces. In 1965 the United States intervened with ground troops to come to the aid of a beleaguered ally again. Still blinded by the myth of "monolithic world communism," the United States operated under the initial premise, as in the Korean War, that North Vietnam was a proxy for communist China, and that Chinese aggression was yet another attempt to spread communism by force of arms. Again, as in Korea, later evidence is that nationalism, not communism, was the primary driving force.

The United States once more covered most of the war's material costs, but statistics reveal that the human costs were paid by the South Vietnamese. At the peak of U.S. strength in April 1969, it had some 543,000 military personnel in Vietnam and the so-called Free World Military Forces had 68,889.[1] Both totals began to decline that year as allied forces were withdrawn; by March 1973 none remained. Yet, the war continued for another two years, and in the end South Vietnamese military forces totaled some 1,110, 000, more than double the number of U.S. forces in the spring of 1969. Casualty figures tell the same story. The United States lost 47,369 killed in action. "Free World Military Forces" lost only 5,218 men, while the South Vietnamese lost 223,748 troops in battle.[2] Furthermore, estimates indicate that some 300,000 South Vietnamese civilians also perished in the war.

In the face of devastating U.S. firepower, "enemy" casualties were horrendous. More than forty years after the end of the Korean War, North Korean and Chinese casualty figures are still highly guarded state secrets. Estimates range from 1.5 million Chinese and North Koreans killed in battle to a low of 500,000. Civilian casualties were beyond calculation, but it is known that some one million North Korean refugees fled south in the winter of 1950–51 to escape the advancing Chinese.

In a 1969 interview, North Vietnamese defense minister Vo Nguyen Giap admitted that he had lost 500,000 soldiers from 1964 to 1969 alone. Estimates reveal that more than 660,000 Viet Cong and North Vietnamese Army soldiers were killed in the course of the war. Numbers for North Vietnamese civilians killed in U.S. bombing raids vary widely, and such figures have been highly politicized.

As former *Washington Post* war correspondent Stanley Karnow found when he visited Hanoi in 1981, "American anti-war activists visiting the city during the [1972 'Christmas bombing'] urged the mayor to claim a death toll of 10,000. He refused, saying that his government's credibility was at stake. The official North Vietnamese figures for fatalities . . . was 1,318 in Hanoi."[3] U.S. official estimates for the entire war maintain that 65,000 North Vietnamese were killed in the bombing raids, while antiwar activists claim a much higher total.

The true figures may never be known, but unquestionably many innocent civilians died.

Unlike Koreans and Vietnamese, who encountered war directly, most Americans, except for the relatively few who served on the front lines, experienced the war vicariously through newsreels and television. While our cities remained unscathed, "[i]n many of the lesser cities of Korea, built of wood and wattle, only the foundations and the vault of the old Japanese bank remained," wrote historian T.R. Fehrenbach. "The people of Chosun, not Americans or Chinese, continued to lose the war."[4] Likewise, it was Ben Tre in the Mekong Delta of Vietnam, not New Orleans in the Mississippi Delta, that "had to be destroyed in order to save it." The majority of Americans witnessed the war in their living rooms, on the television screen, but it was a war sanitized for home consumption; news stories rarely contained combat footage.[5]

Even though the statistics cited reveal stark realities about the amount of human suffering and unequivocal loss for Koreans, Chinese, and Vietnamese, numbers, even invoked in the name of empathy for the other side, the other person, the "enemy," can become impersonal and, indeed, meaningless. As my testimony here gives a face to the experience of war, so do accounts from Korea and Vietnam.[6]

Ahn Junghyo, one of the contributors to this volume, experienced two wars but under very different circumstances—the Korean War as a child and the Vietnam War as a young foreign soldier. Two Vietnamese novelists provide an insight into what the Vietnam War looked like through the eyes of our erstwhile enemies. Bao Ninh's account, *The Sorrow of War,* focuses on a North Vietnamese man who recalls his experience in combat, an experience that continues to haunt him. Duong Thu Huong, a Vietnamese woman who spent seven years living in tunnels and underground shelters with the North Vietnamese troops, uses some of these experiences to craft her *Novel Without a Name.* These accounts also expose the privileged position of Americans abroad, the opportunity to return to a safe, secure, and prosperous America free from the ravages of war. Unlike the official reports, these versions focus on the human and individual dimensions of war. After all, war has to do with people, not things.

Experiences of War in Korea and Vietnam

The War in Korea

No amount of training prepared me for the first shock of combat. It was hard to make myself believe that someone was out there actually trying to kill me. One of the first U.S. troop units ashore, our company arrived in Pusan on July 3, 1950. Moving by rail to Taejon, our tank platoons were dispatched to support the division's infantry units in delaying positions north of the city. Our light reconnaissance tank's 75mm guns were hardly built to stop the Soviet-supplied T-34 main battle tanks of the North Korean Army.

One of the many poignant memories of that war is the devastating loss of our company commander, Lieutenant Leonard Gewin, and two of my garrison roommates, Corporals Tacke and Fields. Gewin, who had been severely wounded as a cavalry officer in World War II and had just months before returned to full duty, went forward with Tacke and Fields in the company's tank retriever to recover one of our tanks that had a mechanical breakdown. As they approached the disabled tank, they were fired on by the North Koreans, and the driver was killed. The retriever went into the ditch and stalled. It could not be restarted because it lacked a starter solenoid that had been on requisition for months. When Gewin and the crew came out through the top hatch, they were killed by the North Koreans, dead for want of a solenoid that probably cost less than a dollar.

I can recall vividly my sense of shame as we retreated into the Pusan perimeter. When we advanced, the streets had been crowded with people waving UN, Republic of Korea, and U.S. flags, and banners hung from the houses welcoming American saviors. But as we pulled back, the streets were deserted, and white flags had replaced the banners. Months later that sense of how badly we had let the people down was reinforced when we saw the bodies of individuals massacred by the North Koreans laid out in shallow graves in Taejon churchyards.

Re-equipped with World War II M4A3E8 76mm-gun *Sherman* medium tanks capable of stopping the T-34s, our company took part in some hard fighting in the Pusan perimeter. Breaking out from the perimeter after the Inchon invasion, we raced north and crossed the 38th parallel into North Korea. Renamed Tank Company, Twenty-First Infantry Regiment, our unit spearheaded Eighth U.S. Army's drive up the west coast of Korea, reaching Chong-go-dong, eighteen air miles from Sinuiju and the Yalu River on November 1, 1950. We were then ordered to retreat in the face of the advancing Chinese army.

Except for the bitter cold, our retreat from North Korea and the Chinese invasion was relatively uneventful since as tankers we rode rather than walked. The most searing memories were of our "scorched earth" policy, imposed by General Walton Walker, the Eighth U.S. Army commander, of burning all dwelling places and destroying all animals and foodstuffs as we retreated. In this way, the Chinese could be prevented from living off the land. In so doing, we also deprived the local civilians of doing so. A million North Koreans—women with babes in arms, children, old men and women with all their worldly possessions arranged in A-frames on their backs—fled south through that terrible winter. It was the most tragic event I have ever seen, made even more so by the necessity to keep the one single road out of North Korea open for Eighth Army's retreat. As a result, the refugees were forced to plod painfully through the snowdrifts along the sides. How many died in that terrible exodus will never be known, but surely they must have numbered in the tens of thousands.

Although I had not realized it, I had been living in the lap of luxury in Tank Company. In February 1951 the company was disbanded, and I ended up as the squad leader of a 57mm recoilless rifle squad in the Weapons Platoon of "L"

Company ("Love" Company in the phonetic alphabet of the time) in the Third Battalion, Twenty-First Infantry. One of my proudest possessions is the combat infantryman badge I won as a soldier in Love Company. I can still remember hugging the earth on Hill 1157 as friendly artillery fire came in short and seeing one of my gunners lose his leg to a shell fragment. Another gunner, who held a master's degree from Harvard, was shot through the throat by a Chinese sniper. Thankfully, both survived their ordeals, but there were many others who did not.

Our plight paled in comparison to that of the enemy. I will never forget the Chinese soldiers coming through a barrage of 4.2–inch mortar fire and through the interlocking bands of our final protective machine gun fire for what seemed like hours. Their bodies were stacked by the hundreds in windrows before they finally called off their assault.

But most of all, I will never forget how heavy my sergeant stripes became in April 1951 in the wake of the Chinese spring offensive, where the Chinese threw 250,000 men and twenty-seven divisions against our front. Soon we found ourselves on an "outpost line of resistance" (OPLR) to delay the Chinese advance. As we watched, they occupied a hill to our front, then encircled it with a concentric ring of trenches in a matter of hours. As soon as they were ready, the Chinese launched a "human wave" attack on our positions. They soon overran "I" Company on the high ground to our right. Our position was turned, and we had to pull back. All my instincts said to retreat since we were already taking fire. But I could not do that. As the acting recoilless rifle section leader, I had to wait until the last of my three squads was out. As I waved the others to the rear, I thought about the enormous price of power, even the meager power I possessed as an infantry sergeant.

By May 1951, I had completed almost four years of experience in the Far East Command and was one of the first allowed to leave the front line. After two weeks at sea aboard a troopship, I was back home. It was not long before the Korean War became the forgotten war for me, like the rest of America. Unlike Vietnam War veterans who went from combat to America by air in a day, I was eased out of the war by a long troopship voyage home. Remaining in the military, I was constantly surrounded by other veterans of the war who provided a kind of "support group" that dissipated the trauma of the war.

For Ahn Junghyo (see chapter 9, "A Double Exposure of the War") the Korean War can never be the forgotten war. Tellingly, it was not the war itself that seems to have traumatized him. As he describes it,

> For us the grass-roots people of the hermit kingdom, the American liberators were like Santa Clauses . . . sacrificing their own lives to fight the Reds for us. . . . But it did not take long for us to realize how the big-nosed liberators behaved after nightfall. They terrorized the villages with nightly visits to molest our mothers, aunts, and sisters. Every night my mother and other village women had to run and hide . . . to escape the UN forces of the night.

That experience of war, contrary to what many would envision, left its impression on Ahn.

Vietnam

Ahn's ruminations on his wartime tour of duty with the Korean White Horse Division in Vietnam, and on his later return to that country, reveal that from his Korean perspective he is no more able to put himself in the shoes of his adversary, the Vietnamese, than the Americans could during the Korean War. His experience as a foreign soldier, however, allows him to understand, if not accept, the behavior of American soldiers in Korea.

As Ahn says, "the war in Vietnam was child's play compared to what the Korean nation had endured during the Korean War."[7] Not only was the war less intense, but the living conditions were infinitely better. During 1950–51, when I was in Korea the front-line troops remained in the field, with only their own pup tents for shelter during that bitter winter. While candy and cigarettes came with the c-ration sundry kits and there was an occasional beer ration, there were no base camps, clubs, or post exchanges on the front lines. But in Vietnam an elaborate base camp system developed, with enlisted and officer clubs, post exchanges, movies, showers, laundry facilities, and other such amenities. Units would deploy to the field for combat operations, but would eventually return to their base camps to rest and refit. Those not involved in combat operations, the overwhelming majority of U.S. military personnel deployed to Vietnam, could remain on these base camps for their entire one-year tour, and except for occasional rocket or mortar attacks, be totally isolated from the war and from Vietnamese society.

In March 1966, I was stationed initially at just such a rear-echelon location, where I was the G-3 operations officer for the night shift and as such was in charge of the Corps Tactical Operations Center (TOC). But, as in Korea where I moved from the relative safety of a tank company to the total vulnerability of a rifle company, in Vietnam I left the comfort of the Corps TOC to become the operations officer of an infantry battalion in the jungle. It is hard to explain this potentially suicidal decision outside the profession of arms. But, by choice, I had been a professional soldier for almost twenty years. My whole career as an infantry officer—platoon and company command, the Infantry School Basic and Advance Course, Ranger School—had all been aimed at preparing me to serve my country in combat. The motto of the Twenty-First Infantry Regiment in whose ranks I served in Korea was "Duty," and "Duty First" was also the watchword of the First Infantry Division. "Duty" it was, and I left the ease of my office chair to join my good friend Major Richard DeWyatt Clark in the First Battalion, Second Infantry, in the jungle south of its base camp at Phuoc Vinh.

In August 1966, Lieutenant Colonel Richard Prillaman, the battalion commander, took a long-deserved R&R (rest and relaxation) trip to Hong Kong, leaving the battalion in the hands of his executive officer, Major Clark. At the moment, our only task was a routine road-clearing operation, but in combat nothing is routine. One of our patrols ambushed the Viet Cong (VC) Phu Loi Battalion, an elite Main Force unit, and a major battle ensued. Our "C" company was first to reinforce, and it penetrated the trench lines of the VC base camp. I moved overland with "A" and "B" companies, while Dick helicoptered in to the "C" company position to take command of the flight. I soon joined him there, and, as we were surveying the situation, a sniper in a tree shot him in the temple, and he was dead before he hit the ground.

Not only had I lost my best friend, but everyone was now looking at me for instructions; as the senior officer present, I was now in command. There was some doubt as to whether in setting up the battalion command post (CP) in the VC trench line, we could hold on, for we were seriously outnumbered and at the extreme range of our supporting artillery. In the midst of that doom and gloom a wounded rifleman was brought in and laid down on the floor of the trench. Catching the sergeant major's eye he asked, "Where in the hell am I?"

"Why son," said the sergeant major, "you're in the battalion CP."

"Whew," said the rifleman, "safe at last!"

To his mind, battalion headquarters was so far back in the rear that nothing bad could possibly happen there. His perspective breathed new life into us, as we got on with fighting the battle.

Another incident raised our morale still further. Captain Nils Johannsen, the "B" Company commander, had been wounded, and I ordered the Battalion S-2 captain, George Downs, to go forward and take command. I told him to give me a situation report as soon as he arrived there. Minutes later, after he had traversed the hundred or so yards to the "B" company CP, Downs radioed in, asking, "Would you believe," he said, in a perfect imitation of Agent 86 in the then-popular "Get Smart" television series, "that we're receiving *intense* automatic weapons fire?"

I listened closely, but I could hear no machine gun fire in that direction. "Negative," I said, "I can't hear any automatic weapons fire."

"Okay then," Downs replied, "how about sporadic small arms fire?"

According to those monitoring our radio traffic in the division command post, that exchange was the best proof that they could have received indicating that everything was under control.

As the battle progressed, other units attempted to come to our relief but were chewed up in the process. At one point the brigade commander, Colonel Sidney Barry, joined the fight and ordered a counterattack to stabilize the lines. Up the trail came our "A" company with a young machine-gunner leading the way. While enemy fire kicked up dirt all around him, he was playing John Wayne. He would take a step, spray the area, take another step, and spray the area again. It was a magnificent performance, one of the bravest acts I had ever seen.

"We need to get that soldier's name," I said, "He really deserves a medal."

"What for?" was Colonel Barry's reply. "That's what machine-gunners are supposed to do."

While we were still under heavy contact the next morning, a napalm strike was called in by the ground commander to force the enemy to disengage. The aircraft came in a bad angle, and the napalm struck our trench line instead. It was an inferno, and the whole world seemed on fire. Screams filled the air. All the radio handset cords melted in the heat, leaving us without means of communication. A case of grenades at my feet was on fire, as was my right arm and left hand. I beat the napalm on my hand out on the side of the trench, and my operations sergeant cut away my burning sleeve. Together we stomped out the fire on the case of grenades. If ever there was a time for panic, that was it. The force of personality of Lieutenant Colonel Paul Gorman, the commander of the First Battalion, Twenty-Sixth Infantry, who had earlier assumed command of all forces in our perimeter, however, had an immediately reassuring effect. Although a map had literally vaporized in his hands when the napalm struck, he remained calm. His example calmed the rest of us as well.

Many Americans, and especially those opposed to the Vietnam War, entertained images of the North Vietnamese soldiers as clear-eyed and determined, posturing heroically, singing victory songs, and being welcomed by the populace wherever they marched. But as former Vietnamese soldiers Bao Ninh and Duong Thu Huong make it clear in their recent novels, those who had dismissed John Wayne in *Green Berets* as hokey propaganda had bought into an even bigger fabrication.

One of only ten survivors of a five hundred-man brigade sent south to fight the war, Ninh in his *Sorrow of War* tells not only of the horrors of combat but also, as few American authors have done, about the courage of his South Vietnamese adversaries. Duong, who also went south to lead a communist youth brigade, shares Ninh's disillusionment. Her *Novel Without a Name* contrasts the realities of combat in the south with the phony heroics of North Vietnamese government pronunciamentos. As San Jose State University professor Larry Engelmann put it, "This perfect cynicism of the party's leaders, described convincingly by Duong, is central to her ongoing theme that the party leadership has little but contempt for the peasant soldiers—a theme embraced also by Ninh—who made all the sacrifices of the war."[8]

Is it surprising that Duong's protagonist spares the life of an American prisoner? This conduct starkly contrasts with Norman Mailer's World War II account of the murder of a Japanese prisoner in *The Naked and the Dead* and with the many horror stories of such actions during the Vietnam War.

Some Concluding Reflections

American ethnocentrism is not confined to the ranks of the military. In a speech at Tulane University in New Orleans on April 23, 1975, President Gerald Ford told students, "America can regain its sense of pride that existed before Vietnam. But it cannot be achieved by fighting a war that is finished as far as America is concerned." The 4,500 students stood and cheered as the word "finished" was spoken. No one in Ford's entourage, least of all the feckless Ford himself, dared remind them of Navy Captain John W. Philip's words as the U.S.S. *Texas* passed the burning hulk of the Spanish cruiser *Vizcaya* at Santiago during the Spanish-American War of 1898: "Don't cheer, men; the poor devils are dying."

Likewise, our erstwhile South Vietnamese allies were dying by the tens of thousands as the eighteen North Vietnamese Army divisions closed on Saigon; our former allies in Cambodia were being slaughtered by the millions in the Khmer Rouge holocaust. But, safe and secure in their American cocoons, the students at Tulane, and the public in general, could not have cared less.

It is fitting to close with a comment by Cambodian minister Sirik Matak shortly before his murder by the Khmer Rouge after he refused U.S. ambassador John Gunther Dean's offer of evacuation from Phnom Penh in April 1975:

> I cannot, alas, leave in such a cowardly fashion. As for you and in particular for your great country, I never believed for a moment that you would have this sentiment of abandoning a people which has chosen liberty. You have refused us your protection, and we can do nothing about it. . . .
>
> But mark it well that, if I should die here on the spot and in my country that I love, it is too bad because we all are born and must die one day. I have only committed the mistake of believing in you, the Americans.[9]

Notes

1. "Free World Military Forces" were troops from Australia, New Zealand, the Philippines, South Korea, and Thailand.

2. This figure does not include the 1975 final offensive because those numbers are not available.

3. Stanley Karnow, *Vietnam: A History* (New York: Viking Press, 1983), p. 653.

4. T.R. Fehrenback, *This Kind of War: A Study in Unpreparedness* (New York: Macmillan, 1963), p. 463.

5. A Twentieth Century Fund report found that "[a] study of Vietnam-related television news film stories from 1968 to 1973 found that only about three percent of the stories contained combat footage, and only two percent showed any dead or wounded"; cited from Peter Braestrup, ed., *Battlelines: Report of the Twentieth Century Fund Task Force on the Military and the Media* (New York: Priority Press Publications, 1985), p. 68.

6. The Korean War sparked few American novels or, for that matter, much literature of any kind. T.R. Fehrenbach's *This Kind of War: A Study in Unpreparedness* is the best nonfiction work about the American experience. A Korean War combat veteran and a distinguished historian, Fehrenback provides a factual yet impressionistic look at Korea that vividly presents the war's human dimensions. Without parallel in the literature of that conflict, his classic is still being "rediscovered" by enthusiastic readers.

7. The propaganda line of the antiwar movement—that the Vietnam War was uniquely horrible, the most terrible and devastating in the history of mankind—was so far from the truth as to be ludicrous. And the degree to which this canard is still believed—as unfortunately it is still believed by many credulous Americans—is evidence that some Americans still do not comprehend the American realities of war, much less the Asian realities.

8. *Vietnam Magazine,* February 1996.

9. Arnold Issacs, *Without Honor: Defeat in Vietnam and Cambodia* (Baltimore: Johns Hopkins University Press, 1983), p. 276.

11

The Korean War at the Dinner Table

Pingchao Zhu

Ever since my childhood, I have cherished a dream that has never been fulfilled. I wanted to be in the army, wearing that elegant uniform; I wanted to follow in my father's footsteps and to pursue a military career. Father had fought for Mao Zedong's military since the 1930s and remained a career army officer until the final moment of his life. I grew up among men and women in uniform and admired that outfit from the day I began to think about my future. When I was old enough, I would often borrow Father's uniform with its insignia and wear it to take pictures. I always felt a kind of satisfaction in being lost in that oversized attire.

When I became eligible for military service, Father forbade me to go, saying that I could do anything except become an enlisted woman. He never told me why and for that reason I did not speak to him for several months. Later, I went to college, got my B.A., and went to the United States to study for a Ph.D. degree in history. Father passed away in 1992 and a letter from my mother finally told me why he would not let me join the military. "All his life," Mother wrote,

> your father fought numerous battles and wars and he fought bravely. In 1949, with the declaration of the People's Republic of China, he thought war was over for good and his family and children could start to live a peaceful life. The coming of the Korean War, however, shattered this hope, and he went to fight one more war before retiring. We should have told you a long time ago about his real intention for preventing you from joining the military. He did not want you to take chances to fight a war like the one in Korea.

It was all about the Korean War, a war eventually forgotten in China. Between 1949 and the eve of the outbreak of the Korean conflict in June 1950, Father's regiment was stationed in Manchuria, an area in the north of China that shares a border with Korea. His troops, then renamed the Chinese People's

Volunteers (CPV), were ordered to cross the Yalu River into Korea a few weeks before the Chinese government officially announced its entry into the war on October 19, 1950.

I belong to the post–Korean War generation and know hardly anything about the war. No sooner had the gunsmoke dissipated on the Korean Peninsula than the memory of the war began to fade away in the minds of most Chinese. Father's experience in the Korean War, therefore, became a very private and personal subject, to be discussed only within our family circle, sometimes at the dinner table. Having experienced the war himself, he told stories that were very different from the ones that we learned in school. Father did not, however, talk often about his experience in Korea. When he did, he was very cautious.

Looking back, I have come to understand why factual accounts of the Korean War often did not conform with those of the Chinese government. Politically, the Korean War was the first war in which China defeated, so it claimed, the joint forces of the West. In the face of the rising tension with the Soviet Union under Stalin's arrogant leadership, China needed to boost its international image by posing as a winner and a defender of peace. Calculated propaganda would help achieve that purpose. Domestically, it was essential to rally the entire nation behind the war effort. A movement known as "Resist America, Aid Korea, defend our country and homes" swept throughout the country during the entire Korean War period. People believed that the American imperialists had conspired the invasion of China, that the CPV was winning many battles in Korea, and that the armistice negotiations were made possible because the CPV triumphed over the American enemy. On the whole, national spirit was with the government propaganda, characterized by its exclusive description of war heroes and positive images. It was in such a political climate that we grew up learning about the Korean War.

One writer particularly well known for his passionate reports on the CPV soldiers was Wei Wei, a journalist who had gone to Korea in 1950 to witness the war and had written many moving essays and stories about the war and its warriors. His writings were widely read, especially among young people in China. One paragraph from Wei Wei's essay entitled "Who Are the Most Beloved People" is still fresh in my memory today:

Dear Friends,

... Are you aware of the happiness all around you? ... Soldiers returning from Korea will tell you that you are living a good life ... since you love our motherland and our leader so much, you must surely love our soldiers deeply.[1]

High school textbooks included Wei Wei's essay, and we were all required to recite it in class. When I practiced my recitation at home, Father would comment: "It sounds really poetic. But what Wei Wei wrote shows you only one side of the coin. The reality in Korea could not be that story-like. War is war, and there was a lot of sadness and cruelty." I wondered what the other side of the coin was. At the dinner table, I pressed my father to tell us what it was really like to be in Korea surrounded by bombings and shellings.

Father had been a dedicated communist and had never had any doubt about what he had been fighting for under the leadership of the Chinese Communist Party (CCP). He wanted to continue doing the right thing and make sure that his children were getting the right education. He had no intention of reversing the general theme of the CCP's propaganda. Having survived the nightmare of the Korean War, Father told us many stories unheard of in either published books or public lectures given by soldiers returning from the war. He told us that war is a monstrosity and that not every soldier died a heroic death on the battlefield as had been portrayed in Korean War movies. Yet even so, according to Father, all the soldiers who died in the war were heroes. Father recalled one incident:

> The bitterly cold winter in Korea was another enemy for us, especially when the CPV troops were not sufficiently clothed. Our soldiers carried only weekly supplies of food and ammunition. Because of difficulties caused by the lack of transportation vehicles, rapid extension of fighting routes, severe weather conditions, and frequent enemy bombings, the CPV logistical supply lines could not move fast enough to fuel the troops. In late November 1950, the CPV soldiers were gathering forces for another big push near Chosin Reservoir, where we encountered the U.S. Marine First Division and the Capital Division of South Korean forces. Many soldiers already suffered from exposure to temperatures lower than thirty degrees below zero Fahrenheit. One night it was reported to me that an entire squad collapsed in the snowstorm. When I rushed to the squad's post in the trench, I was dumbfounded by the scene: all nine soldiers stood firm in their positions cuddling rifles in hands. They were all unconscious and covered by layers of snow. As those bodies under the thin uniforms began to turn cold, I also realized that their food bags were empty. None of them survived to participate in the offensive attack; only their names were sent to the headquarters to be listed as noncombat casualties. The real fighting was yet to begin, and blizzards and starvation had already claimed the lives of numerous soldiers.

I later read about this kind of occurrence in the Chinese official sources regarding CPV campaigns during the Korean War. For the first time the Chinese military admitted that shortages in food and winter uniforms also caused large noncombat losses.[2] Father mourned those who died before they were able to fire a single gunshot in combat. Whether or not a soldier died in actual combat, he viewed all those who perished in the Korean War as heroes who had sacrificed everything for their country.

Father kept a collection of Korean War stories written by CPV soldiers. He often told us that those stories displayed, in most cases, only the bright side of the war. Other, less-positive stories were buried in the minds of many who fought the war. I still have this book today. It presents personal experiences of the Korean War, all heroic ones describing victorious battles and triumphant returns.[3] Having also heard many different war stories from my father and other Korean War veterans, I started to wonder how the public would respond if stories about the other side of the coin were published.

From time to time, Father would recall the experiences of his war buddies. Lieutenant General Wei Jic, who grew up in a neighboring village close to where Father was raised, left home at age fifteen to join the CCP Red Army in 1929. He fought and commanded numerous battles and campaigns, and his military career had since become legendary. In the Korean War he headed the Sixtieth Army under the Third Army Group, one of the first three CPV Army groups that marched across the Yalu River into Korea. Little did he realize, however, that the bitter experience of his Sixtieth Army in the CPV Fifth Campaign between April 22 and June 10, 1951, would change his military as well as his political life forever.

On May 26, the 180th Division of the Sixtieth Army was besieged by the Seventh and Twenty-fourth Divisions of the U.S. Army deep in the mountains between Chunchon and Chichon-ni, some forty miles northeast of Seoul. Other CPV divisions were too far away to come to their rescue. Their radio was damaged by severe enemy bombing; food and ammunition were running out, and fatigue from fighting plagued every soldier. The division headquarters did not organize a counterattack. Instead, the division commanders decided that soldiers and officers were to manage on their own a penetration of the enemy encirclement. Tragically, the 180th Division was nearly wiped out by the American forces. The captured consisted of more than one-third of the entire CPV POWs. Among them was the division Political Commissar Wu Chengde, the highest-ranking CPV officer ever to become a POW in the Korean War.[4] The commander and deputy commander of the division made their way back to the army headquarters, and they were later court-martialed. The Fifth Campaign proved to be the most disastrous setback for the CPV in the Korean War. Within a month the armistice negotiations began.

As the commander of the Sixtieth Army, Wei Jie was held responsible by the CPV Headquarters for the misjudgment and misconduct of the 180th Division commanders and for the loss of the entire division. General Peng Dehuai, the supreme commander of the CPV, severely chastised Wei Jie for not having given timely instructions to the 180th Division to arrange a countersiege offensive.[5] As the war dragged into another year, both the Sixtieth Army and the 180th Division were reorganized into the Twentieth Army Group. Wei Jie returned to China in mid-1952 only to find out that he was to become the chair of the Department of Correspondence Education in a military academy. No promotion was awarded for his contribution in the Korean War. Later in his memoir General Wei wrote: "It was the 180th Division commanders who should be blamed for the disaster. They panicked when facing the threat of the enemy. Our soldiers and officers demonstrated courage. With respect to the accountability, Premier Zhou Enlai in

1953 confirmed personally to me that I should not be held responsible for the loss of the 180th division."[6] The new assignment, however, carried a clear implication that his legendary military commanding career ended with the Korean War. He continued to stay in the army, but from now on only as a political commissar or as secretary of the CCP branch in the army.[7] Military affairs had become history for him. General Wei sometimes joked to Father that if we wanted to study in his military academy, he would keep the "back door" open for us.

Father and many of his Korean War buddies did not receive promotions upon their return from Korea. Homecoming parades, flowers, and handshakes were all they enjoyed. In most cases, they kept similar positions and ranks and went back to where they came from. Life seemed to go on as if little had happened. When Father retired from the military, he was often visited by editors and scholars of military history, who were either writing oral histories or composing historical source books. Stories about the Communist Red Army before 1937 and fighting experiences of the Chinese Liberation Army against the Nationalist forces in the civil war (1945–49) were always the major topics of discussion. Seldom did visitors ask Father about the Korean War, and no one seemed to be enthusiastic about collecting memories of this war.

During the Cultural Revolution in the late 1960s, the period known as the "years of chaos," more visitors from political personnel departments in the military frequented our house. They were not pressing Father for revolutionary stories; they were investigating some of his comrades-in-arms. Questions they often asked were: "Do you know if Comrade so-and-so committed any wrongdoing during the Korean War?" "Have you ever been captured and released by the Americans in the war?" No explanation was given as to how such "wrongdoing" should be defined. One evening at the dinner table, I heard Father mentioning this issue to Mother and wondering, "Maybe elsewhere they are asking others the same questions about me." One of the main features of the Cultural Revolution was to scrutinize society extensively in order to dig out "hidden enemies." Anti-Western and anti-American sentiment, which reached its height during the Korean War years, remained strong and often was rampant. In such a political atmosphere, Korean War veterans were likely to be questioned, and returned Korean War prisoners of war, in particular, became natural targets to be labeled as "traitors" and "American spies."

For the Chinese, the legacy of the Korean War was not just about veterans and returned POWs. The ongoing political conflict at home also affected how the war was remembered. On the one hand, the Chinese government claimed that the Korean War was China's first international victory over an imperialist power in a century. So it was a great war, and the Chinese people should feel proud of their military forces and of their soldiers. On the other hand, the war was deliberately forgotten because of the power struggles within the CCP. The political and ideological splits within the CCP during the late 1950s resulted in the ousting of Marshall Peng Dehuai. To make the situation worse, for the first time in its history the Chinese military faced the issue of POWs. It was also the first time that Chinese soldiers were captured by foreign troops and held on foreign land. Not only the CCP and the military but also the entire nation had to deal with the issue of captivity in an international context. China's five-thousand-year history had not provided the nation with such a precedent. When the armistice agreement was signed in 1953, for the survivors, war was over. But for the POWs, their nightmare had just begun.

In 1986, Da Ying, a military writer, published a book entitled *The CPV POWs and Their Stories*. The book revealed to the Chinese public many untold stories about the CPV POWs, their fighting in POW camps and the treatment they received upon returning home. Of more than 20,000 CPV POWs, some 6,673 came back to China when the armistice agreement was signed in 1953. The rest, 10,400, went to Taiwan.[8] Our cultural vocabulary invests almost exclusively negative meanings in the word "POW," which is generally associated with traitors, cowards, humiliation, and disloyalty. When Father read the book, he said that many CPV were captured when they ran out of ammunition, were wounded, or were surrounded by the enemies. But they were not traitors; they were not cowards or disloyal to our country. Most of the returned POWs received unfair treatment in their political life and employment. Many were accused of betrayal and disloyalty.

The story about the tragic fate of the 180th Division was not released to the public until the late 1980s. Wu Chengde, the political commissar of the 180th Division, was one of those who went back to China after the armistice agreement was signed. He was deprived of his CCP membership, ousted from his military rank, dishonorably discharged, and demoted to work in a farm plantation in Liaoning Province. Throughout the twenty-some years until his retirement in 1975, he wrote numerous confessions and appeals, feeling guilty that his leadership had led to the loss of his division. But, even today, he refuses to tell his story to the public.[9] In the Chinese public and official judgment, Wu Chengde is guilty because he should have led the division to fight to the last man. He did not, either because he could not or because he did not have the guts to face such overwhelming odds. Had he done so, he would have been killed but remembered as a hero. Father once mentioned Wu's case and said he would never abandon his troops should he face a similar situation. He would organize a counterattack to break through the enemy lines. He said he might die as a result, but he would never choose to dismiss the division. But Father also murmured: "I really have no idea how I would feel if I became a POW."

Captive CPV soldiers who came home from Korea faced a fate as dismal as Wu's, as I learned when I was conducting a social survey while I was a college student in the 1970s. Twenty classmates and I traveled to a remote village in the South, and for about a month, we lived and ate at peasants' homes and worked with them in the fields. From the very beginning, we were constantly reminded by the village head, who was also the farm brigade leader, that we should not make any contact with the few "bad guys" in the village, one of them a returned Korean War POW. Ironically, since we could hardly understand the local dialect of those villagers, this returned POW turned out to be one of the few people we could communicate with. One day he approached me and asked if I came from a military family. I wondered what made him think so. "It is because you often wear an army jacket," he replied. It was Father's uniform. Because I liked it, Father had ordered a smaller size for me.[10] The man went on to tell me that he had fought in the Korean War. "Unfortunately, I was captured by the big-nosed Americans"; he sounded quite remorseful. I mentioned to him that my father was also in the war. "He must have been a commanding officer, was he not?" He was so sure, and I concurred. It did not take me long to learn his story. He spent nearly three years in Korea, one year on the battlefield and two in a POW camp. Upon returning home, he was forced to make a confession on why he was captured. In his village, he was classified as a "bad guy" and could only work in the field under surveillance. In all those years he was denied opportunities for employment in factories and receiving a pension for his military service. Villagers despised him because of his POW history. "I could hardly control my fate of becoming a POW because I was wounded when taken captive. I did not want to be a POW, and I did not do anything disloyal to my country." I understood his frustration perfectly, but I could do nothing to help him.

One evening he invited us to have snacks with him at his home. Five of us went, and he made us some delicious rice cakes. The following morning my friends and I were told to report to the political instructor who was with us from the college. The next thing I knew, a "struggle meeting," attended by all villagers and the twenty of us, had been organized to charge this returned POW with conspiring to poison the minds of young people with "honey-coated bombs." He was isolated for a few days, and his workload in the field increased. We were warned not to speak to him any more. The five of us each had to make self-criticisms in front of the entire class; we had not been vigilant enough in our duty to recognize signs of "class struggle." Almost overnight the "rice cake incident" had become a matter of class struggle between "good guys" and "bad guys." I never had another chance to talk to him again during the remaining days there. I left the village with many questions: What made this returned POW a "bad guy"? What if Father had also been captured and returned? Father and this POW shared a similar fate; both had fought in the Korean War. Both were loyal and patriotic Chinese. Why was one good and one bad? They should either be both good or both bad. But there was one thing I was sure of: The rice cakes with peanuts wrapped inside tasted delicious.

I talked about this with my father the following summer when I went home. He seemed to be lost when trying to give me a proper answer. He said we were all helpless in this case simply because government policy had been developed to deal with the issue of returned POWs in this way. He regretted that the returned POW in the village did not receive fair treatment. Finally, news came in 1980 that the People's Liberation Army (PLA), with the help of the civil administration, decided to conduct a nationwide survey of all the returned Korean War POWs and to grant them rehabilitation.[11] Today in many regions, however, the rehabilitation process is yet to be accomplished. For many Korean War veterans and returned POWs, the nightmare of the war—and its legacy—haunts them still.

In the summer of 1995 when the main framework of this paper was formulated, the Korean War Memorial was dedicated in Washington, DC, to veterans of the war as well as the 54,246 Americans killed in Korea. China is believed to have suffered more than one million deaths in the Korean War, and those who survived have to cope with their life at home.[12] The war, however, did promote China's prominence in the international communist movement, and lessons of the war also contributed to the normalization of Sino–American relations two decades later. The Korean War has occupied an important place in contemporary Chinese history. I wish that those who once fought gallantly for the newly established People's Republic of China could also receive the honor they are entitled to and feel proud for having fought in the war.

Upon his removal by President Harry S. Truman from the post as the supreme commander of the UN forces in Korea in 1951, General Douglas MacArthur gave his eloquent speech in Congress. He referred to a popular barrack ballad that proclaimed that "Old soldiers never die. They just fade away." The nature of the Korean War has been controversial because of historical and political complications in both the United States and China. But the "fading away" of the fallen soldiers and veterans of the Korean War, be they American or Chinese, has taught us how important it is to preserve peace and eliminate war.

For me, the war has always been remote. I felt it close only when talking with Father. Although my years of serving in the military have long since passed, I continue to cherish my childhood dream. I still keep the army uniform Father gave to me. But if my child chooses to serve in the military for his country when he grows up, I hope he will never have to fight a war like the Korean War.

Notes

1. Wei Wei, "Who Are the Most Beloved People," in *Kang-Mei yuan-chao sanwen xuanji* [Selection of Essays on the War to Resist American and Aid Korea], ed. Zhang Wenyuan (Beijing: People's Literature Press, 1953).

2. History Department of China Military Science Institute, ed., *History of the Chinese People's Volunteers in the War to Resist America and Aid Korea* (Beijing: Military Science Press, 1990), p. 52.

3. *A Day of the Chinese People's Volunteers* (Beijing: People's Literature Press, 1956).

4. The Chinese military forces did not adopt a military ranking system until 1955. So the rank of a division commander then was equivalent to colonel.

5. Hong Xuezhi, *Recollections of the War to Resist U.S. Aggression and Aid Korea* (Beijing: People's Liberation Army Literature Press, 1990), p. 166.

6. Wei Jie, *Memoir of Wei Jie* (Nanning: Guangxi People's Press, 1989), p. 162.

7. Political positions have always been a part of the Chinese military organization. From the company level up to the unit commander, a political position parallel to the military has been designated from the beginning of its history. Those who hold such positions would be called political instructors at the company level, political commissars at brigade level, and so on. The major responsibilities of the political commander includes conducting propaganda work, keeping soldiers' morale high, and taking care of routine political education of the unit. Both political and military commanders at the same unit level would be granted equal ranking.

8. Da Ying, *Stories About the CPV POWs* (Beijing: People's Liberation Army Literature Press, 1986), p. 3.

9. Ibid., pp. 13–14.

10. The army uniform became fashionable especially among young people during the 1960s and 1970s. Anyone could wear the uniform without the insignia.

11. Da, *Stories About the CPV POWs,* pp. 291–92.

12. The number of total Chinese casualties in the Korean War is believed to be greatly minimized in official documents released to the public. While the Chinese government reported about 360,000 casualties (including dead and wounded soldiers), Western sources estimate a million Chinese deaths in the war. See also History Department of China Military Science Institute, *History of the Chinese People's Volunteers,* p. 2.

12

Myth of the Heroic Soldier and
Images of the Enemy

James Z. Gao

It was late 1978. The news broadcast by the Xinhua News Agency stated that China and the United States were about to establish formal diplomatic relations. After the surprising visit by President Richard Nixon seven years before, such an announcement did not come as a shock to the Chinese audience. People continued their routines, and few foresaw that this news would bring anything remarkable to alter their lives. At the Xinhua Kindergarten in Shanghai where my aunt worked, the children, as usual, sat in a circle, clapping their hands and singing. The teacher leading the songs—my aunt—asked them to sing whatever they knew. Some started to sing:

"Fighters and Cannons / Kill the Americans." My aunt, Yen Ying, hurried to stop the singing. "No, no," she told the children, "We cannot kill the Americans. They are our friends now."

My aunt's story reminded me of my childhood in Shanghai. Not really understanding the meaning of the song, of killing Americans, children had sung it for decades since the Korean War. I did, too, as did my brothers and sisters.

Singing is a principal part of the Chinese preschool education, and many songs taught at nursery schools are political. Their lyrics eulogize Chairman Mao, the Communist Party and the motherland, and condemn American imperialism. Teachers found nothing wrong with songs that included those themes or even endorsed "killing Americans"—until 1979.

While growing up, we liked to sing songs from popular movies. One of our favorites was the song "My Motherland," from a war movie, *Shangganling*. The movie told the story of the bloody warfare that took place at the small town, Shangganling, during the Korean War. The fighting started on October 14, 1952, and lasted for forty-three days. It was reported that more than 100,000 Chinese and American troops were involved, and the total casualty count on both sides was estimated at 50,000. A famous Chinese hero, a Chinese People's Volunteer (CPV) soldier, Huang Jiguang, laid down his life in this battle. He blocked the gunport of an enemy pillbox with his body in order to screen his company's advance, thus becoming a model of patriotism and heroism. During the lulls in the bloody fighting, a nurse and the soldiers in a tunnel sang the song "My Motherland":

> The girls are beautiful as flowers,
> The boys are upright as mountains,
> We entertain friends with wine,
> We deal with wolves with gun.

The music of the song was so beautiful that it immediately became a Chinese favorite after the movie was released. Everyone, including children, understood that the "wolves" in the song meant the Americans.

The mass media and the government offered the same version of the Korean War. Like a pair of chopsticks, they cooperated in harmony, filling our childhood memories with images of cowardly American soldiers and heroic CPV soldiers who went to Korea to fight a just war against America, the aggressor.

These images even left their imprint on the games we played. I lived in a residential compound with six three-storied buildings standing in a row; all the families shared a backyard. My friends and I played war games there many times. We were divided into two mixed-age groups to "fight" against each other. Every time the winners had the privilege of declaring themselves members of the CPV or the People's Liberation Army while the losers were embarrassed by being called "American devils." None of us doubted that the Korean War ended with the Chinese gaining a glorious victory. So every child was "fighting" bravely to avoid losing the game and being humiliated by being labeled an American.

Another favorite game for Chinese boys was "prison's base." Again, the children were divided into two camps by a line drawn on the ground. Each side tried to cross the border to attack the enemy and to catch those from the enemy side who invaded their territory. Such games would always end up with U.S. soldiers being captured by the CPV. The term "POW" was always derogatory because, according to communist teaching, a soldier would rather die in battle than surrender to the enemy. We were sure that only American cowards could be POWs.

China's entry into the Korean War, known in China as the movement to "Resist America and Aid Korea," had created extensive patriotism and intensified anti-American sentiment throughout the country. Since the war was eating up about half the country's budget, China was suffering from a serious shortage of funds. The government encouraged people to donate cash or other valuables to help buy fighter planes. A famous actress of Yuju (Henan Opera), Zhang

Xiangyu, made the headlines in the Chinese press. She held some benefit performances in the name of the war, donated all her income from the box office, and bought a Russian-made MiG-15 fighter for the CPV air force.

Zhang's example inspired children to contribute also to the war effort. In 1951, my older brother started going to primary school. There he and his classmates wrote letters and made gift bags with candies, teacups, pens, or small souvenirs, sending them to the CPV soldiers, who were called "the most beloved people."

College students and people from all walks of life also did something in support of the war. It was reported that the students of Beijing University sent three hundred letters and six thousand gift bags to the CPV within three days. There was a card in one gift bag that said the following:

Dear comrade,

We present to you a towel and soap with which you'll wipe away the sweat and clean your body stained with blood. Take a rest and be ready for the next attack. Let more enemies lie down under your sword.[1]

The Chinese poet Ke Zhongping wrote a poem memorializing China's support of her warriors:

A heart was put into the gift bag,
A heart was sent with the letter,
A million valiant and industrious people
Are showing off to you a million loving hearts.[2]

In the 1950s, there was a famous poster that was a photograph of two smiling children with pigeons in their hands. One was a boy of about six, another a girl of about four. The poster was entitled "We love peace," and thousands of copies were printed and widely posted in Korea and China. It demonstrated the government's interpretation of the Korean War: The CPV were fighting to defend us, the Chinese peace-loving children.

The confrontation between the United States and China clearly made school education "anti-American" in orientation. I distinctly remember English courses disappearing from the curriculum at most schools. Saint Francis College, where I studied for two years, used to be a British missionary school that had its main campus in Shanghai and a branch campus in Hong Kong. Renamed the Shanghai Beihong Middle School in 1949, the board of directors was dismissed, but most teachers, including the best English teachers, were asked to stay. When I went to the school in the 1960s, Russian was a general requirement at the school. The English teachers had been ordered to forget their English and study Russian in order to offer it to the students. Several years later, because of the Sino–Soviet split, many schools, including the Shanghai Beihong Middle School, shifted back to teaching English. But students were not interested in either Russian or English because they saw no use in studying these "enemy languages" in isolated China.

High school textbooks were created to satisfy the demands of the struggle against American imperialism and Soviet revisionism. Korean War literature was suggested as readings for political indoctrination, history, and literature courses. Approaching history with memories of a glorious traditional status as a global power, followed by the humiliation of defeat and division into spheres of economic influence at the hands of the West, China was proud of the CPV who defeated the Western superpower in Korea. The government clearly invoked the war as a convenient wellspring of patriotism.

The students were required to recite some poems and articles extolling the CPV soldiers. The following is an example from an essay by the writer Wei Wei entitled "Who Are the Most Beloved People":

Dear Friends,

When you take the first trolleybus in the morning to the factory, when you plow your fields, when you . . . go to school, when you plan your schedule for the day at your desk, . . . when you enjoy a leisurely walk with your husband or wife—are you aware of the happiness all around you? In response, you might say, "All of these experiences are very common, aren't they?" Soldiers returning from Korea will tell you that you are living a good life. Please realize your own happiness. Only with this awareness can you better understand the selfless fighting of our soldiers in Korea. Friends, since you love our motherland and our leader so much, you must surely love our soldiers deeply. They are indeed our most beloved people.[3]

Like much literature on the Korean War, Wei Wei's essay praised the brave deeds of the "most beloved people" and their North Korean allies and extolled the "Sino–Korean friendship cemented with blood." Since this essay was published in 1951, the "most beloved people" has become the term of endearment for the CPV and the CPV's food—"parched flour plus snow" become a symbol of arduous struggle. As mandatory reading in all schools, Wei Wei's work imbued the students with heroism, patriotism, and a spirit of devotion to internationalism.

In contrast to the "most beloved people," the U.S. military forces were portrayed in the Chinese literature and movies about the Korean War as playboys lacking fighting morale and as cowards. U.S. soldiers were always stereotyped as lovers of jazz music, wild dances, alcohol, and pornographic pictures. In the 1950s and 1960s, anti-American street performances were a regular part of mass demonstrations or holiday festivals. The American soldier was the easiest role to play because his only lines were "I beg your mercy" and "I surrender."

In comparison, many more dramas and movies in China were made about the anti-Japanese War between 1937 and 1945. They showed how Japanese soldiers killed innocents, raped women, and burned villages. The image of the Japanese soldiers as bloodthirsty savages is so graphically presented that in the war-devastated areas of North China rural women use the warning of "Japanese monsters are coming" to silence crying children at night.

According to the Marxist theory of class struggle, those at the lowest levels of the social ladder oppose aggressive wars; therefore, some footage was devoted to poor Japanese working people, especially women, being victimized by their rulers. Yet in the Korean War movies, all Americans, without class distinction, were personified as depraved or cowardly. The image of merciless Japanese soldiers reminds the Chinese of the suffering during war and the deep-seated hatred for Japanese militarism, while the image of American cowards seems to embody Mao's statement that American imperialism was a "paper tiger."[4]

When the "police action" started in Korea, the United States sent the Seventh Fleet to the Taiwan Strait. The Chinese communists saw this as support of Chiang Kai-shek in Taiwan, who sought the end of the communist regime on the mainland. In Beijing's view, the Americans and Chiang Kai-shek were closely linked to each other. "The U.S.-Chiang spies" were, therefore, regarded as the number one threat to the People's Republic of China. Many movies produced in those years repeated a stale story: A spy, trained by the CIA and sent by Chiang Kai-shek, penetrated the mainland. His American boss did not inform him that on the mainland the Korean War was called the "Resist America, Aid Korea" movement. When he referred to the war using the wrong phrase, the U.S.-Chiang spy was immediately caught by the Chinese security forces.

The Korean War also made the Chinese wary of strangers. Those who returned from abroad or had overseas connections were naturally suspected. One of my professors at Beijing University, who was educated in the United States, told me of his experience:

> I decided to return to China when the Korean War broke out. I did not feel right staying in a country that was fighting with my motherland. I believed that I would make a contribution to the country with my knowledge. Upon my arrival in Beijing I was welcomed and praised for my patriotism. But during the Cultural Revolution I was accused of being sent by and working for the CIA. The Red Guards told me that I had been suspected since the first day I came back.

In 1958, the CPV excited the country once again. When the last CPV group withdrew from Korea, the Beijing railway station was splendidly decorated and overflowing with people welcoming them home. The scene was filmed and, with the addition of other pieces from newsreels on the Korean War, a documentary was subsequently produced and shown throughout the country. The place of the CPV as national heroes in Chinese history was fully established.

The public memory of the Korean War, however, soon faded. In the mass media emotional propaganda stopped, names of the CPV heroes were no longer mentioned, and some movies about the war that had been made were not allowed to be shown. Most CPV officers were not promoted as they had been after every battle in the civil war. Many veterans did not get suitable jobs (though 300,000 of them got medals of honor). One of the CPV heroes reported by Wei Wei in his famous essay "Who Are the Most Beloved People" returned to his village and resumed his work as a peasant. It was not until 1994 that anybody knew or asked about what he had done in Korea.

The principal reason for this forgetting was the ongoing power struggle within the Chinese communist leadership. The supreme commander of the CPV, Marshall Peng Dehuai, argued with Mao Zedong over domestic policies at the Lushan Conference. This triggered a party purge in 1959. Peng was ousted from office, and many officers associated with him were persecuted. The glory of the CPV perished as their commander disappeared from the political stage.

In the early 1960s, China experienced an economic depression and famine. One official explanation for this was that the Soviet Union had forced China to pay back its Korean War debt. China had used the Soviet loans mostly for the purchase of war material from the Soviet Union. The total credits were 18.16 billion new rubles (U.S. $4.54 billion), the majority of which was used up in the Korean War. Between 1954 and 1961, China had paid the principal and interest on these loans, mainly by yearly exports of foodstuffs to the Soviet Union. Some say this led to China's internal food shortage.

In the Hundred Flowers Movement of 1957, some people made an anti-Soviet complaint by arguing that "it was unreasonable for China to bear all the expenses of the 'Resist America, Aid Korea War.' "[5] These people were suppressed and labeled as "rightists."[6] In the early 1960s, however, economic depression weakened the government's control, and the people were again able to voice their grievances.[7]

At that time the Sino–Soviet split gradually became an open secret, and people started to criticize the Soviet Union, with which they had long been discontented. It was commonly argued that the CPV shed the blood in Korea while the Soviet Union lent China weapons for which it demanded repayment. The crusade against Soviet revisionism provoked condemnation of the Soviet Union for not keeping its word to provide the CPV with air force support and for the percentage of the shells sold to China that failed to detonate during the fighting.

Beijing never released the total Chinese casualty count in the Korean War.[8] Official statistics of some battles indicate that the enemy–friendly casualty ratio was about 2:1 or 1.6:1. Yet movies and novels fostered military romanticism; people believed that Chinese victory came at a very small cost. In the summer of 1961, I had a chance to visit some family friends who took part in the war. I was surprised at their discontent with the cinematic propaganda. These Korean War veterans told me about the cruelty of the war, the tough American enemy, and how many of their comrade-in-arms died in battle. Their stories coincided with recent emphasis on China's sacrifice in newspapers, revealing higher Chinese casualties.

It was also the first time that I was aware of the POW exchange between the Chinese and the UN forces after the armistice agreement was signed. I was puzzled. The children's version of war was a game of "good guys versus bad guys" and there were no "gray areas." But what about the Chinese POWs? I could hardly connect the image of the heroic CPVs with that of the shameful POWs. Neither the Korean War veterans nor my schoolteachers would answer me when I asked whether the Chinese POWs were traitors or cowards. The question remained with me, and for a long time I, like most Chinese, did not sympathize with those returning Chinese POWs who were socially ostracized.

In the Sino–Soviet dispute of the 1960s, the ambiguous stance of the North Koreans disappointed the Chinese. The image of our comrade-in-arms was darkened. Some people started to doubt whether it had been worthwhile for the Chinese to have paid the heavy toll in the war. In private conversations, college students even challenged the government's version of the war by asking: Who launched the Korean War? Who won the war? Why should the Chinese fight for Kim Il Sung? The political climate soon changed, however, silencing all the whispers. When Mao called to "never forget the class struggle" in 1964, government censorship of public opinion was tightened again.

Two years later, Mao launched the Cultural Revolution. It revived the public memories of the Korean War since the masses were mobilized in the name of anti-American imperialism and anti-Soviet revisionism. Mao needed to use the United States as an enemy to attack and to boast of China's victory in the Korean War in order to encourage the young. It was against this background that Korean War movies and operas reappeared in Chinese theaters.

In the Cultural Revolution, traditional operas were denounced as feudalistic, superstitious, and vulgar. Only five revolutionary Peking operas were allowed to be performed. One was *Qixi baihutuan* (Raid on the White Tiger Regiment), which was based on a battle in the Korean War. It extolled a CPV scout platoon who stealthily raided and destroyed the headquarters of the South Korean "White Tiger Regiment." Their raid contributed to the last Chinese offensive, which destroyed the South Korean Capital Division in July 1953.

This Peking opera was adapted to a movie, *Kuaiban* (a story recited to the rhythm of bamboo clappers), and to many local operas performed by both professional and amateur troupes. The genres of opera and movie reached a wider audience than Wei Wei's essays or any other written literature. They were particularly welcomed in the rural areas, for most Chinese peasants were still illiterate, and their culture was largely oral and localized. Just as John Wayne never died in the American Western movies, the CPV never lost a single battle. The Chinese audience enjoyed quick and easy war victories on the screen and stage. Once again, the CPV soldiers were recast and mythologized.

During the Cultural Revolution, almost all feature films produced before 1966 were withdrawn from public viewing. Only a few films were exceptions, and one of them was *Yingxiong ernü* (The Heroic Sons and Daughters). The movie was adapted from the novel *Tuan yuan* (Reunion) by the famous Chinese writer Ba Jin. The dramatic plot of the original story was a reunion of a separated Chinese family on foreign soil. The hero of the novel was a veteran communist who was in charge of the secret revolutionary activities in Shanghai and was arrested by the Nationalist government. Thus he lost track of his baby daughter in the 1930s. Twenty years later, Chinese people from all walks of life were involved in the Korean War, and people from all corners of China went to Korea. This created a chance for the father to find his missing daughter on the battlefield.

In the movie, the heroes belonged to the second generation of the communist revolution. The missing daughter, Wang Fang, had been brought up by a worker family. She and her stepbrother, Wang Cheng, joined the CPV when the Korean War broke out. Wang Cheng died heroically in battle; in his courageous acts, the audience could see the stories of Huang Jiguang, Yang Gensi, and other CPV martyrs. Wang Fang was a member of the army's art troupe. She wrote a play, a sort of musical, about her stepbrother and performed before the CPV soldiers and commanders. Wang Fang's birth father in the movie was the political commissar of a CPV army. He instructed Wang Fang on how to revise the play not only to mourn her brother but also to call every soldier to follow his heroic example. The commissar then recognized Wang Fang as his missing daughter.

The Heroic Sons and Daughters owed its popularity to the fact that the young audience in the late 1960s readily identified with the characters. The movie portrayed the new generation that eventually inherited the heroic spirit of their fathers and was devoted to the revolution. The movie contained a great deal of romanticism, which impressed the young Chinese, especially the fanatical Red Guards.

During the Cultural Revolution, the fascination of the Red Guards with "revolutionary violence" was embodied in their burning Western and traditional Chinese literature, destroying temples and antiquities, doing house-to-house search for the "four olds,"[9] abusing teachers, and beating and even killing "counterrevolutionaries." In an attempt to relive their fathers' experiences, they took the route of the Red Army's Long March of 1934–35, traveling on foot a thousand miles from Jiangxi to Yan'an and passing through snowy mountains and marshlands. In so doing, these Red Guards believed that they were demonstrating their fathers' distinguished qualities: unyielding revolutionary will, daring to go against authority, showing no pity for the enemy, and standing ready to endure hardship and sacrifice.

In those years of chaos, the fanatical Red Guards declared that their goal was, as Marx and Mao said, "to liberate the whole of humankind." They believed in Mao's teaching that the whole course of world revolution hinged on the anti-American struggle of the world's people. They valued the heroism of the CPV

soldiers highly and criticized North Korea for forgetting its anti-American tradition. The Red Guards condemned the Korean "revisionism" of accepting Soviet
aid and denounced Kim Il Sung as an "aristocrat." Disappointed with North
Korea, they turned their sights on Vietnam. The Chinese and the Vietnamese, as
Ho Chi Minh said, were "comrade-brothers."

The Chinese teenage zealots were eager to join the Vietnam War. Zhao
Jianjun was one such teenager; his story was always on our lips during the
Cultural Revolution.[10] As a student at the Beijing No. 100 High School, Jianjun
and nine other Red Guards (eight boys and two girls) tried to cross the Chinese–
Vietnamese border to join the Vietnam War. These early Red Guards came from
families of military officers or high-ranking cadres who believed in an old Chinese saying: "Dragons bear dragons; phoenixes bear phoenixes; moles bear sons
accomplished in digging holes." A modern version of this traditional proverb
was "the son of a hero father is always a great man; a reactionary father produces
nothing but a bastard."

Jianjun and his friends were brought up in a political environment in which
revolutionary war was regarded as a just and sacred cause. A soldier's glory
excited the youngsters, who wished they had been born earlier so that they could
have fought against the Japanese or the Americans as their fathers had. Jianjun's
plan to join the "Resist America, Aid Vietnam" movement was inspired by Lin
Biao's arguments:

> The Chinese Communist road to the conquest of power was pursuit of national
> and social revolution through armed struggle in the countryside, encircling the
> cities the countryside and finally seizing the cities. The world revolution
> should also follow this road. Taking the entire globe, if North America and
> Western Europe can be called "the cities of the world," then Asia, Africa, and
> Latin America constitute "the rural areas of the world." The center of gravity
> of the world revolution lies in "this world's countryside."[11]

Jianjun and his friends had seen *Shangganling* and *The Heroic Sons and
Daughters* many times, and they carefully studied Lin Biao's article. Two
thoughts were foremost in their minds. First, Vietnam, as a Third World country,
was in the front line of the world revolution, and the heroic Vietnamese desperately needed Chinese help. Second, the "Resist America, Aid Vietnam" movement, like the Korean War, was an excellent chance for the revolutionary
youngsters to fight against U.S. imperialism.

When he left Beijing, Jianjun took with him a Soviet-made Kiev wristwatch
that his father had purchased during the Korean War. The watch, therefore, had a
symbolic meaning for him. The ten Red Guards went to the Chinese–Vietnamese
border by train and then slipped through the line. Six of them were arrested and
sent back to Beijing, while Jianjun and three boys succeeded in crossing into
Vietnam.

Having arrived in Hanoi, Jianjun and his friends went to the Chinese embassy for help. They expressed their determination to fight the Americans and asked the embassy to send them to the South to join the Viet Cong guerrillas. They said that they could not wait, since time was running out and the American aggressor would be wiped out in a couple of months. Their demands reminded the Chinese ambassador, Zhu Qiwen, of the days of his own youth. He promised to help them and asked Beijing for instructions. Premier Zhou Enlai personally reviewed the case and sent Ambassador Zhu this telegram:

> Ambassador Zhu, tell the four revolutionary Red Guards that we are embarrassed by the fact that they slipped through the border without China's or Vietnam's permission. But their determination to "resist America and aid Vietnam" is appreciated. I suggest sending them to our Aid-Vietnam troops for training. . . . This is not to be taken as a precedent.[12]

In November 1966, the four boys joined the Chinese artillery troop in Vietnam and took part in combat. This appealed very much to me and many other Red Guards who were tired of the Cultural Revolution but still pursuing the glory of soldier-heroes.

One month later, Jianjun died in battle at Onhuyen, Vietnam, and was offered a military honor like all other martyrs of the Korean War and the Vietnam War. His death, however, did not stop the march of small groups of Red Guards to Vietnam from sharing the experience of war.

In retrospect, one can find fluctuations in the Chinese memories of the Korean War as political ideas and realities constantly changed. In 1979, the final step for normalization of U.S.–Chinese relations was taken. What happened in my aunt's kindergarten class after the announcement of the U.S.–Chinese agreement was a signal of changes in policy and outlook. The Chinese started to see other images of Americans: the ping-pong players, the Great Wall climbers, physics professors, and smiling IBM salesmen. Although the official interpretation of the Korean War remains intact, the mass media have been reoriented, and scholars have started to look at the war from many perspectives.

In 1986, Da Ying published the book *Zhiyuanjun zhanfu jishi* (Stories About the CPV POWs). Based on intensive interviews with the POWs, he revealed the unfair treatment of the POWs by the government. Da used a traditional tactic to defend the POWs by indicating their unchanging loyalty to China and their suffering at the POW camps. Da Ying has not only won sympathy for the POWs in his readers, but raised fundamental questions about China's cult of CPV heroism.

Recently, love for and interest in the "most beloved people" have diminished among young Chinese people. At nightclubs or *karaoke* bars, the most popular songs are those from Taiwan and Hong Kong. Occasionally, a few people sing the old song "Heroic Sons and Daughters," and the huge screen shows the fighting of the Korean War. In the past, this song, steeped with history, resonated with thousands of Chinese. Today the audience might enjoy the music, but few really care about its historical message and political implications. For most Chinese, memories of the Korean War are too vague and remote.

Notes

1. Quoted from Xie Lifu, *Chaoxian zhanzheng shilu* [Real Records of the Korean War] (Beijing: World Knowledge Press), 1993, p. 729.

2. Ibid.

3. Wei Wei's essay, "Who Are the Most Beloved People," can be found in an eighth-grade Chinese textbook, Zhang Wenyuan, ed., *Kang-Mei yuan-chao sanwen xuanji [The Best of Prose Writings on the Resist-America Aid-Korea movement] (Beijing: People's Literature Press, 1990).*

Wei Wei (b. 1920) went to Korea in 1950 as a military journalist. His reportage on the CPV soon became the most influential reading in the 1950s and 1960s. His novel about the Korean War, *The East,* earned him the Mao Dun Literature Prize, the highest honor a writer can receive in China.

4. Mao Zedong, "Talks with the American Correspondent Anna Louise Strong" (August 1946), *Selected Works of Mao Zedong,* vol. 4 (Beijing: Foreign Language Press, 1966), p. 110.

5. General Long Yun's remarks, quoted in Roderick MacFarquhar, ed., *The Hundred Flowers* (London: Stevens, 1960), p. 50. Long was the Nationalist governor of Hunan Province. In 1949, he rebelled and crossed over to the communists. Because of his anti-Soviet stance, he was denounced as a "rightist" and purged from the government in 1957.

6. After 1957, the "rightists" were ranked with landlords, rich peasants, counterrevolutionaries, and evildoers; all were referred to as the people's enemies.

7. See Editorial Department of *People's Daily and Red Flag,* "Two Different Lines on the Questions of War and Peace—Comment on the Open Letter of the Central Committee of the CPSU(5)," *People's Daily,* November 19, 1963. Also see "Letter of CCP CC to CPSU CC, February 29, 1964," *People's Daily,* May 9, 1964.

8. According to American statistics, the Chinese sustained 909,607 casualties. See Bevin Alexander, *Korea: The First War We Lost* (New York: Hippocrene Books, 1986), p. 483.

9. The "four olds" were old ideas, old customs, old habits, and old culture. See *People's Daily*, August 23, 1966.

10. The name Jianjun means "building up the army," which indicates his family's military background.

11. See Lin Biao's article, "Long Live the Victory of People's War." Lin Biao (1907–1972), a PLA marshall, was elected as the CCP's vice-chairman and Mao's successor but soon lost power. On September 13, 1972, he attempted to escape from China and died in a plane crash.

12. Quoted in Yu Hui, ed., *Hongweibing miwen* [The Secret Records of the Red Guards] (Beijing: Union Press, 1993), p. 128.

Part IV

Comparative and Historical Perspectives

13

The Age of the World Target*

Rey Chow

> They did not want to risk wasting the precious weapon, and de-
> cided that it must be dropped visually and not by radar . . .
> —Barton J. Bernstein, "The Atomic Bombings
> Reconsidered."[1]

For most people who know something about the United States' intervention in
the Second World War, there is one image that predominates and seemingly
preempts the rest: the dropping of the atomic bomb on Hiroshima and Nagasaki,
pictorialized in the now familiar image of the mushroom cloud, with effects of
radiation and devastation of human life at a scale never before imaginable.[2]
Alternatively, we can also say that our knowledge about what happened to Hiroshima and Nagasaki is inseparable from the image of the mushroom cloud. As
knowledge, "Hiroshima" and "Nagasaki" come to us inevitably as representation
and, specifically, as a picture. Moreover, it is not a picture in the older sense of a
mimetic replication of reality; rather it has become in itself a sign of terror, a
kind of gigantic demonstration with us, the spectators, as the potential target.

For someone such as myself, who grew up among survivors of China's war
against Japan in the period 1937–45—the "Eight-Year War" as it is still called
among the Chinese—the image of the atomic bomb has always stood as a signifier for another kind of violence, another type of erasure. As a child, I was far
more accustomed to hearing about Japanese atrocities against Chinese men and
women during the war than I was to hearing about U.S. atrocities against Japan.
Among the stories of the war was how the arrival of the Americans brought
relief, peace, and victory for China; however hard the times were, it was a

---

*This piece was previously published in *Mass Culture and Everyday Life,* ed. Peter
Gibian (London: Routledge, 1997).

moment of "liberation." As I grow older, this kind of knowledge gathered from oral narratives persists in my mind not as proof of historical accuracy but rather as a kind of dissonance, an emotional effect that becomes noticeable because it falls outside the articulations generated by the overpowering image of the mushroom cloud. It is as if the sheer magnitude of destruction unleashed by the bombs demolished not only entire populations but also the memories and histories of tragedies that had led up to that apocalyptic moment, the memories and histories of those who had been brutalized, kidnapped, raped, and slaughtered in the same war by other forces.[3] To this day many people in Japan still passionately deny the war crimes committed by the Japanese military in East and Southeast Asia, and the label "Japanese" is hardly ever as culturally stigmatized as, say, the label "German," which for many is still a straightforward synonym for "nazi" and "fascist."[4]

There are, then, two concerns in this chapter. The first has to do with the significance of the atomic bomb as part of a global culture in which everything has become visual representation and "virtual" reality. The second has to do with the racial politics of knowledge production that may not at first seem related to the dropping of the atomic bomb and that, however, bears crucial ideological connections with the war once we reflect upon them closely.

Seeing Is Destroying

As a journalist recently commented, the bombs that fell on the two Japanese cities in August 1945 ended any pretense of equality between the United States and Japan. It was, he writes, "as if a steel battleship had appeared at Trafalgar, effortlessly and ruthlessly destroying the wooden enemy fleet. There was absolutely no contest."[5] Passages such as this rightly point to the fundamental shift of the technological scale and definition of the war, but what remains to be articulated is the political and ideological significance of this shift.

From a purely scientific perspective, the atomic bomb was, of course, the most advanced invention of the time. Like all scientific inventions, it had to be tested in order to have its effectiveness verified. It was therefore not an accident that the United States chose as its laboratory, its site of experimentation, a civilian rather than military space, since the former, with a much higher population density, was far more susceptible to demonstrating the upper ranges of the bomb's spectacular potential.[6] The mundane civilian space in the early hours of the morning, with ordinary people beginning their daily routines, offered the promise of numerical satisfaction, of a destruction whose portent defied the imagination. Such civilian spaces had to have been previously untouched by U.S. weaponry, so as to offer the highest possible accuracy for the postwar evaluations of the bombing experiments.[7] The fact that there were Christians and U.S. prisoners of war in such spaces, which were therefore not purely Japanese or "enemy" territories, did not seem to matter. And destroying one city was not enough: Since the United States had two bombs, one uranium (which was simple and gunlike, and nicknamed Little Boy) and the other plutonium (which worked with the complex and uncertain means of assembly known as the implosion design, and was nicknamed Fat Man),[8] both had to be tested to see which one should continue to be produced in the future.[9] After the more "primitive" uranium bomb was dropped on Hiroshima, the more elaborate, plutonium one was dropped on Nagasaki a few days later.[10]

There are many ways in which the development of modern science, with its ever-refined criteria for conceptualization, calculation, objectification, and experimentation, led up to these moments of explosion in what Michael S. Sherry calls "technological fanaticism."[11] But what was remarkable in the incident of the nuclear blast was not merely the complexity of scientific understanding.[12] It was rather the manner in which science—in this case, the sophisticated speculations about the relationships among energy, mass, speed, and light—was itself put at the service of a kind of representation whose power resides not in its difficulty but in its brevity and visibility. In a flash, the formula $E = mc^2$, which summarizes Einstein's theory of relativity and from which the bomb was derived, captured the magnitude of the bomb's destructive potential: one plane plus one bomb = minus one Japanese city. Was the formula a metaphor for the blinding flash of the atomic explosion itself, or vice versa?

Precisely because the various units of measurement must be carefully selected for such a formula to be even approximately correct, and precisely because, at the same time, such exactitude is incomprehensible and irrelevant to the layperson, "$E = mc^2$" exists far more as an image and a slogan than as substance, and far more as a political than as a scientific act. If the scientific accuracy and verifiability of this formula remain uncertain to this day, it was nonetheless a supremely effective weapon of persuasion and propaganda. The speed of light is supposed to be a maximum, the fastest anything could possibly travel. The speed of light *squared* is thus clearly and easily perceived as a very large multiplier. Because of its visual representability and simplicity, the formula successfully conveyed the important message that one little bomb could create a whole lot of terror and that one airplane was enough to destroy an entire nation's willingness to resist. It seized the imagination, most crucially, of the *nonscientist* such as the United States president, who consented to dropping the bombs on Hiroshima and Nagasaki.[13]

I should make clear that what I am suggesting is not simply that "science" was replaced by a visual gimmick, that the "real thing" was replaced by a mere representation. Instead, it is that the dropping of the bombs marked the pivot of the progress of science, a pivot that was to continue its impact on all aspects of human life long after the Second World War was over. Science has, in modernity, reached the paradoxical point whereby it is simultaneously advanced and reduced. Having progressed far beyond the comprehension of nonspecialists and with complexities that challenge even the imagination of specialists, science is meanwhile *experienced* daily as the practically useful, in the form of small, simple, matter-of-fact operations that the lay person can manipulate at his/her fingertips. Our daily uses of the telephone, the computer, e-mail, and other types of equipment are all examples of this paradoxical situation of "scientific advancement," in which the portentous disappears into the mundane, the effortless, and the intangible.[14] We perform these daily operations with ease, in forgetfulness of the theories and experiments that made them possible. Little do we think of the affinity between these daily operations and a disaster such as the atomic holocaust. To confront that affinity is to confront the terror that is the basis of our everyday life.

The gigantic impact of the explosion literally expressed itself—as if without effort—in a neat little formula that anyone could recall and invoke. An epochal destruction based on the speed of light became, for the ordinary person, an instantly visible, graspable, portable thing, like a control button at his command. The logic of the ending of this particular war was hence encapsulated in the formulaic elegance of "$E = mc^2$": the most rarefied knowledge of science became miniaturized and transmissible, and thus *democratized* as a weapon of attack.

From a military perspective, the mushroom cloud signals the summation of a history of military advancement and invention that has gone hand in hand with the development of representational technologies, in particular the technologies of seeing. As Paul Virilio asserts, "For men at war, the function of the weapon is the function of the eye."[15] Virilio argues time and again in his work that there are close affinities between war and vision. Since military fields were increasingly reconfigured as fields of visual perception, preparations for war were increasingly indistinguishable from preparations for making a film: "The Americans prepared future operations in the Pacific," Virilio writes, "by sending in filmmakers who were supposed to look as though they were on a location-finding mission, taking aerial views for future film production."[16]

In a well-known essay, "The Age of the World Picture," Martin Heidegger argues that in the age of modern technology, the world has become a "world picture." However, he adds, this "does not mean a picture of the world but the world conceived and grasped as a picture."[17] By this, Heidegger means that seeing and objectification have become so indispensable in the age of modern technology that understanding—"conceiving" and "grasping" the world—is now an act inseparable from visuality. Supplementing Heidegger, we may say that in the age of bombing, the world has been transformed into—is essentially conceived and grasped as—a target. To conceive of the world as a target is to conceive of it as an object to be destroyed. As W.J. Perry, a former U.S. under-secretary of state for defense, is known to have said: "If I had to sum up current thinking on precision missiles and saturation weaponry in a single sentence, I'd put it like this: once you can see the target, you can expect to destroy it."[18] Increasingly, war would mean the production of maximal visibility and illumination for the purpose of maximal destruction. It follows that the superior method of guaranteeing efficient destruction by visibility during the Second World War was aerial bombing, which the United States continued even after Japan had made a conditional surrender.[19]

If the dropping of the atomic bomb created "deterrence," as many continue to believe to this day, what is the nature of deterrence? (We can ask the same question about "security," "defense," "protection," and other similar concepts.) The atomic bomb did not simply stop the war; it also stopped the war by escalating and democratizing violence to a hitherto unheard of scale. What succeeded in "deterring" the war was an ultimate (am)munition; destruction was now outdone by destruction itself. The elimination of the actual physical warring activities had the effect not of bringing war to an end but instead of promoting and accelerating terrorism, and, importantly, the terrorism of so-called deterrent weaponry. The mushroom cloud, therefore, is also the image of *this* transfer, this blurring of the boundary between war and peace. The transfer ushered in the new age of relativity and virtuality, an age in which powers of terror are indistinguishable from powers of "deterrence," and technologies of war indissociable from practices of peace. These new forces of relativity and virtuality are summarized in the following passages from Virilio:

> There is no war, then, without representation, no sophisticated weaponry without psychological mystification. Weapons are tools not just of destruction but also of perception—that is to say, stimulants that make themselves felt through chemical, neurological processes in the sense organs and the central nervous system, affecting human reactions and even the perceptual identification and differentiation of object. . . .
>   . . . By demonstrating that they would not recoil from a civilian holocaust, the Americans triggered in the minds of the enemy that *information explosion* which Einstein, towards the end of his life, thought to be as formidable as the atomic blast itself.
>   . . . even when weapons are not employed, they are active elements of ideological conquest.[20]

This merging of war and representation, war technology and peace-time technology has brought about a number of changes.

First, the visual rules and boundaries of war altered. While battles in the olden days tended to be fought with a clear demarcation of battlefronts versus civilian spaces, the aerial bomb, for instance, by its positionings in the skies, its intrusion into spaces that used to be off-limits to soldiers, and its distance from the enemies (a distance that made it impossible for the enemies to fight back), destroyed once and for all those classic visual boundaries that used to define battle. Second, with the transformation of the skies into war zones from which to attack, war was no longer a matter simply of armament or of competing projectile weaponry; rather, it became redefined as a matter of the logistics of perception, with seeing as its foremost function, its foremost means of preemptive combat.

Third, in yet a different way, the preemptiveness of seeing as a means of destruction continues to operate as such even after the war. Insofar as the image of the atomic blast serves as a peacetime weapon to mobilize against war, it more or less precludes other types of representation. *Nuclear* danger becomes the predominant target against which peace coalitions aim their efforts, while the equally disastrous effects caused by chemical and biological weapons (nerve gases such as sarin and bacteria such as anthrax) seldom receive the same kind of extended public consideration. Because of the overwhelming effect of the continual imaging of the mushroom cloud, the world responds to the nuclear blast as if by mimicry, by making the nuclear horror its predominant point of identification and attack, and by being oblivious to other forms of damage to the ecosphere that have not attained the same level of *visibility*.

The World Becomes Virtual

The dropping of the atomic bomb effected what Michel Foucault would call a major shift in *epistemes,* a fundamental change in the organization, production, and circulation of knowledge.[21] War after the atomic bomb would no longer be the physical, mechanical struggles between combative oppositional groups, but would more and more come to resemble collaborations in the logistics of perception between *partners* who occupy relative, but always mutually related, positions.[22] As in the case of the competition between the United States and the Soviet Union for several decades, war was more and more to be fought in virtuality, as an exchange of defensive positionings, a mutually coordinated routine of upping the potential for war, a race for the deterrent. Warring in virtuality meant competing with the enemy for the stockpiling, rather than actual use, of preclusively horrifying weaponry. To terrorize the other, one specializes in representation, in the means of display and exhibition. As Virilio writes, "A war of pictures and sounds is replacing the war of objects (projectiles and missiles)."[23] In the name of arms reduction and limitation, the SALT and START agreements served to promote, improve, and multiply armament between the United States and the Soviet Union, which were, strictly speaking, allies rather than adversaries in the "star wars" (Strategic Defense Initiative).

Moreover, war would exist from now on as an agenda that is infinitely self-referential: "War" represents not other types of struggles and conflicts—what in history classes are studied as "causes"—but "war" itself. From its previous conventional, negative signification as a blockade, an inevitable but regretted interruption of the continuity that is "normal life," war shifts to a new level of force. It has become not the cessation of normality but, rather, the very definition of normality itself. The space and time of war are no longer segregated in the form of an other; instead, they operate from within the here and now, as the internal logic of the here and now. From being negative blockade to being normal routine, war becomes the positive mechanism, momentum, and condition of possibility of society, creating a hegemonic social space through powers of visibility and control.

It is important to note that the normativization of war and war technology takes place as well among—perhaps especially among—the defeated. As John W. Dower writes, in Japan, deficiency in science and technology was singled out as the chief reason for defeat, and the atomic bomb was seen simultaneously as "a symbol of the terror of nuclear war and the promise of science."[24] Since it was forbidden to advance in militarism, postwar Japan specialized in the promotion of science and technology for "peace" and for the consolidation of a "demo-cratic" society. Instead of bombs and missiles, Japan became one of the world's leading producers of cars, cameras, computers, and other kinds of "high-tech" equipment.[25] With Honda, Toyota, Nissan, Hitachi, Toshiba, Sony, Sanyo, Nikon, Mitsubishi, and their likes becoming household names throughout the world, the "victim" of the war rises again and rejoins the "victor" in a new competition, the competition in bombarding the world with a different type of implosion—information.[26]

With the preemptiveness of seeing-as-destruction and the normativization of technology-as-information, thus, comes the great epistemic shift, which has been gradually occurring with the onset of speed technologies, and which finally *virtualizes* the world. As a condition that is no longer separable from civilian life, war is thoroughly absorbed into the fabric of our daily communications—our informational channels, our entertainment media, our machinery for speech and expression. We participate in war's virtualization of the world as we use—with-out thinking—TV monitors, remote control buttons, computer interfaces, and other digital devices that fill the spaces of everyday life. We no longer notice the terrorism of, say, watching news episodes of the most violent bloodshed on television while having dinner, nor are we shocked by the juxtaposition of TV commercials with reports of mass slaughters that are happening on another conti-nent. Our consumption of war, bloodshed, and violence through our communica-tion technologies is on a par with our consumption of various forms of merchandise.

There is, furthermore, another side to the virtualization of the world that most of us do not experience but that is even more alarming: When a war does occur, such as the Gulf War of 1991, the ubiquitous virtualization of everyday life meant that war could no longer be fought without the skills of videogames. The aerial bombing of Iraq meant that the world was divided into an above and a below in accordance with the privilege of access to the virtual world. Up above in the sky, war was a matter of maneuvers across the videoscreen by U.S. soldiers who had been accustomed as teenagers to playing videogames at home; below, war remained tied to the body, to hard work, to the random disasters falling from the heavens. For the U.S. men of combat, the elitism and aggressive-ness of panoramic vision went hand in hand with distant control and the instant destruction of others; for the women and children of Iraq, life became more and more precarious—immaterial in the sense of a readiness for total demolition at any moment.[27]

The Orbit of Self and Other

Among the most important elements in war, writes Karl von Clausewitz, are the "moral elements."[28] From the U.S. point of view, this phrase does not seem at all ironic. The bombings of Hiroshima and Nagasaki, for instance, were considered pacific acts, acts that were meant to save lives and save civilization in a world threatened by German nazism. (Though, by the time the bombs were dropped in Japan, Germany had already surrendered.) Even today, some of the most educated, scientifically knowledgeable members of U.S. society continue to believe that the atomic bomb was the best way to terminate the hostilities.[29] And, while the media in the United States are quick to join the media elsewhere in reporting the controversies over Japan's refusal to apologize for its war crimes in Asia or over France's belatedness in apologizing for the Vichy government's persecution of the Jews, no U.S. head of state has ever visited Hiroshima or Nagasaki or expressed regret for the nuclear holocaust.[30] In this—the perpetual conviction and self-legitimation of its own superiority, leadership, and moral virtue—lies perhaps the most deeply ingrained connection between the dropping of the atomic bombs and the foundation myth of the United States as a nation, as well as all its subsequent interventions in nationalist struggles in Asia, Latin America, and the Middle East.[31]

In the decades since 1945, whether in dealing with the Soviet Union, the People's Republic of China, Korea, Vietnam, countries in Central America, or during the Gulf War, the United States has been conducting war on the basis of a certain kind of knowledge production and producing knowledge on the basis of war. War and knowledge enable and foster each other primarily through the collective fantasizing of some "foreign" or "alien" body, usually communist or Muslim, that poses danger to the "self" and to the "eye" that is the nation. Once the monstrosity of this foreign body is firmly established in the national consciousness, the United States feels it has no choice but war.[32] War, then, is acted out as a moral *obligation* to expel an imagined dangerous otherness from the United States' self-conception as the global custodian of freedom and democracy. Put in a different way, the "moral element," insofar as it produces knowledge about the "self" and "other"—and hence "eye" and "target"—as such, justifies war by its very logic. Conversely, the violence of war, once begun, fixes the other in its attributed monstrosity and confirms the idealized image of the self.

In this regard, the racist stereotyping of the Japanese during the Second World War—not only by U.S. military personnel but also by social and behavioral scientists—was simply a flagrant example of an ongoing ideological mechanism that had accompanied Western treatments of non-Western "others" for centuries. In the hands of academics such as Geoffrey Gorer, writes John W. Dower, the notion that was collectively and "objectively" formed about the Japanese was that they were "a clinically compulsive and probably collectively neurotic people, whose lives were governed by ritual and 'situational ethics,' wracked with insecurity, and swollen with deep, dark currents of repressed resentment and aggression."[33] At the same time, as Dower cautions:

> The Japanese, so "unique" in the rhetoric of World War Two, were actually saddled with racial stereotypes that Europeans and Americans had applied to nonwhites for centuries: during the conquest of the New World, the slave trade, the Indian wars in the United States, the agitation against Chinese immigrants in America, the colonization of Asia and Africa, the U.S. conquest of the Philippines at the turn of the century. These were stereotypes, moreover, which had been strongly reinforced by nineteenth-century Western science.
>
> In the final analysis, in fact, these favored idioms denoting superiority and inferiority transcended race and represented formulaic expressions of Self and Other in general.[34]

The moralistic divide between "self" and "other" constitutes the production of knowledge during the U.S. occupation of Japan after the Second World War as well. As Monica Braw writes, in the years immediately after 1945, the risk that the United States would be regarded as barbaric and inhumane was carefully monitored, in the main by cutting off Japan from the rest of the world through the ban on travel, control of private mail, and censorship of research, mass media information, and other kinds of communication. The entire occupation policy was permeated by the view that "the United States was not to be accused; guilt was only for Japan":[35]

> As the Occupation of Japan started, the atmosphere was military. Japan was a defeated enemy that must be subdued. The Japanese should be taught their place in the world: as a defeated nation, Japan had no status and was entitled to no respect. People should be made to realize that any catastrophe that had befallen them was of their own making. Until they had repented, they were suspect. If they wanted to release information about the atomic bombings of Hiroshima and Nagasaki, it could only be for the wrong reasons, such as accusing the United States of inhumanity. Thus this information was suppressed.[36]

As in the scenario of aerial bombing, the elitist and aggressive panoramic "vision" in which the other is beheld means that the sufferings of the other matter much less than the transcendent aspirations of the self. And, despite being the products of a particular culture's technological fanaticism, such transcendent aspirations are typically expressed in the form of selfless universalisms. As Sherry puts it, "The reality of Hiroshima and Nagasaki seemed less important than the bomb's effect on 'mankind's destiny,' on 'humanity's choice,' on 'what is happening to men's minds,' and on hopes (now often extravagantly revived) to achieve world government."[37]

Once the relations between war, racism, and knowledge production are under-lined in these terms, it would no longer be possible to assume, as many still do, that the recognizable features of modern war—its impersonality, coercion, and deliberate cruelty—are "divergences" from the "antipathy" to violence and to conflict that characterize the modern world.[38] Instead, it would be incumbent upon us to realize that the pursuit of war—with its use of violence—and the pursuit of peace—with its cultivation of knowledge—are the obverse and reverse of the same coin, the coin that I have been calling "the age of the world target." Rather than being irreconcilable opposites, war and peace are coexisting, collab-orative functions in the continuum of a virtualized world. More crucially still, only the privileged nations of the world can afford to wage war and preach peace at one and the same time. As Sherry writes, "The United States had different resources with which to be fanatical: resources allowing it to take the lives of others more than its own, ones whose accompanying rhetoric of technique dis-guised the will to destroy."[39] From this it follows that, if indeed political and military acts of cruelty are not unique to the United States—a point that is all too easy to substantiate—what is nonetheless remarkable is the manner in which such acts are, in the United States, usually cloaked in the form of enlightenment and virtue, in the form of an aspiration simultaneously toward technological perfection and the pursuit of peace. In a country where political leaders are always held accountable for their decisions by an electorate, violence simply cannot—as it can in totalitarian countries—exist in the raw. Even the most violent acts must be adorned with a benign, rational story.

It is, then, in the light of such interlocking relations among war, racism, and knowledge production that we may make the following comments about "area studies," that academic establishment which crystallizes the connection between the epistemic targeting of the world and the "humane" practices of peacetime learning.[40]

As its name suggests, "area studies" as a mode of knowledge production is, strictly speaking, military in its origins. Even though the study of the history, languages, and literatures of, for instance, "Far Eastern" cultures existed well before the Second World War (in what Edward Said would term the old Orien-talist tradition), the rigorous systematization of such study under the rubric of special "areas" was a postwar and North American phenomenon. The "areas" that needed to be studied were those that, in the aftermath of the Second World War, when the United States competed with the Soviet Union for the power to rule and/or destroy the world, required continued, specialized super-*vision*. Thus countries of East Asia, Southeast Asia, Eastern Europe, Latin America, and the Middle East took on the significance of "target fields"—as fields of information retrieval and dissemination that were necessary for the United States' continual political and ideological hegemony. The "scientific" and "objective" production of knowledge about these "other" cultures during peacetime—often under the modest claims of fact-gathering and documentation—became the institutional practice that substantiated and elaborated the militaristic conception of the world as target.[41] In other words, despite the claims about the apolitical and disinterested nature of the pursuits of higher learning, activities undertaken under the rubric of area studies, such as language training, historiography, anthropology, economics, political science, and so forth, are fully inscribed in the politics and ideology of war. To that extent, the disciplining, research, and development of so-called academic information are part and parcel of a *strategic* logic.

If the production of knowledge in area studies (with its vocabulary of aims and goals, research, data, analysis, experimentation, and verification) in fact shares the same scientific and military premises as war, is it a surprise that it is doomed to fail in its avowed attempts to "know" the other cultures? Can "knowledge" that is derived from the same bases as war put an end to the violence of warfare, or is such knowledge not simply warfare's accomplice, destined to destroy rather than preserve the forms of lives at which it aims its "focus"?

As long as knowledge is produced in a self-referential manner, as a circuit of targeting or *getting* the other that ultimately consolidates the omnipotence and omnipresence of the "self" and "eye" that is the United States, the other will have no choice but remain just that—a target whose existence justifies only one thing, its destruction by the bomber. As long as the focus of our study of Asia remains the United States, and as long as this focus is not accompanied by knowledge of what is simultaneously happening elsewhere, such study would ultimately confirm once again the already self-referential function of virtual worlding that was unleashed by the dropping of the atomic bomb, with the United States always being the bomber and other cultures being the military and information target fields. In this manner, events whose historicity does not fall into the orbit of the atomic bomb—such as the Chinese reactions to the war from a primarily anti-Japanese point of view that I alluded to at the beginning—would never receive the attention that is due them. "Knowledge" would lead only to further silence and the silencing of diverse experiences.

The truth of the continual targeting of the world as the fundamental form of knowledge production is, as I already suggested, xenophobia, the inability to handle the otherness of the other beyond the orbit that is the bomber's own visual path. For the xenophobe, every effort must be made to sustain and secure this orbit—that is, by keeping the place of the other-as-target always filled. Hence, with the end of the Cold War and the disappearance of the Soviet Union, the United States by necessity seeks other substitutes for war. As it has often been pointed out, drugs, poverty, and illegal immigrants have since become the new targets. Like the communists and the Muslims, drugs, poverty, and illegal immigrants now occupy the place of that ultimate danger which must be "deterred" at all costs.

Even then, xenophobia can still backfire. When the anxiety about the U.S. loss of control over its own target fields—and by implication its own boundaries—becomes overwhelming, bombing takes as its target the United States itself. This is so because, we remember, bombing the other was the means to end the war, the violence to stop violence, and, most important of all, the method to confirm moral virtue. Why, then, when the United States is perceived to be threatened and weakened by incompetent leadership, should bombing not be the technique of choice for correcting the United States itself? And so, in spite of all the racist conspiracy suspicions about "foreigners," it was U.S. minutemen who were revealed to have been, apparently, the bombers of the federal office building in Oklahoma City on April 19, 1995. Spurred by a moral determination to set things right, the targeting of "others" turned into the targeting of innocent American men, women, and children, with a violence that erupted from within the heart of the country. The worst domestic terrorist incident in U.S. history,[42] the bombing in Oklahoma City, took place with the force of an emblem. The vicious circle of "the world as target" had returned to its point of origin.[43]

Notes

1. Barton J. Bernstein, "The Atomic Bombings Reconsidered," *Foreign Affairs* 74, no. 1 (January/February 1995): p. 140.
2. For an account of the immediate consequences of the dropping of the bombs in Hiroshima, see John Hersey, *Hiroshima* (New York: Alfred A. Knopf, 1946). (Hersey's account was first published in *The New Yorker,* August 31, 1946. An excerpt from the account was reprinted on the fiftieth anniversary of the end of the war in *The New Yorker,* July 31, 1995, pp. 65–67.) For accounts of the censorship of information about the atomic bomb in the aftermath of the Second World War, see Monica Braw, *The Atomic Bomb Suppressed: American Censorship in Occupied Japan* (Armonk and London: M.E. Sharpe, 1991), in particular chapters 1, 2, 8, 9, and 10.
3. "To the majority of Japanese, Hiroshima is the supreme symbol of the Pacific War. All the suffering of the Japanese people is encapsulated in that almost sacred word: Hiroshima" (Ian Buruma, *The Wages of Guilt: Memories of War in Germany and Japan* [New York: Farrar Straus Giroux, 1994]). Buruma criticizes the manner in which Hiroshima has become the exclusive sacred icon of martyred innocence and visions of apocalypse in Japan, often in total isolation from the rest of the history of the war. In this process of sanctifying Hiroshima, he writes, what has been forgotten is the city's status as a center of military operations during Japan's period of active aggression against other countries such as China—"At the time of the bombing, Hiroshima was the base of the Second General Headquarters of the Imperial Army (the First was in Tokyo)" (p. 106). Buruma offers accounts of the Rape of Nanjing and the varied postwar Japanese reactions to Japanese war crimes; see Parts Two and Three of his book. See also John W. Dower, "The Bombed: Hiroshimas and Nagasakis in Japanese Memory," *Diplomatic History* 19, no. 2 (Spring 1995): 275–95, also reprinted in this volume. Dower writes: "Hiroshima and Nagasaki became icons of Japanese suffering—perverse national treasures, of a sort, capable of fixating Japanese memory of the war on what had happened to Japan and simultaneously blotting out recollection of the Japanese victimization of others. Remembering Hiroshima and Nagasaki, that is, easily became a way of forgetting Nanjing, Bataan, the Burma–Siam railway, Manila, and the countless Japanese atrocities these and other place names signified to non-Japanese" (p. 281).
4. See Buruma, *The Wages of Guilt,* for comparative accounts of the significance of Hiroshima and Auschwitz. In chapter 15 in this volume, "Controversies Surrounding the

Asian–Pacific War: The Tokyo War Crimes Trial," Kentaro Awaya argues that the stigmatizing of Japan, though different from that of Germany, is widely felt in Japanese discussions, including those in the Diet itself.

5. "The Mushroom Cloud Over Art," *The Economist,* February 25, 1995, pp. 87–88.

6. The testing of the plutonium bomb on July 16, 1945, at the Trinity site in New Mexico was mainly a concept test: What was tested was the nuclear device but not the precise delivering mechanisms or the blast effects on a real target. "Between Trinity and Hiroshima, the bomb remained [to the scientists] a kind of awesome abstraction, now tested to be sure, but not yet imaginable as a weapon of war" (Michael S. Sherry, *The Rise of American Air Power: The Creation of Armageddon* [New Haven and London: Yale University Press, 1987], p. 343). In his notes, Sherry appends information on calculations that were made at Trinity about possible hazards to occupying personnel (notes 112 and 113, p. 417).

7. For an account of the shift, among U.S. military decision-makers, from the older morality of not killing noncombatants to the emerging morality of total war, see Bernstein, "The Atomic Bombings Reconsidered," pp. 135–52. Murray Sayle writes that the moral line of not bombing civilians was in fact already crossed with the bombing of Dresden in February 1944; see his essay "Letter from Hiroshima: Did the Bomb End the War?" *The New Yorker,* July 31, 1995, pp. 40–64. For a long and detailed history of the events leading up to the use of the atomic bomb, including the major scientific and political figures involved, see Richard Rhodes, *The Making of the Atomic Bomb* (New York: Simon and Schuster, 1986).

8. The gender politics of the naming of the bombs is noted by Sherry as follows: "Dominated by men, Western science has aspired to unlock the secrets of the natural world. Often its practitioners have also sought immortality through escape from that world, a world so often associated with women and femininity. By their colloquial language, the men at Los Alamos hinted at such aspirations. . . . Femininity was weakness, masculinity was the power to transcend nature and its mortal reality. If these men entertained a male fantasy of ultimate potency, it was perhaps not coincidence that they gave their bombs masculine names (Fat Man, Little Boy)" (*The Rise of American Air Power,* pp. 202–3). By contrast, crews often gave their own bombers feminine names since such bombers were regarded as "the symbolic repository of feminine forces of unpredictable nature which men could not control" (*The Rise of American Air Power,* p. 215).

9. For a personal account of these events, see Philip Morrison, "Recollections of a Nuclear War," *Scientific American* 273, no. 2 (August 1995): 42–46. A neutron engineer, Morrison was one of the many physicists enlisted to work on the Manhattan Project in Chicago and Los Alamos.

10. See Hersey, *Hiroshima,* pp. 107–8. Buruma: "There was . . . something . . . which is not often mentioned: the Nagasaki bomb exploded right over the area where outcasts and Christians lived" (*The Wages of Guilt,* p. 100). See also Evan Thomas, "Why We Did It," *Newsweek,* July 24, 1995: "If there was little debate over the moral rights and wrongs of atomizing Hiroshima, there was even less over Nagasaki; indeed, no debate at all. The operation was left to [General Leslie R.] Groves, who was eager to show that an implosion bomb, which cost $400 million to develop, could work as well as the trigger-type bomb that had destroyed Hiroshima. Exploding over the largest Roman Catholic cathedral in the Far East, the Nagasaki bomb killed an additional 70,000 people. The victims included as many Allied prisoners of war as Japanese soldiers—about 250" (p. 28).

11. See Sherry, *The Rise of American Air Power,* especially chapters 8 and 9 (pp. 219–300).

12. For detailed philosophical reflections on science and modernity, see, for instance, Martin Heidegger's *The Question Concerning Technology and Other Essays,* translated

and with an introduction by William Lovitt (New York: Harper Colophon Books, 1977).

13. "According to President Truman, on his part the decision to use the atomic bomb was taken without any second thoughts" (Braw, *The Atomic Bomb Suppressed,* p. 138; Braw's source is Harry S. Truman, *Year of Decisions,* p. 302). Sayle writes, "No one ever made a positive decision to drop the bomb on Hiroshima, only a negative one: not to interfere with a process that had begun years before, in very different circumstances. Truman later described it as 'not any decision that you had to worry about,' but a decision implies a choice, and Truman never contemplated, or even heard suggested, any delay, or any alternative to the bomb's use on a Japanese city" ("Letter from Hiroshima," p. 54). See also Osborn Elliott, "Eyewitness," *Newsweek,* July 24, 1995: "Harry Truman . . . buried any qualms he might have had. At a press conference in 1947 he told reporters, 'I didn't have any doubts at the time.' He said the decision had saved 250,000 American lives. In later years Truman would raise the number of lives saved to half a million or a million. 'I'd do it again,' Truman said in 1956. In 1965, seven years before he died, he repeated that he 'would not hesitate' to drop the A-bomb" (p. 30). For a detailed account of the decision-making process (by top military personnel and scientists as well as Truman) that led up to the dropping of the bombs, see Bernstein, "The Atomic Bombings Reconsidered."

14. This is the situation Heidegger is referring to in a passage such as this: "everywhere and in the most varied forms and disguises the gigantic is making its appearance. In so doing, it evidences itself simultaneously in the tendency toward the increasingly small. We have only to think of numbers in atomic physics. The gigantic presses forward in a form that actually seems to make it disappear—in the annihilation of great distances by the airplane, in the setting before us of foreign and remote worlds in their everydayness, which is produced at random through radio by a flick of the hand" (Heidegger, *The Question Concerning Technology,* p. 135). Elsewhere, I have discussed in greater detail the manner in which modern technology, which is aimed at facilitating global "communication" in the broadest sense of the word, has paradoxically led to the increasing intangibility, and for some, the disappearance, of the material world. See Chapter VIII, "Media, Matter, Migrants," in *Writing Diaspora: Tactics of Intervention in Contemporary Cultural Studies* (Bloomington and Indianapolis: Indiana University Press, 1993).

15. Paul Virilio, *War and Cinema: The Logistics of Perception* (1984), trans. Patrick Camiller (New York and London: Verso, 1989), p. 20. Virilio's other works, in particular *Pure War* (with Sylvère Lotringer), trans. Mark Polizzotti (New York: Semiotext(e), 1983), are also germane to the present topic.

16. Virilio, *The Vision Machine* (1988), trans. Julie Rose (Bloomington and Indianapolis: Indiana University Press, 1994), p. 49.

17. Heidegger, *The Question Concerning Technology,* p. 129.

18. Quoted in Virilio, *War and Cinema,* p. 4.

19. "On August 10, the day after the Nagasaki bombing, when Truman realized the magnitude of the mass killing and the Japanese offered a conditional surrender requiring continuation of the emperor, the president told his cabinet that he did not want to kill any more women and children.

. . . After two atomic bombings, the horror of mass death had forcefully hit the president, and he was willing to return partway to the older morality—civilians might be protected from the A-bombs. But he continued to sanction the heavy conventional bombing of Japan's cities, with the deadly toll that napalm, incendiaries, and other bombs produced. Between August 10 and August 14—the war's last day, on which about 1,000 American planes bombed Japanese cities, some delivering their deadly cargo after Japan announced its surrender—the United States probably killed more than 15,000 Japanese" (Bernstein, "The Atomic Bombings Reconsidered," pp. 147–48. In *The Rise of American*

Air Power, Sherry argues that the U.S. aerial attacks on Japan stemmed from strategic and emotional reasons: "The ultimate fury of American aerial devastation came against Japan not because it was more fanatical, but because it was relatively weaker. Germany's strength and tenacity gave the Allies little choice but to resort to invasion because Germany would not surrender without it. It was the relative ease of attacking Japan by air that tempted Americans into the fullest use of air power. As an image, Japan's fanaticism was real enough in the minds of many Americans. But it served mainly to justify a course of bombing rooted in strategic circumstances and the emotional need for vengeance" (p. 246).

20. Virilio, *War and Cinema,* p. 6; emphasis in the original.

21. See Michel Foucault, *The Order of Things: An Archaeology of the Human Sciences* (translated from the French) (London: Tavistock Publications, 1970). Foucault means by "episteme" not simply a concept or an idea but a particular relation between "reality" and representation, a relation that produces knowledge (i.e., that exists as a condition for the possibility of knowledge) and that shifts with different historical periods.

22. Ironically, this partnership attests to what Freud, in the famous exchange with Einstein, discusses as the ambivalence of war, which for him advanced as much as threatened civilization. See the section "Why War?" (1932/33), in *The Standard Edition of the Complete Psychological Works of Sigmund Freud,* vol. 22 (London: Hogarth Press, 1964), pp. 197–215.

23. Virilio, *War and Cinema,* p. 4.

24. Dower, "The Bombed," p. 7.

25. Dower points out that Japan's conversion to nonmilitary manufacturing activities in the postwar years was greatly facilitated by its previously diverse and sophisticated wartime technology. See the chapter "The Useful War" in his *Japan in War and Peace: Selected Essays* (New York: New Press, 1993), in particular pp. 14–16.

26. Notably, Japan's rise to economic power triggers in the United States a new rhetoric of anxiety and hostility—a rhetoric that is, Dower argues, in fact rooted in the racist attitudes toward Japan in the Second World War. See his discussion of this point in *War Without Mercy: Race and Power in the Pacific War* (New York: Pantheon Books, 1986), pp. 311–17. I will discuss the relations between racism and postwar knowledge production in the pages to follow.

27. See Sherry, *The Rise of American Air Power,* pp. 204–18, for an account of the *distance* from the enemy that occurs both because of the nature of air combat and because of the demands of aviation that arise outside combat. In the history of air war, airmen were conditioned to "see themselves as an elite for whom performance of professional skills—a mastery of technique—was more important than engaging an enemy. Before they went into combat and again when they came out of it, powerful factors of class, education, and policy strengthened their status and their elite image" (p. 213).

28. Karl von Clausewitz, *On War,* ed. and trans. Michael Howard and Peter Paret (Princeton: Princeton University Press, 1976), p. 184. See also Book 1, Chapter 3, "On Military Genius" (pp. 100–112) for more extended discussions.

29. Buruma reports that at a United Nations Conference on Disarmament Issues in Hiroshima in July 1992, "an American Harvard professor argued that the Hiroshima bombing 'ended World War II and saved a million Japanese lives.' He also added that the horror of this event had helped to prevent nuclear wars ever since, and thus in effect Hiroshima and Nagasaki saved millions more lives" (*The Wages of Guilt,* p. 105). See also the account by Mary Palevsky Granados, "The Bomb 50 Years Later: The Tough Question Will Always Remain," *Los Angeles Times Magazine,* June 25, 1995, pp. 10–11, 28–30. Granados was shocked to hear Hans Bethe, the man who was the head of the Los Alamos Lab's Theoretical Physics Division during the time of the war and "who has been called America's most influential advocate of nuclear disarmament," emphatically con-

firm that "the first use of nuclear armaments was necessary and correct" (p. 28).

30. Richard Nixon visited Hiroshima in 1964, four years before he became president, and Jimmy Carter visited Hiroshima during the late 1980s, on one of his many trips to Japan after he left office. Neither expressed regret for what was done by the United States during the war. In April 1995, Bill Clinton declared that the United States did not owe Japan an apology for using the atomic bombs and that Truman had made the right decision "based on the facts he had before him." See Robert Jay Lifton and Greg Mitchell, *Hiroshima in America: Fifty Years of Denial* (New York: Grosset/Putnam, 1995), pp. 211–22.

31. It should be pointed out, however, that, despite the massive destructions over the decades, attitudes toward the United States in some of these areas remain ambivalent rather than straightforwardly hostile. For instance, in a country that was devastated by U.S. military forces such as Vietnam, there is, ironically, widespread welcome of the return of the Americans today.

32. See Jacqueline Rose's persuasive discussion of this point in " 'Why War?' " the first chapter of *Why War?—Psychoanalysis, Politics, and the Return to Melanie Klein* (Oxford, UK, and Cambridge, MA: Blackwell, 1993), pp. 15–40.

33. Dower, *War without Mercy,* p. 127. Besides Gorer, the notable scientists who studied the Japanese national character listed by Dower include Margaret Mead, Gregory Bateson, Ruth Benedict, Clyde Kluckhohn, and Alexander Leighton (p. 119). Of course, these scientists did not come to the same conclusions.

34. Dower, *War without Mercy,* p. 10.

35. Braw, *The Atomic Bomb Suppressed,* p. 142.

36. Ibid., p. 151. Notably, such suppression of information took place *even as Supreme Commander Douglas MacArthur publicly emphasized the virtues of the freedom of the press and freedom of speech.* (MacArthur issued a Directive for the Freedom of Speech and Freedom of the Press in Tokyo on September 10, 1945, and reimposed censorship on the Japanese press on September 18.) From being simply a routine military undertaking that was negative in its function, censorship was transformed into a positive, essential tool, a tool that would assist in the virtuous task of helping Japan emerge from defeat as a democratic, peace-loving nation. See pp. 143–56 of Braw's book for an extended discussion.

37. Sherry, *The Rise of American Air Power,* p. 351.

38. See, for instance, the discussion of the "inhuman face of war" in John Keegan, *The Face of Battle* (London: Jonathan Cape, 1976), pp. 319–34.

39. Sherry, *The Rise of American Air Power,* p. 253.

40. The most controversial argument on this connection remains that of Edward Said's *Orientalism* (New York: Pantheon Books, 1978).

41. I shall not repeat arguments about the politics of Asian studies in American universities that I have already made elsewhere. Interested readers are asked to see my discussions in chapters I and VI of *Writing Diaspora.*

42. See the exclusive prison interview with the prime suspect, Timothy McVeigh, in David H. Hackworth and Peter Annin, "The Suspect Speaks Out," *Newsweek,* July 3, 1995, pp. 23–26.

43. I am very grateful to Beth Bailey, David Farber, James A. Fujii, Austin Meredith, and Susan Neel for their valuable contributions to this chapter. Conversations with them not only helped me revise my arguments but also directed me to crucial references on a topic on which I had not done previous research. My thanks also go to Jackie Hiltz and Peter Gibian for their constructive editing comments and suggestions.

14

Controversies Surrounding
the Asia–Pacific War

The Tokyo War Crimes Trials

Kentaro Awaya (translated by Barak Kushner)

The year 1995 marked the fiftieth anniversary of the end of World War II, a war that brought untold suffering to countless individuals throughout the world. The passage of time that now amounts to half a century compels us to mourn for all of the war's victims, regardless of their loyalties during the war, and to reaffirm our resolution never again to repeat the tragedy of war. In spite of the various events planned worldwide in solemn commemoration of this anniversary, there are still some individuals and groups who wish to fan the flames of mutual distrust by emphasizing wartime differences and, in so doing, eclipse efforts aimed at creating a more peaceful world.

Japan's Diet Resolution

Both as a concerned individual and as a Japanese engaged in academic pursuits and cultural activities in Japan, I believe that it is essential for Japan to promote reflection on and examination of its own responsibility in the Asia–Pacific War.[1] Accordingly, in March 1995, a group of scholars from many different countries, including me, presented an international appeal outlining a common basis for working toward global peace.[2] By obtaining the support of like-minded citizens around the world, we hoped to turn the fiftieth anniversary into an opportunity to strengthen international public opinion in support of world peace.[3]

The appeal demands serious reflection on all sides of the Pacific. For Japan, the obvious starting point for reflection seems to be aggression in China, beginning with the so-called Manchurian Incident of September 1931 and the subsequent military invasion into Southeast Asia. In fact, examination should commence with an investigation of Japanese colonial rule, dating back one hundred years to its victory in the first Sino–Japanese War. The process of colonization that began in Formosa, currently known as Taiwan, in 1895 and extended to Korea in 1910 has all too often been overshadowed by the Asia–Pacific War. Japan launched war against the Allied powers on December 8, 1941, with a surprise attack on Pearl Harbor and a military assault on the Malay peninsula.[4] If Japan is to become a leader in promoting worldwide peace, the Japanese people must clearly reflect upon their colonial rule in Asia as well as their responsibility for starting war in the past.

During the Asia–Pacific War, individuals in many other Asian countries suffered tremendously. Two of the most atrocious events, the Nanking massacre (sometimes referred to as the Rape of Nanking) and the Bataan death march, are etched forever in the memories of Chinese, Filipinos, and Allied POWs. The Japanese people, too, endured much. Hiroshima and Nagasaki, the noncombatant sites of the unleashing of atomic weapons, have become the most poignant symbols of their suffering. By the time of the Japanese surrender in August 1945, many of Japan's cities had been ravaged by aerial bombing; the country's economy was in shambles and people disillusioned. Out of this unequivocal loss developed a consciousness stressing "no more war." Economic recovery replaced militarism, and foreign disputes were avoided whenever possible.

Until just a decade ago, the Japanese identified themselves as victims and overlooked Japan's role as aggressor, terrorizing civilians and invading foreign countries alike.[5] This self-centeredness has limited the development of a "peace consciousness" in Japan. For example, in the past, the postwar Japanese government policies for compensation of war victims have applied only to Japanese nationals. In the 1990s, however, information on issues such as the "military comfort women" has been more widely disseminated, and Japanese public opinion in support of apologizing to foreign war victims and providing compensation has gradually increased. On the fiftieth anniversary of Japan's defeat, many Japanese citizens now recognize that it is imperative to expand the recognition of Japan's complete role in the Asia–Pacific theater in World War II.

The appeal draft committee of scholars from around the world demanded a resolution from the Japanese Diet outlining the exact position of the current government with regard to the war. On June 9, 1995, the lower house of the Japanese Diet passed a resolution and the full text reads as follows:

> This Diet, in the fiftieth year since the war, offers its sincere tribute to the memory of the war dead throughout the world and victims who have suffered because of war and other deeds.
>
> Recalling the many instances of colonial rule and acts of aggression in the modern history of the world, we recognize those acts which our country carried out and the unbearable suffering inflicted on the peoples of other countries, particularly the nations of Asia, and express deep remorse.
>
> Transcending differences in historical views of the past war, we must hum-

bly learn the lessons of history and build a peaceful international community.

This Diet links hands with the countries of the world, under the doctrine of lasting peace enshrined in the Constitution of Japan, and expresses its determination to open up a future of coexistence for humankind.

We affirm the above.[6]

The resolution passed, but it infuriated rather than appeased the public. Diet rules require a quorum of 501 total votes for the passage of any legislation. The resolution garnered only 230 votes but was still approved as the result of large-scale abstentions. One cannot help but view this as an example of partisan party politics rather than a desire to advance the wishes of the people. Furthermore, the resolution itself did not clearly define Japan's role in the Asia–Pacific War. Not only did the government avoid admitting that the war was one of aggression; it made no explicit mention of apology or compensation to victims of the war abroad but merely ended with an expression of "remorse." The omissions in the resolution of the Diet underscore the real state of Japanese politics.

The final Diet resolution faced stiff opposition within the ruling Liberal Democratic Party (LDP) and opposition Shinshinto (New Frontier Party). These groups rejected the explicit reference to reflections about Japan's past "colonial domination" and "actions of aggression." Lower House representative Seisuke Okuno, the figure who most clearly represents the opposing faction, stated that it was America and England that instigated the war of invasion. He claimed that Japan fought the United States and England, not Asia. Japanese civilians were the ones who suffered the horrors of the atomic bomb and the forced deportation of 600,000 men to Siberia. Although Okuno admitted that Japan made mistakes during the war, he questioned why only Japan is labeled as aggressor. He represents a faction that contends that Japan, a late-comer in the game of modernization and empire building in a region dominated by the great powers, fought the war in order to defend itself and to liberate Asia from the West. The same faction also argues that even the admission of wartime excesses does not alter the true nature of the war, simply because Japan was defeated.

The Politics of Naming the War

Okuno's faction endorses the "affirmative theory of the Greater East Asian War," or, in other words, the conviction that Japan fought the Asia–Pacific War, or the "Greater East Asian War" as these individuals still identify it, for positive reasons—to liberate Asia. The various names for the war are informed by basic underlying assumptions. The ambivalence in the Diet resolution can be clarified by a brief discussion of the politics of naming Japan's involvement in World War II.

The Japanese government of the 1940s coined the term "Greater East Asian War" to describe the conflict that began on December 8, 1941, with the Japanese surprise attack on Pearl Harbor and the landing on the Malay peninsula. The "China Incident"—the war with China—was also included under the rubric of that name. The term itself was steeped in ideology that called for the "defense for self-preservation" of Japan and "the establishment of the Greater East Asian Co-Prosperity Sphere" with Japan at the vanguard leading East Asia into a hopeful future, free from decades of humiliation at the hands of the West. As we know, the reality was quite different.

However, Japan lost the war, and American forces occupied Japan. In December 1945 the General Headquarters (GHQ) of the Supreme Command Allied Powers (SCAP) prohibited use of the term "Greater East Asian War" in all public documents. Instead, the United States enforced the use of the "Pacific War." Although not as ideological, this name still hinges on the American historical perspective, and, as the label indicates, is a description that centers on the American involvement in the Pacific region of the war between Japan and the Allied powers. It ignores the anti-Japanese wars in China and the rest of Asia or simply treats them lightly. Therefore, in recent years, the opinion among Japanese researchers is that the label "Asia–Pacific War" describes the reality more accurately and should be used. There is a growing consensus in favor of this usage, one that I support.

On the heels of the American occupation, Japan experienced great economic growth in the 1960s and went on to become an economic superpower. The nation's increasing conservatism and awareness of its status in the international economy once again spawned a renaissance of the term "Greater East Asian War."[7] Symbolizing this reemergence was a series of articles, written by Fusao Hayashi and loosely translated as "The Affirmation Theory of the Greater East Asian War," which appeared in the September 1963 issue of *Chuokoron* magazine. Hayashi wrote that the "Greater East Asian War" was the final phase of a "one hundred year war in East Asia" initiated by Commodore Perry's arrival in Japan in 1854. Hayashi asserted that "it [the war] was something that happened because it was inevitable and during the hundred years it was Japan's destiny to carry this burden."

In response to Hayashi's assertions, progressive historians, beginning with Professor Saburo Ienaga, criticized approval of the aggressive nature of Japan's involvement in World War II.[8] The "Affirmative Theory of the Greater East Asian War" did not make it into the mainstream of historical scholarship. The theory did, however, resonate among conservative and ultra–right-wing Japanese politicians. As Japan achieved the status of economic superpower, reactionary nationalism gained in popularity, and the label "Greater East Asian War" once again found support in Japan.

The antiresolution faction, which includes Representative Okuno, is composed mainly of individuals who directly experienced the war. One might say that, having failed to face the reality of the Asia–Pacific war—that is, what caused it and what it truly was—they merely continue to parrot the wartime propaganda of "Asia for Asians" and "liberation from European and American colonialism." While Okuno and his supporters did not succeed in persuading a majority of conservative politicians to support the "Affirmation Theory of the Greater East Asian War," there are a number of vocal proponents whose influence cannot be ignored.

The Tokyo War Crimes Trials

The defenders of the "Affirmative Theory of the Greater East Asian War" share feelings of hostility and strong opposition toward the Tokyo war crimes trials, properly known as the International Military Tribunal for the Far East, or IMTFE. These individuals frequently criticize the way in which the trial was held and how the image of Japan's guilt later affected its international relations. For them, the Tokyo war crimes trials are nothing more than "victors' justice." They stress that Japan was a victim unilaterally judged by the Allied countries. While pointing out the faults of the trials, the group is unable to admit Japan's own culpability in the war. The issue and conflict over the historical reading of the Asia–Pacific War in postwar Japan is intimately linked to an interpretation of the Tokyo war crimes trials.

The trial convened from May 1946 to November 1948, featured twenty-eight Japanese war leaders charged as "Class-A war criminals," and was presided over by an international tribunal composed of eleven judges from the victorious nations. In court the prosecution targeted the period from 1928 to September 2, 1945, and focused on the traditional war transgressions of "conventional war crimes" and "murder" as well as two new designations, "crimes against peace" and "crimes against humanity." The twenty-eight Class-A war crimes defendants faced criminal and personal liability charges as individuals and representatives of Japan. By making them representatives of the nation, the court also judged Japan's responsibility for waging a war of aggression.

In opposition, immediately after the commencement of the trials, the defense counsel delivered a motion objecting to the court's jurisdiction. The defense counsel protested that, according to international law, "crimes against peace" or "crimes against humanity" did not exist before the war; therefore, the prosecution had created the designation retroactively or what lawyers define as ex-post facto or retroactive law. Nonetheless, the motion was rejected. The prosecution and defense argued laboriously, but by 1948 the judgment was in sight. Most of the judges contended that "crimes against peace" or "crimes against humanity" were not affected by the issue of retroactive law but were instead acknowledged under existing international law. Tojo Hideki and six other defendants were sentenced to hang, and the remainder were found guilty and punished with fixed-term prison sentences.[9]

My own evaluation of the Tokyo war crimes trial addresses a different consideration. If Japan's acceptance of the Potsdam declaration and unconditional surrender to the Allied forces are acknowledged, one can only view the trial as an historical inevitability. Like the German Nuremberg trials, the Tokyo trials, on the basis of international law, added to "conventional war crimes" the new categories of "crimes against peace" and "crimes against humanity." As a result, the tribunals could indeed judge German and Japanese war crimes and the personal criminal liability of war leaders. In the wake of unprecedented atrocities in warfare and the resulting desire to inaugurate an era of peace in the postwar world, one can assess this as a significant development.

In his book *What Are War Crimes?* international law expert Professor Hisakazu Fujita explores the tensions of the new developments at that time.[10] He raises important questions that identify the essence of the matter: Should one discredit the new philosophy of criminality in war because of its link to "victors' justice" or retroactive laws? One could say that it was wrong to judge the individuals on the basis of these new designations. Or one could say that the unparalleled barbarity of World War II demanded an expansion of international law to establish the criminality of those actions. If one interprets the legality of "war crimes" as reflecting the development and progress of the legal code in the postwar international community, Professor Fujita's latter evaluation is appropriate. Throughout the world, the concept of "war crimes" as defined by the United Nations is generally accepted and continues to gain support.

I support Professor Fujita. To be sure, the Nuremberg and Tokyo trials posed various problems and ignored important issues, some of which are described below. Fifty years after the end of World War II, however, one can say that the verdicts of both trials helped develop international law in ways that would deter and punish perpetrators of future war crimes. Therefore, I affirm the positive historical significance of the Tokyo trials.

Other individuals in Japan attach significance to different areas of the trials. For example, the assertions of the defendants' lawyers regarding retroactive law were given little attention. However, Justice Radhabinod Pal, the Indian judge, delivered a long minority opinion. Arguing from the position of a legal positivist and as one of the few judges who had any training in international law, he ruled that a war of aggression is not illegal and insisted that all the accused were innocent. Judge Pal did not deny that Japan had carried out large-scale massacres of civilians and abused prisoners of war. He did, however, emphasize the cruelty of the American atomic bombings of Hiroshima and Nagasaki as "the only near approach to the directives of the Nazi leaders during the Second World War."[11] Since that time, Judge Pal's ruling has been enthusiastically championed by those who affirmed the "Greater East Asian War." Even today, it circulates as proof that Japan is not guilty.

At any rate, contemporary advocates of the "Greater East Asian War" simultaneously entertain Judge Pal's opinion and the statements that Counsel Ichiro Kiyose, Tojo Hideki, and other army defendants used in court at the Tokyo trials—that for Japan, the Asia–Pacific War was a war of "self-defense." In addition, they deny that the Japanese army committed atrocities documented at the Tokyo war crimes trials, including the Rape of Nanking and the Japanese wars of invasion starting with the "China Incident." The San Francisco treaty of 1951, which heralded the end of the American occupation and the renewal of Japan's independence, would make it impossible to take a stand as they have; the treaty's article 11 states that "Japan accepts the judgment of the International Military Tribunal for the Far East." Fortunately, the position described above is not tenable in the academic community of Japan today.

In 1956 Japan joined the United Nations and since then, as a member of an international society whose political policies are influenced by the tone the UN sets, Japan has become the nation it is today. The United Nations acknowledges the decision of the Nuremberg trials, known as the Nuremberg principle, and for Japan there is no choice but to respect the philosophy of the Tokyo trials as espoused in the decisions, which are based on the same Nuremberg principle. This information confronts the advocates of the "Greater East Asian War" with a complete antithesis of their logic. Proponents would be forced to abandon the San Francisco peace treaty and retreat from the United Nations. Certainly, they do not intend to act in this way. Yet, the mentality suggests none other than the reemergence of the same type of Japanese international isolation apparent in the 1930s.

Through the testimony of witnesses and presentation of evidence, the prosecution staff of the Tokyo trials documented the course of the Japanese war of aggression from around the time of the "Manchurian Incident" to the time of the Sino–Japanese war, and then on to the Asia–Pacific War. This information was more or less acknowledged even in the verdict. The truth revealed in the public decision shocked the nation's populace, especially the testimony in court concerning Japanese opium and drug trafficking in the Sino–Japanese war, the Rape of Nanking, the Bataan Death March in the Philippine arena of the Asia–Pacific War, the murder of ethnic Chinese in Singapore, and so on. Appalling, too, was evidence concerning the murder and maltreatment of Allied prisoners of war and barbarous acts committed in areas occupied by the Japanese Army.

The truth regarding Japanese atrocities and aggression, documented at the Tokyo war crimes trials, later became the starting point for further elucidation and inquiry into these incidents. One case in particular that later developed into a hotly contested issue was the Rape of Nanking. In the 1970s journalist Katsuichi Honda, the first Japanese to conduct both an oral inquiry of Chinese war victims and to investigate the Nanking massacre, published a book, *Chugoku no tabi* (Voyage to China [Asahi shimbunsha, 1972]), which greatly influenced the Japanese public. In opposition Japan's largest publisher, Bungei Shunju, in one of its magazines embarked on a campaign of denial that the Nanking massacre had taken place. Although the investigation began in this manner, most Japanese today accept the truth of the massacre of several tens of thousands. The Tokyo trials estimated that 200,000 people were killed during the Nanking massacre; this figure was later accepted by researchers as close to the real numbers.

The cruelty of the Japanese army did not stop with citizens of Nanking but included Allied prisoners of war as well. The Tokyo trials officially acknowledged that, of the 130,000 officers and enlisted men who were prisoners of war, 35,000 died, reflecting a death rate of 27 percent. In contrast, the death rate of Allied prisoners of war captured by the German forces was about 4 percent. These figures underscore the Japanese policy of maltreatment of prisoners of war. Recently in Japan, debate has clearly developed in regard to atrocities committed against Asia; nonetheless, interest concerning transgressions against Allied prisoners of war remains low.

In any case, while affirming the historical significance of the Tokyo war crimes trials, it is still necessary to examine the problematic issues and limitations of the trials as history.

Historical Limitations and Lingering Questions

To illuminate the complexity of the Tokyo trials, I would like to examine some of the problems surrounding the application and execution of indictment and immunity and the issue of "victors' justice."

Closer examination of the Tokyo war crimes trials reveals the subtle intermingling of prosecution and immunity. Unlike in the war crimes trials in Germany, beginning with the Nuremberg trials, in the Tokyo trials many war leaders and significant events escaped judgment. Of course, historical limitations at the time rendered certain investigations impossible, and one should not ignore the intentions of the prosecution, discussed in more detail below. The Nuremberg trials were jointly administered by four nations, the United States, England, France, and the Soviet Union. However, in the Tokyo trials, the United States firmly held the leadership, and the prosecution was drawn from the American prosecutorial staff. Most individuals who were granted immunity received it because of American political policy.

The motives for granting immunity at the trials and the results of that immunity were not fully understood at the time and, in fact, were concealed. As a result, this information has not been a part of the historical memory of the Japanese. Only recently has the truth been investigated by researchers and journalists. In response the Japanese government, through its control of textbooks used uniformly across the country in schools, has chosen to cover up the truth. The omissions of the Nanking Massacre and the activity of Unit 731 (see below) by the Ministry of Education are powerful illustrations of this tendency. The government is supported by members of the conservative faction, which includes virtually all members of the LDP, who are resolutely trying to suppress these realities. At present, the issue is not open to public debate.

One of the important players who did not become a defendant in the Tokyo Trials was the Showa emperor, Hirohito. How the prosecution wrestled with the complex problem of the emperor was the focal point of the defendant selection process. Since the details of why he was not brought to trial have been painstakingly investigated in recent years, I will highlight the conclusion. The American government had to consider the explosive nature of the issue and balance it with political necessity in order to proceed smoothly forward in the occupation of Japan. Thus, it accepted the advice of General Douglas MacArthur and did not pursue the wartime responsibility of the emperor but acknowledged his reign and preserved the system that he represented.

As a monarchy, England agreed that prosecuting the emperor would be a grave political mistake and led its fellow nations of the British Commonwealth on this point. The only member of the prosecution that formally proposed the indictment of the emperor was Australia. Neither the Soviet Union nor China demanded that legal action be taken against the emperor. After MacArthur rejected the Australian proposal, the issue was further avoided. Later in Japan, a political myth circulated that the "Showa emperor was a pacifist and constitutionalist." Debating the emperor's wartime responsibility in public became taboo.[12]

Many Japanese people who experienced the war had a strong desire to cover up the emperor's responsibility. They harbored feelings of complicity and, as such, felt subconsciously that trying the emperor would be tantamount to judging themselves. Therefore, the emperor's responsibility is important not only in itself but because it has allowed the Japanese people to avoid directly confronting their own war responsibility.

In addition to the emperor, members of the financial world and bureaucrats from the Home Ministry and Judiciary Departments were not indicted. Although the accountability of the charged army and navy soldiers was later debated, no such discussion over the responsibility of those granted immunity has emerged.

Japan's colonial domination was another area of willful oversight at the Tokyo trials. The countries that judged Japan possessed colonies, and if they had put the issue of colonial control under scrutiny, it might have rebounded and possibly snowballed out of control. The prosecution did not charge Japan with wartime atrocities in Korea, which was not yet an independent nation. Chinese representatives did not pursue legal action aimed at reducing Japanese colonial domination of Taiwan either. Forced deportation of Koreans, the "comfort women," and other similar matters could have been classified under "crimes against humanity" but were not pursued.

Other important facts that escaped prosecution at the Tokyo trials are the biological and chemical warfare activities of the Japanese armed forces. Initially, the International Prosecution Section investigated the problem, but in the end it was not heard in a court of law. The Kanto Army Unit 731 and every regional Japanese Army germ warfare battalion used Chinese and other prisoners of war, numbering more than three thousand, as subjects for germ infection experiments, gas effectiveness experiments, and vivisections. At the Chinese front line as well, the Japanese army engaged in germ warfare. Moreover, the Japanese Army had developed large-scale gas warfare for use in every area of the Chinese territory.

As mentioned, the Japanese Army was not formally charged in its use of germ and gas warfare. However, with regard to germ warfare, the General Staff Second Division of GHQ, which placed Unit 731's commanding officer, Lieutenant General Shiro Ishii, under detention, refused the prosecution's request to interrogate Ishii. General C.A. Willoughby, head of the General Staff Second Division, and MacArthur had already agreed to a policy guaranteeing full immunity for involved battalion members of Unit 731 in exchange for a complete investigation of their activities. As a result, the prosecution section could not prepare enough documentary evidence to charge and prove the war crimes of Unit 731 and abandoned its goal of indicting the unit. In reality, ulterior motives by the United States informed the decision not to prosecute. The American government wished to monopolize the research results obtained in Unit 731's human experiments and, therefore, did not release the information to the public.

The prosecution section also obtained appropriate documents and witnesses for its charge against the Japanese Army in its use of gas warfare on the Chinese front line and attached an addendum to the indictment. However, at the trial the prosecution section did not verify the use of gas warfare. It is believed—but has not been substantiated—that an order had been delivered from the upper echelons of the American government to stop interrogation of the matter and grant immunity to involved individuals. One can risk making an educated guess as to the means for this conduct. The legal exploration of the use of gas warfare by the Japanese would have opened up a Pandora's box of connections, the most obvious association being the use of the atomic bomb by the Americans. In addition, the American government had intended to implement a strategy of chemical warfare in future wars. If, at the Tokyo trials, chemical warfare had been proved to be in conflict with international law, America would have been thwarting its own designs. Consequently, the United States abandoned the idea of charging responsible individuals.

In the Tokyo war crimes trials, as in the Nuremberg trials, the war crimes of the victors, the Allied countries, were not broached. American responsibility for dropping the atomic bomb was raised by the defense counsel but later ruled out of the court's jurisdiction. One cannot deny that the lack of discussion of the use of the atomic bomb demonstrates the one-sided nature of "victors' justice." In both the Nuremberg and Tokyo trials, the Allied countries assumed that their job was to judge the war crimes and responsible individuals of the Axis countries—not their own deeds or compatriots.

Professor John Dower, also a contributor to this volume, in his book *War Without Mercy* graphically illustrates that the war was not just about Japanese war crimes. American forces also committed war crimes, not limited to the dropping of the atomic bomb.[13] The Americans indiscriminately air-bombed Japanese civilians and massacred Japanese prisoners of war. Motivating these actions was a firmly embedded American prejudice against the Japanese. American forces were not the only Allied perpetrators; the Soviet forces also committed war crimes. Abuse and violence against Japanese civilians occurred in Manchuria. In addition, at the conclusion of the war, the Soviet Union interned more than 600,000 Japanese soldiers in Siberia and elsewhere, forcing them into labor camps on the pretext of postwar management; this behavior certainly corresponds to a war crime.[14] Eventually, the Japanese frustration with the failure to judge the wartime behavior of the Allied powers built up over time and came to generate the twisted social consciousness among some individuals within postwar Japanese society.

An analysis of the Tokyo war crimes trials shows that there were lasting positive effects, as evidenced by the strengthening of international law, in addition to major drawbacks, epitomized by the one-sided judgment of war crimes by the victorious nations. It *is* possible to affirm the historical significance of the trials, but it is essential to continue clarifying and refining the historical limitations at work.

Notes

1. Below I discuss the difficulties in naming World War II in the Pacific arena and the history of that naming.

2. The appeal appeared in *Sekai* magazine in August 1995.

3. The appeal was supported by 204 individuals from around the world, most of whom are university researchers. Of the many professors endorsing it, 112, including Carol Gluck, Barton Bernstein, Tetsuo Najita, and John Dower, are from the United States.

4. In the United States, the attack is said to have occurred on December 7. According to Japanese time, however, the offensive happened on December 8.

5. See chapter 2 in this volume by John Dower, "The Bombed: Hiroshimas and Nagasakis in Japanese Memory," for a discussion of "victim-consciousness" in Japan.

6. *Japan Times,* June 10, 1995.

7. At this time, several books appeared that reflected this trend. One example is Ezra F. Vogel's *Japan as Number One* (Cambridge: Harvard University Press, 1979).

8. Ienaga's reading of Japanese involvement in World War II is explored in *The Pacific War: World War II and the Japanese, 1931–1945,* trans. Frank Baldwin (New York: Pantheon Books, 1978).

9. There are several studies in English that focus on the Tokyo war crimes trial. See Richard Minear's *Victor's Justice: The Tokyo War Crimes Trial* (Princeton: Princeton University Press, 1971) and Arnold Blackman's *The Other Nuremberg: The Untold Story of the Tokyo War Crimes Trial* (New York: Morrow, 1987).

10. Hisakazu Fujita, *Senso hanzai to wa nanika* [What Are War Crimes?] (Tokyo: Iwanami shoten, 1995).

11. Blackman, *The Other Nuremberg,* p. 393.

12. See my article, "Emperor Showa's Accountability for the War," *Japan Quarterly* (October–December 1991), for a discussion of this very controversial issue.

13. John Dower, *War Without Mercy* (New York: Pantheon Books, 1986). See also his latest work, *Japan in War and Peace: Collected Essays* (New York: New Press, 1994).

14. Toyoko Yamasaki's novel *The Barren Zone* (Tokyo: Kodansha International, 1993) tells the story of a Japanese army officer who survived Siberia and prisoner-of-war camps. Japanese POW deaths in Siberia are officially estimated at 55,000. However, Major Viktor Karpov of the Russian army suggests that many more Japanese POWs died on Soviet territory than either side has acknowledged. He estimates that as many as 113,000 soldiers may have died during the period 1945 to 1956, when the last group of captured soldiers was repatriated (*Far Eastern Economic Review,* November 11, 1993).

15

Tutoring Democracy

Michigan State University and the Politics of Reform in South Vietnam

John Ernst

Between 1954 and 1962, Michigan State University (MSU) played the role of junior partner in an ambitious but ultimately unsuccessful effort to develop a reform-minded, anticommunist government in South Vietnam that could serve as a reliable American ally in the global struggle against communism. An examination of the collaboration between MSU and the Republic of Vietnam reveals many of the assumptions and values underlying U.S. policies toward Southeast Asia on the eve of the massive American military intervention in the Vietnam War. The chief players in this peculiar drama were South Vietnam's president, Ngo Dinh Diem (1901–1963), a reclusive and imperious mandarin, and Wesley Fishel (1919–1977), a young MSU assistant professor of political science. An odd couple if ever there was one, Diem and Fishel, both firm anticommunists, nevertheless represented divergent political systems. Ultimately, the fundamental incompatibility of the values associated with each not only doomed the collaboration between the Saigon government and MSU but also contributed to wrecking the entire American project of building an anticommunist nation in the southern half of an artificially divided Vietnam.

In the beginning, American optimism overcame the misgivings of those who doubted the American mission in Vietnam almost from the start. Reflecting on the American decision to intervene in South Vietnam, President Dwight D. Eisenhower acknowledged that significant obstacles existed to constructing an anticommunist, democratic nation there, but none so serious that "good old Yankee ingenuity" could not overcome. Following France's defeat at the hands of Ho Chi Minh's communist-led insurgents, Eisenhower and Secretary of State John Foster Dulles overrode the warnings of intelligence officials who argued that Vietnam was the wrong place for the United States to make a stand against communist expansion in Southeast Asia. Emboldened by their recent success in suppressing other communist-led insurgencies, notably the Huk Rebellion in the Philippines, American policymakers, untainted by the colonialism that plagued the French, hoped to achieve similar results in Vietnam.[1]

Eisenhower and Dulles were not alone in their optimism. The partnership between American higher education and the U.S. government, born in World War II, matured during the Cold War when the federal government poured money into the universities for defense-related research and the training of "foreign-area specialists" and technical assistance personnel to serve in the Third World.[2] For both financial and patriotic reasons, most universities eagerly participated in Pentagon-funded programs that, in the mid-1950s, funneled about $300 million a year into college coffers. Many university presidents had served in the federal government during and after World War II. Most of them, including Michigan State's John Hannah, were staunchly anticommunist and barred members of the Communist Party from serving on their faculties.[3]

Hannah's desire to better the world by exporting U.S. values and ideas while stamping out communism was supported in the 1950s by numerous American social scientists. They sought to restructure developing nations into modern, democratic societies by providing them with technology and training. Theorists and policymakers alike believed that U.S. security depended on the emulation by Third World countries of Western rather than communist economic and political systems. Scholars like Walt W. Rostow, later an adviser to John F. Kennedy and Lyndon B. Johnson, contended that "economic assistance promote[d] economic development" and "economic development promote[d] political stability."[4] Rostow identified "the threat of communism in the Third World as a modernization problem" and called for America to provide Third World nations with extensive financial and material assistance in order to inoculate them against communism, which fed on poverty and underdevelopment.[5]

To address this situation in Vietnam, the Eisenhower administration embraced the concept of nation building. Viewing "modernity as incompatible with tradition," most advocates of modernization believed that established mores, practices, and institutions were obstacles to modernization and needed to be superseded. In attempting to restructure South Vietnam according to American economic, military, and political models, U.S. policymakers tried to minimize cultural disruption in order to reduce the risks of backlash, but they failed. American efforts at nation building alienated the South Vietnamese.[6]

President John Hannah, steeped in the ethic of public service, was eager to enlist MSU in the nation-building process. As head of the Association of Land-Grant Colleges and Universities, he offered the Truman administration complete cooperation with Point Four, "a 'bold new program' for making the benefits of American science and industrial progress available to 'underdeveloped' countries."[7] MSU sent staff to train counterparts in agricultural colleges in Colombia,

India, and Taiwan. As one faculty member observed, "it could be said, the world was its campus, and seldom did the university regard any clientele—domestic or foreign—beyond the range of its responsibility or the pale of respectability."[8]

The Michigan State University Group (MSUG), a technical-assistance program in Vietnam, was the most significant operation the school undertook in partnership with the federal government. The MSUG provided training and consulting in both police and public administration. The police administration staff worked with South Vietnamese law enforcement agencies assigned to internal security: the civil guard, municipal police, and the Sureté. The MSUG's public administration division was less well defined and far more diverse. Projects included a school for civil servants, the National Institute of Administration, overseas participant training, refugee resettlement, and cultural studies of the South Vietnamese highlanders, the Montagnards. MSUG originated in Hannah's commitment to public service and South Vietnamese president Ngo Dinh Diem's friendship with Wesley Fishel, whom Diem had first encountered in Tokyo in July 1950. They had followed very different paths to arrive at that point of intersection.[9]

Born in Cleveland in 1919, Fishel graduated from Northwestern University in 1941 and served in the Pacific during World War II as a military language specialist.[10] After receiving his Ph.D. in international relations from the University of Chicago in 1948, Fishel went to Japan as a member of the UCLA faculty to teach American servicemen.[11] In 1952, the University of California Press published *The End of Extraterritoriality in China,* a revision of his doctoral dissertation. About this time, Fishel joined a U.S. Army classified research project on communist media portrayals of American race relations. In 1953, he received a medal from the United Nations for his work.[12]

Ngo Dinh Diem, the son of a Vietnamese imperial official, studied at French Catholic academies and Hanoi's public school of administration. Cosmopolitan and highly educated, he was courted by Vietnam's French colonial rulers as well as by the Vietminh, their communist-led opponent. The Vietminh's murder of his brother, Ngo Dinh Khoi, in 1945, combined with his own Catholic faith, dissuaded Diem from turning to communism. At the same time, as a Vietnamese patriot, he refused to cooperate with the French. Instead, he went into self-imposed exile abroad. While touring Japan, he was introduced to Fishel by a Japanese friend who had saved his life in 1945.[13]

When Fishel went to Michigan State in 1951 as assistant director of MSU's Governmental Research Bureau, Diem followed. Two years later Fishel appointed his friend the bureau's Southeast Asian consultant.[14] Fishel's support of Diem came at a pivotal point in the latter's career. A persuasive advocate of his own cause, Diem portrayed himself to American policymakers as an ardent anticommunist sympathetic to the West. His irreproachable nationalist "credentials" were seen as ensuring him significant political support in Vietnam while his firm anticommunist views dovetailed with American geopolitical goals.

During his sojourn in the United States, Diem cultivated enough American support to enable himself to assume power in South Vietnam in July 1954. Until the early 1960s, when the relationship soured, Washington continued to support Diem, viewing him as an effective agent of Vietnamese modernization. Soon after Diem returned to Vietnam, he made Fishel his unofficial adviser. In his memoirs, John Hannah recalls that Secretary of State Dulles personally called him to request that Fishel accompany Diem to the 1954 Geneva Conference. In the end, Diem did not attend, but representatives of his fledgling government did, including several relatives.[15]

During the Diem regime's chaotic early years, Fishel acted as a consultant to the president and promoter of his cause. To the South Vietnamese president, Fishel was a trusted adviser. To the U.S. State Department, he was a useful informant. In 1954–55, Fishel served on the staff of General J. Lawton Collins, Eisenhower's special representative in South Vietnam, functioning as a liaison between Collins and Diem. Collins noted that "Dr. Fishel did a splendid job while he was here and enjoyed both Ngo Dinh Diem's and my confidence and respect."[16] Unsure whether his initially shaky government would survive, and lacking other confidants, Diem turned to Fishel, whose advice he valued. For a time, Fishel lived in the presidential palace, as did Wolf Ladejinsky, an American land reform expert. The three often discussed government affairs over breakfast. In September 1954, Fishel wrote his department chair at MSU, "I go in and out of the palace so often these days I'm treated as one of his staff by the guards. Yesterday I was there for 15 hours, and on Saturday for 19 hours."[17]

Fishel was not to be a one-man mission much longer. Later, in September, at Diem's request, several other MSU faculty joined Fishel in Saigon. A three-person team composed of James H. Denison, Hannah's administrative assistant and head of public relations, Arthur F. Brandstatter, chairman of the police administration department, and Charles C. Killingsworth, chairman of the economics department, were tasked with evaluating whether a technical assistance program would benefit both the university and South Vietnam.[18] During its two-week trip, the "special mission" visited Washington, DC, the Philippines, and Vietnam and conducted numerous interviews with American, Philippine, and Vietnamese officials, including Presidents Diem and Ramon Magsaysay. The latter, with American assistance, had recently suppressed the communist-led Huk movement in the Philippines. The mission justified its brief two-week visit by claiming that in the existing crisis situation a six-month or year-long study was impossible. Mistakes would be made in "any emergency program," they contended, "but the important thing is to get a program under way that has a least at reasonable chance of success."[19]

In its October 1954 report to the U.S. Foreign Operations Administration (FOA), the group recommended that Michigan State, in joint agreement with South Vietnam and the FOA, provide technical assistance to the South Vietnamese government under four major headings: (1) public administration; (2) police administration; (3) public information; and (4) public finance and economics. MSU's eagerness to get started reflected a postwar "can-do hubris" that clouded the judgment of U.S. academicians and policymakers alike, leading them to overestimate American capabilities and become involved in inappropriate endeavors.[20] As former defense secretary Robert S. McNamara admitted in his memoirs:

> I had never visited Indochina, nor did I understand or appreciate its history, language, culture, or values. The same must be said, to varying degrees, about . . . many others. When it came to Vietnam, we found ourselves setting policy for a region that was terra incognita.[21]

In this respect, McNamara and his colleagues resembled the protagonist of Graham Greene's novel *The Quiet American* (1955), Alden Pyle, a naive young Bostonian, on government assignment in Vietnam, who was "determined . . . to do good, not to any individual person but a country, a continent, a world."[22] Pyle's profound ignorance of Vietnam as well as his naiveté resulted in the death of many innocent persons.[23]

Like Pyle and McNamara, MSUG personnel had only the barest knowledge of Vietnam, acquired during a three-week language and culture orientation conducted on the Michigan State campus. Although fully half of this brief orientation was devoted to language study, MSUG participants never mastered Vietnamese and were dependent on local Vietnamese interpreters. Reflecting on this experience many years later, a member of one of the early groups commented that "we didn't" really have an orientation program.[24] Of course, even a much more extensive orientation would not have prevented all of Michigan State's difficulties in South Vietnam, many of which stemmed from cultural misunderstandings. But more intensive language instruction might have reduced the language barrier and facilitated communications between MSUG teams and their Vietnamese counterparts.[25]

South Vietnam's government under Ngo Dinh Diem was a complex of patriarchal and tradition-bound bureaucracies that valued age, formal education, and political loyalty above competence and efficiency. In this environment, the introduction of new training methods and procedures proved very difficult indeed. Vietnamese officials dug in their heels against change and accepted assistance from MSUG only under duress.

The resettlement of refugees from the north is a case in point. Following the 1954 Geneva accords some 900,000 Catholic, Buddhist, and Protestant refugees from North Vietnam fled south. At one point, five thousand refugees were entering the south every day. Lacking the means to assimilate them, South Vietnam's Commissariat for Refugees, better known by its French acronym, COMIGAL, turned to MSUG. Michigan State personnel worked well with COMIGAL's Vietnamese staff and made a significant contribution by providing technical assistance and introducing a decentralization plan that placed greater responsibility for resettlement in the hands of the refugees themselves. Within the relatively brief space of two years (1955–57), the vast majority of northern refugees had been successfully relocated. MSUG member Ralph Smuckler praised COMIGAL director Bui Van Luong for his cooperative attitude, which distinguished him as "an unusual person . . . [who] did accept advice and read the reports that we prepared."[26] As a new organization, COMIGAL was not hampered by the same bureaucratic restraints that MSUG encountered in established government agencies.[27]

Diem's willingness to accept American advice concerning refugee issues receded once the initial crisis was over. By 1957, South Vietnam's resettlement policies focused on the highlands, where Diem sought to resettle northern refugees as a barrier to communist infiltration of this upland region. The Vietnamese president dispatched Gerald C. Hickey and Fred Wickert, the only MSUG members with anthropological training, to the highlands to study Montagnard land policies. Visiting numerous Montagnard villages in the course of their difficult travels—at one point their jeep was attacked by an eight-foot cobra—the Americans submitted a report, written by Hickey, that displeased Diem because it argued that the highlanders perceived the South Vietnamese as colonialists. Disregarding Hickey's and Wickert's advice to refrain from settling refugees in the highlands, Diem wound up creating the scenario he had tried to avoid. His actions "facilitated rather than hindered the subsequent subversion of the tribes" by the communists.[28]

Another area where MSUG officials differed on occasion with their South Vietnamese counterparts was over the training of police forces. A clash of values and perspectives caused Michigan State's association with the civil guard to fail. Diem officially organized the guard into a 60,000–member paramilitary organization in April 1955. An impasse occurred a year later when MSUG, going against Diem and the U.S. Army's wishes, tried to convert the guard into a civil agency operating on the village level and equipped with simple weaponry. Conceiving of it as a Vietnamese equivalent of American state police units, MSUG advocated training the guard to handle burglaries and homicides in Vietnam's countryside. Diem and the U.S. Army wanted to maintain the guard as a paramilitary unit capable of exercising national police duties *and* providing support for the South Vietnamese army. This clash of views engendered bureaucratic infighting and a lack of preparedness when insurgency threatened the south in 1959. In retrospect, several MSUG police advisers admitted to having misjudged the situation. Ralph Turner remarked in a 1992 interview that "obviously the Vietnamese were right" in insisting on a paramilitary unit.[29]

Police training was more effective in situations such as weapons instruction, where verbal communication and methodology were less important. Because such activities were more concrete, they had a "lower cultural barrier to cross." MSUG training specialist Paul Shields, a former FBI agent, recalled that "[i]t was difficult to teach using an interpreter," because one could not always tell from facial expression or questions whether the Vietnamese were "getting the message." Shields stuck to technical training and avoided anything that smacked of politics. Emerging from colonialism and facing an increasingly powerful communist insurgency, Vietnam's national law enforcement agency, the Sureté, resisted any attempt to transmit American constitutional and legal norms to South Vietnam. Shields noted that the Sureté "had no trouble in accepting equipment such as revolvers, ammo, [and] communication equipment but being receptive to American democratic principles, that's something else."[30]

Diem's regime resisted efforts to restructure South Vietnam's police along democratic lines. Seeing political control as its top priority, the Sureté routinely employed extreme methods with no regard for the rights of those against whom these methods were directed. Diem approved the use of repressive tactics against political rivals and communists and enlisted Michigan State's aid in doing so. To ferret out suspected communist agents living in South Vietnam, the Vietnamese police and the MSUG created the National Identity Card Program (NIC), supplying an ID for every Vietnamese eighteen years or older. Michigan State provided advice and equipment to this project, which led to the arrest of fifty Viet Cong and 163 military deserters, unimpressive numbers considering the efforts involved. MSUG police administration adviser Ralph Turner later recalled that NIC was the only project that the United States did not "ram down the throat of the Vietnamese."[31]

Some MSUG personnel objected to Diem's repressive methods, but since Michigan State was in Vietnam at his invitation, it could do little more than protest individual cases of police brutality. Wesley Fishel was among those MSUG advisers who openly defended the government's use of repression. Still other Americans kept their views to themselves. Eventually, however, this issue culminated in MSU's departure from Vietnam. How this happened is worth exploring.

The partnership between Michigan State and the Diem regime began to unravel in the early 1960s, when several MSUG advisers returned home from Vietnam and began writing critically about the Vietnamese government. Two articles appearing in *The New Republic* were instrumental in arousing Diem's anger. The first was a collaborative effort between two close friends, Adrian Jaffe, a visiting professor of English as the University of Saigon, and Milton C. Taylor, an MSUG economist.[32] Taylor, a devout Catholic, had gone to Vietnam to "help a regime loyal to the West, a regime run by Catholics," but he returned disillusioned with Vietnam and the MSUG project in particular.[33]

In their *New Republic* article, Jaffe and Taylor argued that Diem had alienated the Vietnamese people by using oppressive methods (including secret police, informants, and concentration camps) against communist and noncommunist political opposition alike. These methods, they said, had sapped the people's will to resist the communist guerrillas. Jaffe and Taylor also criticized their MSUG colleagues for refusing to speak out against Diem, charging that many of their colleagues did not wish to give up the prestige and benefits of overseas service.[34]

Whether this was a valid indictment is debatable, but there were advantages. Because Washington designated Vietnam as a "hardship" assignment that merited special pay incentives, Michigan State professors could almost double their regular salaries while benefiting from access to low-cost groceries and liquor at American commissaries.[35] The nightlife in Saigon was also much more exciting than that in East Lansing. From time to time, Michigan State hosted large receptions attended by top Vietnamese and American officials, where the subsidized liquor flowed freely and Vietnamese servants catered to the Americans' needs and desires. Ordinary professors were corrupted by a lifestyle well beyond their normal means at home.[36]

Diem was outraged by the *New Republic* articles. An autocrat who tolerated no criticism, he informed MSUG chief adviser Guy Fox that the authors "would have been tried ... for fomenting an insurrection" had they published their pieces while still in Vietnam.[37] Diem put Michigan State on warning that its contract would not be renewed unless the university guaranteed that its faculty would refrain from criticizing his government. Hoping to continue their work in public administration, Michigan State officials tried unsuccessfully to placate Diem. They informed the South Vietnamese president that while academic freedom made it impossible to censor former project members, future staff would be carefully screened to prevent any such problem from recurring. Diem remained unmoved. He carried out his threat to discontinue MSUG.[38]

On the Michigan State campus, termination of the Vietnamese connection provoked angry discussions among some faculty and administrators. Taylor and Jaffe, at the center of the controversy, published another article in *The New Republic* just one month after Diem's decision to axe MSUG. Anything but contrite, they attacked university administrators for accepting government contracts too readily. "What is alarming about university operations abroad," they asserted, "is that the schools have been caught up in endeavors which are often irreconcilable with serious scholarship and which have caused deterioration in the ethical and professional standards of many participating faculty members."[39] Taylor's and Jaffe's remarks went to the heart of the conflict over academic participation in foreign affairs.

During the mid- to late 1960s, as American intervention in the Vietnam War escalated dramatically, the role of universities in promoting American foreign policy goals received greater attention. Campus demonstrations increased dramatically as faculty and students joined in protesting the war. Michigan State was no exception. In 1962 the campus divided over whether the university should have supported a dictatorship like Diem's. Wesley Fishel and John Hannah adhered to the official U.S. government view that the American presence in Vietnam was vital to stopping the spread of communism. For several years, they defended Diem's actions as necessary evils toward this positive goal. Other

Michigan State faculty disagreed sharply, arguing that Diem's methods were destroying South Vietnam and that he had to be replaced. Joining this debate, Taylor and Jaffe chastised Hannah and the MSU administration for their willingness to "accept unquestioningly, even joyously, the point of view of the [State] Department" and to "assist dictatorial, venal regimes."[40]

Use of American modernization methods in developing nations also came under scrutiny in the 1960s. Opponents argued that tradition might be advantageous to growth and that Third World countries should "pursue their own paths of development."[41] American policy in South Vietnam became a matter of contention. Without taking into account indigenous customs and mores, critics charged, American policymakers often imposed their will on South Vietnam. Michigan State was said to have engaged in activities that offended Vietnamese sensibilities and damaged the prospects of nation building.[42]

Michigan State's predicament reflected the basic dilemma of American policy. Eisenhower backed Diem in order to halt the spread of communism, hoping that the South Vietnamese government would implement desperately needed economic and political changes. Lacking leverage, Fishel and Hannah counted on Diem's recognition of what they believed would be in his own best interest—a moderate course of reform to preempt revolution. When Diem failed to behave in the prescribed manner, the Eisenhower administration, fearful of weakening South Vietnam, refrained from applying the only leverage it possessed, namely, its threat to withhold aid.[43] A war-torn nation suffering from a legacy of colonialism, South Vietnam was an implausible place for taking a stand against communist expansion in Southeast Asia. Nation building would have been difficult under the best of conditions. Diem's authoritarian rule made it impossible. Although the Vietnamese president assumed power "largely under American auspices," numerous U.S. policymakers at the time cautioned that his legitimacy as a leader was suspect.[44] A self-imposed exile and devout Catholic, Diem appeared an unlikely choice to establish a noncommunist government in a predominately Buddhist country. He was, however, in Dulles's words, the "best available man," so his flaws were overlooked.[45] Diem fit the necessary American criteria: nationalist credentials coupled with firm anticommunist views.[46] Diem remained in office until 1963, when dissident South Vietnamese generals assassinated him. John F. Kennedy's administration was aware of the impending coup but declined to intervene.[47] Following the Vietnamese president's death, the United States sponsored several leaders who also failed to establish a workable government. Fearful of just such an eventuality, Diem's American supporters, such as Fishel, had hesitated to break with the president. In 1965, Lyndon Johnson sent U.S. combat forces to South Vietnam to prevent its fall to the communists.[48]

Notes

1. George C. Herring, *America's Longest War: The United States and Vietnam, 1950–1975,* 2d ed. (New York: Knopf, 1986), pp. 47–48; George Kahin, *Intervention: How*

America Became Involved in Vietnam (New York: Knopf, 1986), pp. 69–70.

2. In this volume, see chapter 14 by Rey Chow, "The Age of the World Target," for a discussion of "area studies."

3. Kenneth J. Heineman, *Campus Wars: The Peace Movement at American State Universities in the Vietnam Era* (New York and London: New York University Press, 1993), pp. 13–19; *Saturday Evening Post,* September 15, 1956; Walter Adams and John A. Garraty, *Is the World Our Campus?* (East Lansing: Michigan State University Press, 1960), p. 2; Paul L. Dressel, *College to University: The Hannah Years at Michigan State, 1935–1969* (East Lansing: Michigan State University Publications, 1987), pp. 11–12. See also Sigmund Diamond, *Compromised Campus: The Collaboration of Universities with the Intelligence Community, 1945–1955* (New York and Oxford: Oxford University Press, 1992).

4. Samuel P. Huntington, *Political Order in Changing Societies* (New Haven and London: Yale University Press, 1968), p. 6.

5. Alvin Y. So, *Social Change and Development: Modernization, Dependency, and World-System Theories* (Newbury Park, London, and New Delhi: Sage Publications, 1990), pp. 261–62, 30, 34, 36; Max F. Millikan and W.W. Rostow, *A Proposal: Key to an Effective Foreign Policy* (New York: Harper & Brothers, 1957), pp. 1–4; Huntington, *Political Order in Changing Societies,* p. 6; Samuel P. Huntington, "The Goals of Development," in *Understanding Political Development,* ed. Myron Weiner and Samuel P. Huntington, (Boston and Toronto: Little, Brown, 1987), p. 6.

6. So, *Social Change and Development,* p. 262.

7. David McCullough, *Truman* (New York: Simon & Schuster, 1992), p. 730.

8. Walter Adams, *The Test* (New York: Macmillan, 1971), p. 18; Dressel, *College to University,* pp. 3, 5, 7–11, 14, 276–300; East Lansing (Mich.) *State News,* February 25, 1991; John A. Hannah, *A Memoir* (East Lansing: Michigan State University Press, 1980), p. 138; Richard Niehoff, *John A. Hannah: Versatile Administrator and Distinguished Public Servant* (Lanham, MD.: University Press of America, 1989), pp. 133, 214–16; Heineman, *Campus Wars,* p. 21.

9. *Saturday Evening Post,* September 15, 1956; Detroit *Free Press Magazine,* June 11, 1972, Box 677, Michigan State University Vietnam Project Papers, Michigan State University Archives and Historical Collections, East Lansing, Michigan (hereafter cited as Vietnam Project Papers); Bio-Data File 1974 and New York *Times* Bio-Service, both in Wesley R. Fishel Papers, Michigan State University Archives and Historical Collections, East Lansing, Michigan (hereafter cited as Fishel Papers).

10. Bio-Data File 1974 and New York *Times* Bio-Service, both in Fishel Papers.

11. Bio-Data File 1974, Fishel Papers; Detroit *Free Press Magazine,* June 11, 1972, Box 677, Vietnam Project Papers; author's interview with Fred Wickert, July 20, 1992.

12. *Saturday Evening Post,* September 15, 1956; Bio-Data File 1974, Fishel Papers; Detroit *Free Press Magazine,* June 11, 1972, Box 677, Vietnam Project Papers; Wesley Fishel, *The End of Extraterritoriality in China* (Berkeley and Los Angeles: University of California Press, 1952); American Friends of Vietnam Biographical File, Box 3, Folder 18, Gilbert Jonas Collection 166, Gilbert Jonas Papers, Michigan State University Archives and Historical Collections, East Lansing, Michigan; Herbert Garfinkel to Wesley Fishel, July 8, 1952, John Davis to Wesley Fishel, November 16, 1954, Wesley Fishel to John Davis, November 19, 1954, all in Box 1184, Fishel Papers.

13. *Saturday Evening Post,* September 15, 1956; Herring, *America's Longest War,* pp. 47–48; David Anderson, *Trapped by Success: The Eisenhower Administration and Vietnam, 1953–1961* (New York: Columbia University Press, 1991), p. 8; Detroit *Free Press Magazine,* June 11, 1972, Box 677, Vietnam Project Papers; Wickert interview.

14. *Detroit Free Press Magazine,* June 11, 1972, Box 677, Vietnam Project Papers.

15. Anderson, *Trapped by Success,* pp. 52, 59; Hannah, *Memoir,* 130; Herring, *America's Longest War,* pp. 48–49; *Michigan State News,* September 27, 1954.

16. J. Lawton Collins to John A. Hannah, March 11, 1955, Box 42, John A. Hannah Papers, Michigan State University Archives and Historical Collections, East Lansing, Michigan (hereafter cited as Hannah Papers).

17. Fishel to Weidner, September 20, 1954, Box 628, Folder 101, Vietnam Project Papers; Collins to Hannah, March 11, 1955, Hannah Papers; Wickert interview; "The Vietnam Lobby," *Ramparts* (July 1965), p. 20; Anderson, *Trapped by Success,* p. 75.

18. *Michigan State News,* September 27, 1954.

19. Arthur F. Brandstatter, James H. Denison, Charles C. Killingsworth, and Edward W. Weidner, Chief of Mission, *Report of the Special FOA Mission from Michigan State College for Public Administration, Public Information, Police Administration, and Public Finance and Economics* (Saigon, October 16, 1954), pp. i–3, Vietnam Project Papers; Robert Scigliano and Guy H. Fox, *Technical Assistance in Vietnam: The Michigan State University Experience* (New York: Praeger, 1965), p. 2.

20. Kahin, *Intervention,* pp. 69–70.

21. Robert S. McNamara with Brian VanDeMark, *In Retrospect: The Tragedy and Lessons of Vietnam* (New York: Times Books, 1995), pp. 32.

22. Graham Greene, *The Quiet American* (New York: Penguin Books, 1977; orig. pub. 1955), p. 18.

23. Ibid., pp. 17, 28, 41; Scigliano and Fox, *Technical Assistance in Vietnam,* p. 2; Brandstatter et al., *Report of the Special FOA Mission,* I-3.

24. Author's interview with John Hunter, July 22, 1992.

25. Ibid.; Status Report from L.E. Traywick, Assistant Coordinator, to C.C. Killingsworth, Coordinator, July 29, 1955, pp. 1–6, Box 648, Folder 87, Vietnam Project Papers; Office Diary, July 21, 1955, ibid.

26. Author's interview with Ralph Smuckler, May 13, 1993.

27. Ibid.; *Final Report of the Michigan State University Advisory Group,* 1962, 6, Vietnam Project Papers; Gertrude Samuels, "Passage to Freedom in Viet Nam," *National Geographic* (June 1955: 866–67; Louis Wiesner, *Victims and Survivors: Displaced Persons and Other War Victims in Viet-Nam, 1954–1975* (Westport, CT: Greenwood Press, 1988), p. 6; Precise figures on the refugees are unobtainable because COMIGAL's files burned in May 1955 during a battle between Diem's troops and the Binh-Xuyen, a group of Saigon criminals. The best estimates on the number of refugees who migrated south appear in a 1959 article by COMIGAL's commissioner, Bui Van Luong, and are debatable. See Bui Van Luong, "The Role of Friendly Nations," in *Viet-Nam: The First Five Years, An International Symposium,* ed. Richard Lindholm (East Lansing: Michigan State University Press, 1959), pp. 49, 52–53.

28. Quoted in Kahin, *Intervention,* p. 99; Wickert interview; Wiesner, *Victims and Survivors,* pp. 15–16, 20, 361; Gerald Hickey, *Free in the Forest: Ethnohistory of the Vietnamese Central Highlands, 1954–1976* (New Haven: Yale University Press, 1982), pp. 32–41, 44, 47–54; Gerald C. Hickey, *Preliminary Research Report on the High Plateau* (Saigon: MSUG, 1957), p. 29; Gerald C. Hickey to author, January 28, 1993.

29. Author's interview with Ralph Turner, July 9, 1992; Ronald H. Spector, *The United States Army in Vietnam: Advice and Support: The Early Years of the U.S. Army in Vietnam, 1941–1960* (Washington, DC: Government Printing Office, 1983), pp. 375–78; Chief of Police Advisor's Report to the Minister of Interior, 6, Box 680, Folder 9, Vietnam Project Papers; Analysis of the Role of Security Services, 2–4, Box 680, Folder 8, Vietnam Project Papers; Arthur Brandstatter to Ralph Turner, February 3, 1961, Box 680, Folder 48, Vietnam Project Papers.

30. Paul Shields to author, April 5, 1994; Scigliano and Fox, *Technical Assistance in Vietnam,* pp. 18–19.

31. Author's conversation with Ralph Turner, March 16, 1994; *MSUG Final Report,* 49; Chief Advisor's Report to the Minister of Interior, pp. 16–17; Scigliano and Fox, *Technical Assistance in Vietnam,* p. 21; Chief Advisor's Project Status Report, July 29, 1960, p. 2, Vietnam Project Papers; E.H. Adkins, Jr., "Monthly Report," July 1961, 1, Box 680, Folder 13, Vietnam Project Papers.

32. Adrian Jaffe and Milton C. Taylor, "A Crumbling Bastion: Flattery and Lies Won't Save Vietnam," *The New Republic* (June 19, 1961): 17.

33. Author's interview with Walter Adams, August 10, 1993.

34. Jaffe and Taylor, "A Crumbling Bastion," pp. 17, 19.

35. *Ramparts,* April 1966, p. 17.

36. *Ramparts,* April 1966, p. 17; *Milwaukee Journal,* January 13, 1957; author's interview with Milton Taylor, May 11, 1993; Request for Reimbursement, October 5, 1961, Box 643, Folder 106, Vietnam Project Papers; ibid., May 9, 1958, Box 643, Folder 101, Vietnam Project Papers.

37. Guy Fox to James B. Hendry, February 19, 1962, Box 656, Folder 72, Vietnam Project Papers.

38. New York *Times,* February 20, 1962; Scigliano and Fox, *Technical Assistance in Vietnam,* p. 53.

39. Milton C. Taylor and Adrian Jaffe, "The Professor-Diplomat: Ann Arbor and Cambridge Were Never Like This," *The New Republic,* March 1962, pp. 28–30.

40. Ibid., p. 29.

41. So, *Social Change and Development,* p. 262.

42. Huntington, *Political Order in Changing Societies,* p. 3.

43. See Anderson, *Trapped by Success.*

44. Douglas J. Macdonald, *Adventures in Chaos: American Intervention for Reform in the Third World* (Cambridge: Harvard University Press, 1992), pp. 248, 2.

45. Quoted in Herring, *America's Longest War,* p. 72.

46. Ibid., pp. 49, 72.

47. Ibid., pp. 104–7.

48. Anderson, *Trapped by Success,* p. 209.

16

American Wars Within World History

G. L. Penrose

This chapter situates both the Indian wars and America's wars in Asia within the context of world systems and refines that context with reference to Marshall G.S. Hodgson's analysis of Western exceptionalism. According to Hodgson, the West institutionalized methods of economic and technological change that gave Westerners an essentially insurmountable advantage in relations with other cultures, including those of Native Americans and Asians. In this way the Indian wars and conflicts in Asia become instances of the same basic power dynamic.

World-systems history strongly suggests technological parity among the major centers of civilization until the seventeenth century. Premodern technological change and innovation gave no culture or world area long-term strategic superiority over its neighbors or enemies. Janet Abu-Lughod states the obvious fact that no particular culture held a monopoly on technological or social inventiveness.[1] Innovations such as agriculture, domestication of animals, writing, iron, the wheel, the recurved bow, riding astride, various sailing technologies, the stirrup, and many others spread evenly and at a moderate pace. In other words, the vast majority of such inventions could be easily duplicated. Once a person saw the stirrup employed, it was a simple matter to go back home and make a pair for one's own use. The same was generally true as well even for fairly complex processes, such as agriculture. In general, pre-modern innovations could be easily duplicated, or borrowed, across distance and over cultural boundaries. The very few of these inventions that were not readily understood, borrowed or duplicated, as was evidently the case with Greek fire, were only locally decisive and remain something of a mystery even at the present.

Then, something happened to transform the world into a place where the difficulty of understanding, borrowing, and duplication escalated dramatically. It became strategically significant to possess new technology, to have the use of complex inventions that gave long-term advantage to those who owned them.

This transformation continues down to the present. What happened was the process that we know as the industrial revolution.

The past quarter-century has seen some fresh efforts to understand what this European and North American event has meant for the rest of the world, that is, for those cultures from whose perspective we are striving to understand American wars in Asia.[2]

The Western industrial revolution was the result of the long accumulation of civilizational knowledge on the rough frontier that Europe was, in relation to much older centers of human culture such as the eastern Mediterranean and China. What would become Europe had an advantage over the older centers because of its fertile virgin land, small population, and relatively abundant natural resources. Although the debate over Hodgson's explanation for the origins of the revolution will continue, his understanding of the process itself once under way and of its results for the rest of the world seems compelling.

First, he identifies a cultural shift that features the institutionalization of innovation. That is, for the first time in human history people were rewarded directly, socially, for finding new ways to do things. This accelerated the rate of change. The result was an end to the earlier technological parity among civilizations. Europe got ahead, fast. And then, faster. Indeed, the rate of change is such that nowhere else can it be "paralleled independently nor . . . borrowed wholesale."[3] This means accepting the very real possibility that nobody can ever duplicate what the Western industrial revolution has produced over the past two centuries. This is "exceptional" in the most profound sense of the world.

The evidence for this is all around us in the world today. It is possible to argue that nobody will ever have as much of the most obvious products of the revolution—wealth and the power that it buys—as the West has enjoyed. We have set a standard of material well-being and political clout that has become the yardstick by which the rest of the world has learned to measure itself. And never will the rest of the world measure up. Just to emphasize the exceptional nature of the process, recall that twice in this century (1914–18, 1939–45) Westerners tried to destroy themselves by concentrating their wealth and power against one another. Still, try as they might, they could not damage themselves enough to lose their collective power, which was merely shifted to North America, and, in the late 1980s America, without even breathing hard, drove the Soviet economy into revolution when the last of the Soviet Union's numerous attempts to measure up failed again.[4]

There are serious moral issues here, especially for late twentieth-century Americans who, though they no longer produce very much new wealth, still enjoy the power it has bought. It is worth recalling Theodore H. von Laue's provocative discussions of the possibility that there may be some room for moral thinking about how we ought to use the power that the wealth has generated.[5]

The current essay does not depend totally upon whether or not this rather dark thesis is accepted. That the rest of the world has struggled and is struggling to make itself secure relative to the West is not debatable. That the natives of the Americas faced a similar set of issues in their confrontation with us is similarly beyond question. The point here is that, by looking again at our interaction with Native Americans as an experience we believe that we know well, we may derive additional insight into the Asian interaction with us, an experience that we know less well.

It should be clear by now where this chapter is headed. It will be fruitful to compare the Native American and Asian experiences with the powerful, wealthy, industrialized, white, North American and European cultures. What Asians and Native Americans share is an experience of contact and conflict with a technologically and materially overwhelming culture. This is not to suggest that Asian and Native American cultures are necessarily in any other ways equivalent except in their experiences with us. One finds in them responses to the West that are similar enough to invite comparison

Changes in non-Western cultures involved with the West begin with mere, initial contact, most often in the direction of an increased level of violence and lethality. The most striking example may be what happened to Native American culture upon the arrival together on these shores of the horse, the iron age, firearms, and new diseases. A good deal of energy was expended in 1992 debating the Columbian legacy, so only the horse will be emphasized here. Many Americans of descent other than Native American—and one might suspect no small number of Native Americans as well—imagine the Plains Indian as the epitome of "Indianness." Yet, that epitome is the product of an innovation that arrived only in 1492. It would destroy the culture of agriculturists and hunter-gatherers, and the balance among them, by giving strategic advantage to those who could get and use horses. The warrior society that resulted degraded all other cultural options for their failure in warfare. It is well known what happens to societies that adopt riding astride.[6] It is not all good, and it is especially injurious to the status of women. In any case, the point is only to suggest that what might be called "merely passive contact" can produce profound results.[7] So that if counting coup (the act of touching an enemy, as a deed of bravery) is the cultural preference of the horseless hunter-gatherer armed with stone and sinew, it is not the pragmatic choice of the light cavalryman armed with a firearm. It is interesting to speculate whether it might have made a difference if, before the Native Americans were drawn into mortal combat astride, they had been able to experiment with the horse for two thousand years, as the Turks and Mongols had done.

The Manchus provide a useful springboard for beginning the comparison from the Asian side. The Manchus ruled through a great transmutation of their own that flows from the firearm. It is not the result of "mere contact," since the Russians had shot at them and thereby initiated conflict.[8] Still, the firearm alone is responsible for a revolution in Chinese strategic understanding of their place in the world. For two thousand years the horsemen of Inner Asia had been the prime strategic threat to Chinese civilization. No sedentary state could afford to maintain enough horses to challenge the nomads in their own element, the steppe, until the firearm as a personal weapon finally gave the infantryman, in this case the Manchu, parity, and then dominance, on the battlefield, especially as light artillery developed. Wellington's infantry squares defeated Napoleon's cavalry at Waterloo; Custer (dismounted) is a fine negative example.

If the Inner Asian frontier of China was now, in the mid-eighteenth century, for the first time ever, secured against the nomads by firearms, the Manchus were still not fully aware that a new strategic threat existed. However, they would soon learn that and, again, the threat would involve firearms along with other technological factors from the West. That is, the arrival of the British at Canton with the "new European approach to trade-cum-plunder," and with heavier and more numerous weapons, completed the Manchu strategic revolution.[9] It became increasingly clear that an unprecedented, strategic, but now seaborne threat to Chinese civilization had forced revision of the strategic thinking of two millennia.

In the case of Japan, initial contact bled into conflict as well. It is of interest to note, by the way, that the career of a single empire builder could encompass chronologically Commodore Perry's arrival in Japan (1854), Grant's "total war," Seward's purchase of Alaska (1867), and the Battle of the Little Bighorn (1876).[10] Perry, Grant, and Seward represent the high national confidence that came to accompany the growing wealth and power of the developing industrial society. Custer is a negative example, stunning as an exception, only because by any reasonable standard he should have won. In any case, Perry forced the Japanese to look at themselves, especially to compare themselves with what they saw happening to China.

For reasons having to do with Japanese politics and development, the *tozama* daimyos of Satsuma and Chosen moved first and fastest to adopt what they could of the technology that Perry so ostentatiously displayed. They built ships and fortifications and made weapons and then proceeded to use them against one another to greater effect than when they were employed against Westerners.[11] They also understood, as some others would not immediately, that it was essential to be able to make and repair their own Western weapons lest they become dependent upon Western sources with the political strings that always come attached to such supply.

The major point in this case, however, is the level of violence. It is hard to know for sure how to measure such a level with any precision, but common sense can suggest an answer. One can mentally compare the probable level of violence resulting from the confrontation between two samurai forces armed with "cold" weapons and a deep cultural tradition "regulating" conduct with the level that results from reequipping the samurai with firearms and naval guns, which are culturally out of place. This is not to suggest that premodern war was somehow better; rather that it took greater physical, cultural, and psychological effort to kill.

In each of these cases, so far the Indians and the horse, the Manchus and the firearm, the Japanese and Perry, it seems reasonable to assert that for the non-Western culture "mere contact" likely results in profound cultural transformation, an increase in the level of violence, and probably an increase in lethality of that violence as well. The violence also begins by way of the new technology that makes it possible to escape cultural tradition, which had been a means of regulating violence, if not controlling it. In the stages of intercourse that are beyond initial contact, there is steady need to cope with the conflict that it has provoked.

The most obvious source of Western technological superiority is the gun in whatever permutation in which it is employed: as cannon, as pistol, as long rifle, as naval artillery. The response of the non-Western culture, therefore, is to get guns. But it has already been suggested that to simply acquire the guns from Western sources creates strategic dependence. True, if one can get enough guns in the right place at the right time, one can kill Custer or sink battleships in Pearl Harbor. However, the only chance for long-term security is to sustain the supply by producing guns, ammunition, and spare parts from a resource, demographic, and technical base under one's own control. Otherwise—and this is the history of both Native American and Asians in relations with America over the past two centuries—sooner or later the Western industrial revolution will prevail because, recall, in the end, it can be neither duplicated nor borrowed wholesale. Can there be much doubt that the Vietnam War, lost on the battlefield or on the evening news, was won in the post exchange?

That is, responses to the West in Western terms have tended to fail. The cultural effort and economic disruption required to acquire the weapons that will provide strategic security have regularly proved to be more than non-Western societies could afford. Nor, having gotten the machines, could those societies match the accelerating pace of change and innovation that seemed to be built into the Western industrialized nations.

The result has often been a sense of hopelessness, of doom, that has developed in the face of technological inferiority. This response has several permutations. The first, perhaps the most common, and one certainly shared by Native Americans and Asians, is an invocation of superior spiritual powers for service against Western machines.

The ghost dancers were confronted by their clear inability to defend their way of life, by the destruction of their culture, and by the loss of the buffalo; they are a good example of the attempt to substitute for machines with spiritual power. With proper attention to their own tradition and, not incidentally, an admixture of the new Christian theology, they sought a great victory of the Indian spirit over the mechanical pressure of the whites. The last of them, the Lakotas at Wounded Knee, paid an awful price for their desperation.

In China, both the Taiping and the Boxer "rebels" mixed spiritual revelation with protection from the Western intrusion. The Taipings, like the ghost dancers, added a shot of Christian revelation to older formulas as if, having failed at borrowing or duplicating the machines, they might succeed in appropriating the Western spiritual essence. In contrast, the "Self-Strengthening Movement" was led by serious reformers determined to change China in order to meet the Western threat without losing what they understood to be the essential elements of Chinese culture. They had already suspected that cultural loss was a very real possibility if one went too far in the direction of Westernization, so they sought a formula that would invest Western machines with Chinese "essence," thereby remaining Chinese while also becoming capable of defense in the face of both Western and Japanese encroachment. In the wake of the failure of self-strengthening and of reform in general, the Boxers appeared. Self-consciously and, one might postulate, dialectically anti-Christian,[12] they were to be protected from Western bullets by the careful practice of newly mixed elements of traditional faith. In 1900 they fared no better than the Lakota did in 1890.

Even, late in this current century, Mao Zedong can be characterized as a "military romantic" who was determined to overcome Western, or Soviet (!), technology with Chinese bodies. In the well-known film *The Manchurian Candidate,* we have nothing but a formulation of the contest between machines and cleverness, an instance of the near-victory of mind over matter.

In Asian novels and films, especially Japanese films on the Pacific War, one rarely, if ever, sees Western faces shown as enemies in the way that *The Sands of Iwo Jima* or a hundred other similar American films demonize the Japanese. Rather, the appeal is to Japanese spirit, which will prevail over that of the Westerners because it is superior. This is contrasted in the popular mind with our "native" American comfort with technology and our own conviction that it will finally prevail over anybody else's spirit.

We know, for instance, that the Pacific War began with Japanese technical superiority. They had better torpedoes and better fighter aircraft, at least. Imperial naval gunnery was also superior, certainly at night, if only because of better training.

Here we slide into the superior spirit realm, for the training was matched, the technological edge was lost, the resource and demographic base for replacement was insufficient. We are left with the kamikaze attacks as the penultimate Pacific War event that pitted spirit against machines. The ultimate events happened at Hiroshima and Nagasaki, which in the long term may be seen as brutal punctuation marks to the sentence that begins with Western contact.

The comparison of Native American and Asian experiences with Westerners can be broadened to include what might be called patterns of Western behavior. These patterns consist of ways the West went about, or attempted, its domination. For instance, we find a parallel between the Indian School system and the strategic hamlet in Vietnam. Both were designed to make over the subjects of the policy into something we could understand and control by making them as much like us as was possible.[13] In this context gender issues are meaningful analytically. On balance, "native" women are more likely to enter Western society than are males. One of the results of this is the emasculation of the men, who, diminished by their role under Western domination, make their women objects of blame and violence. The dynamics of Native American gender relations with the advancing whites seems quite consistent with, say, the Korean experience as it is addressed in Ahn Junghyo's novel, *The Silver Stallion,* which has also enjoyed great success as a feature film in Korea.[14]

Vietnam may be the best example of the end of direct colonial rule often leading to "native" oppression of fellow non-Westerners that is no longer moderated or modulated by outside, imperial interests. In connection with this is the favorite Western solution to big-power rivalry over a single country partition. Partition has the dubious benefit of providing political positions for twice as many people as unity does, but it always fails to solve anything and creates new problems in its wake. The parallel with the Native Americans runs through this as well, where "partition" into geographically separated reservations and willingness to accept sometimes despotic rule causes as many problems as it solves.

The Western presence also divides families and peoples and forces unpleasant choices upon the subject population even when the Western rule is only exploiting preexisting rivalries. The Crows who fought for Custer have their counterpart in the South Koreans who fought for the United States in Vietnam. That is, there is a pattern, a shared Asian–Native American experience that sees non-Westerners drawn into larger wars as allies or surrogates of imperial powers whose interests are not at all likely to be congruent with those of the host culture.

A final generalization and comparison has to do with the very high probability that contact and conflict with the generally victorious West divides the people who think deeply in the non-Western culture into two opposing factions. All may agree that something has gone seriously wrong. The disagreement, the divisions, appear in the debate about just what has happened and how to fix it.

There are some Native Americans, evidently a minority, who think it is okay to do sacred dances for white dollars and, further, who would not hesitate to teach the Native American religion to nonnatives. Their argument is that, since the whites have almost destroyed the land and the native people while following their own religion, maybe the only way to reverse the damage is to teach them the spiritual system that, presumably, honors the land and the creatures more than it does human dominion over them. They are opposed by those who would keep something sacred, something uniquely theirs.

This current Native American discussion can be seen as another angle on the debate that arises among all people who have been subjected to Western dominance. If everybody agrees that something has gone wrong because the West has won, non-Western intellectuals have regularly found themselves divided into two opposing camps about what to do about it: the iconoclastic Westernizers and the nativist romantics. The Westernizers say that what has gone wrong is that Westernization has not progressed far enough and that it is "traditional" society itself that is responsible. The only hope for strategic security in the face of Western domination is to become more Western. The romantics reject this, most often because they sense how damaging it may be to abandon traditional culture. They argue a psychologically and emotionally satisfying alternative to iconoclasm that finds all the answers needed already present in traditional culture if it were only properly understood and attended to.

In conclusion, it needs to be said that Americans are merely lucky, not superior. The exceptional quality of this nation's experience consists of having fortuitously arrived in one of the fairest portions of the earth's surface at precisely the moment that Europeans were devising the technology to exploit the given land, colonial labor, and their capital to an unimaginable degree. The optimal mix of land, labor, and capital came naturally as Americans swept across the continent isolating the native cultures encountered on the way. Americans then leapt across the Pacific to treat others, the Asians, in essentially the same way as the Indians, often using the same words and the same techniques. Although it may be mistaken to imagine that Americans really understand the Native American experience, we certainly know it better than the Asian experience. If we undertake to understand the Asian experience, we may find the readiest insights already a part of our own national culture.

This chapter does not depend upon what most would understand to be the pessimistic view of the prospects for non-Western development with which it began.[15] Whatever the prospects may be, the history of the past two centuries is unchanged. It seems hard to deny, however, that even the most vigorous of the new Asian economies are resource-poor or dependent, feature uneven mixes of capital, land, and labor that will not sustain indefinite growth, and most important are ultimately dependent on the consuming wealth of the first industrialized societies, Europe and North America, as markets for machines whose technical and intellectual genealogies remain Western.

Notes

1. Janet Abu-Lughod, *Before European Hegemony, The World System* A.D. 1250–1350 (New York and Oxford: Oxford University Press, 1989), p. 354.

2. All of us who do what we may still call "area studies" have been sent deep into reflection about our calling by Edward Said's *Orientalism* (New York: Pantheon Books, 1978). Many of us have been most influenced by Marshall G.S. Hodgson, a quirky and difficult scholar. His major work is *The Venture of Islam*, 3 vols. (Chicago and London: University of Chicago Press, 1974). A more readable exposition of his ideas is found in Marshall G.S. Hodgson, *Rethinking World History*, ed. Edmund Burke III (Cambridge: Press Syndicate of the University of Cambridge, 1993).

3. Hodgson, *Rethinking World History*, 313. Elsewhere in the same volume (p. 124) he expands on this thought, "unless the other blocs had undergone the same transformations—by some improbable historical sleight-of-hand—at exactly the same moment, they must necessarily quickly be left hopelessly behind; for, before being transformed themselves, they could not even borrow at the requisite pace of innovation." In an altogether

different context, but making the same point, J.M. Coetzee recently said, "The underlying question is whether a culture can become modern without internalizing the genealogy of modernity, that is, without living through the epistemological revolution, in all its implications, out of which western science grew." (J.M. Coetzee, "Fabulous Fabulist," a review of Naguib Mafouz, *The Harafish,* in *The New York Review of Books,* September 22, 1994, p. 30).

4. "Forced since the 1870s to substitute the horse for the machine and 'magic for technology,' war planners were powerless to correct the disjuncture between 'policy objectives, strategy, and the military system derived from Russia's society and economy.'" (Elsie Kimerling Wirtschafter in her review of William C. Fuller, *Strategy and Power in Russia 1600–1914* [New York: Free Press, 1992] in *Slavic Review,* 53, no. 3 [Fall 1994]: 870–71).

5. Theodore H. von Laue, *The World Revolution of Westernization: The Twentieth Century in Global Perspective* (New York: Oxford University Press, 1987); and also his *Why Lenin? Why Stalin?: A Reappraisal of the Russian Revolution, 1900–1930,* 2d ed. (Philadelphia, New York, and Toronto: J.B. Lippincott, 1971).

6. David Waller Anthony, "The Social and Economic Implications of the Domestication of the Horse" (Ph.D. dissertation, University of Pennsylvania, 1985).

7. In a severely understated manner, McNeill makes this point as follows: "Historical change was largely provoked by encounters with strangers followed by efforts to borrow (or sometimes to reject or hold at bay) especially attractive novelties. This, in turn, always involved adjustments in other established routines" (William McNeill, "The Changing Shape of World History," *History and Theory,* 34, no. 2 [1996]: 15).

8. See G.L. Penrose, "Inner Asian Influences on the Earliest Russo-Chinese Trade and Diplomatic Contacts," *Russian History,* 19, nos. 1–4, (1992): 361–92.

9. Abu-Lughod, *Before European Hegemony,* p. 361.

10. It is worthwhile to drive home here two points about the American Civil War. First, that despite the awful destruction and loss of life the war caused, the damage was insufficient to stay the growth of American power in the wider world because of the enormous wealth that the industrial system produced. Second, of course, is the more obvious point that an industrial North defeated an agricultural, "traditional" South.

11. It should be noted that the *tozama* daimyo, Satsuma and Chosen, joined forces in the Meiji Restoration (1868), which was relatively nonviolent. The two groups turned against each other—the Chosen joined by many other former daimyo armies—only in 1877.

12. Western spiritual values were inextricably bound together with the spread of Western wealth, power, and dominance. The result was an especially difficult marginalization of Christian converts in times of conflict.

13. Both systems were rooted in the rational optimism of Locke and Voltaire that held humans to be perfectible creatures if they can only be removed from bad influences. What did not advance the Western agenda was bad.

14. Ahn Junghyo, *The Silver Stallion* (New York: Soho Press, 1990). In a conversation with Ahn Junghyo during the 1995 NEH Summer Institute in Missoula, Montana, "American Wars in Asia: A Cultural Approach," the author made the connection explored here. He related that in his childhood, dominated by the American presence he came to understand that "Indians and Japanese were all evil." *White Badge: A Novel of Korea* (New York: Soho Press, 1989) is Ahn's searing account of Korean combat forces under U.S. command in Vietnam.

15. Surely, if it could have been made to happen, our Cold War efforts over the half-century since World War II to create democratic and industrial societies throughout the world would have produced better results.

17

The Indian Wars and the Vietnam War

David Trask

Images drawn from the Indian wars of the late nineteenth century permeate America's experience with war in Asia in the twentieth century. This observation may seem unremarkable when applied to the U.S. quelling of the Philippine "insurrection" at the turn of the century. At that juncture the Indian wars were the most recent American experience of war. They were widely discussed in the nation's newspapers and by American citizens. Therefore it is not surprising to find Theodore Roosevelt comparing Filipinos to "Apaches" and identifying anti-imperialists as "Indian-lovers" or to read in *Harper's* that the best way to win the war would be to find the Philippine equivalent to the buffalo and exterminate it. The significance of American Indian war imagery grows, however, when we reflect on its use during the Pacific War and later in Vietnam.

In the spring of 1942 the War Department printed 2,000 copies of the famous "Budweiser lithograph" of Custer's Last Stand and distributed them to army recruiting offices. During the Vietnam War participants (as well as subsequent novelists) referred to the combat zones of Vietnam as "Indian country" and characterized their patrols as "playing cowboys and Indians."[1] The echoes of the past become louder when we remember the creation of a hybrid fighting force for Vietnam—the Air Cavalry. If the vocabulary of the Vietnam War recalled the Indian wars, this is so at least in part because the Asian experience of war with the United States has several points in common with that of the natives of the new world.

This chapter looks at the values of modern Western civilization to identify the cluster of ideas, common to both eras and drawn from Enlightenment thinking, that facilitated or retarded the prosecution of the wars against Native Americans in the nineteenth century and in Vietnam. In both instances the outcomes were "unsatisfactory" in the sense that a policy stalemate led to an ambiguous resolution of the conflict. The destruction of the enemy fell short of the total victory sought by some proponents of war although it overwhelmed the efforts of the opponents of war to ameliorate or end the hostilities. A study of this "unsatisfactory" situation, using Graham Greene's *The Quiet American* as a starting point, emphasizes the ways that contradictions within American culture, as much as conditions in the field, led to this outcome.

The vacillation of American policies between military and humanitarian efforts characterized both the Indian wars of the nineteenth century and the Vietnam War. In Vietnam the government pursued an incremental escalation of armed force according to a calculus of pain in the search for the right amount of force to tip the situation in favor of American objectives. The acceptance of zones where bombing was not allowed, coupled with alternations between bombing forays and bombing halts, emphasizes the importance to Americans, or at least policymakers, of being "humanitarian" in combat. The injection of teams from American universities to teach people better agricultural and political techniques was part of this approach.[2] In the nineteenth century the United States passed the management of Indians back and forth between the Department of the Interior and the Department of War. The former was regarded as ineffective in controlling its wards while the latter was seen as too harsh in dealing with them. On the reservations, forerunners to Vietnam's strategic hamlets, government farmers and missionaries brought the education deemed necessary by the United States to "civilize" the "savages." Ultimately, however, the connection between these wars runs deeper.

The examination of specific traits of Western culture and their relationship to the Indian and Vietnam wars begins with language. One of the most remembered statements from Vietnam asserted that "we had to destroy the village in order to save it." This echoed the thinking of some late nineteenth-century "friends of the Indian" who touted the efficacy of off-reservation Indian education to create citizens out of the "nation's wards"; their program, however, was predicated on the need to "kill the Indian to save the man."[3] In Vietnam the soldiers themselves conjured the spirit of the nineteenth century when they labeled the areas beyond fortified compounds as "Indian country." These connections are significant because they link both conflicts to some of the core values of modern Western culture. An analysis of Graham Greene's *The Quiet American,* focusing on the ideals and actions of the American Alden Pyle, underscores this relationship for students.[4] Although the novel has been widely praised for its accurate anticipation of American attitudes and actions in Vietnam, its story could also be regarded as a portrayal of the direct application of American policies for the "Indian problem" to another place and time.

Alden Pyle's mission in Vietnam combined two major elements of American dealings with Native Americans—economic development and, more importantly in the novel, the application of military force. His promotion of General The as a "third force" to meet the need for a pro-American alternative to French and communist forces recalls the many nineteenth-century efforts to circumvent the structure of Native American leadership by designating and working with "chiefs" who were willing to sign the treaties put forward by the U.S. government. Pyle's acceptance of the loss of innocent life to create a "national democratic front" in the bombing in the Place Garnier (p. 163) parallels many of the military actions that killed Indians in order to move the rest onto reservations for "their own good."

Furthermore American feelings toward either Indians or Vietnamese are reflected in Pyle's relationship with Phuong, the Vietnamese woman whom he plans to marry. The romance is a curious one. When Pyle decides to marry Phuong, he first announces his intention to Fowler, the British journalist who is having an affair with her; Pyle has not yet asked his intended wife because he cannot conceive of the possibility she will turn him down. His motivation is rescue: "I want to protect her"; her love for him will come later. With no understanding of Vietnamese culture, he visualizes her taking part in the round of middle-class social activities that will comprise her life once she moves to America. This denial of Phuong's identity and culture is thorough: "I want to give her a decent life. This place-smells" (p. 133). She is a child to be rescued just as the American Indians were to be saved from their "plight." In these attitudes Pyle underscores America's long-standing allegiance to modern Western values of the control of nature and the malleability of human traits that date back to the philosophies of Francis Bacon and John Locke.

The term "Indian country," taken seriously, is a condition as well as a place. While the first half of the term, "Indian," emphasizes racial themes in American history, the addition of "country" expands the focus to include the total endeavor of American soldiers and settlers, justified by themes in Enlightenment ideology, in which "wilderness" and native peoples could be subdued to enhance economic opportunity for white settlers. Bacon's contribution to the foundation of the modern world was in part his emphasis on the importance of dominating nature through technology in order to relieve human misery. The natural environment was not a "given" to be accommodated but was rather a repository of secrets that could be used to improve life through the proper application of technology. The acceptance of "machines as the measure of men" by Europeans facilitated the labeling of low-technology societies as inferior and immediately subject to modification.[5] This approach also ensured that any knowledge possessed by Native Americans would be ignored in the process by which people could become objects of study and manipulation like the land itself.

Nineteenth-century Americans as well as Graham Greene's Alden Pyle exhibit their allegiance to these views in diverse ways. Greene emphasizes repeatedly Pyle's lack of understanding of or even interest in the people and their culture; this emphasizes the American belief that the culture of the "other" is only a starting point on the journey of Americanization. Pyle's attraction to technique—the belief that success can be guaranteed by following the step-by-step recipes developed by "experts"—is evident in his reliance on York

Harding's *The Role of the West* to guide his activities in Vietnam despite the fact that Harding had never been to that country. It is, of course, not to be omitted that Pyle does not just apply recipe knowledge to the lives of others; in the novel Fowler finds a sex manual among Pyle's belongings after the American is killed.[6]

Bacon's agenda accompanied the colonists to the new world. In contrast to recent definitions in American discourse that categorize wilderness as "unspoiled" nature or settled territory, earlier Americans from colonial times on believed that the appropriate categories were "wasteland," which was lying idle, and "redeemed land," which had been put to the "good" purposes of farming, mining, or lumbering. Bacon's ideas went far beyond the point of the story of Genesis in which God gave Adam dominion over the earth and its creatures in the Garden of Eden. Bacon argued that mankind could restore the earth to its "perfect and original condition" and its role of serving human needs—through the workings of science. Max Oelschlaeger describes Bacon's position:

> People had long existed through ignorance in a fallen condition—a result of the revolt against God's law. Through science, however, humankind could escape; a way had been "opened for the human understanding entirely different from any hitherto known," a way to "exercise over the nature of things the authority which properly belongs to it." ... One interpretation of Bacon's philosophy is that virtually any technological transformation of the wilderness is an improvement, an almost automatic enhancement of civilized life.[7]

For European settlers of the future United States, "Indian" and "country" were both to be transformed into something better—the land into useful production and the Indian into Christian, farmer, and, later, citizen. European values predominated, and few settlers made any effort to learn about Indian culture. For example, because Puritan New Englanders classified hunting and fishing as recreational pursuits that could lure people into ungodly sloth, they regarded Indians who practiced these pursuits as lazy and ungodly even though hunting and fishing were essential for survival.[8] Indians were not going to be allowed to pursue their traditional activities in their then-current haunts; they were sitting on resources with economic and material value that they failed to appreciate. One need only read some of the classic accounts of Manifest Destiny to see that Americans justified their claims to the land of others by asserting that their willingness to use fully the soil and minerals gave them a "higher," if not prior, claim to land held by Mexicans and Indians, who were not using land for its highest possible purpose.[9] Similarly, for Americans in Vietnam, like Alden Pyle, neither nature nor society were "given" or intractable. Rather, both were to yield to and be transformed by human effort, violent human effort if necessary.

The attempt by Americans to alter Vietnam as "country" finds an illuminating parallel with approaches used in the Indian wars. Americans, to be sure, were ambivalent about Indian culture. They admired it while at the same time destroying the environment that sustained it. The writings of George Catlin illustrate this ambivalence. On the one hand, the idea of the Indian as part and parcel of nature prompted Catlin to propose "a magnificent park, where the world could see for ages to come, the native Indian in his classic attire. . . . A nation's Park, containing man and beast, in all the wild and freshness of their nature's beauty."[10] On the other hand, the Native American mind, according to Catlin, had the malleability characteristic of humanity in general: The Indian's "mind is a beautiful blank slate on which anything can be written if the proper means be taken."[11] This phrasing ties Catlin directly to the ideas of John Locke, one of the foundational thinkers for modern, Enlightenment values, who formulated many ideas at the core of American political thought.

Locke presented all humans as possessors of a contradictory natural endowment. Although all people at birth were endowed with the inalienable natural rights of life, liberty, and property (this last right was transformed into the "pursuit of happiness" in the Declaration of Independence), they also came into the world with "blank slate" minds that could be shaped by education and experience. Because, to Locke, there was no such thing as an innate human nature that put limits on human malleability, people could be transformed into any type of person that society desired.

Indians, like all people, could be seen not only as fully human and deserving of respect because of their natural rights but also as fully malleable because of their chalkboard minds onto which could be written "ennobling" messages once their "uncivilized graffiti" had been erased. Thus, the phrase "to kill the Indian" meant to erase the board in order to start over. In Vietnam the destruction of the village in order to save it was part of a process to ensure that communist insurgents could not slip in at night to eradicate the "correct" messages written by the United States and the government of South Vietnam during the day. Nature and the particular sense of place in Vietnamese culture were linked to ancestor worship, which was destroyed as families and whole villages were relocated with the justification that the uprooting was simply and rightly the erasure of "superstition."

The notion of "Indian country" is the bridge between these philosophical reflections and America's wars, both in Asia and in the West. Indian country is at once flawed and perfectible, savage and salvageable. It is the ideal object for an American culture willing to offer, or to impose if necessary, "improvements" on land and people. These same values, however, impose limits on American action. The impact on the land must be for the better, and the indigenous residents must be helped, not destroyed. American policymakers had to devise strategies to accommodate an American public that saw Native Americans and Vietnamese both as residents of "Indian country" and as possessors of fundamental natural rights overlaid with erroneous mind-messages from their cultures. This condition justified harsh treatment but simultaneously required respect for and created obligation toward these people. Indian policy in the late nineteenth century contained conflicting goals in the mandate simultaneously to eradicate savages and improve them. A similar contradiction characterized American policy in Vietnam. It is not surprising that the wars resulted in ambiguous outcomes that pleased neither the eradicators nor the civilizers.

The Big Hole Battlefield in southwestern Montana illustrates this cross-pressuring in late nineteenth-century Indian policy. The battle had limited objectives. The battle of 1877 was one of a series in which soldiers sought to capture Nez Percé Indians who evaded efforts by the U.S. government to relocate them onto a reservation in Idaho. The prime objective of the attacking soldiers, as readers of the park's interpretive literature and signs can readily see, was limited to depriving the Nez Percé of their horses and their food supplies in order to break their resistance, stop their flight, locate them on their assigned reservation and place them under the tutelage of missionaries, government farmers, and other "civilizers." However, the placement of markers showing where each victim on both sides fell and the maps indicating lines of attack and retreat emphasize only the military dimension to the casual visitor.[12] Although Indian reformers were often appalled by the physical bloodshed of massacres or limited military actions, they were not reluctant to "kill Indians" in a cultural sense by taking the children to off-reservation schools and banning the use of Indian languages. To reformers, the creation of a "civilized" person offset the violence of destroying a savage culture.

The war in Vietnam offers striking parallels and near parallels that reveal the cultural complexity accompanying American involvement in Southeast Asia. Although the Vietnamese were not regarded as savages, their culture had to be changed. They became, in succession, the objects of French and American efforts to transform them into French Catholics or, subsequently, modernized members of a democratic society. The introduction of Western educational curriculum in-country coupled with overseas study for promising Vietnamese nationals parallels the off-reservation education used in the United States; strategic hamlets isolated some Vietnamese from outside influences in ways reminiscent of reservations; and university extension projects from America's agricultural colleges assumed the role of government farmers employed on reservations to teach Indians about the best farming techniques. There was an effort to "kill the Vietnamese" culturally that recalled earlier attitudes toward Native Americans.

But there was also an effort to kill the Vietnamese as a people, just as earlier there had been efforts to kill Indians. Novelists retelling their war experiences go beyond the language of cowboys and Indians; readers encounter tales of the accumulation by American soldiers of enemy ears as war trophies. This activity recalls both scalping during the Indian wars and the taking of the ears of predator or nuisance animals in order to qualify for bounty payments during the effort to make "wild" lands suitable for "civilized" life. The value contradictions of the Indian wars revisited Americans during Vietnam.

The confidence of the nation in its ability to make sweeping changes in human affairs—most notably apparent in the willingness to try to override culture—was tempered by widespread American recognition that, deep down, there were limits to how far these efforts should go. People, including Vietnamese, possess fundamental human rights. Consequently the outcome of the war was neither military victory nor the creation of a Western democracy nor a Vietnamese society left in its precontact condition.

Analyses of the "unsatisfactory outcomes" of both the Indian wars and the Vietnam War should reflect American culture as well as concrete developments in specific wars. Many critiques look outward from American culture to conditions-on-the-ground to identify the mistaken judgment or misassessment that opened the door to policy failure. For example, those who believe that a broader military escalation, including the use of more powerful weapons, or the identification and support of a different, better leader stood between the nation and victory reveal their allegiance to a Baconian approach. This approach ignores the contradictions within American culture by holding that if the nation had selected the "right" tools, unambiguous victory would have followed. Presumably the nation failed to find the solution that would have met all our policy goals and forestalled the bitter debates and protests of the 1960s.

There were parallel debates about Indian policy in the nineteenth century. Control of Indian policy was passed back and forth between the War Department and the Department of the Interior as faith in the efficacy of military solutions competed with the protest over the failure of the army to protect Native Americans' natural rights. President Ulysses Grant's "peace policy" turned the direction of many reservations over to the control of churches. The army carried out a variety of missions where the goal, such as at the Battle of the Big Hole, was to force fleeing Indians to settle on reservations in order to "enjoy" the benefits of a civilized life. The 1876 campaign in Wyoming and Montana that resulted in the Battle of the Little Bighorn was similarly motivated. Within ten years national policy became law as embodied in the Dawes Severalty Act, which attempted to turn Indians into farmers. Three years later, in 1890, the massacre at Wounded Knee Creek, South Dakota, killed more than two hundred Native Americans. Although the time frame for these nineteenth-century events was not as compact as the one for Vietnam, parallels in the ambiguities of positions are useful in teaching American history.

The national tendency in American debates since the 1960s has been to divide people into camps according to who is right or wrong, patriotic or traitorous, smart or dumb. Missing in this oversimplification is the fact that these ambiguities and conflicts are embedded in American culture itself. The desire to respect the natural rights of others and the wish to transform the world of these others in the name of civilization and progress are both culturally sanctioned in the Western world.

Exploring the contradictions in this historical legacy places the acrimonious debates of the Vietnam era into a larger context. The military can believe that it was given an unclear mission, received fickle citizen support, and did not get permission to use the full potential of its weaponry. Although this situation was defined by some as "stabbing the army in the back," the military focused instead on problems of technique and leadership within the army.[13] In contrast, some citizens think that the military must be controlled or it will trample the natural rights of others. The military, of course, has many defenders within the civilian population. The inability to find the broadly acceptable solution in the midst of conflicting values is proof for some that the political system cannot provide effective leadership. Any rehash of the mistakes of the Vietnam era must include the study of the major traditions within American culture. Student awareness of the dynamics of American culture is as important for understanding the conduct of foreign policy and military operations as is the awareness of how other peoples define their worlds. This nation and its citizens must not act like Alden Pyle, pursuing policies with significant consequences, while blind to the cultural contexts of all parties involved, including his own.

Notes

1. Richard Slotkin, *Gunfighter Nation: The Myth of the Frontier in Twentieth-Century America* (New York: HarperPerennial, 1993), pp. 106, 109–11, 318–26. For Vietnam references, see Slotkin, *The Fatal Environment: The Myth of the Frontier in the Age of Industrialization 1800–1890* (New York: HarperPerennial, 1994), pp. 16–18. For a source on the Native American experience of the Vietnam War, see Tom Holm, *Strong Hearts, Wounded Souls: Native American Veterans of the Vietnam War* (Austin: University of Texas Press, 1996). The work grew out of the author's experience working with Native Americans suffering post-traumatic stress syndrome from fighting in the Vietnam War. Many of these veterans have made sense of their experiences by reconnecting with the warrior traditions of their respective tribes.

2. See chapter 15 of this volume, John Ernst, "Tutoring Democracy: Michigan State University and the Politics of Reform in South Vietnam."

3. For a reference to "killing Indians," see Patricia Limerick, *Legacy of Conquest: The Unbroken Past of the American West* (New York: W.W. Norton, 1987), p. 196.

4. Graham Greene, *The Quiet American* (Hammondsworth, UK: Penguin, 1973). Numbers in parentheses below refer to this edition.

5. This distillation of Bacon draws on several sources, including Albert Borgman, *Crossing the Postmodern Divide* (Chicago: University of Chicago Press, 1992), p. 23; Morris Berman, *The Reenchantment of the World* (Ithaca: Cornell University Press, 1981), pp. 29–31, and Michael Adas, *Machines as the Measure of Men: Science, Technology and Ideologies of Western Dominance* (Ithaca: Cornell University Press, 1989).

6. Greene, *The Quiet American*, p. 29.

7. Max Oelschlaeger, *The Idea of Wilderness from Prehistory to the Age of Ecology* (New Haven: Yale University Press, 1991), pp. 80–85; quotation is from p. 83.

8. William Cronon, *Changes in the Land: Indians, Colonists, and the Ecology of New England* (New York: Hill and Wang, 1983), p. 56.

9. One of the most comprehensive lists of these rationalizations is Albert Weinberg, *Manifest Destiny: A Study of Nationalist Expansionism in American History* (Chicago: Quadrangle Books, 1963).

10. Lee Clark Mitchell, *Witnesses to a Vanishing America: The Nineteenth Century Response* (Princeton: Princeton University Press, 1981), p. 96; italics are in the original.

11. Limerick, *Legacy of Conquest,* p. 185.

12. For the full story, see Alvin Josephy, Jr., *The Nez Percé Indians and the Opening of the Northwest,* abr. ed. (New Haven: Yale University Press, 1971), pp. 558–627. The relations of the Nez Percé with white settlers and with other Indians is interesting and complicated. The fleeing Indians often traveled peacefully through the countryside replenishing their supplies by purchase from stores. On some occasions settlers visited Nez Percé camps at night while other settlers joined civilian forces in pursuit of the band. After capture, the Indians were greeted warmly in Bismarck, Dakota Territory, as heroes, according to Josephy (p. 617).

13. Harry Summers, Jr., *On Strategy: The Vietnam War in Context* (Carlisle Barracks, PA: Strategic Studies Institute, U.S. Army War College, 1981), p. 7.

Selected Bibliography and Filmography

The Pacific War

Historical Overview

Awaya, Kentaro. "Emperor Showa's Accountability for War." *Japan Quarterly* (October–December 1991).

Bernstein, Barton J. "The Atomic Bombings Reconsidered." *Foreign Affairs* 74, no. 1 (January/February 1995): 135–52.

Blackman, Arnold. *The Other Nuremberg: The Untold Story of the Tokyo War Crimes Trial.* New York: Morrow, 1987.

Boyle, John Hunter. Chapters 6–8, "The Downward Spiral," "The Pacific War," and "Hiroshima." In *Modern Japan: The American Nexus,* 201–302. New York: Harcourt Brace Jovanovich, 1993.

Buruma, Ian. *The Wages of Guilt: Memories of War in Germany and Japan.* New York: Farrar Straus Giroux, 1994.

Daniels, Roger. Chapters 4–6, "The Coming of the Japanese and the Anti-Japanese Movement," "Japanese America, 1920–1941," and "Asian Americans in World War II." In *Asian America: Chinese and Japanese in the United States Since 1850,* 100–282. Seattle: University of Washington Press, 1988.

Dower, John. *War Without Mercy.* New York: Pantheon Books, 1986.

———. *Japan in War and Peace: Collected Essays.* New York: New Press, 1993.

Gluck, Carol. "Entangling Illusions: Japanese and American Views of the Occupation." In *New Frontiers in American East Asian Relations: Essays Presented to Dorothy Borg,* edited by Warren I. Cohen, 169–236. New York: Columbia University Press, 1983.

———. "The Past in the Present." In *Postwar Japan as History,* edited by Andrew Gordon, 64–95. Berkeley: University of California Press, 1993.

Gong, Gerrit W., ed. *Remembering and Forgetting: The Legacy of War and Peace in East Asia.* Washington, DC: Center for Strategic and International Studies, 1996.

Havens, Thomas, *The Valley of Darkness: The Japanese People and World War Two.* Lanham, MD: University Press of America, 1986.

Hein, Laura, and Mark Selden, eds. *Living with the Bomb: American and Japanese Cultural Conflicts in the Nuclear Age.* Armonk, NY: M.E. Sharpe, 1997.

Hsiung, James, and Steven I. Levine, eds. *China's Bitter Victory: The War with Japan, 1937–1945.* Armonk, NY: M.E. Sharpe, 1992.

Ienaga, Saburo. *The Pacific War: World War II and the Japanese, 1931–1945.* Translated by Frank Baldwin. New York: Pantheon Books, 1978.

Iriye, Akira. *Across the Pacific: An Inner History of American-East Asian Relations.* Chicago: Imprint Publications, 1992 (1962).

———. *Power and Culture: The Japanese-American War, 1941–1945.* Cambridge, MA: Harvard University Press, 1981.

Linenthal, Edward T. "Rust and Sea and Memory in This Strange Graveyard." In *Sacred Ground: Americans and Their Battlefields,* 173–212, 2nd ed. Urbana: University of Illinois Press, 1993.

———. "Anatomy of a Controversy." In *History Wars: The Enola Gay Controversy and Other Battles for the American Past,* edited by Edward T. Linenthal and Tom Engelhardt. New York: Metropolitan Books, 1996.

Minear, Richard. *Victor's Justice: The Tokyo War Crimes Trial.* Princeton: Princeton University Press, 1971.

Oral History/Biography

Cary, Otis, ed. *From a Ruined Empire: Letters-Japan, China, Korea, 1945–1946.* Tokyo: Kodansha, 1984.

Cook, Haruko Taya, and Theodore F. Cook. *Japan at War: An Oral History.* New York: New Press, 1992.

Gibney, Frank, ed. *Sensō: The Japanese Remember the Pacific War.* Translated by Beth Cary. Armonk, NY: M.E. Sharpe, 1995.

Hersey, John. *Hiroshima.* New York: Vintage Books, 1989. (See chapter 2 by John Dower for a discussion of Hersey's work).

MacArthur, Douglas. *Reminiscences.* New York: McGraw-Hill, 1964.

Minear, Richard, et al. *Hiroshima: Three Witnesses.* Princeton: Princeton University Press, 1990.

Morris, Ivan. "If Only They Should Fall." In *The Nobility of Failure: Tragic Heroes in the History of Japan.* New York: Holt, Rinehart, and Winston, 1975.

Terkel, Studs. "The Good War," *An Oral History of World War II.* New York: Pantheon Books, 1984.

Literature—Overview

Keene, Donald. "The Barren Years: Japanese and War Literature." *Monumenta Nipponica,* 33, no. 1 (Spring 1978): 67–112.

———. "Japanese Writers and the Greater East Asia War." In *Landscapes and Portraits: Appreciations of Japanese Culture.* New York: Kodansha International, 1981.

Kimball, Arthur G. *Crisis in Identity and Contemporary Japanese Novels.* Rutland, VT: C.E. Tuttle Co., 1973.

Ōe, Kenzaburō. *Hiroshima Notes.* New York: Grove Press, 1996.

Treat, John Whittier. *Writing Ground Zero: Japanese Literature and the Atomic Bomb.* Chicago: University of Chicago Press, 1995.

Literature

Ch'ae Man-Sik. *Peace Under Heaven.* Translated by Chun Kyung-Ja. Introduction by Carter J. Eckert. Armonk, NY: M.E. Sharpe, 1993.

Choe Chong-hui. *The Cry of the Harp and Other Korean Short Stories.* Seoul: Si-sa-yong-o-sa Publishers, 1983.

————. *The Cruel City and Other Korean Short Stories.* Translated by Genell Y. Poitras. Seoul: Si-sa-yong-o-sa Publishers, 1983.

Ding Ling. "When I Was in Hsia Village." Translated by Gary Bjorge. In *Modern Chinese Stories and Novellas, 1919–1949,* edited by Joseph Lau, C.T. Hsia, and Leo Ou-fan Lee. New York: Columbia University Press, 1981.

Endo, Shusaku. *The Sea and Poison.* Translated by Michael Gallagher. New York: New Directions, 1992.

Go, Shizuko. *Requiem, A Novel.* Translated by Geraldine Harcourt. Tokyo: Kodansha International, 1985.

Hino, Ashihei. *Barley and Soldiers.* Translated by K. and L.W. Bush. Tokyo: Kenkyusha, 1939.

Hsiao Hung. *The Field of Life and Death and Tales of Hulan River.* Translated by Howard Goldblatt. Bloomington: Indiana University Press, 1979.

Hsu Kai-yu, ed. *Twentieth Century Chinese Poetry: An Anthology.* Translated by Hsu Kai-yu. Ithaca: Cornell University Press, 1970 (1963).

Ibuse, Masuji. *Black Rain.* Translated by John Bester. Tokyo: Kodansha International, 1990.

Jones, James. *The Thin Red Line.* New York: New American Library, 1962.

Kojima, Nobuo. "The American School." Translated by William Sibley. In *Contemporary Japanese Literature: An Anthology of Fiction, Film, and Other Writing Since 1945,* edited by Howard Hibbett. New York: Alfred A. Knopf, 1977.

Mailer, Norman. *The Naked and the Dead.* New York: Holt, Rinehart and Winston, 1968 (1948).

Mo Yan. *Red Sorghum.* New York: Viking Press, 1993.

Ōe, Kenzaburō. *The Pinch Runner Memorandum.* Translated by Michiko N. Wilson and Michael K. Wilson. Armonk, NY: M.E. Sharpe. 1994.

Ōe, Kenzaburō, ed. *The Crazy Iris and Other Stories of the Atomic Aftermath.* Introduction by Kenzaburō Ōe. New York: Grove Press, 1985.

Ōe, Kenzaburō. *The Catch and Other War Stories.* New York: Kodansha International, 1990.

Ooka, Shohei. *Fires on the Plain.* Translated by Ivan Morris. Tokyo: Charles E. Tuttle Co., 1967.

Nagai, Takashi. *The Bells of Nagasaki.* Translated by William Johnston. New York: Kodansha International, 1994. (See chapter 2 by John Dower for a discussion of the author Takashi Nagai and his work.)

Richler, Mordecai, ed. *Writers on World War II: An Anthology.* New York: Alfred A. Knopf, 1991.

Son So-hui. *The Wind from the River.* Seoul: Si-sa-yong-o-sa Publishers, 1988.

Takeyama, Michio. *Harp of Burma.* Translated by Howard Hibbett. Rutland, VT: Charles E. Tuttle, 1966.

Xiao Jun. *Village in August.* New York: Smith & Durrell, 1942.

Wang, C.C., ed. *Stories of China at War.* New York: Columbia University Press, 1947.

Yamasaki, Toyoko. *The Barren Zone.* Tokyo: Kodansha International, 1993.

Film—Overview

Sato, Tadao. "Japanese War Films." In *Currents in Japanese Cinema.* Tokyo: Kodansha, 1982.

Chow, Rey. *Primitive Passions: Visuality, Sexuality, Ethnography, and Contemporary Chinese Cinema.* New York: Columbia University Press, 1995.

Documentary Films

America, the Way We Were: The Homefront 1940–1945. 180 min. Reader's Digest Home Entertainment in association with CEL Communications, Inc., 1989. 3 videocassettes.

In the Name of the Emperor. Directed by Christine Choy and Nancy Tong. Produced by Nancy Tong. Distributed by Christine Choy and Nancy Tong, Film New Now Foundation, 230 East 15th Street, Apt. 10N, New York, NY 10003, Tel/Fax: (212) 777–7813.

Isoroku Yamamoto: Grand Admiral, Imperial Japanese Navy. 62 min. Time-Life Video, 1976. Videocassette.

Know Your Enemy: Japan. Produced by Frank Capra and Army Pictorial Services, Signal Corps. 63 min. United States Army Pictorial Service, 1945. Videocassette.

CBS. *The Pacific War Begins.* Four segments narrated by Walter Cronkite. 95 min. CBS, 1981. Videocassette.

"Reinventing Japan," In *The Pacific Century.* Co-produced by PBI/Jigsaw Productions in association with NHK-Japan [and] KCTS/Seattle. Directed by Frank Gibney. 60 min. Annenberg/CPB Collection, 1992.

Feature Films

Black Rain. Produced by Hisa Iino. Directed by Shohei Imamura. 123 min. Fox Lorber, 1991. Videocassette.

Bridge on the River Kwai. Directed by David Lean. 162 min. Columbia Pictures, 1993 (1957). Videocassette.

Burmese Harp. Directed by Kon Ichikawa. 116 min. Nikkatsu Kabushiki Kaisha, 1956. Videocassette.

Come See the Paradise. Produced by Robert F. Colesberry. Directed by Alan Parker. 135 min. Twentieth Century Fox, 1991.

Fires on the Plain. Directed by Kon Ichikawa. 105 min. Embassy Home Entertainment, 1987 (1959). Videocassette.

From Here to Eternity. Produced by Buddy Adler. Directed by Fred Zinnemann. 118 min. Columbia Pictures Corporation, 1953. Videocassette.

Guadalcanal Diary. Produced by Bryan Foy. Directed by Lewis Seiler. 93 min. Twentieth Century-Fox, 1990 (1943). Videocassette.

The Human Condition (Ningen no joken). Produced by Shigeru Wakatsuki. Directed by Masaki Kobayashi. 190 min., 200 min., 180 min. Shochiku Co., 1988. 3 videocassettes. For an extended discussion of this film, see chapter 8 by Van Symons.

The Naked and the Dead. Directed by Raoul Walsh. 131 min. Video Communications, 1987 (1958). 2 videocassettes.

No Regrets for Our Youth (Waga seishun ni kui nashi). Directed by Akira Kurosawa. 112 min. Toho Kabushiki Kaisha, 1946. Videocassette.

Red Sorghum. Directed by Zhang Yimou. 91 min. New Yorker Video, 1988. Videocassette.

Rhapsody in August (Hachigatsu no kyoshikyoku). Directed by Akira Kurosawa. 98 min. Orion Home Video, 1991. Videocassette.

Teahouse of the August Moon. Produced by Jack Cummings. Directed by Daniel Mann. 124 min. MGM, 1956. Videocassette.

Twenty-four Eyes. Directed by Keisuke Kinoshita. 158 min. Shochiku Kabushiki Kaisha, 1954. Videocassette. (For a discussion of the film, see chapter 4 by Tadao Sato).

The Korean War

Historical Overview

Chen Jian. *China's Road to the Korean War: The Making of the Sino-American Confrontation, 1948–1950.* New York: Columbia University Press, 1994.
Cumings, Bruce. *The Origins of the Korean War.* 2 vols. Princeton: Princeton University Press, 1990 (1981).
Fehrenbach, T.R. *This Kind of War: A Study in Unpreparedness.* New York: Macmillan, 1963.
Gibney, Frank. *Korea's Quiet Revolution: From Garrison State to Democracy.* New York: Walker and Co., 1992.
Goldman, Eric F. *Crucial Decade: America, 1945–1955.* New York: Alfred A. Knopf, 1966 (1960).
Halliday, Jon, and Bruce Cumings. *Korea: The Unknown War.* New York: Pantheon, 1988.
Hunt, Michael. "Beijing and the Korean Crisis, June 1950–1951." *Political Science Quarterly* (Fall 1992): 453–78.
Hunt, Michael, and Steven I. Levine. "The Revolutionary Challenge to Early U.S. Cold War Policy in Asia." In *The Great Powers in East Asia, 1953–1960,* edited by Warren I. Cohen and Akira Iriye, 13–34. New York: Columbia University Press, 1990.
John Merrill. *Korea: The Peninsular Origins of the War.* Newark: University of Delaware Press, 1989.
Steuck, Williams. *An International History of the Korean War.* Princeton: Princeton University Press, 1995.
Suh, Dae-sook. *Kim Il-sung: The North Korean Leader.* New York: Columbia University Press, 1988.
Weathersby, Kathryn. "The Soviet Role in the Early Phase of the Korean War: New Documentary Evidence." *Journal of American East Asian Relations,* 2, no. 4 (Winter 1993): 425–58.
West, Philip. "Confronting the West: China as David and Goliath in the Korean War." In *A Revolutionary War: Korea and the Transformation of the Postwar World,* edited by Williams J. Williams, 225–43. Chicago: Imprint Publications, 1994.
Whitfield, Stephen J. *The Culture of the Cold War.* Baltimore: John Hopkins University Press, 1991.
Yang, Sungchul. *North and South Korean Politics: A Comparative Analysis.* Boulder: Westview Press, 1994.

Oral History/Biography

Knox, Donald. *The Korean War: Pusan to Chosin, An Oral History.* 2 vols. New York: Harcourt Brace Jovanovich, 1985.
Marshall, S.L.A. *The River and the Gauntlet.* New York: Time Incorporated, 1962.
Wills, Morris. *Turncoat: An American's Twelve Years in Communist China.* New York: Prentice-Hall, 1968.

Literature—Overview

Kim Chong-un. "Introduction." In *Postwar Korean Short Stories,* translated and edited by Kim Chong-un. Seoul: Seoul National University Press, 1983.
Suh Ji-moon. "America and Americans as Depicted in Korean Fiction." *Journal of American Studies,* vol. 28, no. 2 (Winter 1996): 371–89.

Literature

Ahn Junghyo. *Silver Stallion.* Translated by Ahn Junghyo. New York: Soho, 1990. (See chapter 8 by Van Symons for an extended discussion of the novel.)

Ch'ae Man-sik. *Peace Under Heaven.* Armonk, NY: M.E. Sharpe, 1993.

Choi In-hoo. *A Grey Man.* Translated by Chun Kyung-ja. Seoul: Si-sa-yong-o-sa, 1988.

Kang Sok-kyong, Kim Chi-won and O Chong-hui. *Words of Farewell: Stories by Korean Women Writers.* Translated by Bruce and Ju-Chan Fulton. Seattle: Seal Press, 1989.

Kim, Richard. *The Innocent.* Seoul: Si-sa-yong-o-sa, 1968.

———. The Martyred. Seoul: Si-sa-yong-o-sa, 1960.

Kim, Won-il. *The Wind and the River.* Seoul: Si-sa-yong-o-sa, 1988.

Lee, Peter H. *Flowers of Fire.* Honolulu: University of Hawaii Press, 1974. (Contains Kim Tongin's short story "Potato," discussed in chapter 5 by David McCann.)

Pihl, Marshall R., and Bruce and Ju-Chan Fulton. *Land of Exile: Contemporary Korean Fiction.* Armonk, NY: M.E. Sharpe, 1993.

Suh Ji-moon, ed. *The Rainy Spell and Other Korean Short Stories.* Translated and introduced by Suh Ji-moon. Armonk, NY: M.E. Sharpe, 1997. (See especially Yun Heung-gil, "The Rainy Spell" and Choe Yun, "My Father's Keeper.")

Documentary Films

Home Apart: The Two Koreas. 1992. Choy, Christine. (For information on how to preview this documentary, contact Christine Choy, Chair, Graduate Film Department, New York University, Tisch School of the Arts; fax: 212–995–4063; telephone: 212–998–1740.)

The Korean War. Produced by Korean Broadcasting System and Ahn Dae Won. Korean Broadcast System, 1992. 5 videocassettes, 120 min. each. Distributed by West Long Branch, NJ: White Star.

Film—Overview

Standish, Isolde. "Korean Cinema and the New Realism: Text and Context." *East West Film Journal,* 7, no. 2 (July 1993): 54–79.

———. "United in HAN: Korean Cinema and the 'New Wave.' " *Korea Journal* (Winter 1992): 109–18.

Films

The Manchurian Candidate. Produced by George Axelrod and John Frankenheimer. Directed by John Frankenheimer. 126 min. MGM/UA Home Video, 1988 (1962). Videocassette.

M.A.S.H. Produced by Ingo Preminger. Directed by Robert Altman. 117 min. Twentieth Century-Fox Film Corporation. 1990 (1970). Videocassette.

Pork Chop Hill. Produced by Sy Bartlett. Directed by Lewis Milestone. 98 min. United Artists Corporation, 1959. Videocassette.

Silver Stallion. Produced by Han Kapchin. Directed by Chang Kilsoo. 123 min. Han Jin Enterprises (fax: 82–2–277–3644), 1995. Videocassette. (Film version of the novel by Ahn Junghyo.)

Steel Helmet. Produced and directed by Samuel Fuller. 84 min. Lippert Pictures, Inc., 1951. Videocassette.

To the Starry Island. Produced by Park Kiyong. Directed by Park Kwang-su. 102 min. Park Kwang-su Film, Ltd., 1994. Videocassette.

The Vietnam War

Bibliography

Schafer, John, Lady Borton, Alan Riedy, and Dan Duffy. *Lac Viet 17.* New Haven: Yale University, 1997. (Vietnam in English: two indexes and a bibliography. John Schafer's annotated bibliography "Vietnamese Perspectives on the Vietnam War" provides an introductory essay and list of references for eleven categories.)

*Historical Overview**

Allen, Douglas, and Ngô Vinh Long, eds. *Coming to Terms: Indochina, the United States, and the War.* Boulder: Westview Press, 1991.
Chanda, Nayan. *Brother Enemy: The War After the War.* New York: Harcourt Brace Jovanovich, 1986.
Herring, George. *America's Longest War: The United States and Vietnam, 1950–1975.* 3d ed. New York: McGraw Hill, 1996,
Iriye, Akira. *Across the Pacific: An Inner History History of American-East Asian Relations.* New York: Harcourt, Brace & World, 1992 (1967).
Kahin, George M. *Intervention: How America Became Involved in Vietnam.* New York: Anchor Books, 1987 (1986).
Karnow, Stanley. *Vietnam: A History.* New York: Viking Press, 1991 (1983).
Katsiaficas, George, ed. *Vietnam Documents: American and Vietnamese Views of the War.* Armonk, NY: M.E. Sharpe, 1992.
Macdonald, Peter. *Giap: The Victor in Vietnam.* New York: W.W. Norton, 1993.
McMahon, Robert J. *Major Problems in the History of the Vietnam War.* 2d ed. Lexington, MA: D.C. Heath and Company, 1990.
Sheehan, Neil. *After the War Was Over: Hanoi and Saigon.* New York: Random House, 1992.
Summers, Harry. *On Strategy: The Vietnam War in Context.* Carlisle Barracks, PA: Strategic Studies Institute, U.S. Army War College, 1981.
Williams, William Appleman, Lloyd Gardner, and Walter LaFeber, eds. *America in Vietnam: A Documentary History.* New York: W.W. Norton, 1989 (1985).
Young, Marilyn. *The Vietnam Wars, 1945–1990.* New York: HarperPerennial, 1991.

Oral History/Biography

Borton, Lady. *After Sorrow: An American Among the Vietnamese.* New York: Viking, 1995. (See chapter 7 by James Soular for a discussion of Lady Borton's work.)
Englemann, Larry, ed. *Tears Before the Rain: An Oral History of the Fall of South Vietnam.* New York: Oxford University Press, 1990.
Halberstam, David. *Ho.* New York: Random House, 1971.

---

*Special thanks to John Ernst for his suggestions on historical works about the Vietnam War.

Truong Nhu Tang, with David Chanoff and Doan Van Toai. *A Vietcong Memoir.* New York: Vintage, 1986.
Tom Holm. *Strong Hearts, Wounded Souls: Native American Veterans of the Vietnam War.* Austin: University of Texas Press, 1996.

Literature—Overview

Durand, Maurice M., and Nguyen Tran Huan. *An Introduction to Vietnamese Literature.* New York: Columbia University Press, 1985.
Palmer, William J. "The Literature and Films of the Vietnam War." In *Forgotten Warriors: Combat Art from Vietnam,* edited by Dennis L. Noble. Westport: Praeger, 1992.
Lockhart, Greg. "Introduction." In Nguyen Hy Thiep, *The General Retires and Other Stories.* London: Oxford University Press, 1991.
Rowe, John Carlos, and Rick Berg. *The Vietnam War and American Culture.* New York: Columbia University Press, 1991.

Novels

Ahn Junghyo. *White Badge: A Novel of Korea.* New York: Soho Press, 1989.
Bao Ninh. *The Sorrow of War: A Novel of North Vietnam.* Translated by Phan Thanh Hao. Edited by Frank Palmos. New York: Riverhead Books, 1996 (1995). (See chapters 11 and 6 by Colonel Harry Summers, Jr., and Leslie Adams for discussions of this novel.)
Butler, Robert Olen. *A Good Scent from a Strange Mountain: Stories.* New York: H. Holt, 1992.
Del Vecchio, John M. *The 13th Valley: A Novel.* New York: Bantam Books, 1982.
Duffy, Dan, ed. *North Viet Nam Now: Fiction and Essays from Ha Noi.* Introduction by Dan Duffy. New Haven: Yale University Council on Southeast Asia Studies, *Viet Nam Forum 15,* 1996.
Duong Thu Huong. *Novel Without a Name.* Translated by Phan Huy Duong and Nina McPherson. New York: William Morrow, 1995. (See chapters 11, 8, and 6 by Colonel Harry Summers, Jr., Van Symons, and Leslie Adams for discussions of this novel.)
Greene, Graham. *The Quiet American.* New York: Penguin Books, 1955/1977. (See chapters 16 and 12 by John Ernst and David Trask for discussions of the novel.)
Hayslip, Lee Ly. *When Heaven and Earth Changed Places: A Vietnamese Woman's Journey From War to Peace.* New York: Penguin Books, 1990.
Heinemann, Larry. *Paco's Story.* New York: Penguin Books, 1989. (See chapter 6 by Leslie Adams for a discussion of the novel.)
Herr, Michael. *Dispatches.* New York: Avon, 1978. (See chapter 6 by Leslie Adams for a discussion of this novel.)
Karlin, Wayne, and Le Minh Khue. *The Other Side of Heaven: Postwar Fiction by American and Vietnamese Writers.* Willimantic, CT: Curbstone Press, 1995.
Lang, Daniel. *Casualties of War.* New York: McGraw-Hill, 1969.
Lederer, William J., and Eugene Burdick. *The Ugly American.* New York: Fawcett Crest, 1960.
Nguyen Du. *The Tale of Kieu.* Translated and annotated by Kuynh Sanh Thong (bilingual edition). New Haven: Yale University Press, 1983.
Nguyen Hy Thiep. *The General Retires and Other Stories.* Translated by Greg Lockhart. London: Oxford University Press, 1993.
O'Brien, Tim. *Going After Cacciato: A Novel.* New York: Dell, 1992. (See chapter 6 by Leslie Adams for an extended discussion of this novel.)

————. *If I Die in a Combat Zone.* New York: Delacrote Press/Seymour Lawrence, 1973.

————. *In the Lake of the Woods.* New York: Houghton Mifflin, 1994.

————. *The Things They Carried.* New York: Penguin, 1991. (See chapter 6 by Leslie Adams for a discussion of this novel.)

Wright, Stephen. *Meditations in Green.* New York: Charles Scribner's Sons, 1983.

Poetry

Komunyakaa, Yusef. *Dien Cai Dau.* Middletown, CT: Wesleyan University Press, 1988. See chapter 7 by James Soular for a discussion of Komunyakaa's poetry.

————. *Neon Vernacular: New and Selected Poems.* Hanover, NH: Wesleyan University Press; University Press of New England, 1993.

Thanh T. Nguyen, and Bruce Weigl, ed. and trans. *Poems from Captured Documents.* Amherst: University of Massachusetts Press, 1994. (See chapter 7 by James Soular for a discussion of these poems.)

Raffel, Burton, ed. and trans. *From the Vietnamese: Ten Centuries of Poetry.* New York: October House, 1968.

Rottmann, Larry, Jan Barry, and Basil T. Paquet, eds. *Winning Hearts and Minds: War Poems by Vietnam Veterans.* New York: McGraw-Hill, 1972.

Soular, James. *The Thousand-Yard Stare.* Canton, CT: Singular Speech Press, 1997.

Thich Nhat Hanh. *Love in Action.* Berkeley: Parallax Press, 1993.

————. *Call Me by My True Names.* Berkeley: Parallax Press, 1994.

Van Devanter, Lynda, and Joan A. Furey, ed. *Visions of War, Dreams of Peace.* New York: Warner Books, 1991.

Weigl, Bruce. *Song of Napalm.* New York: Atlantic Monthly Press, 1988. (See chapter 7 by James Soular for a discussion of Weigl's work.)

Film-Overview

Lanning, Michael Lee. *Vietnam at the Movies.* New York: Fawcett Columbine, 1994.

Palmer, William J. "The Literature and Films of the Vietnam War." In *Forgotten Warriors: Combat Art from Vietnam,* edited by Dennis L. Noble. Westport, CT: Praeger, 1992.

Documentary Film

Anderson Platoon. Produced and directed by Pierre Schoendorffer. 60 min. Films Inc., 1987 (1966). Videocassette.

Hearts and Minds. Produced by Bert Schneider and Peter Davis. Directed by Peter Davis. 115 min. Touchstone and Audjeff, 1992 (1974). Videocassette.

Legacies. Written and directed by Richard Ellison. 60 min. Films Incorporated, 1983. Videocassette.

Victory at Dien Bien Phu. Produced and directed by Tran Viet. 75 min. 1964.

Vietnam: A Television History. Produced and directed by Richard Ellison. 780 min. WGBH (Boston), 1987. 7 videocassettes.

Feature Films

Apocalypse Now. Produced and directed by Francis Ford Coppola. 153 min. Zoetrope Studios, 1977. Videocassette.

Born on the Fourth of July. Produced by A. Kitman Ho and Oliver Stone. Directed by Oliver Stone. 145 min. Universal City Studios, 1990. Videocassette.

Brothers and Relations. Directed by Tran Vu and Nguyen Huu Luyen. 1986. Contact UCLA Film and Television Archive for information on how to preview this film.

The Deer Hunter. Produced by Barry Spikings et al. Directed by Michael Cimino.183 min. Universal Pictures Corporation, 1978. Videocassette.

Full Metal Jacket. Produced and directed by Stanley Kubrick. 117 min. Warner Brothers, 1988. Videocassette.

The Green Berets. Produced by Michael Wayne and directed by John Wayne and Ray Kellogg. 135 min. Warner Brothers, 1968. Videocassette.

Hamburger Hill. Produced by Marcia Nasatir and Jim Carabatsos. Directed by John Irvin. 94 min. Paramount Pictures, 1987. Videocassette.

Heaven and Earth. Produced and directed by Oliver Stone. 142 min. Warner Home Video, 1993. Videocassette

Platoon. Produced by Arnold Kopelson and directed by Oliver Stone. 120 min. Vestron Video, 1986. Videocassette.

Scent of Green Papaya. Produced by Christophe Rossignon. Directed by Tran Ahn Hung. 104 min. First Look Pictures Releasing, 1993. Videocassette.

When the Tenth Month Comes. Directed by Dang Nhat Minh. 1984. Contact UCLA Film and Television Archive for information on how to preview this film.

White Badge, 1992. Produced and directed by Chong Cook. 120 min. 1995. Videocassette. (Based on Ahn Junghyo's novel of the same name.)

Contributors

Leslie Kennedy Adams is assistant professor of English at Houston Baptist University. She is particularly interested in the study of war literature and films and teaches two courses on the subject: War in Literature and the Vietnam War in Fiction and Film.

Ahn Junghyo is a veteran of Korea's Ninth White Horse Division and served in the Vietnam War. Since graduating from Sogang Jesuit University, he has worked as a reporter, columnist, editor, and translator of books into Korean and English. His novels include *White Badge* (1983), and *Silver Stallion* (1987)—both published in the U.S.—as well as *Life and Death of the Hollywood Kid* (1992). Mr. Ahn is currently working on a novel about Korean women mobilized by the Japanese to work as prostitutes or "sex slaves" during Japanese colonial rule.

Kentaro Awaya is professor of modern Japanese history at Rikkyo (St. Paul's) University in Tokyo. Among his publications are "Emperor Showa's Accountability for War" (*Japan Quarterly,* October–December 1991) and *Miketsu no Sensosekinin* (The Unconvicted War Responsibility 1994).

Rey Chow is professor of English and comparative literature at the University of California, Irvine. Her writings include many scholarly essays and articles that have appeared in anthologies and journals published in Australia, Canada, France, Hong Kong, Japan, Spain, and Taiwan, as well as the United States. She is the author of *Woman and Chinese Modernity: The Politics of Reading Between East and West* (1991), *Writing Diaspora: Tactics of Intervention in Contemporary Cultural Studies* (1993), *Primitive Passions: Visuality, Sexuality, Ethnography, and Contemporary Chinese Cinema* (1995), *Xie zai jia guo yi wai* (in Chinese) (1995), and *Ethics After Idealism: Theory-Culture-Reading* (forthcoming in 1998).

Merrel Clubb is professor emeritus of English at the University of Montana, where he taught for thirty-two years and was chairman of the English Department. In World War II he was a naval gunfire liaison officer attached to army or marine combat units. He fought in the Pacific theater, earning four battle stars, a Bronze Star (with V), and is entitled to wear a presidential citation and a navy commendation.

John W. Dower is Elting E. Morison Professor of History at the Massachusetts Institute of Technology. His books include the award-winning *War Without Mercy: Race and Power in the Pacific War* (1986), *Empire and Aftermath: Yoshida Shigeru and the Japanese Experience* (1979), and *Japan in War and Peace* (1994). Currently, Professor Dower is completing a study of Japan in the period immediately after World War II.

John Ernst is assistant professor of history at Morehead State University, where he teaches courses on American foreign policy, Asian history, and military history. He is the author of *Forging a Fateful Alliance: Michigan State University and the Vietnam War* (forthcoming, 1998).

James Zheng Gao is assistant professor of history at Christopher Newport University, where he teaches courses on world civilization, American–East Asian relations, and classical and modern East Asian civilization and history. His major publications include *Shijie wenhua zhi mi* (Myths of World Civilization) (with Xu Xiaoguang, 1986) and *Meeting Technology's Advance: Social Changes in China and Zimbabwe in the Railway Age* (1997).

Jackie Hiltz is research associate at the Maureen and Mike Mansfield Center at the University of Montana, where she is coordinator of the "American Wars in Asia" project. She has taught courses on Asia at the University of Montana.

Steven I. Levine, senior research associate at Boulder Run Research in Hillsborough, North Carolina, taught courses on Chinese and East Asian politics for many years. He wrote *Anvil of Victory: The Communist Revolution in Manchuria* (1987), co-edited with James C. Hsiung *China's Bitter Victory: The War with Japan, 1937–45* (1992), and has published numerous chapters, articles, and review essays.

Edward T. Linenthal is professor of religion and American culture at the University of Wisconsin, Oshkosh. His books include *Symbolic Defense: The Cultural Significance of the Strategic Defense Initiative* (1989), *Sacred Ground: Americans and Their Battlefields* (2d ed. 1993), and *Preserving Memory: The Struggle to Create America's Holocaust Museum* (1995), and he is co-editor of *History Wars: The Enola Gay and Other Battles for the American Past* (1996).

David R. McCann is the Korean Foundation professor of Korean language and literature at Harvard University. He is the editor of *Korea Briefing: Toward Reunification* (1997) and the co-editor (with Oh Se Young) of the Korean (1997) and English (forthcoming) editions of *Anthology of Modern Korean Poetry*. He has published thirteen books (in translation) of or about Korean literature.

G.L. Penrose is professor of history at Hope College, where he teaches courses on Russian and East Asian history. His current research includes work on the diary of a Montana National Guard soldier in the Philippine insurrection.

Tadao Sato is a film critic and author who published his first movie review in 1956. Since then he has written more than 150 books on Asian film and has also served as editor-in-chief of the film magazines *Eiga byoron and Shiso no kagaku*. In 1989, Mr. Sato and his wife, Hisako, were awarded the Kawakita Prize for their contribution to international cultural exchange through movies. He has been president of the Japan Academy of Moving Images since April 1996. His book *History of Japanese Films* (4 vols.) was awarded the Mainichi Publication Culture Award in 1995 and the Art Encouragement Prize of the Ministry of Education.

James Soular served in the Vietnam War as a crew chief for the First Cavalry Division of the U.S. army. He currently works as a contract administrator for the U.S. Forest Service and teaches courses on poetry and American and Vietnamese literature of the Vietnam War at the University of Montana. His collection of poetry, *The Thousand-Yard Stare* was published in 1997.

Colonel Harry Summers, Jr., is a veteran of the Korean and Vietnam Wars. He was twice decorated for valor and twice wounded in action. His award-winning critique of the Vietnam War, *On Strategy: The Vietnam War in Context* (1981), is used as a student text by the war and staff colleges and by many civilian universities. His other works include *Vietnam War Almanac* (1985) and *Korean War Almanac* (1990). Currently, he is a syndicated columnist for the Los Angeles *Times* and editor of *Vietnam Magazine*.

Van Jay Symons is professor of history at Augustana College. He is author of *Ch'ing Ginseng Management: Chinese Monopolies in Microcosm* (1981) and co-author, with Sechin Jagchid, of *Peace, War, and Trade Along the Great Wall* (1989). During the 1997–98 academic year he will be chairman of the board of directors of ASIANetwork, a consortium of about one hundred colleges seeking to strengthen Asian programs on college campuses.

David Trask is a member of the history department at Guilford Technical Community College in Jamestown, NC, with research interests in late-nineteenth century U.S. history and the American West. He was an elected member of the Council of the American Historical Association (1995–97) and served as a council representative to *Perspectives,* the newsletter for AHA, with responsibility for the "Teaching" column.

Philip West is director of the Maureen and Mike Mansfield Center at the University of Montana, Missoula, where he is also Mansfield Professor of Modern Asian Affairs. He teaches courses on Chinese and Japanese history and American–East Asian relations. Professor West is author of "China as David and Goliath in the Korean War," in William J. Williams, ed., *A Revolutionary War: Korea and the Transformation of the Postwar World* (1994).

Pingchao Zhu is visiting assistant professor of history at the University of Idaho. She teaches courses on world civilization, U.S. diplomatic history, and modern Chinese and Japanese history. In summer 1995 Professor Zhu taught at Guangxi Teachers University in Guilin, China.

Index